T0205673

PROCEEDINGS OF THE THIRD EUROPEAN CONFERENCE ON
COMPUTER-SUPPORTED COOPERATIVE WORK - ECSCW '93

Proceedings of
the Third European Conference
on
Computer-Supported Cooperative Work
13-17 September 1993, Milan, Italy

ECSCW '93

Edited by

GIORGIO DE MICHELIS and CARLA SIMONE
Laboratory for Cooperation Technologies,
Department of Information Sciences, University of Milan, Italy

and

KJELD SCHMIDT
Cognitive Systems Group,
Risø National Laboratory, Denmark

SPRINGER-SCIENCE+BUSINESS MEDIA, B.V.

ISBN 978-94-010-4928-3   ISBN 978-94-011-2094-4 (eBook)
DOI 10.1007/978-94-011-2094-4

A C.I.P. Catalogue record for this book is available from the Library of Congress.

Cover Design by Giulio Ceppi

Printed on acid-free paper

ECSCW '93 Organization

Conference Committee

Chair: Carla Simone (University of Milano)

ECSCW '91 Past Chair: Mike Robinson (University of Aarhus)

Technical Program: Giorgio De Michelis (University of Milano)

Workshops/Panels: Steve Benford (University of Nottingham)

Tutorials: Fiorella De Cindio (University of Milano)

Demonstrators/Videos: Francesco Tisato (University of Milano)

Treasurer: Dario Tognazzi (Digital Equipment SpA, Milano)

Proceedings: Kjeld Schmidt (Risø National Laboratory)

Local Arrangements: Buni Zeller (Istituto RSO, Milano)

Organization Office: (University of Milano)
    Alessandra Agostini
    Giuseppe Omodei Salè
    Monica Divitini
    Stefano Patriarca
    Antonia Grasso
    Alberto Pozzoli

International Committee Steve Scrivener (Loughborough University of Technology)

USA Publicity: John King (University of California, Irvine)

LIAISONS

SIGOIS: Clarence Ellis (University of Colorado)

SIGCHI: Brad Hartfield (University of Hamburg)

SIGLINK: Norbert Streitz (GMD - IPSI, Darmstadt)

CSCW '92: Marylin Mantei (University of Toronto)

Program Committee

Martin Ader (Bull, France)

Robert Anderson (Rank Xerox Cambridge EuroPARC)

Liam Bannon (University of Limerick, Ireland)

Claudio Ciborra (University of Bologna)

Giorgio De Michelis (University of Milano) - Chair

Peter Docherty (Stockholm School of Economics)

Pelle Ehn (Lund University)

Clarence Ellis (University of Colorado, Boulder)

Anatol Holt (University of Milano)

Hiroshi Ishii (NTT, Japan)

Simon Kaplan (University of Illinois, Urbana)

Robert Kraut (Bellcore, Morristown)

Wolfgang Prinz (GMD, Bonn)

Mike Robinson (University of Aarhus)

Tom Rodden (Lancaster University)

Thomas Schäl (Istituto RSO, Milano)

Kjeld Schmidt (Risø National Laboratory, Roskilde)

Carla Simone (University of Milano)

Lucy Suchman (Xerox PARC, Palo Alto)

Gerrit van der Veer (Free University, Amsterdam)

Sponsors of ECSCW '93

Microsoft, Italy

Digital Equipment, Italy

Elsag Bailey, Italy

Rank Xerox Cambridge EuroPARC

Sun Microsystems Italia

A.I.C.A. (Associazione Italiana Calcolo Automatico)

Commission of the European Communities (General Directorate XII)

Consiglio Nazionale delle Ricerche, Italy
('Information Systems and Parallel Computing' Project)

University of Milano, Italy

From the editors

It is a pleasure to welcome all the participants to ECSCW '93 as well as those who may read these Proceedings after the conference.

We hope that you find the papers contained in these Proceedings stimulating and informative. They have been selected from among more than 80 submissions for the Scientific Program of ECSCW '93 by the Program Committee, with the help of more than fifty reviewers. The review process has been very careful. Each paper has had at least three reviews and the final decision of the Program Committee is the result of deep and passionate discussions. Many papers of interest could not be accommodated in the final program. The choice to maintain a single-track program imposed limitations that did not allow the Program Committee to accept them.

We are certain you will find the selected papers stimulating and representative of the diverse approaches and cultures of this multi-disciplinary field.

It is important to underline that the papers that you find in these Proceedings constitute the Scientific Program of an international conference. They are only the most prominent manifestation of a wider set of activities. ECSCW '93 is also Workshops, Tutorials, Demos and Videos. We hope, therefore, that all participants, both professionals and academics, will find rich opportunities for discussing, learning and opening their minds.

If ECSCW '93, and therefore these Proceedings, meets its aims, we must gratefully thank many persons. Let us list all of them.

First, all those who submitted a paper, in particular those whose papers were not accepted. Receiving many good submissions is the basis for a good conference, and accepting a rigorous selection procedure is the basis for good research practice.

Second, all those who proposed and participate in Workshops, Tutorials, Demos and Videos. A rich program is important for embedding paper presentation in a stimulating environment.

Third, all those who contributed to the organization of ECSCW '93. An international conference is a complicated event that requires careful attention to many details, from the publicity that precedes it to the organizational tasks that are needed to make it run smoothly.

Fourth, all those who sponsored ECSCW '93. While an international conference such as ECSCW '93 requires a lot of resources, the help of sponsors allowed us to maintain affordable tariffs.

Fifth, all those who contributed to the definition of the scientific program. The Program Committee members, together with the reviewers who helped them, did a very difficult job. We hope that the written comments that all authors of the submitted papers (whether accepted or not) received back have helped them in their research work.

Sixth, the publishers of the Proceedings. A well designed, printed and distributed book is an important medium for the transfer of knowledge in the international community.

Seventh and finally, the promoters and organizers of the American conferences on CSCW. The tacit agreement between them and us, on interleaving their and our conferences, as well as the practice of announcing the conferences as if they were on a single track has greatly contributed to make ECSCW an international conference that is held in Europe, thereby reducing the geographical barriers between the different research communities.

Giorgio De Michelis, Kjeld Schmidt, Carla Simone

Special Thanks

We gratefully acknowledge the asssistance provided to the Program Committee by the many reviewers whose names are listed here below:

Samy Ababatein, Alessandra Agostini, Amy Baltzer, Steve Benford, Richard Bentley, Jacques Bicard-Mandel, Elsa Bignoli, Ruth Bittingher, Richard Blumenthal, Terry Boger, Doug Bogia, Catharine Brand, Thomas Brink, Dan Brodsky, Monica Divitini, Paul Dourish, Simo El-Khadiri, Jeff Frankestein, Louis Gomez, Maria Antonia Grasso, John Hughes, Grant Jacob, Mark Kendrat, Val King, Anita Levinson, Christopher Lewis, Carlos Maltzahn, John Mariani, John McAlister, Giuseppe Omodei Salè, Daniele Pagani, Uta Pankoke-Babatz, Stefano Patriarca, Ted Phelps, Alberto Pozzoli, Dave Randal, Horst Santo, Federico Serrana, Borre Steen, Scott Stornetta, A.Tepper, Bill Tolone, Micheal Twidale, Esmerelda Wijngaarde, Wayne Wilner, E. Vance Wilson, Gerd Woetzel, Toshihiko Yamakami.

Table of Contents

Do Categories Have Politics? The Language/Action Perspective
Reconsidered
Lucy Suchman (Xerox Palo Alto Research Center) 1

COLA: a Lightweight Platform for CSCW
Jonathan Trevor, Tom Rodden, and Gordon Blair
(Lancaster Univ.) 15

Sharing To-Do Lists with a Distributed Task Manager
Thomas Kreifelts, Elke Hinrichs, and Gerd Woetzel
(GMD) 31

Supporting The Design Process Within An Organisational
Context
Bob Anderson, Graham Button (Rank Xerox EuroPARC)
and Wes Sharrock (Univ. of Manchester) 47

Improving Software Quality through Computer Supported
Collaborative Review
Philip Johnson and Danu Tjahjono (Univ. of Hawaii) 61

Design for Privacy in Ubiquitous Computing Environments
Victoria Bellotti (Rank Xerox EuroPARC), and Abigail
Sellen (Rank Xerox EuroPARC and MRC Applied
Psychology Unit) 77

The Designers' Notepad: Supporting and Understanding
Cooperative Design
Michael Twidale, Tom Rodden, and Ian Sommerville
(Lancaster Univ.) 93

A Spatial Model of Interaction in Large Virtual Environments
Steve Benford (Univ. of Nottingham) and Lennart Fahlén
(SICS-Kista) 109

Culture and Control in a Media Space
Paul Dourish (Rank Xerox EuroPARC) 125

TOSCA Providing organisational information to CSCW
applications
Wolfgang Prinz (GMD) 139

Unpacking Collaboration: The Interactional Organisation of
Trading in a City Dealing Room
    Christian Heath (Univ. of Surrey and EuroPARC),
    Marina Jirotka (Univ. of Oxford), Paul Luff (Univ. of
    Surrey), and Jon Hindmarsh (Univ. of Oxford)   155

Analyzing Cooperative Work in a Urban Traffic Control Room
for the Design of a Coordination Support System
    Geneviève Filippi and Jacques Theureau (URA CNRS)   171

Design for Unanticipated Use...
    Mike Robinson (Univ. of Aarhus)   187

Low Overhead, Loosely Coupled Communication Channels in
Collaboration
    Dorab Patel and Scott D. Kalter (Twin Sun, Inc.)   203

A Model for Semi-(a)Synchronous Collaborative Editing
    Sten Minör and Boris Magnusson (Lund Univ.)   219

Informed Opportunism as Strategy: Supporting Coordination in
Distributed Collaborative Writing
    Eevi E. Beck (Univ. of Sussex and Rank Xerox
    EuroPARC) and Victoria Bellotti (Rank Xerox
    EuroPARC)   233

Support for Collaborative Authoring via Electronic Mail: The
MESSIE Environment
    Martina Angela Sasse, Mark James Handley (Univ.
    College London) and Shaw Cheng Chuang (Cambridge
    Univ.)   249

Participation Equality and Influence: Cues and Status in
Computer-Supported Cooperative Work Groups
    Suzanne P. Weisband, Sherry K. Schneider and Terry
    Connolly (Univ. of Arizona)   265

The Use of Breakdown Analysis in Synchronous CSCW
System Design
    Silvia Pongutá Urquijo (Univ. of Technology,
    Loughborough), Stephen A.R. Scrivener (Univ. of
    Technology, Loughborough and Univ. of Derby), and
    Hilary K. Palmén (Heriot-Watt Univ., Edinburgh)   281

An Ethnography Studies of Graphic Designers
    Dianne Murray (Univ. of Surrey)   295

Building Shared Graphical Editors Using the Abstraction-Link-
View Architecture
    Tom Brinck and Ralph Hill (Bellcore)   311

Beyond Videophones: TeamWorkStation-2 for Narrowband
ISDN
  *Hiroshi Ishii, Kazuho Arita, and Takashi Yagi (NTT
  Human Interface Lab.)*   325
Bringing Media Spaces into the Real World
  *Daniele S. Pagani (Lucrezio Lab - Formative Networks
  and Rank Xerox EuroPARC) and Wendy E. Mackay
  (Rank Xerox EuroPARC)*   341

ECSCW '93 Directory: Authors and Committee Members   357

Proceedings of the Third European Conference on Computer-Supported Cooperative Work
13-17 September, 1993, Milan, Italy
G. De Michelis, C. Simone and K. Schmidt (Editors)

Do Categories Have Politics?
The language/action perspective
reconsidered

Lucy Suchman
Xerox Palo Alto Research Center, U.S.A.

Abstract: Drawing on writings within the CSCW community and on recent social theory, this paper proposes that the adoption of speech act theory as a foundation for system design carries with it an agenda of discipline and control over organization members' actions. I begin with a brief review of the language/action perspective introduced by Winograd, Flores and their colleagues, focusing in particular on the categorization of speakers' intent. I then turn to some observations on the politics of categorization and, wiith that framework as background, consider the attempt, through THE COORDINATOR, to implement a technological system for intention-accounting within organizations. Finally, I suggest the implications of the analysis presented in the paper for the politics of CSCW systems design.

No idea is more provocative in controversies about technology and society than the notion that technical things have political qualities. At issue is the claim that machines, structures, and systems of modern material culture can be accurately judged not only for their contributions to efficiency and productivity ... but also for the ways in which they can embody specific forms of power and authority. Winner 1986, p. 19.

By teaching people an ontology of linguistic action, grounded in simple, universal distinctions such as those of requesting and promising, we find that they become more aware of these distinctions in their everyday work and life situations. They can simplify their dealings with others, reduce time and effort spent in conversations that do not result in action, and generally manage actions in a less panicked, confused atmosphere. Flores et al 1988, p. 158.

The world has always been in the middle of things, in unruly and practical conversation, full of action and structured by a startling array of actants and of networking and unequal collectives ... The shape of my amodern history will have a different geometry, not of progress, but of permanent and multi-patterned interaction through which lives and worlds get built, human and unhuman. Haraway 1991, p. 11.

Introduction

Since the inception of CSCW as an explicit research agenda in the early 1980's, a class of systems has been under development that attempt to structure computer-based message systems into tools for the coordination of social action. Some of these have been concerned with affording flexible support for a diverse and changing ensemble of communicative practices (for example COSMOS/Bower and Churcher 1988). Others have been aimed at using system design as a mechanism for the prescription of *a priori* forms of social behavior. Arguably the most influential of the latter efforts has been the language/action perspective of Winograd, Flores and their colleagues and the system, trademarked THE COORDINATOR, designed to implement it .[1]

This paper is an attempt to contribute to a critical re-examination of the place of coordination technologies in CSCW research and development, in particular that class of technologies that seeks to develop canonical frameworks for the representation and control of everyday communicative practices. Among the latter, I take the language/action perspective of Winograd, Flores *et al* and its embodiment in THE COORDINATOR as exemplary. Of particular concern is the problem of how the theories informing such systems conceptualize the structuring of everyday conversation and the dynamics of organizational interaction over time. To anticipate, I will argue that the adoption of speech act theory as a foundation for system design, with its emphasis on the encoding of speakers' intentions into explicit categories, carries with it an agenda of discipline and control over organization members' actions. Alternatively, we might embrace instead something closer to the stance that historian Donna Haraway recommends; namely, an appreciation for and engagement within the specificity, heterogeneity and practicality of organizational life.

My strategy for developing this argument will be to juxtapose what might at first seem unrelated discussions, drawn on the one hand from influential writings within the CSCW community and on the other from recent social theory. Specifically, I begin with a brief review of the language/action perspective introduced by Winograd, Flores and their colleagues, focusing in particular on the place of speech

---

[1] Both the language/action perspective and THE COORDINATOR have been described in numerous publications. The present discussion relies upon Winograd and Flores 1986, and Flores et al 1988.

act theory and the categorization of speakers' intent in that perspective. I then turn to some observations on the politics of categorization offered by the sociologist Harvey Sacks, and on disciplinary practice by the philosopher Michel Foucault. The point of this latter move is to look at the place of categorization as an instrument in the control of social relations. With that sociological framework as background, I consider the attempt, through THE COORDINATOR, to implement a technical system for intention-accounting in organizations. Finally, I suggest the implications of the analysis presented for the politics of CSCW systems design.

Speech Act Theory

In their book *Understanding Computers and Cognition: A New Foundation for Design* (1986) Winograd and Flores present speech act theory as the basis for a particular doctrine of communication, and an associated machinery for the training and improvement of members' participation in organizational life. From the language/action perspective they describe, the "ontology" of organizational life comprises speech acts combined into "recurrent patterns of communication in which language provides the coordination between actions" (1988, p. 156). Through their development of this perspective, speech act theory has come to be a dominant framework for the conceptualization of communicative action within the CSCW community. To understand the underpinnings of that conceptualization requires a closer look at just what speech act theory takes to be its basic premises and what makes those premises compelling for computer research. The two aspects of the theory most relevant to the present argument are a) the premise that language is a form of action and b) the assumption that a science of language/action requires a formal system of categorization.

The observation that language is social action is due originally to Austin (1962) and the later Wittgenstein (1958), who argue for the impossibility of theorizing language apart from its use. Somewhat paradoxically, however, their observations have been taken by subsequent theorists as grounds for assuming that *a theory of language constitutes a theory of action*. Rather than setting up as a requirement on theorizing about language/action that it be based in investigations of talk as a form of activity, the observation that language is action has been taken to imply that action is, or can be theorized as, the use of language *qua* system to get things done. And language taken as a system provides a tractable core phenomenon for disciplines whose theory and methods best equip them for formal systems analysis. The proposition that dealing with language is dealing with action has consequently become a means of extending the scope of such disciplines while requiring little if any change to their organizing premises and practices.

Moreover, as Bowers & Churcher summarize it "[s]ince Austin, the development of speech act theory has been largely associated with Searle ... Searle has been at pains to formalise the notions introduced by Austin, to classify the conditions under which different kinds of speech acts can be appropriately ("felicitously") issued, and to explicate a typology of illocutionary acts. It is Searle's work which has proved particularly influential in CSCW" (op cit., p. 126). Language in this scheme is an instrumentality, a technology employed by the individual to express his or her intentions to others. The taxonomy of utterances that speech act theory after Searle proposes seeks to provide a comprehensive ordering of the available communicative tools, represented as a formalized "grammar of action" (Agre 1993, pp. 26-27).

In response to the popularity of speech act theory a number of cogent critiques have appeared in recent years based on observations drawn from the analysis of actually occurring conversation (see for example Bogen 1991, Bowers & Churcher 1988, Schegloff 1988, Levinson 1983.) These critiques turn on the interactional and circumstantially contingent character of meaning and intention. Briefly, the argument is that speech act theory takes communication as an exchange of speakers-hearers' intent, while conversation analyses underscore the irreducibly interactional structuring of talk. So, for example, conversation analysts have documented the ways in which a speaker's intent is observably shaped by the response of hearers over the course of an utterance's (co)production (see for example Goodwin 1981, chpt. 4; Goodwin & Goodwin 1992, Schegloff 1982.) Bowers and Churcher argue that the consequent "radical indeterminacy" of the unfolding course of human interaction presents a problem for any system designed automatically to track an interaction's course by projecting expected or canonically organized sequences. This, they argue, "cannot be ignored by designers of systems for CSCW without unwittingly coercing their users" (op cit, p. 137).

A related criticism of speech act theory turns on the difficulty, for the hearer/analyst, of categorizing the illocutionary force or perlocutionary effect of an utterance given its interactional and contingent character. THE COORDINATOR dispenses with this problem by enrolling speakers themselves in categorizing their utterances with explicit illocutionary tags. As Winograd and Flores explain it:

> We are not proposing that a computer can 'understand' speech acts by analyzing natural language utterances ... What we propose is to make the user aware of this structure and to provide tools for working with it explicitly. This is being done experimentally in a computer program that we are developing called a 'coordinator', designed for constructing and controlling conversation networks in large-scale distributed electronic communication systems ... An individual performs a speech act using THE COORDINATOR by: selecting the illocutionary force from a small set of alternatives (the basic building blocks mentioned above); indicating the propositional content in text; and explicitly entering temporal relationships to other (past and anticipated) acts (1986, p. 159).

So in the face of otherwise intractable uncertainties in accounting for the "illocutionary force" of a given utterance, THE COORDINATOR enlists participants in a coding procedure aimed at making implicit intent explicit. The premise of this procedure is that explicitly identified speech acts are clear, unambiguous, and preferred.[2] Whether based in the assumption that intent is somehow there already in the utterance and that what is being done is simply to express it, or that left to themselves people will remain vague as to their own intent and that of others and will benefit from the discipline of being pressed for clarity, the strategy of THE COORDINATOR is to remedy the carelessness of organization members regarding their commitments to each other through a technologically-based system of intention-accounting. According to Winograd and Flores the motivation here is explicitly self-improvement:

> In their day-to-day being, people are generally not aware of what they are doing. They are simply working, speaking, etc. more or less blind to the pervasiveness of the essential dimensions of commitment. Consequently, there exists a domain for education in communicative competence: the fundamental relationships between language and successful action... People's conscious knowledge of their participation in the network of commitment can be reinforced and developed, improving their capacity to act in the domain of language (ibid, p. 162).

The machine thus becomes the instructor, the monitor of one's actions, keeping track of temporal relations and warning of potential breakdowns. It provides as well, of course, a record that can subsequently be invoked by organization members in calling each others' actions to account.

Categorization as discipline

Speech act theory brings us into the presence of categorization as a basic device for modern analytic sciences, including the longstanding search for a science of intentionality. Within recent social science, in particular ethnomethodology, this tradition has been challenged through a conceptually simple but consequentially complex inversion of the status of categorization devices as analytic resources. Briefly, categorization has been taken up not just as a resource for analysts but as part of their topic or subject matter; that is, as a fundamental device by which all members of any society constitute their social order. With this move has come a rich corpus of theorizing and of empirical study about just how they do so (see for example Sacks 1979, Sacks and Schegloff 1979, Schegloff 1972.)

In his consideration of members' categorization devices, the sociologist Harvey Sacks was concerned among other things with the role that categorization plays in contests over the control of social identities. As a way in to his analysis we can take a passage from a 1966 lecture published under the title "Hotrodder: A Revolutionary Category" (1979). The problem Sacks sets up for himself in this

---

[2] See Bowers 1992, pp. 3-4 for a discussion of the modernist preference for the "clear and distinct"and its relation to agendas of explicitness, formalisation and control.

lecture is to understand what is going on with teenage kids and cars. Sacks himself is working with a piece of transcript, in which kids are talking about the relative likelihood of getting picked up by the police depending on what kind of car you are driving and, within that, just how you are dressed when driving it. Of this bit of talk and its implications Sacks says:

> We could work at it by asking such questions as, why do kids go about making up all those typologies of cars – and the typologies they have are really enormously elaborate, and they use those typologies to make assessments of other drivers, and the assessments are not always very nice, as we've seen. Now the question to ask is why do they do it? Aren't the terms that are used before they go to work good enough? And what's the matter with them if they aren't? (ibid, p. 8)

For my own present purposes, then, what I want to ask is: What is it about speech act theory that makes it so irresistably attractive as a way for practitioners of computer science and systems design to come to grips with organizational communications? Why do computer scientists go about making up all these typologies of interaction? Aren't the typologies used by practitioners themselves before the computer scientists go to work, enormously elaborate and used to make assessments of each other, good enough? And what's the matter with them if they aren't?

I have already suggested how a particular interpretation of language as action could contribute to the attractiveness of speech act theory for the computer sciences. To get more specifically at the question of categorization, we might begin by asking as Sacks does in relation to kids what it is that categorization provides for those making use of it in some domain of activity. Sacks frames his analysis of "hotrodders" in terms of acts of resistance, specifically how persons assigned to a place in a system of categorization not of their own making, e.g. "teenagers," can develop categories for themselves, e.g. "hotrodders" as, in Sacks' terms, a revolutionary act. That is to say, systems of categorization are ordering devices, used to discipline the persons, settings, events or activities by whom they are employed or to which they refer. Non-compliance with the use of a particular category scheme, particularly one imposed from outside, or the adoption of an alternative are in this sense acts of resistance.[3]

If membership categorization is appropriable as a technology of control by some parties over others, acts of resistance involve a taking back of systems of naming

---

[3] Liam Bannon points out that this is part of the wider phenomenon of "naming as a form of control ... the missionaries banning the use of native names and giving natives 'Christian' names to make them lose their sense of history, or the British in Ireland re-naming villages and counties in English terms that did not preserve the original Gaelic meanings, thus disinheriting future generations of their past folklore and roots" (1993, personal communication). Anthropology is replete with further examples, drawn from colonial encounters between European and indigenous cultures throughout the world.

and assessment into indigenous categorization schemes developed by the "others" themselves. In Sacks' words "that means, for example, that *they* will recognize whether somebody is a member of one or another category, and what that membership takes, and *they* can do the sanctioning ... what's known about hotrodders – what they do with their cars, how they look, how they behave – these are things that hotrodders can enforce on each other and defend against nonmembers" (ibid. pp. 11-12)

Sacks' analysis identifies the relation of categorization devices to social identity, including assessments of persons' adherence to the moral and aesthetic sensibilities associated with a particular category. It points as well to the ways in which categorization can be taken up as a resource in the development of more elaborated and formalised systems of social control. These systems form a kind of technology whether or not they are literally inscribed in a machine. In *Discipline and Punish* (1979) Michel Foucault traces the historical development of a figurative machinery of disciplinary practice, the military, and takes as a case in point the soldier, treated in the 17th century as an intrinsically honorable entity whose character was reflected in his bearing, becoming in the 18th century a technical body to be trained via exercise:

> These methods, which made possible the meticulous control of the operations of the body, which assured the constant subjection of its focus and imposed on them a relation of docility-utility, might be called 'disciplines' ... The historical moment of the disciplines was the moment when an art of the human body was born ... A 'political anatomy,' which was also a 'mechanics of power' ... it defined how one may have a hold over others' bodies, not only so they may do what one wishes, but so that they may operate as one wishes, with the techniques, the speed and the efficiency that one determines. Thus discipline produces subjected and practiced bodies, 'docile' bodies (pp. 137-38)

Foucault further points out that disciplinary practices invariably develop in response to specific problems in the administration of power. With these perspectives in mind, we can return to the idea of taking the categorization devices of speech act theory as a discipline for organizational communications. Like many of the cases reviewed by Foucault, this regime is to be administered technologically. That is to say, troubles diagnosed as breakdowns in communication are to be addressed through a technological solution involving a new communicative discipline. Speech act theory and its attendant technologies are offered as a remedy to perceived flaws and inadequacies in organization members' communicative practices, by providing a discipline enforced through the technology. The 20th century then might be seen as a return to the analysis and manipulation of what Foucault calls the 'signifying elements of behavior,' through the training of the body's intentions as reflected in its talk.

The Conversation for Action

To see how the discipline of intention-encoding plays out in the technology of THE COORDINATOR we can turn to Winograd and Flores' "theory of management and conversation," centered around the "conversation for action" pictured as Figure 5.1 (1986, p. 65) in their text:

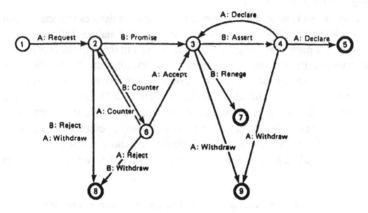

Figure 1. The basic conversation for action

As Winograd and Flores explain this figure in their text:

> As an example of conversational analysis we will consider in some detail the network of speech acts that constitute straightforward *conversations for action* – those in which an interplay of requests and commissives are directed towards explicit cooperative action. This is a useful example both because of its clarity and because it is the basis for computer tools for conducting conversations ...
>
> We can plot the basic course of a conversation in a simple diagram like that of Figure 5.1, in which each circle represents a possible state of the conversation and the lines represent speech acts (1986, p. 64, original emphasis).

This picture is central to Winograd and Flores' exposition and, perhaps even more importantly, to the machinery of THE COORDINATOR presented as its logical consequence. In a paper titled "Pictures of Nothing? Visual Construals in Social Theory" (1990) Michael Lynch suggests that representations like that of "the basic conversation for action" as he puts it "both describe the operations of 'rationality' and display 'rationalistic commitments'." Such pictures, he explains:

> ... do not propose to resemble observable phenomena, nor do they present readers with puzzles to be worked out in a visible workspace. Instead, they mobilize formal elements to exhibit and authorize a certain 'impression of rationality' ...

This impression of rationality is associated with at least the following formal elements: bounded labels, quasi-causal vectors, and spatial symmetries and equivalences ... The spatial separation between the labels contributes to a sense of their conceptual discrimination, and the coherent two-dimensional arrangement provides a unitary 'ground' for linking together the heterogeneous factors ... The labels are detached from the relative seamlessness and polysemy of discursive writing, taking on the appearance of stable concepts or even of names for things positioned in space ... The entire array of cells and vectors in the picture look somewhat like an electrical wiring diagram; a tracing of a tightly contained flow of an homogeneous force from one well-defined component to another (ibid, pp. 20-22).

The picture of the basic conversation for action unifies and mathematizes the phenomena it represents. It works by transforming a set of colloquial expressions into a formal system of categorization that relies upon organization members' willingness to re-formulate their actions in its (now technical) vocabulary (Agre 1993).[4] Once encapsulated and reduced to the homogeneous black circles and arrows of the diagram the "conversation" is findable anywhere. At the same time, specific occasions of conversation are no longer open to characterization in any other terms.

Winograd and Flores' figure of a conversation claims to be a reduction of the intentional structure of any conversation for action, while also providing the rendering that is required by the computer system, called THE COORDINATOR, that they present as a logical consequence of their analysis. In displaying categorical action types and their logical relations, the representation sets up the grounds for just the kind of menu-driven procedures for intention-encoding and accounting that the technology of THE COORDINATOR embodies and prescribes. The Conversation for Action, in contrast to conversations in the course of ongoing activity, is bounded and ready-to-hand for translation into the machine. And for management, the machine promises to tame and domesticate, to render rational and controllable the densely structured, heterogeneous texture of organizational life. As Flores *et al* put it in the citation with which this paper begins:

By teaching people an ontology of linguistic action, grounded in simple, universal distinctions such as those of requesting and promising, we find that they become more aware of these distinctions in their everyday work and life situations. They can simplify their dealings with others, reduce time and effort spent in conversations that do not result in action, and generally manage actions in a less panicked, confused atmosphere (1988, p. 158).

The assumption that "universal" distinctions such as requesting and promising are simple, however, conflates the simplicity of the category with the subtlety and complexity of the phenomenon categorized. One could imagine by analogy a

---

[4] Agre further points out that in the formalization provided by speech act theory the categories employed are not different from members' own so much as different in kind; that is, they are technical renderings of familiar terms.

system of painting that trained artists to follow a "simple" scheme of primary colors. But our sense of artistry in any field is precisely the ability to move, in more and less articulable ways, effectively through the circumstances in which one finds oneself. This is not done through reductions but through complex forms of highly skilled practice, involving an ability to bring past experience to bear in creative ways upon an unfolding situation.

There seems something of a contradiction, moreover, between the premise that THE COORDINATOR is a tool for introducing order into an otherwise "panicked, confused atmosphere," and the subsequent statement by Flores *et al* that

> [w]e are primarily designing for settings in which the basic parameters of authority, obligation and cooperation are stable ... THE COORDINATOR has been most successful in organizations in which the users are relatively confident about their own position and the power they have within it. This does not mean that the organization is democratic or that power relations are equal. It means that there is clarity about what is expected of people and what authority they have (ibid., p. 173).

Rather than being a tool for the collaborative production of social action, in other words, THE COORDINATOR on this account is a tool for the reproduction of an established social order.

Winograd and Flores argue that theory-driven design will produce coherent systems and practices. They report that implementations of THE COORDINATOR have been used to manage large software engineering enterprises, in which they claim the participants report that "by providing a computer tool to maintain the structure of the requests and commitments, they were able to greatly improve productivity" (1986, p. 161). Other reports of COORDINATOR use from the field, however, indicate that users selectively appropriate and ignore aspects of the system in an *ad hoc* fashion (see for example Johnson et al 1986; Bullen & Bennett 1990). On the one hand, users' failure in these cases to use the system as intended by its designers could be seen as a failure of the design, or of the discipline or compliance of users. On the other hand, it could be taken to reflect the desirability of systems that lend themselves to various *ad hoc* forms of customization in use (Bannon & Robinson 1991). The success that THE COORDINATOR has enjoyed, on the latter interpretation, would be understandable less as a result of its theory-driven coherence than of its practical adaptability.

Conclusion

The language/action perspective takes off from the observation that technologies comprise both artifacts and associated practices. From this it follows that "technology is not the design of physical things. It is the design of practices and possibilities to be realized through artifacts" (Flores *et al* 1988, p. 153). What ties together hotrodders, Foucault's soldier and the users of THE COORDINATOR is the belief by others that they must be brought into compliance with a particular conventional order. For technical systems it is the computer scientist (presumably assisted by organizational development consultants and the managers who employ them) who is now cast into the role of designer not only of technical systems but of organizations themselves. And implicit in the endeavor of professional organizational design is the premise that organization members, like the components of the technical system, require a strong, knowledgable hand that orders them, integrates them and brings them effectively into use.

Organizational design from a language/action perspective takes place within the context of a technological imperative that leads inexorably to change and, if done well, to progress. As Flores puts it:

> When we accept the fact that computer technology will radically change management and the nature of office work, we can move toward designing that change as an improvement in organizational life (*Flores et al* 1988, p. 154).

Before we accept this imperative, however, I would argue that we should subject it to the following questions:

First, what kind of a fact is it "that computer technology will radically change management and the nature of office work"? Computer technology, the directionality and dynamics of change, and the forms of work that are the objects of change are treated as self-evident, homogeneous and naturalized entities. But what if we were to open up this proposition to the uncertainties, heterogeneities and practical expediencies of the categories it invokes? We would need to specify then just what technologies concerned us, and how; whether, or even how those technologies are implicated in what processes of change; just what forms of managerial work we are concerned with and why; and what other forms of work, in what kinds of settings, we assume are getting done.

Second, who are "we"? From what position do we claim or are we granted rights to design change? In what sense is change designed? From what perspective do we assess the results of our actions as "improving organizational life," and for whom?

Throughout the history of communications technologies within organizations we find the imposition of regimes of action in the name of individual self-improvement and organizational efficiency (Yates 1989). At the same time, organization members are subjected to ever more elaborated systems of record-keeping, measurement and accountability.[5] Instead of the emancipating alternative that

---

[5] For a discussion of the relation of new regimes of "quality" and "empowerment "to such systems, and the ways in which they have become incorporated into the very doing of the work itself, see Agre 1993 and Suchman 1993.

Winograd and Flores would seek, they seem to offer yet another technology designed to create order out of "nature" by, as Haraway would put it, "policing her unruly embodiments" (1991, p. 20).

I have proposed that speech act theory offers to computer and management sciences a model of the communicative order compatible with the prior commitments of those enterprises – a model of speech that promises a universal basis for the design of technologies of accountability. By technologies of accountability I mean systems aimed at the inscription and documentation of actions to which parties are accountable not only in the ethnomethodological sense of that term (Garfinkel and Sacks 1970), but in the sense represented by the bookkeeper's ledger, the record of accounts paid and those still outstanding. If this promise of speech act theory is consistent with the intellectual antecedents and aspirations of computer and management science, however, it is also increasingly difficult to maintain in the face of a growing challenge from culturally and historically-based studies of talk as it is specifically located in space and time. Schegloff has stated this challenge in terms of the contest over "context" among disciplines:

> There is, to my mind, no escaping the observation that context ... is not like some penthouse to be added after the structure of action has been built out of constitutive intentional, logical, syntactic, semantic and pragmatic/speech-act-theoretic bricks. The temporal/sequential context rather supplies the ground on which the whole edifice of action is built (by the participants) in the first instance, and to which it is adapted 'from the ground up' ... (nd. p 21).

With the emergence of technologies like THE COORDINATOR, this contest is no longer over intellectual terrain alone. The inscription of formal representations of action in technical systems transforms the debate more clearly into a contest over how our relations to each other are ordered and by whom. Sacks' discussion of membership categorization draws our attention to the ways in which categorization devices are devices of social control involving contests between others' claims to the territories inhabited by persons or activities and their own, internally administered forms of organization. In the case of hotrodders, the move is to develop indigenous categories through which kids are able to claim back ownership of their social identities from the adult world that would claim knowledge of them. In the move to inscribe and encode organization members' intentions, as commitments or otherwise, we find a recent attempt to gain members' compliance with an externally imposed regime of institutional control. Sacks' insight can help us make sense of the abiding interest that those committed to the reproduction of an established institutional order might have in replacing the contested moral grounds of organizational commitment and accountability with a scheme of standardized, universalistic categories, administered through technologies implemented on the desktop.

References

Agre, Philip (1993) From high tech to human tech: on the sudden market for social studies of technology. In the proceedings of the workshop *Social science research, technical systems and cooperative work.* Paris, France, pp. 17-30.

Austin, J. L. (1962) *How To Do Things With Words.* Oxford: Clarendon Press.

Bannon, Liam and Robinson, Mike (1991) Questioning Representations. In *Proceedings of the European Conference on Computer-Supported Cooperative Work*, Amsterdam, The Netherlands, pp. 219-234.

Bogen, David (1991) Linguistic Forms and Social Obligations: A critique of the doctrine of literal expression in Searle. In *Journal for the Theory of Social Behavior*, Vol. 21, No. 1, pp. 31-62.

Bowers, John The Politics of Formalism. (1992) In M. Lea (ed.) *Contexts of Computer-Mediated Communication.* Hassocks: Harvester.

Bowers, John and Churcher, John (1988) Local and Global Structuring of Computer-Mediated Communication. In *Proceedings of the ACM Conference on Computer-Supported Cooperative Work*, Portland, OR, pp. 125-139.

Bullen, Christine and Bennett, John (1990) Learning from user experience with groupware. In *Proceedings of the ACM Conference on Computer-Supported Cooperative Work*, Los Angeles, CA, pp. 291-302.

Duranti, Alessandro (1991) Intentionality and Truth: An Ethnographic Critique. unpublished ms, Department of Anthropology, University of California, Los Angeles.

Flores, Fernando, M. Graves, B. Hartfield, and T. Wonograd. (1988) Computer Systems and the Design of Organizational Interaction. In *ACM Transactions on Office Information Systems*, Special Issue on the Language/Action Perspective. Vol. 6, No. 2, pp. 153-172.

Foucault, Michel (1979) *Discipline and Punish: The Birth of the Prison.* NY: Random House.

Garfinkel, Harold and Sacks, Harvey (1970) On Formal Structures of Practical Action. In J. McKinney and E. Tiryakian (eds.) *Theoretical Sociology.* New York: Appleton-Century-Crofts, pp. 337-366.

Goodwin, Charles (1981) *Conversational Organization: Interaction between Speakers and Hearers.* New York: Academic Press.

Goodwin, Charles and Goodwin, Marjorie (1992) Assessments and the construction of context. In A. Duranti and C. Goodwin (eds.) *Rethinking Context: Language as an interactive phenomenon.* Cambridge, UK: Cambridge University Press, pp. 147-190.

Haraway, Donna J. (1991) Science as Culture, Science Studies as Cultural Studies? Paper prepared for the volume *Cultural Studies Now and in the Future*, P. Treichler, C. Nelson, and L. Grossberg (eds.), in prep. , presented at a conference on Disunity and Contextualism: New Directions in the Philosophy of Science Studies. Stanford University, March31-April 1.

Johnson, B., G. Weaver, M. Olson, & R. Dunham (1986) Using a computer-based tool to support collaboration: A field experiment. In *Proceedings of the ACM Conference on Computer-Supported Cooperative Work*, Austin, TX, pp. 343-352.

Levinson, S. (1983) Speech Acts. Chapter 5 in *Pragmatics*. Cambridge, UK: Cambridge University Press.

Lynch, Michael Pictures of Nothing? Visual Construals in Social Theory. (1990) Paper presented at the 85th Annual Meeting of the American Sociological Association, Washington, D.C., August.

Sacks, Harvey (1979) Hotrodder: A Revolutionary Category. In G. Psathas (ed.) *Everyday Language: Studies in Ethnomethodology*. NY: Irvington, pp. 7-14.

Sacks, Harvey and Schegloff, Emanuel (1979) Two Preferences in the organization of references to persons in conversation and their interaction. In G. Psathas (ed.) *Everyday Language: Studies in Ethnomethodology*. New York: Irvington, pp. 15-21.

Schegloff, Emanuel (nd) To Searle on Conversation: A Note in Return. Prepared for a volume of essays in response to the work of John Searle, unpublished manuscript, Department of Sociology, University of California, Los Angeles.

Schegloff, Emanuel (1972) Notes on a Conversational Practice: Formulating place. In D. Sudnow (ed.) *Studies in Social Interaction*. New York, Free Press, pp. 75-119.

Schegloff, Emanuel (1982) Discourse as an Interactional Achievement. In D. Tannen (ed.) *Analyzing Discourse: Text and Talk*. Georgetown Roudtable on Language & Linguistics, Washington, D.C.: Georgetown University Press, pp. 71-93.

Schegloff, Emanuel (1988) Presequences and Indirection: Applying speech act theory to ordinary conversation. In *Journal of Pragmatics* 12, pp. 55-62.

Suchman, Lucy (1993) Technologies of Accountability: On Lizards and Aeroplanes. In G. Button (ed.) *Technology in Working Order: Studies in work, interaction and technology*. London: Routledge, pp. 113-126.

Winner, Langdon (1986) Do Artefacts Have Politics? In *The Whale and the Reactor*. Chicago: University of Chicago Press, pp. 19-39.

Winograd, Terry and Fernando Flores (1986) *Understanding Computers and Cognition: A New Foundation for Design*. Norwood, NJ: Ablex.

Wittgenstein, Ludwig (1958) *Philosophical Investigations*. Oxford: Blackwell.

Yates, JoAnn (1989) *Control through Communication*. Baltimore and London: Johns Hopkins University Press.

Proceedings of the Third European Conference on Computer-Supported Cooperative Work
13-17 September, 1993, Milan, Italy
G. De Michelis, C. Simone and K. Schmidt (Editors)

COLA: A Lightweight Platform for CSCW

Jonathan Trevor, Tom Rodden, Gordon Blair
Department of Computing, Lancaster University, U.K.

ABSTRACT: Despite the reliance of cooperative applications on the facilities provided by distributed systems, little consideration is given by these systems to the support of cooperative work. This paper examines the provision of appropriate mechanisms to represent cooperative work within a distributed platform. Based upon a examination of existing models of cooperative activity and the experiences of their use, a lightweight model of activities is suggested as the basis for the supporting platform. Rather than concentrate on the exchange of information, this lightweight model focus on the mechanisms of sharing of objects. This focus enables a clear separation between the mechanisms provided by the distributed platform and the policy which is the responsibility of the cooperative applications.

1. Introduction

The technologies currently exploited to construct cooperative applications were designed and developed prior to the emergence of CSCW and its associated applications. The facilities provided by these systems and the manner in which they are presented seldom sit easily with cooperative applications (Rodden, 1992). The needs of the application domain, the nature of the work and the mechanisms to support cooperation are intertwined within the development process. The developers of CSCW systems are forced to juggle all these factors in an attempt to realise a cooperative system. This is a painfully slow and problematic task resulting in a set of similar services replicated across a collection of applications in a manner that is confusing to both developers and users alike.

It our belief that a key requirement for developers of CSCW applications is the need for specific support for the development of these applications. Applications programmers should be free to concentrate on the semantics of the application and what should be provided. The programmer should not need to worry about how the mechanisms employed obtain the required result. The development of this support is essential to the future of CSCW and we would agree with (Patterson, 1991) when he argues:-

> "If multi-user applications are to flourish in the future, then programmers will require support for building these applications".

This paper presents a platform to support group working by providing mechanisms for sharing Cooperating Objects in Lightweight Activities (COLA). The COLA platform provides the means to allow applications to externalise appropriate features of cooperative activities in such a way that these can be shared across applications. Previous activity models have adopted a modelling perspective based on communication and its influences on work flow or document flow. In contrast, our approach is based on mediating the sharing of information rather than controlling its exchange. Consequently, the emphasis is on the provision of suitable supporting mechanisms within the platform. This approach allow the details of policy and the associated control of this policy to be administered by the applications being supported.

2. The Nature of Support

The need for support has been addressed within computing in a variety of ways relevant to CSCW. At the lowest level, existing distributed systems provide support for many features of cooperative applications, for example, object migration and location transparency. In addition, some distributed system designers are considering more advanced features which could prove useful to CSCW. These include multimedia objects, group multicasting and high performance networks.

Distributed systems are far removed from cooperative applications which embody a set of assumptions of why people work together and often characterise how they should work. These applications contain considerable information about the domain in which they are applied. A number of CSCW *application toolkits* have emerged to support application development in different cooperative domains. These toolkits provide a set of existing facilities for a particular domain which can be reused by developers in the construction of new applications. Examples of this form include RENDEZVOUS (Patterson et al., 1990) and LIZA (Gibbs, 1989) which support the development of multi-user interfaces and DISTEDIT (Knister and Prakash, 1990) a development toolkit to support the construction of shared editing systems.

These toolkits provide little or no support for representing the cooperation taking place. However, a number of *cooperative environments* exist which focus on representing cooperative work and how these representations can support the work taking place. Tremendous variety exists within these environments and a number of different classes can be identified. Some indication of the classes and the diversity of cooperative environments embrace are shown in figure 2 .

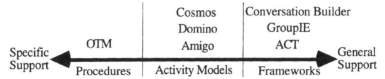

Figure 1. Spectrum of cooperative environments

In general, cooperative environments tend to be *goal oriented*; in that they include some conception of an activity or task which has some goal marking its completion. The more specific the support , the more specialised and narrow the goals. The majority of these systems are both computational and procedural in nature, However, *conceptual frameworks* exist where support is limited to the provision of models, outlines and frameworks upon which more specific instances can be built.

Procedural models describe well defined and understood tasks, almost exclusively in an office environment. The models control who takes part in a task, what operations they should perform in order for a task to be completed and what documents need to be exchanged. The model enforces what the user does and "runs" the procedure. Examples include OTM (Office Task Manager) (Lochovsky et al., 1988) and the systems currently being developed by action technologies based upon the COORDINATOR(Medina-Mora et al., 1992).

Activity models expand the horizons of procedural models by presenting a more general approach to task specification. In a similar manner to the procedure models, activity models have specific goals for the cooperation they are supporting. The main difference is that these models are general enough to be applicable to more than just those specific goals. The models concentrate on what and how information is exchanged between members of the activity and attach more significance to what these people can actually do. Many different systems offer these features, some of the most well known being COSMOS (Dollimore and Wilbur, 1991) , DOMINO-W (Kreifelts and Woetzel, 1987) and the AMIGO ACTIVITY MODEL (Danielson and Pankoke-Babatz, 1988).

Frameworks are the most general form of cooperative environment, they aim to provide support for cooperation, but without any specific domain in mind. The ACT (Activity CoordinaTion) model (Kreifelts et al., 1991) supports the coordination of activities in groups or teams. The ACT model differs from activity models (such as AMIGO and COSMOS which focus on coordinating the communication flow) by concentrating on coordinating the execution of actions. Other examples adopting particular perspectives on group work include GROUPIE (Rudebusch, 1991), CONVERSATION BUILDER (Kaplan et al., 1992) and OVAL (Malone et al., 1992).

2.1. Shortcomings of Existing Support

All applications, interfaces and tools rely, to a greater or lesser extent, on the underlying services provided. However, any problems with this support will inevitably be propagated upwards when the service is used. This is one of the major reasons why CSCW applications are so difficult to build. Not only do the applications contain many issues single user applications do not, but support can be unstable and often unsuitable for the demands that are placed on them.

The most obvious drawback of existing cooperative environments is that they are closed applications rather than open platforms and do not provide facilities to support a number of different approaches to cooperative work. In addition, the particular problems of merely extending or augmenting existing support models include:

i)Unrealistic Models of the real-world

One of the biggest shortcomings of existing support for cooperation is that they start from a set of unrealistic assumptions about work. For example, OM-1 (Ishii and Ohkubo, 1991) and other activity models represent well structured cooperative work knowledge. These assume that the information necessary for a task is know in advance and that the work follows a set procedure. In reality, work is not well structured or defined (i.e. the handbook is not followed and procedures are used as a resource rather than merely interpreted (Suchman, 1983)). Ishii and Ohkubo (1991) have also found this to be true in their experience of office tasks:

> "we found that office workers made many short-cuts and modifications to the standard procedures defined in the handbook. Therefore, it was no easy task to determine the actual standard procedure, even when it was defined clearly in the handbook".

Given that cooperative applications are intended to support the actual work of groups, unrealistic assumptions about that work will have tremendous impact upon the success of CSCW systems. Many authors have commented on the variability of work within natural settings and the difficulty of modelling this; interested readers are referred to (Bannon and Schmidt, 1992) for a full discussion of the issues involved. To minimise these problems we wish to reduce the set of assumptions within our support platform to the minimal set necessary to support cooperation.

ii) Constraining models of control

One of the main stumbling blocks of many activity models are that they rely on people behaving methodically and working to some plan. However, by constraining their actions users are being restricted by the model intended to help them. In fact, users often circumvent procedures and do the unexpected (Schmidt, 1991). This variability needs to be reflected in the support structure to allow applications to cope with variance from the expected norm. The handling of procedural exceptions in existing approaches is symptomatic of the problems of control. If exceptions are allowed, they can at best only be handled in a very general way. This leads to prescriptive models, which eliminate the possibility of exceptions and increase the burden upon the user.

Services and support tools should assist and augment higher levels of abstraction, and not prescribe particular viewpoints. The purpose of a support platform is to aid both the programmer and user, not to force them to do things in a particular manner. Consequently, a platform needs to provide the *mechanisms* necessary to represent cooperation. Policy surrounding control and coordination remains the exclusive responsibility of users or where appropriate applications.

iiii) Lack awareness of "groups"
With the possible exception of a few CSCW environments, existing computer platforms, tools and services provide only limited awareness of others, thus users are unaware of who is cooperating on what. It is often the case that people gain new insights and ideas from others and there is no reason why this shouldn't be the case when people cooperate together on a computer. A supporting platform should provide a high level of *"group awareness"*, with users aware of the actions of others.

iv) Limited support for "sharing"
Cooperative work relies on people *sharing* information (ideas, files, etc.). However, the majority of activity models attempt to coordinate people in cooperative work through a model of cooperation based on asynchronous message passing (for example, forms based systems). Little support is provided for the sharing of objects to support the cooperation taking place.

We would therefore, characterise much of the existing support as heavyweight with a high degree of application specific semantics encoded, and enforced, by a model based on message passing. We wish to consider the development of a lightweight model which adopts a perspective to cooperation based on sharing.

3. A Lightweight Approach

Future CSCW applications will desire a great deal more than current support can provide. Using the problems above as a basis, we can identify three major desirable characteristics for cooperative support platforms:

i)   A lightweight and flexible representation of cooperation

ii) A separation of the application semantics from the support features

iii) The provision of increased group awareness

Our approach is to design a platform which directly addresses these requirements. This will allow additional services to develop more realistic models of cooperation and allow further study into suitable and realistic underlying support for cooperation. In essence, this lightweight approach needs to provide useful *mechanisms* for describing cooperative situations, while relying only on *minimal semantic knowledge* in order to interpret these mechanisms.

Our focus is on the representation of cooperation which augments existing distributed services and communication systems. The COLA (Cooperating Objects in Lightweight Activities) platform provides a lightweight service which *aids users and applications in the cooperative use of objects*. The central part of the platform is a lightweight activity model which is used to provide a context in which objects can be shared. Unlike many cooperative environments, the bias of this platform is towards providing mechanisms to support sharing but with limited semantics. This means the platform acts as a "veneer" between semantically laden cooperative environments and distributed systems.

COLA presents mechanisms to cooperative applications and environments building upon the general mechanisms provided by distributed systems. With this approach:

- the only semantic information put into the activity are the events that change the state of the activity and the stages that an activity goes through.

- an activity can move forward and backwards or jump to any stage. The lightweight model does not specify when this occurs.

- objects can be shared amongst activities, and can be accessed from many different contexts (even from outside any activities)

- objects are context dependent and can present different interfaces to different people at different times.

- every change in an activity produces an event. Events are delivered to anyone who has specified some interest in it. Therefore, anyone in the system can be as aware as they like.

- users can move between activities as they wish and may undertake some roles local to an activity.

Activity *policy* rests exclusively with the application - the enforcement of deadlines and other features of activity control are contained within the application. The COLA platform can be considered as providing a set of *policy free mechanisms* to allow different features of activities to be represented. With a clean mechanism and policy separation the platform not only allows existing models to be built on top of it, but enables users to circumvent applications and directly interact with the platform.

The platform provides two important interfaces. The first is through a defined service interface available to cooperative applications. This allows applications to register activities and update the information within the activity model using remote procedure calls. An equally important component is the lightweight activity browser which provides a user interface to the activity model which allows activity information to be directly accessed and manipulated by users.

4. Components of a Lightweight Model

The lightweight model adopted within the COLA platform focuses on providing mechanisms to allow the externalised nature of activities to be represented and shared. Consequently, the platform is less concerned with either the structure or intent of the cooperation taking place but more with representing external effects of the cooperation. A number of distinct components exist within the lightweight model.

- *Activities*, provide a structure for the cooperation.

- *Roles*, limit object access and presentation in an activity.

- *Objects*, which are unaware of their context and Object *Adapters*, which present objects in context sensitive manner.

- *Events*, enable any objects registered in the platform to be kept group aware.

This section explains these main aspects of the platform in the following sections, for each, a brief example is given to illustrate its use.

4.1 Activities

A lightweight activity is defined as *a process in which users and objects interact and exhibit a public state.* A number of people participate in activities and an activity has a *life-cycle*, subdivided into *stages*, which it moves through before completion. Advancement and retreating of stages in an activity is done by the applications involved in the activity through the activity service provided by the platform. There are several reasons why the conditions required for a change of stage are not recorded in the definition of the activity (the "activity template"):

- this information is the sort of semantic information which may not be known in advance

- exceptions may arise outside of the activity which means a stage may need to be skipped or retraced.

- often, even simple events are not fixed and are open to negotiation within a cooperative setting.

As an example, consider the setting of an examination associated with an undergraduate course. The question paper should be created and approved before the examination takes place. The paper may be submitted for approval and edited any number of times. The exam commences at a given time and lasts a set duration.

Answer papers cannot be created before the exam starts, after the exam is completed no further additions to the answer papers can be made.

In this scenario, heavyweight activity models would focus on the construction of this activity and its decomposition into constituent subtasks. A traditional activity model would attempt to capture the dependencies between sub tasks, the deadlines associated with different tasks and the behaviour exhibited by different roles. In contrast, the lightweight model within the COLA platform focuses on the external effects of this activity by defining only the stages the activity must move through and the objects and people associated with it. The stages to an examination setting activity could be described as:

CREATEPAPER STAGE

Purpose	To create an exam paper for students to complete
People involved	Writers (of the paper), Reader (to check the paper)
Objects	Exam paper and Sample Solutions

DOPAPER STAGE

Purpose	For students taking the course to read and complete an answer paper using the exam paper previously created
Roles involved	Student (of the course), Examiner (to solve problems with the paper)
Objects	Exam paper and Answer sheets.

MARKPAPER STAGE

Purpose	To mark all the answer papers produced by the students
Roles involved	Marker
Ends	Answer sheets and Sample Solutions

4.2 Roles

In an activity, people do different things to contribute to the work taking place. For example, within the examination activity their exists people who:

- set the exam paper.
- check/proof read the paper to make sure it is satisfactory.
- answer the questions
- mark the answer papers

In order to represent this variability, people can take on different *roles*. Some roles may be taken by more than one person, some may only be assumed by one. Previous activity models have used roles to explicitly describe the behaviour of different people, in contrast, roles are used within the lightweight model as a means of access control. This access control is sufficient to represent within the framework the profiles of the different people taking part in an activity. That is not to say that the application using the activity model cannot *prescribe* activity related actions or conditions on that role but this is not within the platform model which wishes to remain semantically neutral.

Within the examination activity a number of distinct roles can be identified:-

WRITER	The role concerned with writing and creating the question paper
READER	This role makes sure the paper is satisfactory.
STUDENT	The users taking this role create and write the answers during the exam.
MARKER	Anyone in this role marks the students answer papers.

Many of these roles may be occupied by the same person (e.g. in reality the writer of an examination paper and the marker are often the same) and at each stage any roles are free to participate. However, the roles within an activity need to be encoded in such a manner as to highlight illegal[1] access operations, such as a student reading the exam paper before the exam starts.

4.3 Objects

Objects present the largest problem in a lightweight activity model. They can be accessed in several ways, from within an activity where they were created, from inside another activity or from outside of any activity. In each case the object may present a slightly different interface to reflect the invoking users rights. Objects in a lightweight activity model may also present a different set of operations (an interface) to each role during an activity. Thus an object exhibits a degree of *activity sensitivity*. However the basic object itself may still be activity unaware, but is merely presented in different ways to different roles and at different stages of the activity.

Accessing an object from within the context of an activity, through a role, means that the object must respond differently depending on the accessing role and the stage an activity is in. Accessing an object from inside another activity requires more rules for different roles for the second activity. More importantly the security of the object could be easily compromised as two activities may have no knowledge of the restrictions each has placed on the objects. Clearly it is cumbersome in the extreme, if not impossible, to define huge sets of rules on each object operation for every potential eventuality. The solution adopted within the COLA platform is the use of *Object Adapters*. which provide a clear interface between the objects within the platform and the entities which can access them.

4.3.1 Object Adapters

Object adapters have attempted to capture aspects of both object presentation and access control, and as such, have much in common with many methods in both of the presentation and access areas (such as capabilities and proxy objects (Shapiro, 1986)). However, object adaptors in COLA embody a set of concepts concerning the cooperative sharing of the object. Every object has a basic set of operations.

---

[1]Although appearing illegal, access might not necessarily be invalid. For example, it could be a matter of policy that dyslexic students are allow to read exam scripts in advance.

When an object is created from an activity that activity is given an object adapter that abstracts the basic object into a set of activity meaningful operations, together with a set of access rules for that object. The object adapter is initially defined as part of the activity and is stored, along with existing pre-defined activity templates (such as an exam activity) in an information store.

When an object is used, an instance of an object adapter is created which as far as the user within an activity is aware acts as the object and presents an appropriate interface to the them (as illustrated in figure 2). The object adapter provides several operations beyond normal interface filtering:

- *Extended operational semantics:* These methods masquerade as standard object interface operations insofar as the client would view the object interface without the adapter. However these new methods have deliberate side effects which change the underlying object into an object which is contextually sensitive. e.g. a normal "write" operation on a file will look the same to a client as the "write" operation on the underlying object, but will also perform some locking information.

- *Dynamic Contextual Filtering*: Unlike a normal interface to an object, which cannot change once it has been assigned, an object adapter provides a set of rules based on an associated activity's state and the client's current status within the system. These rules dictate what operations a user can invoke at any time during the activities life cycle.

- *Extendible Interfaces*: These are new operations specially provided by the adapter which use and act upon the semantic knowledge of what the object is supposed to represent with the activity.

- *Interface amalgamation*: No assumption is made that an adapter only presents one object interface. This means that an adapter can present a combination of more than one interface (and hence more than one object) to a client. The client only sees one object through the adapter

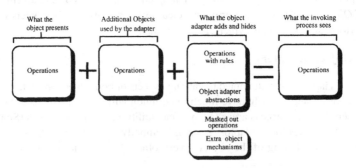

Figure 2. Presentation of an object

Each set of basic adapters and objects are managed and controlled by a master adapter, or simply a master. In effect the master adapter distinguishes the objects owner. This "ownership" can be transferred to any other activity or user at any time.

The rules describing which operations are usable by who, and when, inside the basic adapter and master are defined using a combination of the rules based upon the activity context, the role of the client, and the clients status in the overall system. If the object is *activity dependent*, e.g. an exam paper, then the set of allowable operations in the basic adapter will be very small. If the object is highly *activity independent*, e.g. a shared whiteboard application, then this set of operations may be large. One basic adapter is created per client of an object in order to allow the adapters to customise themselves towards particular clients.

It is up to the original activity, through the master, to promote clients to allow access to higher privilege operations. For each combination of user, role and activity which may access the adapter there is a corresponding rule and *access level*. Levels are a less cumbersome way of defining which operations can be performed on an object. Instead of listing the operations with each potential access, they are listed one (or more times) in the adapter and are ordered into one or more *"ladders"* of importance. Therefore the greater the degree of access you have, the "higher" up on a particular ladder you are, and the more operations you can perform. When the client invokes an operation on the object, through the adapter, the first rule which can be applied to the user (starting at the most specific) is applied. If no rules are applicable then the invocation fails. It is up to the original activity, through the master, to promote users and other activities to use higher privileged operations.

From the examination example, we can identify three necessary objects; the question paper, the sample solutions and the answer scripts. The following tables define the question paper as an abstraction of a text file which, for example, can only be read by someone in a student role when the activity is in the "DoPaper" stage.

UNDERLYING OBJECT: TEXT FILE

OBJECT OPERATION LADDER: 1

Level	Operation(s)
1	Write
2	Append
3	Read

QUESTION PAPER RULE SET:

User	Role	Activity	Required condition	Level	Ladder
any[2]	Student	*local*	stage = DoPaper	3	1
any	Reader	*local*	stage = CreatePaper	2	1
any	Writer	*local*	*none*	1	1
any	*any*	*any*	stage>= MarkPaper	3	1

2Keywords in italics have special meanings. "any" in the user column for instance matches any user.

4.4 Events

Events are small structured messages that are propagated around the environment in order to make environment objects aware of any changes of state. Events which the user or application are interested in and can generate are kept and managed by the platform. The awareness that events provide is primarily achieved by allowing users to register *interests* in certain types of event with the platform. When an event that matches this "interest" arrives at an activity it is delivered to the user (as well as the actual specified destinations). Events addressed to one activity from another, or events which are generated locally within an activity, are always seen by members of the activity.

An event is delivered according to three levels of addressing, the most general being to all the people registered to an activity. The next level is the role within an activity and finally the user themselves. It is not necessary to always specify the activity if a role is specified, nor a role or activity if a user is specified.

Events themselves all contain several standard fields. Each event must be *named* uniquely (within an activity) and contain a *description* that outlines what the purpose of the event is. Two addressing fields are used, the *source* and *destination*. Each of the addresses can be decomposed into *user* (which may be an object ID and therefore does not always refer to a human user), a *role* and an *activity*. The final part of an event is the *contents* field which can contain any number of text sub-fields which can have activities, roles and users tagged onto them to restricted reading and writing.

Any activity will have access to a core set of events. These include event which are commonly used between objects (e.g. for synchronisation) and by the user. One such event is the *notify* event, a very general message which can be passed between users, objects and a mixture of the two. Most events are a specialisation of this event. Within the examination example there are a few possible specialisations, for example:

PAPERREADY? EVENT

Purpose	To ask the READER role to check that the question paper is suitable of the exam.
Contents fields	The location / name of the question paper object
S'rce restrictions	Writer role
Dest' restrictions	Reader role

PAPERREADYREPLYEVENT

Purpose	To confirm to the READER that the paper is satisfactory or needs further work
Contents fields	Approval field and a text field indicating what work needs doing
S'rce restrictions	Reader role
Dest' restrictions	Writer role

EXAMSTART EVENT

Purpose	To inform the students taking the course that the exam is about to start
Contents fields	Examination start time and name of object holding the examination paper
S'rce restrictions	Reader, Writer and Marker roles
Dest' restrictions	-

COLA Events resemble *semi-structured messages* (Malone et al., 1986) (Ishii and Ohkubo, 1991) in many ways. These are text messages with identifiable types. Each type contains a known set of fields, but with some fields containing unstructured text or other information. The difference between events and semi-structured messages is in approach. Semi-structured messages concentrate more on the semantic nature of the information being sent in the message and its destination(s) whereas events are simpler. In effect, semi-structured messages can be viewed as a semantic extension and specialisation of events with events in COLA are closer to the use of events in Kronika (Lövstrand, 1991).

5. Functional Architecture and Services

The COLA platform, a number of simple applications and a *platform browser* which allows direct user access are currently being developed beyond an existing prototype. The prototype contains a fully working event model and a set of skeleton support services, coupled with a number of initial browser interfaces. ISIS (Birman and Marzullo, 1989) was chosen as a suitable toolkit to support the development in a distributed environment because of its use of process "groups" and associated multicast facilities. We want to compare and contrast ISIS as an underlying distributed support system with others, such as the ANSA TESTBENCH (ANSA, 89) and CHORUS (Rozier et al., 1990), in order to address two concerns:

- what are the distributed systems requirements of CSCW applications?

- what aspects of existing systems are useful in supporting these requirements?

Figure 3 shows the various objects that make up the functional architecture (circles) and the interprocess communication streams used to link them (lines and arrows). The most important conceptual aspects are controlled by the existence of corresponding managers. There is one activity manager and event manager per activity and an overall object manager, called an object trader.

Each *activity manager* maintains an activity template, which describes the associated components of the activity, and acts as the central point of coordination and reference for the activity. The activity manager responsibilities include membership, role allocation and activity update.

The *event manager* provides event propagation to both activity members and other event managers as well as providing facilities to allow event interests to be

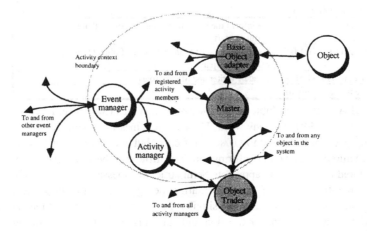

Figure 3. IPC calls between objects

registered and filters on these event registers. In the examination example suppose a user wished to see what events were going from Joe to Thomas, specifically in the activity known as "Examination course 123". The user would make up an event template with only the destination activity, destination user and source user fields completed (with the values "Examination course 123", "Thomas", "Joe" respectively) and then register this with *any* event manager, as all events are seen by every activity.

The *object trader* is split into two parts, the *finder* (where all objects in the COLA platform are registered) and *binder*. In order to obtain access to an object a user must put in a request or query to the binder (which take the form of an object template and a client context). The binder is the main point of access control and attaches a user to an object adapter to the underlying object.

6. Conclusion

This paper has highlighted the need to provide appropriate support for CSCW applications and has indicated that existing support is inadequate because of a number of problems. A platform to address these problems, COLA, has been described which acts as a bridge between distributed systems (which provide many mechanisms for sharing but without any knowledge of *why* people work together) and cooperative environments (which contain a great deal of semantic information, and often prescribe *how* people ought to work together). It consists of a flexible lightweight activity model, roles for access control, events for group awareness and object adapters, which enable objects to be context sensitive.

The platform is unconcerned with the semantics of what happens when information is passed around, and provides the means to share the information, relying on either social protocols or further computer management to ensure the information is used appropriately. This approach is still relatively new, but it is clear that if the wide range of future CSCW applications are to become adopted as useful everyday tools, then lightweight support is essential.

It remains to be seen how much of the CSCW application developers overhead has actually been removed by the COLA platform and how much, in terms of performance, the developer will have to pay in order to reap the possible gains that COLA provides.

References

ANSA (1989): "ANSA: An Engineer's Introduction to the Architecture", Release TR.03.02, Projects Management Limitied, Poseidon House, Castle Park, Cambridge, CB3 0RD UK. November.

Bannon, L., Schmidt, K. (1992): "Taking CSCW seriously", CSCW: An international Journal, vol. 1, no. 1, Oct 1992, Kluwer.

Birman, K., Marzullo, K. (1989): "ISIS and the META project." *Sun Technology*, Summer,1989, pp.90-104.

Danielson, T., Pankoke-Babatz, U. (1988): "The Amigo Activity Model.", in R.Speth (ed.):*Research into Networks and Distributed Applications.* Elsevier Science Publishers B.V., North Holland, pp.227-241.

Dollimore, J., Wilbur, S. (1991): "Experiences in Building a Configurable CSCW System.", in J.M.Bowers and S.D.Benford (eds.):*Studies in Computer Support Cooperative Work.* Elsevier Science Publishers B.V, North Holland, pp.173-181.

Gibbs S.J. (1989): "LIZA: An extensible groupware toolkit." in*Proceedings of the SIGCHI Human Factors in Computing Systems,* Austin, Texas, ACM Press, pp. 29-35.

Ishii, H., Ohkubo, M. (1991): "Message Driven Groupware Design Based on an Office Procedure Model, OM-1." *Journal of Information Processing*, vol.14, no. 2,1991, pp.184-191.

Kaplan, S.M., Tolone, W.J., Bogia, D.P., Bignoli, C. (1992): "Flexible, Active Support for Collaborative Work with Conversation Builder." in: *Proceedings on the conference for CSCW''92,* Toronto, Canada, 1992, pp.378-385.

Knister, M.J., Prakash, A. (1990): "DistEdit: A distributed toolkit for supporting multiple group editors." in: *Proceedings of the Conference on Computer Supported Cooperative Work October 7-10,* Los Angeles, California, 1990, ACM Press,

Kreifelts, T., Licht, U., Seuffert, P., Woetzel, G. (1984): "Domino: A system for the specification and automation of cooperative office processes." in: *EUROMICRO.,* 1984, pp.33-41.

Kreifelts, T., Pankoke-Babatz, U., Victor, F. (1991): "A Model for the Coordination of Cooperative Activities." in: *Proceedings of the International Workshop on CSCW,* Berlin, 1991, pp.85-100.

Kreifelts, T., Woetzel, W. (1987): "Distribution and Error Handling in an Office Procedure System.", in D.Tsichritzis and G. Bracchi (eds.):*Office Systems: Methods and Tools.* Elsevier Science Publishers B.V., North-Holland, pp.197-209.

Lochovsky, F.H., Hogg, J.S., Weiser, S.P., Mendelzon, A.O. (1988): "OTM: Specifying Office Tasks." in: *ACM Proceedings on the Conference on Office Information Systems,* Palo Alto, CA, 1988, pp.46-54.

Lövstrand, L. (1991): "Being selectively aware with the Khronika System," in L. Bannon, M. Robinson and K. Schmidt (eds.):*ECSCW '91. Proceedings of the Second European Conference on Computer-Supported Cooperative Work,* Kluwer Academic Publishers, Amsterdam, 1991, pp. 265-279.

Malone, T.W., Grant, K.R., Lai, K., Rao, R., Rosenblitt, D. (1986): "Semi-Structured Messages are Surprisingly Useful for Computer-Supported Coordination." in: *Proceedings of conference on CSCW'86,* Austin, Texas, 1986, pp.102-114.

Malone T.W., Lai K., Fry C. (1992): "Experiments with Oval: A Radically Tailorable Tool for Cooperative Work." Proceedings of CSCW'92: ACM 1992 conference on Computer Supported Cooperative Work, October 31 to November 4, 1992, Toronto, Canada, ACM press, pp. 289-297.

Medina-Mora, R., Winograd, T., Flores, R., Flores, F. (1992): "The Action Workflow Approach to Workflow Management Technology." in: *Proceedings of the conference on CSCW'92,* Toronto, Canada. November, 1992, pp.281-288.

Patterson, J.F. (1991): "Comparing the Programming demands of Single-User and Multi-User applications."*User Interface Software and Technology (UIST),* November 11-13, 1991, pp.87-95.

Patterson, J.F., Hill, R.D., Rohall, S.L., Meeks, W.S. (1990): "Rendezvous: An architecture for synchronous multi-user applications." in (eds.): *Proceedings of the Conference on Computer Supported Cooperative Work October 7-10,* Los Angeles, California, 1990, ACM Press, pp.317-328.

Rodden, T., Blair, G.S. (1991): "CSCW and Distributed Systems: The Problem of Control." in L. Bannon, M. Robinson and K. Schmidt (eds.):*ECSCW '91. Proceedings of the Second European Conference on Computer-Supported Cooperative Work,* Kluwer Academic Publishers, Amsterdam.

Rodden T., Mariani J., Blair G. (1992): "Supporting Cooperative Applications", CSCW: An international Journal, vol. 1, no. 1, Oct. 1992, Kluwer

Rozier, M., Abrossimov, V., Armand, F., Boule, B., Gien, M., Guillemont, M., Herrmann, F., Kaiser, C., Langlois, S., Leonard, P., Neuhauser, W. (1990): "Overview of the CHORUS Distributed Operating Systems", CS/TR-90-25, Chorus Systemes. April 15.

Rudebusch, T.D. (1991): "Supporting Interactions within Distributed Teams." in: *International Workshop on CSCW,* April 9-11, 1991, pp.17-33.

Schmidt, K. (1991): "Riding a Tiger, or Computer Supported Cooperative Work," in L. Bannon, M. Robinson and K. Schmidt (eds.):*ECSCW '91. Proceedings of the Second European Conference on Computer-Supported Cooperative Work,* Kluwer Academic Publishers, Amsterdam.

Shapiro, M. (1986): "Structure and encapsulation in distributed systems: The proxy principle." in:*6th International Conference on Distributed Computer Systems,* May, 1986, pp.198-204.

Suchman, L.A. (1983): "Office Procedures as Practical Action: Models of Work and System Design", *ACM Transactions on Office Information Systems,* vol.1, no.4, October 1983, pp. 320-328.

Proceedings of the Third European Conference on Computer-Supported Cooperative Work
13-17 September, 1993, Milan, Italy
G. De Michelis, C. Simone and K. Schmidt (Editors)

Sharing To-Do Lists with a Distributed Task Manager

Thomas Kreifelts, Elke Hinrichs, Gerd Woetzel
Gesellschaft für Mathematik und Datenverarbeitung, Germany

Abstract: We describe a simple and powerful tool for the management of distributed work: the Task Manager. Common tasks may be shared and manipulated independently by a number of people. They are represented as shared to-do lists at the user interface. With the help of the tool, users may organize cooperative tasks, monitor their progress, share documents and services, and exchange messages during task performance. The paper gives the motivation for the development of the Task Manager, implementation details, and a first assessment of its usefulness.

1 Introduction, or: Why do we need tools for the management of distributed work

Working in large and geographically distributed business organizations and government agencies requires that individuals and groups at different sites engage in intensive cooperative activity. Business teams are formed from different parts of an organization, and agencies in non-centralized government settings have to cooperate over large distances. There is a trend towards formation of joint ventures and consortia to carry out large projects across organizational and national boundaries. All this leads to an increasing need for computer tools to support distributed task management in order to provide better overview and to avoid expensive inefficiency, errors, and delay.

Another incentive for the development of support tools for distributed task management is the emergence of alternative forms of the organization of labour: on the one hand we have an increasing number of people working "on the move", e.g. at a customer or on a construction site. On the other hand we observe a tendency towards people working at home in order to avoid commuter traffic and enable more effective part-time working.

The EuroCoOp project set out to provide the required support by developing facilities for distributed work management, including tools for the scheduling and coordination of cooperative activities, progress monitoring, formal reporting, and joint authoring of documents. Within this project, over the period of the past two years, we have developed the Task Manager as a tool to share and manage common tasks in a community of distributed users[1].

The Task Manager is a prototype software system for specifying and managing cooperative activity. With its help, users may organize (create, refine, and modify) cooperative tasks, monitor their progress, share documents and services, and exchange messages during task performance. The Task Manager distributes task specifications, attached documents, and messages to the involved users in a consistent way. It is meant to support the management of work distributed in time and/or space by providing

- support of organization and planning of collaborative work (who does what, with whom, until when, using what?),
- up-to-date overview of collaborative activity and work progress,
- dynamic modification of work plans during performance,
- availability and exchange of documents and messages within groups of people involved in task performance.

The Task Manager organizes distributed work in tasks which have a person responsible, a deadline, other participants, the material necessary for task performance, and possibly subtasks. The primary user interface of the Task Manager is a hierarchically structured to-do list which displays all tasks a user is involved in and which allows direct access to the relevant information attached to a task.

2 Motivation, or: Why develop coordination tools

There has been considerable research on coordination tools; recently also a number of commercial products has appeared claiming to support coordination.

Commercially available products come in different flavours: some cover certain aspects of the problem like personal productivity tools, group calendars for local networks, project management systems (which are single user applications for project managers). Others represent closed "groupware" solutions with no clear concept of, and not particularly tuned to, coordination. The integration of, or interoperability with, existing computer support (like word processors, data base sys-

---

[1] Research reported in this paper has partly been funded by the Commission of the European Communities within the project no. 5303 "EuroCoOp - IT Support for Distributed Cooperative Work" of the ESPRIT Programme in 1991 and 1992. Project partners were TA Triumph-Adler, Århus Universitet, BNR Europe, empirica, GMD, Jydsk Telefon, NeXor, and Storebæltsforbindelsen.

tems, spreadsheets etc.) usually presents a serious problem. Consequently, there is not much support available on the market that provides the comprehensive coordination functionality and the necessary amount of "openness" to third-party software that we consider essential.

Within academic research, quite a number of models, prototypes, and systems have been developed with the explicit goal of coordination. Not many of these approaches have ever been implemented or even put to use; so there is not much experience with coordination tools in spite of the obvious need for such tools. The few experiences reported on computer support for coordination exhibited a number of difficulties with those systems, particularly the lack of flexibility and interoperability. This has also turned out to be true for the office procedure system DOMINO (Kreifelts et al. 1991) that we had implemented and assessed. Consequently, we focused on two problems:

*   the *rigidity* of pre-defined procedures and imposed structures which lead to a limited application domain and non-adequate exception handling in a number of situations
*   the *isolation* from informal communication, information sharing, and other forms of computer support.

To avoid the implications of rigidity, it has been argued in (Hennessy, Kreifelts and Ehrlich 1992) that future coordination support systems should focus on Schmidt's proposal (1991) of treating models of cooperative work as *resources* to be defined, modified, and referred to for information purposes instead of as *prescriptions* to be adhered to. To overcome the relative isolation future coordination support systems have to be able to interface to existing computer systems that support the actual work — coordination is never an end in itself.

Another aspect that so far seems to have been largely neglected is the effort needed to make use of coordination systems: most systems require *pre-organization* of the cooperative work by some sort of systems administrator before a system may be put to use by an ordinary user. Instead, one would like to have coordination systems that encourage *self-organization* of cooperative work by the end-users themselves. In order to overcome this initial barrier of using coordination systems, the genericity and simplicity of the underlying coordination model are of primary concern.

3   Description, or: What are the basic concepts of the Task Manager

We now describe the framework on which the Task Manager is based: its components and their attributes, and the operations to create and modify task structures. We then give a picture of how all of this is presented at the user interface.

3.1 Components

The central notion of the Task Manager is that of a *task*. In order to perform a task, *people* use shared *documents* and/or *services* and communicate by sending *messages* to each other.

- Tasks

   The Task Manager's notion of a task has various aspects: one could think of a task as of a project, i.e. a common goal of a set of people (*result-oriented*). A task may be broken up into several sub-tasks and dependencies may be defined between them and their documents. The more detailed specifications are given, the more a task resembles an office procedure with causal dependencies between subtasks and documents of a task (*procedure-oriented*). A task may also be used as a simple folder with little or no structure defined: in that case a task is simply a shared container of subtasks, documents and/or services, and messages that people exchange about in a common task (*information-sharing-oriented*).

- Documents/services

   In everyday office life, there are generally resources of some sort needed in order to achieve the goal of a task; therefore, each task may have resources attached to it. Resources are "pointers" to various kinds of computerized objects: the first kind of resource one could think of would of course be documents that are shared between the participants of a task. But there are also other resources like rooms, budgets, machinery, etc. that may be crucial to the performance of a common task. In our system those resources are handled by services that are implemented outside of the actual Task Manager, but may be referred to and shared by the participants of a task.

- People/users

   The most important "resource" are the people involved in a common task. We distinguish between various levels of participation and of competence. There is a set of people involved in a task, the *participants*, that all have equal access rights to the attributes of a task, its documents and services and its messages. Participants may invite other people to take part in the task, i.e. to become new participants or observers. *Observers* are people interested in the completion of the task with read access only to any information and the right to participate in the informal message exchange associated with the task.

   One of the persons involved in a task is "more equal" than the others: the *person responsible* for the performance and the outcome of the task. S/he has exclusive write access to some of the tasks attributes, e.g. state, start date and deadline, and only s/he may reassign the responsibility of the task to another person.

- Messaging

   Participants and observers may freely exchange informal electronic mail messages within the context of a task. By integrating and facilitating extensive message exchange we give more room to flexible social protocols in contrast to regulations dictated by the system.

3.2 Attributes

Tasks, participants, documents, and services are specified in more detail by a set of attributes each. The *title* of a task both identifies a task to its participants and gives a short and concise description of its goal. The title of a task is the only mandatory attribute — thus, the user is not forced to fill out long forms before s/he can actually start working on a task. All other attributes are either optional or set to a default value by the system. E.g., when a user initially creates a task s/he automatically is the *person responsible* for it.

As mentioned above, the person responsible for a task has special rights; in particular s/he may set the *state* of a task. We only distinguish between the completion state of *not finished* and *finished*. This state is set by the user. Apart from the completion state, a task can be *pending*, i.e. there is a causal dependence on another task not yet finished, or *not pending*. This state is set by the system automatically, and should help the user decide when best to start with the actual work on a task. As a third kind of state information, a task can be *acknowledged* by the responsible actor. This is to inform the co-workers of the responsible person's awareness and acceptance of the task s/he has been assigned to.

Another important attribute is the envisioned *deadline* of a task. The system reminds the user of approaching deadlines, but does not enforce any actions with respect to overdue tasks.

Besides those most important attributes there are a number of other attributes that allow the user to specify in more detail how a task should be performed: time-related data, such as *start date*, data that describes causal *dependencies* between tasks and between tasks and documents, and *personal data* attached to a task, such as notes etc. The latter attributes are purely local and are not distributed to and shared by the other participants.

Documents and/or services may be attached to any task in which the user participates at any time. They consist of a name, a history of who did what and when, the owner of the document and other data. After discussions with prospective users we added the *abstract* attribute of a document: it contains an informal text description of the document and it frees the user of having to transfer, open and read the entire document when s/he is only interested in a resume. For reasons of simplicity, we decided to implement a semi-transparent file transfer service (cf. section 5). Other resources as mentioned above are handled by separately implemented services; the system keeps an account of so-called service requests, but leaves other details to the respective service.

Participants are people that work together on a common task. They are worldwide and uniquely determined by a pair of ids or by an X.500 distinguished name.

We also support more user friendly names, individual address books, and access to the X.500 directory service.

3.3 Operations

Users can create tasks and subtasks, dependencies between tasks and between tasks and documents, they may set and modify attributes, add, modify, and remove documents and service requests. Persons responsible for a task may refuse responsibility and they may reassign it to another user. Any participant can introduce new participants or observers to a task. Tasks may be copied and pasted or moved around freely. All of this may be done at any time, thus allowing dynamic modification of the work situation at run-time.

Basically, the system distributes information on tasks, makes available resources across the (world-wide) network, keeps the data up-to-date, and resolves conflicts of synchronization. Each user has instant access to the shared tasks s/he is involved in. The system guarantees a consistent view on tasks for each participant. Additionally, the system keeps track of the actions the users take. Thereby monitoring and task tracking at execution time as well as report generation after completion of a task is rendered possible.

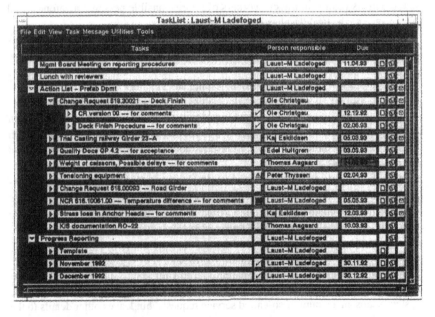

Figure 1. Task List user interface

3.4 User interface

The set of tasks a user participates in is presented at user interface level as a *Task List*, very similar to conventional outliner programs (Figure 1). The Task List gives an overview of the hierarchically ordered tasks along with a condensed view of the most important attributes: *title, person responsible, deadline, documents/services, participants, state*, and a list of *messages* that have been exchanged within that task. Operations are invoked by selecting menu commands and/or by directly typing in the attribute fields. In most cases, the Task List will suffice to display the information and to perform the necessary operations.

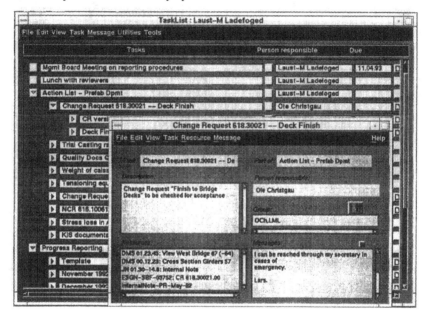

Figure 2. Task Editor user interface

For more detailed information, we provide a form-oriented *Task Editor*; it may be used to view and edit in detail all of the attributes (Figure 2). The Task Editor also provides access to a local address book as well as to external addressing information such as the X.500 directory.

The *Dependency Editor* represents groups of sub-tasks and documents in a net-like way; it mainly serves the purpose of graphically displaying and editing dependencies between tasks and resources. The dependency structures are similar to those used in workflow systems, but are interpreted differently: instead of driving a workflow with a strict sequencing of steps, dependencies in the Task Manager represent recommendations which may be changed or overridden by the users at any time.

The *Logging Tool* gives a complete history of events with respect to all or to selected tasks, and lets the user acknowledge new events (Figure 3). Thereby, s/he may find out what's new since "last Tuesday".

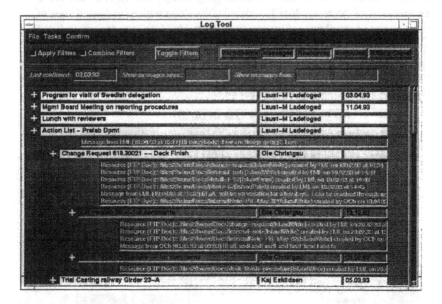

Figure 3. Logging Tool user interface

Other views are possible and desirable, but are not yet implemented: filters on the Task List on the basis of selection criteria, sorting according to other criteria, Gantt or milestone charts for a group of sub-tasks in order to facilitate time management, etc.

4 Usage, or: What can you do with the Task Manager

In the following, we describe in more detail how we envisage the usage of the Task Manager — this will also include other forms of system usage not generally associated with the term "task coordination".

4.1 Different Kinds of Usage

We have chosen some typical forms of usage which will demonstrate the versatility of the Task Manager tool; like with ordinary paper to-do lists, such different types of usage may be mixed with one another.

- Personal To-Do List
  This is the simplest form of use: tasks in the Task Manager's task list are not shared with other users, but serve as reminders for actions to be taken; that may range from trivial tasks simply represented by their title to specifications of complex projects. Entries in the task list may also simply represent "folders" for a set of tasks.
- Brainstorming, Conferencing
  A task may be thought of as an environment for off-line brainstorming. Prospective contributors are added as participants to the task and offered a short description as to the purpose of this activity. They may add their ideas as text messages or documents of any kind. The person responsible acts as a moderator and may form subconferences if necessary. A passive observer status is possible.
- Meeting Preparation
  The preparation of a meeting can be made a task: the invitation and other important documents will be distributed to the participants as documents attached to such a "meeting task", the participants can give their feedback via the task conference, the organization of the meeting, the writing of the minutes or other follow-up activities can be made subtasks of the meeting task.
- Project Planning and Monitoring
  The support of this activity is a natural for the Task Manager: it supports a gradually and dynamically refinable and restructurable structure of tasks and subtasks, the responsibility may be assigned and reassigned, the completion state is reported by the responsible persons as tasks are carried out, and deadlines can be set and monitored.
- Project Execution
  Also the project work itself can be coordinated, because relevant material and applications may be attached to the respective tasks and subtasks of the project in order to be shared and worked upon by the project members. The somewhat primitive document access and version control mechanisms would have to be complemented for more sophisticated applications by special services.
- Repetitive Tasks
  The Task Manager supports the reuse of task specifications which may be first edited to fit the current situation and then "pasted" into the list of tasks. Templates for repetitive tasks may be stored privately or copied from organizational databases.
- Bulletin Board
  This again is a very "simple" use of the Task Manager: a task represents a topic described by the title, the bulletins are added as messages or documents to the task and are then available to all participants. Hierarchical structuring of topics is possible via creating subtasks. New participants may be introduced by existing ones. Participants no longer interested may leave the topic in question.

The above is not meant to prove that almost every kind of collaborative (or even non-collaborative) activity may be supported by the Task Manager; of course we are aware of collaborative tasks which would require more specialized support, like e.g., the joint authoring of documents. We want to show that the Task Manager can be used in various ways not just for the management of clearly defined tasks.

The various kinds of usage are not necessarily to be kept separate from one another but can dynamically develop from one kind to another. For instance, a task in the personal to-do list ("Should develop a productivity tool for our software production") can be turned into a brainstorming item by adding a few more participants. Documents attached to such a personal to-do list item, e.g. a draft proposal ("A Distributed Task Manager for Software Production") are distributed to the other participants and may now be commented on. Eventually, a project plan could develop from this activity; some persons involved in the planning activity drop out of the task, new participants are introduced which have special skills needed for the project. A senior manager is added as an observer of the top level task so as to be informed of the essentials of the project, and so on.

4.2 Synchronous and Colocated Usage

Within the well known two-by-two matrix of CSCW systems introduced by R. Johansen which distinguishes systems along the dimensions of temporal and spatial distribution, the Task Manager clearly falls into the asynchronous, geographically distributed category: the Task Manager does not require that its users sit in front of their workstations at the same time nor in the same room. On the other hand, it does not forbid this, i.e. the Task Manager may also be used in the colocated or synchronous case.

For instance, a user may realize that another user is actively manipulating tasks around the same time s/he does and could react by sending a message or even call the other participant and discuss rearranging or rescheduling a group of subtasks while both would look at the task list and do some editing. They could also sit in front of the same display and work together on some tasks; the results of such a session would be automatically distributed to each of them (and any other participants).

Another example is that of a project meeting where the task structure is discussed by the participants equipped with the Task Manager on mobile computers. So, while mainly meant for work situations distributed in time and space, the Task Manager may also be used synchronously or in colocated situations.

4.3 Scalability of Use

The Task Manager may not only be used by a limited number of users over a local network. Special attention has been paid during its development to its scalability with regard to the number of users, the number of tasks, and the dimensions of geographical distribution. The Task Manager is not limited in this respect other than by the availability of computer storage and store-and-forward communication facilities. It may be used for the support of large user communities over large geographical distances without restrictions or deterioration of functionality.

5 Implementation, or: How does the Task Manager work

Starting with the conception of the coordination model, the Task Manager was developed over a period of two years, with a first prototype after about 15 months. The subsequent phase of evolutionary development included: stabilization of the prototype; evaluation in simulated work situations by potential users which brought valuable feedback to the developers; essential enhancements of functionality and user interface towards a workable system.

Having had an early working prototype paid in terms of quality of the present system. Now that the Task Manager is rather stable it is in use within the developers' group, among other things for project management and the development of the next version of the system itself. We plan to gradually extend this system usage to different types of settings, e.g. with the partners of our present European project.

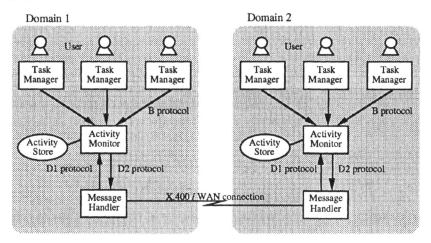

Figure 4. Software Architecture of the Task Manager

Figure 4 gives an outline of the software architecture. It shows two domains linked by standard X.400 store-and-forward message transfer — however, the number of domains is not restricted. The concept of domains reflects the different speed of

LAN or WAN communication. Within a domain, a client-server approach is used to update a shared task structure, while X.400 messages are used to distribute changes to other domains. Every user of the system is located in a specific domain and uses his/her own instance of the Task Manager. This tool manages user specific views of the user's task list. Using remote procedure calls, the Task Manager talks to the Activity Monitor to get up-to-date data and to request changes to the domain-wide shared Activity Store. In each domain, there is one instance of the Activity Monitor that serves multiple Task Manager instances.

When a user modifies a specific task or the task structure, the Task Manager sends an operation request to the Activity Monitor. The monitor executes the operation in the Activity Store and broadcasts the request to the remote domains involved via the Message Handler. When an operation request arrives from a remote domain, the Message Handler passes it over to the Activity Monitor which then updates the corresponding task objects in the Activity Store accordingly.

The task objects are actually replicated in different domains. This is needed because user operations on tasks should be immediately reflected in local changes. A user will not wait for operation requests or results transported over WAN connections, but requests a fast response — even if the response is preliminary in some cases as discussed below. Strictly speaking, tasks have to be replicated not only in those domains where participants of the task itself are located but also in domains where participants of supertasks can observe a task (a task can be subtask of more than one supertask). Therefore, the replication of task objects depends on task participants and the hierarchical task structure which both may change dynamically. Task replication is completely transparent at the user interface. The essential purpose of the Activity Monitors is exactly the distributed control of the replication and modification of task objects in spite of WAN connection breakdowns between Activity Monitors and lost or duplicated messages on WAN connections.

Obviously, a concurrency problem has to be solved for this architecture: operation requests arrive asynchronously at the Activity Monitors from local and remote domains, while all users in their different domains should eventually have a compatible view of the task structure (which needs not necessarily be the same view). As a solution, we have designed the D protocols between the Activity Monitor and the Message Handler in such a way that the causal order of operations on task objects is preserved[2]. As a main feature, our protocols enable the Activity Monitor to detect concurrent updates of task attributes, and to resolve conflicting assignments by assuming a linear order on those events.

Of course, all Activity Monitors must reach the same belief about the linear order eventually. The effect of this strategy for users is that sometimes local changes be-

---

[2] Our approach is similar to the *cbcast* method within process groups in the ISIS system (Birman, Schiper and Stephenson 1991). But in contrast to the ISIS system, we only need causal order to deal with changes of a tasks' participant set, such changes are not atomic (membership changes of process groups in ISIS are atomic).

come "overwritten" by changes due to remote participants. Because all changes are highlighted at the user interface, a user at least gets aware of what has happened.

The asynchronous distribution mechanism for tasks is also used for the distribution of messages, documents and services. Lists of messages, document references, and service access points are attached to tasks and technically managed as task attributes. In order to attach or to change a document, the document or new version is copied with a new filename to a host in the local domain, and the pair "host/filename" is distributed. When accessed remotely, the documents are ftp'ed (a cache can be used on the remote site to avoid multiple remote copies).

While the distribution of new versions of documents admits only an asynchronous, coarse-grain update of documents, the usage of services allow for distributed editing and synchronous communication. Task Manager and service use a simple protocol to agree upon what X server the service is to be used when it eventually contacts the user. All services integrated in our system must obey this start-up protocol.

The concept of documents and services renders the system "open-ended". We support documents of any kind as long as their associated tools, like word-processors or graphical editors, run on the underlying UNIX operating system.

The Activity Monitor is implemented as an ISO-ROS service (Rose, Onions and Robbins 1991) supporting two access protocols B and D_1. The Message Handler offers another ROS service: via the D_2 protocol the Activity Monitor propagates its data across domains. The protocols are defined in ASN.1 (Steedman 1990). All clients and services of the system are implemented in C++ using ISODE (Rose, Onions and Robbins 1991).

6 Evaluation, or: Does the Task Manager live up to the expectations

Here we report on first assessments of the usability and usefulness of the Task Manager. First, we take a look at our design goals.

Flexibility : we have already shown that the Task Manager is a versatile tool that may be useful in a variety of work situations. Tasks may be performed by just one user or shared by any number of users in the same way, a shared task may be structured to various degrees of refinement and causal dependency, and all attributes, including the participating users, may be changed dynamically.

The only restriction to flexibility perceived so far is the rather egalitarian model of task sharing: all participants share the same view. Extensions to the tool might be needed in order to adapt to rather different organizational cultures than we originally had in mind.

Interoperability: the concept of attaching documents and services to tasks opens up various ways in which existing tools or applications to be created may interoperate with the Task Manager. First, arbitrary documents attached to tasks may be opened and worked on without leaving the task management context. Secondly, services offer specific cooperation support not covered by the Task Manager within the task management context.

Self-Organizability: users of the Task Manager may organize their collaboration as they see fit, the only prerequisite being the installation of the tool in the user community. There is the possibility of using and adapting task templates from an organizational database, or reusing old task specifications.

Simplicity, Genericity: the Task Manager in its present form is basically a very simple tool, and is usually very quickly understood by novice users as a distributed to-do list. It may be applied to any kind of collaborative activity, because it has not been tuned to any specific application domain.

Early designs and a first prototype of the Task Manager were evaluated in user workshops conducted in the spirit of the Scandinavian approach of user-centred design (Kyng and Greenbaum 1991). Our user organization is a company which manages a very large technical project, and our users at the workshops were managers, engineers, and support personnel; details on the organization may be found in (Grønbæk, Kyng and Mogensen 1992).

The main goal of the user involvement was to find out whether the Task Manager addressed the problems of distributed work management found in the user organization, and what might improve its design. The prospective users regarded the Task Manager as potentially useful for coordination within their organization, but thought *overview* and *efficiency* of the tool should be improved. This criticism has led to considerable enhancements of the Task Manager. We are sure that the planned real-world use will offer further occasions for improvements.

Finally, we found it interesting to compare our Task Manager with the check-list for a successful CSCW tool which recent analyses of cooperative work — computer-supported or not — came up with. Robinson (1993) claims that a tool should have a clear functionality to do a job and in addition should support the following features which we think are also present in the Task Manager.

Peripheral awareness: is offered by the task list interface which at a glance notifies of events in shared work the user should attend to.

Implicit communication: is supported via sharing documents and services attached to a task.

"Double level language", i.e. the complementary and mutually supportive use of implicit and explicit communication: is provided for by the conference of informal messages attached to a task.

Overview: of distributed work is one of the main features of the shared to-do list.

Multifunctionality: could be claimed as demonstrated in section 4, but still has to be proven in real use.

Our first assessments showed that distributed to-do lists can contribute to the management of distributed work. It also became clear that there still remains a lot to be done with regard to flexibility and interoperability of the tool. All of this has encouraged us to proceed with the further development of the Task Manager.

7 Conclusion, and: Where do we go from here

There is a still growing need for tools to manage distributed work. The coordination models and systems developed over the last years suffered from the *rigidity* of predefined procedures and imposed structures, and the *isolation* from informal communication and other forms of computer support.

With the Task Manager we have presented a simple, powerful, and generic tool for the management of distributed work that addresses these problems by its flexibility to adapt to a broad variety of collaborative work situations, and by the possibilities it offers to interoperate with other computer support.

The present prototype of the Task Manager will be the starting point for further evolutionary development. By putting the prototype to actual use we will further evaluate the tool and try to gradually add features that improve its usefulness as a coordination instrument. Additionally, we will address the problems connected with the mobile use of the Task Manager, i.e. intermittent disconnection from the base system, and further open it up by creating facilities to interoperate with other types of CSCW systems like distributed hypermedia and shared window conferencing.

Acknowledgements

We would like to thank all members of the EuroCoOp project team who participated in the design and implementation of the Task Manager, Andreas Bäcker, Ute Ehrlich, Pippa Hennessy, Karl-Heinz Klein, Ernst Lutz, Peter Seuffert, Alan Shepherd, and those who prepared and evaluated the user workshops, Kaj Grønbæk, Morten Kyng, Preben Mogensen and our users at Great Belt Link in Knudshoved.

References

Birman, K., Schiper, A., Stephenson, P. (1991): "Light weight causal and atomic group multicast," *ACM Transactions on Computer Systems*, vol. 9, no. 3, August 1991, pp. 272 - 314.

Grønbæk, K., Kyng, M., Mogensen, P. (1992): "CSCW challenges in large-scale technical projects: A case study," in J. Turner, R. Kraut (eds.): *CSCW '92*, Proc. Conf. on Comp.-Supp. Coop. Work, (Toronto, Oct. 31 - Nov. 4 1992), ACM, New York NY, pp. 338-345.

Hennessy, P., Kreifelts, Th., Ehrlich, U. (1992): "Distributed work management: activity coordination within the EuroCoOp project," *Computer Communications* vol. 15, no. 8, October 1992, pp. 477-488.

Kreifelts, Th., Hinrichs, E., Klein, K.-H., Seuffert, P., Woetzel, G. (1991): "Experiences with the DOMINO office procedure system," in L. Bannon, M. Robinson, K. Schmidt (eds.): *ECSCW '91*, Proc. 2nd European Conf. on Comp.-Supp. Coop. Work, Kluwer, Dordrecht, pp. 117 - 130.

Kyng, M., Greenbaum, J. (eds.) (1991): *Design at Work*, Lawrence Erlbaum, London.

Robinson, M. (1993): "Keyracks and computers: An introduction to 'common artefact' in Computer Supported Cooperative Work (CSCW)," *Wirtschaftsinformatik* vol. 35, no. 2, April 1993, pp. 157 - 166.

Rose, M. T., Onions, J. P., Robbins, C. J. (1991): "The ISO Development Environment: User's Manual," version 6.24, vols. 1 - 5.

Schmidt, K. (1991): "Riding a tiger, or computer supported cooperative work," in L. Bannon, M. Robinson, K. Schmidt (eds.): *ECSCW '91*, Proc. 2nd European Conf. on Comp.-Supp. Coop. Work, Kluwer, Dordrecht, pp. 1 - 16.

Steedman, D. (1990): *Abstract Syntax Notation One, The Tutorial Reference*, Technology Appraisals, Isleworth.

Proceedings of the Third European Conference on Computer-Supported Cooperative Work
13-17 September, 1993, Milan, Italy
G. De Michelis, C. Simone and K. Schmidt (Editors)

Supporting The Design Process Within An Organisational Context

Bob Anderson, Graham Button
Rank Xerox EuroPARC, England

Wes Sharrock
University of Manchester, England

Abstract: This paper attempts to take what has been essentially abstract thinking about how to support the design process and relocates it within the working and organisational context of design. Through a single case analysis we analyse how organisational exigencies affect design activities and design train of thought. On the basis of this study we consider how tools that have been developed to support the design process do not take account of the collaborative, interactional, and organisational ordering of the design process and make recommendations as to the features that one family of support tools, design rational tools, should poses.

Introduction

We begin this paper with three simple observations about design work. First, design work often involves collaboration. The design of software and computer systems usually involves a design team and this inevitably means that the work of design is, in part, organised in the interactions and negotiations between team members. Second, designers use tools in and as part of their design work. For example, they use development methodologies for structuring and organising their design work; they have originated conceptual tools for ordering their reasoning activities such as, to mention one that will figure in this examination, "design rationale"; and they use technologies such as CASE.

Third, there is often a conflict between the fact that design is done collaboratively and the nature of the tools that are used to support design. The tools do not systematically take account of the collaborative organisation of their work. For example, development methodologies are cohort independent and thus do not take account of the numbers involved in a project. Consequently, whilst they provide for a modularised development process they say nothing about how different individuals or groups within a team can co-operate when the modules are being developed concurrently. Yet, as any engineering team or any observer of such teams will readily testify, communication, collaboration and co-operation between different engineers within the team is essential for the successful ordering of the development process.

Further, CASE technology tends to individuate the development process at a critical point in its cycle: the specification of requirements. As Fisher has suggested with respect to the use of CASE: "The goal is to provide freedom for the lone designer, or the most skilled team member, allowing this person to concentrate fully on developing the requirements and design specifications" (Fisher, 1991: 33).

Concepts that have been used to support design reasoning have also often emphasised the individual designer rather than the design team. One concept that we have become particular familiar with as a result of our work at EuroPARC is that of "design rationale" and design rationale tools. In the main design rational has been articulated with respect to the deliberations and decisions of individual designers. Even where the focus is on team design, less attention is paid to the role of the group *as a group*.

We believe that the contradictions mentioned have their origins in the way in which the various forms through which the design process is supported have been developed by thinking about the design process *in the abstract* as opposed to thinking about the design process as a real worldly phenomenon. Thinking about the design processes in the abstract has tended to separate design issues from the features of working and organisational context within which the design activities are placed, and this in turn has invariably tended to strip the design process of the features through which it is constituted as an organisational phenomena. We believe, from our observations of design teams at work, that an essential feature of that work is the way in which the organisational context is played out in the interactions and collaborations of design teams.[1]

We maintain that our arguments here have a relevance to thinking about CSCW related topics in a number of ways. First, they attempt to make a direct

---

[1] Our interest in the organisational context of design is also shared by Jirotka, Gilbert and Luff (1992) who examine the social basis of organisations and its relationship to CSCW. Also of relevance is Bucciarelli (1988) who furnishes a good ethnographic description of engineering design and March (1991) who examines decision making in organisations.

allowance for reiteration of phases of the project. However, there were aspects of the scheduling which looked unrealistic. The company has a complex design and development methodology - its Product Development Process (PDP)- and this has a complex pattern of phases and reviews. It looked, from the outset, as if there would be problems in complying with the review process. The PDP procedures very much prescribe that one stage of work be unequivocally and successfully completed before the next phase is undertaken, and it is therefore formally the case that the working out of the design and the preparation for production should be completed before money was made available to initiate production processes. The tight schedule of this project, however, set it in conflict with the formal procedures, since the 'lead times' necessary for the manufacturing processes were so long that their successful initiation would antedate the earliest possible time at which the formal review of the initial design's adequacy could be initiated.

The project had, however, even in its inception, been organised through bypassing the formal development processes. It had been put together through informal agreements with the marketing department. These procedures were to be satisfied, but after the fact. The failure to follow these through, however, meant that at crucial moments within the project there was uncertainty as to what requirements the design needed to satisfy, and there were, in addition, those common consequences of informal agreements within organisational settings: one of the individuals who was an important party to them had moved on.

2 Staffing

This site had recently been through a restructuring, and many staff had been laid off or relocated within the company. The need to reduce staff had taken priority and those who had gone had been those who could and would go, and there had been no way in which the target reductions could be obtained whilst maintaining a balance in the structure of staff available. This meant that the staffing of project teams could be problematic, and this certainly was the case with Centaur which was 'top heavy' with senior and very experienced staff . The skill mix available on the team was not fully congruent with the project's work requirements, and some more junior members of the team were only partially skilled in the work they would be called upon to do. Finally, this site's deficiencies in staffing could be compensated for by deployment of staff from other sites. However, the requirements of different sites are not necessarily either integrated or synchronised, and the capacity of one site to come across with just what the other one needs as and when it needs it is not assured. A site in Holland was required to provide expertise in electronics, but the individual who brought this was not available at the moment at which work began and so a 'stand in' from the local site had to contribute to the early work .

link between design rationale which has been an influential concept in thinking about the design process and the essentially collaborative and organisational context of real worldly design. Second, they attempt to give a concrete substance to the relationship between the design process and organisational context. That is, we are not merely interested in making a programmatic point about context but with actually investigating of what that context can consist of as an empirical matter. Third, we are concerned with explicating actual work practices of design. Fourth we make specific recommendations concerning the features of design rational tools that can support the work of design as that is ordered within an organisational context.

The Project....

The project 'Centaur' (which is producing an 'add on' high capacity feeder for one of the photocopiers the company under investigation produced) was a comparatively small 'fast track' operation. The company was concerned to reduce its inventory, and one of their recent models had not been selling well. The possibility arose that a significant number of machines - a few thousand - could be moved through sale to US educational libraries, where it was considered a good machine for book copying but only if its paper holding capacity was increased.

In use, the machines would be contained within an outer casing in order for them to operate on a payment basis, and the small paper holding capacity meant that such use would make excessive demands on key holders for replenishment. If the machine could be provided with a much increased paper holding capacity, and if it could be marketed at the right point in the purchasing cycles of the libraries, then this could meet a significant demand. If the project was to be undertaken then it would have to be carried through unusually quickly: from the 'concept' phase of the project - in which the design idea was initially worked out - to its launch on the market was to take a little over a year and the target launch date would be a rigid one.

....And Its Problems:

1 Time

Though a schedule could be prepared for the project which showed that it could meet the deadline, there was always uncertainty amongst the project members as to how realistic this could be. It had been designed on the assumption that everything on the project would 'go right the first time' and there was no

3 Costs

The company's projects are targeted against an estimated cost, the 'unit manufacturing cost' (or UMC). Centaur faced the fact that, as conceived, its target manufacturing cost was utterly unrealistic, some hundreds of dollars out of line with the actual cost. The product was aimed at a market which, in production terms, was small, with some 4000 items being projected. Such a production run was nowhere near long enough to defray the costs of tooling it.

Practical Management Of The Design Space.

As the design team saw it, they were faced with two sets of problems. One was to design a specific device, the feeder. The other was to find ways of reducing production costs to a level which would be acceptable and to initiate manufacturing work early enough to meet their launch dates. The first appeared to be relatively straightforward - since this was only the production of an add on to a machine that had already been marketed - though this would, of course, have its own wrinkles. The second looked to be a killer. Given this was the case, the problems readily priorities themselves, with almost all the innovative energy being directed to finding ways of managing the cost and time constraints.

For the purposes of this discussion, we will concentrate on just three of the innovative strategies which members of the Centaur project used to tackle these problems:

1 Improvising on the formal procedures

Within the design organisation which we studied, standard procedures and protocols are used for every stage in the Product Delivery Process (PDP). As we have seen, if Centaur were to have followed these procedures to the letter, it would be impossible for them to have delivered on their targets in time. The team's response was not to disregard the formal steps and processes. Rather, they sought to fulfil them whilst at the same time reducing the constraints they imposed on the team's room for manoeuvre. Here are some of the ways this was done.

a)   Informalising the review

One of the major problems was that of bringing the project to a point at which a formal review was possible. This meant both achieving the conditions required for review and organising the allocation of time to be taken from other project work in order to prepare for such a review. One way of dealing with this might be to arrange a relatively early and informal review. In particular, this offered the possibility of a timely commitment to manufacturing spending. By being able to hold an informal review, the team were able to get "in principle" permission to proceed before they were actually ready to ask for definitive permission.

b)   Opportunistically exploiting the black economy

The problem of unit cost was constantly with them. Though it seemed they could not make more than marginal differences to the discrepancy between the target and projected cost, matters of detailed costings were nonetheless carefully attended to. Much satisfaction was derived from anything that was judged 'low cost'. Complaints were registered about and close scrutiny given to anything that made a 'hit' against costs.

A chance conversation between managers at the local site revealed that, as one of the by-products of restructuring mentioned earlier, the Procurements Department was short of work, and was casting about for things to do. Through its knowledge of and relations with suppliers, a 'shadow' operation was set up by which the Procurements Department compiled an alternative costing and scheduling of parts production to that being provided by the official manufacturing operation. The aim was to see if lead times (and costs) could be significantly cut by "contracting out".

c)   Massaging the UMC

The UMC was affected by two principal things, the cost of developing tooling for the manufacture of non-standard parts and the size of the production run. Since these were the only two things which could be varied, ways of varying them had to be considered.

The extension of the production run was one possibility. Lifting the run from 4000 to 10000 units, would have brought the UMC considerably closer to target. It would still be high, but by a 'reasonable' sum.

The cost of tooling was usually looked at in two parts: the development of 'soft tooling', that is, tools made out of inferior materials for producing the parts required for the prototype; and the development of 'hard tools' for use in the production run. Since this project had only 'one shot' at the prototype and since the production run was short, the possibility of using soft tools in production was considered.

d)   Adopting a deflationary approach to problems

The organisation uses a 'management by problem solving' approach to the conduct of projects. Part of this means that problems are classified by "seriousness". There are three levels: ordinary, major and critical. The 'ordinary' are effectively minor problems: they have not been solved, but only routine measures are required for their resolution. Major problems are ones whose solution will have consequences for the cost, quality or delivery of the product. Critical ones are felt to be difficult to solve and may even be insoluble, and to which attention must be given. The existence of critical problems calls the continuation of the project into question.

Given the position in which it found itself, Centaur adopted a 'go ahead anyway' approach even to critical problems. They were known to exist and strategies for dealing with them were underway. But they were not as yet resolved. In the meanwhile, it was necessary to get on with the project's other tasks. In addition, Centaur's schedule was, as we have mentioned, constructed on a 'right first time' basis. When things, as they inevitably did, failed to go right first time, it was impossible to halt work on dependent problems because, then, the schedule would slip irrevocably. The net result was that the formal requirements of problem solving were circumvented from the start.

2 Working with and around the normal work practices

The culture of design in this organisation is, as with any work group, composed of the patterns of normative activity and the value systems espoused by those who identify with it. These are what any designer in the organisation knows about how things are to be done. In the course of actual designing, the making of decisions and the solving of problems, this knowledge is deployed not as procedural rules or even as rules of thumb, but as ways of making design sense of the issues on hand, and therefore deciding just what to do. Knowing, then, how long some activity should take to complete or what quality of output from some process one should expect is determined in *media res*. As the design goes along, and as the design tasks are encountered, the configuration of this knowledge changes. In turn, this dynamism resonates back onto the ordering of design decisions, the possibilities explored, and the route to be taken. On the Centaur project, this reciprocal fitting of work practice and workplace knowledge to the design tasks in hand could be seen in a number of ways. We will detail just a few.

a) Cutting corners and watching for potholes became a way of design life

Schedules are usually compiled more in hope than expectation. The interlocking of steps in sequences means that exceeding the estimated time always has knock-on effects which have to be either anticipated or actively managed. One case that occurred on Centaur involved working out the detailed features of the design and the production of the technical drawings. The concern was to get decisions to the point at which technical drawing could begin whilst at the same time attempting both to truncate the process of producing usable drawings and to prevent any slippage at that point. To do this, a policy was adopted of using less-than-finished drawings wherever possible. Where it was thought that the supplier of a part was well enough known to be relied upon to understand and implement a rough drawing, it was agreed these could be issued at an early stage.

b) Problems were traded off against one another

We mentioned that the composition of the Centaur team was affected by the contraction of the site's work-force. The team was made up of individuals all of whom were senior and long serving, and who regarded themselves as equally experienced in project leading as their Project Manager. These individuals treated their mutual relations as delicate. There was a ready possibility for misreading motives, and especially for disagreement to be construed as personal criticism. Any attempt to force disagreements to conclusions in design meetings might well have been taken as attempts to 'show up' the Project Manager in front of colleagues. This does not mean disagreements did not occur, but they were muted. If dissent on some point revealed that the Project Manager had a strong preference, then this was deferred to. This display of restraint as a way of handling this issue had one crucial consequence for the development of the project.

'Timing diagrams' are a particularly important tool for the design of photocopiers. They involve working out the precise timings for the movement of paper sheets through the machine. One important aim in photocopier design is to achieve maximum possible speed in the copying of sheets and, thus, to keep the sheets moving through the 'paper path' as close together as possible, but without leading to overlaps or conflicts and hence mis-feeds or a paper jams. The production of the timing diagram for Centaur was, then, a matter of some importance. However, there was disagreement on just how urgent it was. The Project Manager appreciated the task was important, but did not feel it was quite as critical or urgent as did some of his colleagues.

From the Project Manager's point of view, although working out the timings would be a difficult task, the team had no-one who was experienced or appropriately skilled in it. On the other hand, the feeder was to be compatible with a machine which had already been built, and for which there would or ought to be extant timing diagrams. He also knew there was someone on the site who was experienced in the work. Furthermore, she had done the very timing diagrams for the relevant copier. The Project Manager set about tracking down these diagrams and tried to 'borrow' the relevant skilled person from the project to which she was currently attached. In his view, the diagrams were in hand. He had other more pressing issues to resolve.

Other members of the team did not agree. They regarded the timing diagrams as critically important, and thought that they should be produced as soon as possible. When it became clear that the Project Manager did not share their view, they acceded to his argument, without accepting it for one moment. They foresaw problems resulting from delay in getting the timing diagrams out. However, their choice was between two kinds of trouble on the project; that which would result from late availability of the diagrams, and that which would result from creating personal animosities.

c)   Necessity was the mother of re-deployment

Relative to the project's life, the search for the copier's timing diagrams and the negotiations with the other project for assistance in working them out was protracted. The necessary diagrams were eventually found and then only by happy coincidence. The negotiations to borrow the skilled person were not successful, and so the work had to be done — now belatedly — by someone within the team. Even here, the one who had the most relevant skills was not the one who did the work. He already had his hands full with other, equally critical tasks, such as designing the printed wiring boards (PWB). These tasks were not further deferrable, so working out of the timings had to be assigned to someone who had just enough skill to do them effectively, albeit with difficulty, and who had other tasks which could be deferred.

3 Revising the design requirements from within the design

Clearly, one of the ways to find an achievable route through Centaur's design space, would be to relax some of the constraints encapsulated in the design requirements. A several points a number of attempts to relax these constraints were made.

a)   Amending the customer requirements

 A key feature of the project was that the attachment of the Centaur feeder should not require any communications with the central processor of the host machine. This meant that the design was constrained to use the communications facilities already designed into the host. This gave rise to one of the tricky design problems, namely the use of the host's sensors to communicate the various states of the paper trays. It became apparent that all possible combinations could not be accommodated, and so one of the immediate responses was to see if the range of possibilities could be constricted in some way.

The issue could only be resolved at the level of marketing strategy. The design had been developed on the assumption that the machine was to be produced in the routine way to meet the requirements of various markets of an international company. It would have to operate in different climatic conditions, with different sizes and qualities of paper, with instructions in different languages, and so on. The difficulties in accommodating all these possibilities without independently communicating with the central processor led the team to ask if this was realistic. The project was, as everyone was well aware, designed to solve a specific problem by exploiting a specific market niche, one most prominently based in the USA. How many actual markets, therefore, was the machine to be designed for? How much variability in paper sizes and climatic conditions should be involved? What was the actual pattern of paper use within the main projected market? Answers to these questions might allow a drastic reduction in the range of alternatives to be designed for. And that might enable them to design the communications systems according to specification.

This example illustrates the ways in which the various strategies the team engaged in, interacted with each other and how problems can move in and out of the foreground of the design team's attention. We pointed out earlier that the project had been initiated relatively 'informally'. This informality now began to have consequences, in that there was no formal mechanism to clarify the actual requirements for the design. There were informal contacts with relevant parties in the local marketing function, but these were rendered problematic by changes in personnel. In the event, an agreement was made with someone in the main marketing organisation to collate information on the actual pattern of paper types, sizes etc. in the target market. The need to obtain clarification of the marketing policy and to establish whether the feeder could be launched in one or two countries only was also recognised. Launching the machine for specific markets offered the possibility not only of restricting the combinations to be designed for — and thus simplifying the task — but also of being able to dispense with the need to design packaging and arrange translations for all the different markets. This promised cost savings. However, though this information was badly needed, it could not be speedily obtained. There appeared to be no easy way to clarify market potential. Personnel in the international marketing arm were changing positions, and the steps involved in moving informal support for Centaur to formal decisions about its launch policy had not been taken.

b) Assuming the best solution will be available

Obviously decisions are interdependent. Designers seek to line them up so that one decision can determine the character of others. On Centaur one issue was how much power it was going to need. This would depend upon the size of motor required which, in its turn, would fix the amount of space available for the installation of the PWBs. Engineering lore lays down that the final size of a motor is always greater than that envisaged or wanted. Hence, the size of the motor could not be determined prior to decisions about the power supply or about the architecture of the boards. The investigation of the available motors, the decision about the power supply and the design of the PWBs all had to proceed simultaneously, with decisions about each involving a certain amount of risk. Allowing for the worst possible outcome with respect to the size of the motor was not possible because there was a constraint on the space into which the motor and PWBs had to go. The risk was in judging what one would get away with in terms of motor size and then hoping that this estimation would be fulfilled.

It is this kind of problem which puts designers in 'no choice' situations. There are things they would like to know, and decisions they would like to have settled, but the speed of the formal 'decision loops' and the time scale of design tasks mean that important considerations cannot be resolved. The designers have no choice save to go on working out the design — even its detailed features — whilst awaiting the resolution of issues upon which the effectiveness of their decisions depend.

c) Adopting an Alexandrian approach to requirements

The final production of the timing diagrams revealed serious problems in the timing and tracking of sheet movements. There were, too, still unresolved questions about the capacity to communicate between the feeder and the host machine. These were both 'life threatening' problems for the project. To enter a review (even and informal one) with two 'critical' problems of this order would almost certainly be fatal. Time was running out. It was becoming clear that a drastic solution was needed. As various possibilities were examined to solve the paper feeding problems, it became increasingly apparent that the main obstacle was the requirement about communication with the central processor. If that requirement was not in place, then there was a simple solution. All that would be needed to solve the timing problems successfully, was a single wire between the feeder and the central processor. The installation of such a wire would make only marginal difference to the installation work. (Minimising the installation task was a prime reason for the prohibition on communication with the central processor). But if communication with the central processor was available then other outstanding problems would also be solved. Signalling the state of paper and trays could also be done through that connection (and with minimal alteration to the software). The only way forward was to go back upon what had hitherto been treated as an immutable constraint, and cut the gordian knot it had created. Once it was accepted that this must be done, the outstanding problems evaporated and the project entered the review in sufficiently good condition to have its mechanical and electrical designs approved.

Conclusion

One of the purposes of our study was to consider the implications of the actualities of collaborative work in projects for the development of tools to support such work, particularly the kinds of tools that seek to improve 'design capture', and these considerations confirm what Karat and Bennett (1991) say when they argue that "maintaining a user-centred perspective during design must be done in concern with engineering realities of function to be provided, schedules to be met, and development costs to be managed" (Karat and Bennett, 1991: 270).

From the point of view of designers it is design considerations which should, take precedence but in their practice, and certainly from the point of view of others in the design and development process, design considerations must often be subordinated to organisational priorities. Designers and everyone else involved in managing the project recognised that the conditions of the project were a good deal less-than-ideal but simply took it that nothing much could be done to alleviate those difficulties in the face of the organisation's need to shift its inventories. restructure its work-force, and revise its operating procedures. The fact that the composition of the project team is generally changing - as people are circulated from one project to another, move position in the organisation or are simply laid off on a large scale in mid project - is something that those who continue working on the project have to contend with. Similarly, the fact that the members of the project will be dividing their time and effort between different projects is an organisational fact of life, and the capacity of individuals to satisfy the often competing priorities of projects and departments may be problematic.

These facts of "organisational life" have a consequence for the way in which we might consider the design of support tools for designers. This can be illustrated by briefly returning to one family of support tools that we mentioned in the introduction: design rational tools. From the point of view that we have been arguing which is that design has to be placed within the collaborative working and organisational context then support tools such as design rational tools need to take account of the following[2]:

1) Abstractly thinking about the design process has resulted in tools that provided for detailed documentation of the process. However, in practice designers facing time constraints need less not more record keeping. Support tools should provide for this. 2) Because a project team is interactionaly dynamic with, for example, project team membership generally changing any tool will have to mark the variability of skills available and the courses of action decided upon as a response to the variability of membership. 3) Because design teams are organisational objects every member of a project team is simultaneously a member of other project teams. The prioritisations of activities are not always in the hands of the designers concerned and can be affected by a multitude of exogenous forces. Tools should be adaptive to the consequences for design scheduling of potential discontinuities in the management of the prioriatisation process. 4) Organisationally defined procedures such as the product delivery process (PDP) are constantly under review and subject to 'upgrade', 'improvement', 'reconfiguration' at almost any level of granularity. Design rational tools should indicate just how such changes impact design decisions and those reformations of the formal procedures.

Acknowledgements

We would like to thank Tom Moran, Victoria Bellotti, Alan MacLean and Paul Luff for their extensive comments on previous drafts of this paper.

---

[2]The following points are presented only as preliminary outlines of issues to be attended to.

References

Bucciarelli, L.L. (1988), "An Ethnographic Perspective On Engineering Design", *Design Studies*, 9, pp. 159-168.

Fisher, A.S. (1991): *CASE: Using Software Development Tools.*, John Wiley & Sons Inc, New York.

Jirotka, M., Gilbert, N. and Luff, P. (1992), "On The Social Organisation Of Organisations", *CSCW* 1-2, pp. 95-118.

Karat, J. & Bennett, J.L. (1991), "Working With The Design Process: Supporting Effective and Efficient Design", in J. Carroll, (ed.), *Designing Interaction.* Cambridge University Press, Cambridge.

March, J.G. "How Decisions Happen In Organisations" Human Computer Interaction, Vol. 6 no. 2 pp. 95-117.

Proceedings of the Third European Conference on Computer-Supported Cooperative Work
13-17 September, 1993, Milan, Italy
G. De Michelis, C. Simone and K. Schmidt (Editors)

Improving Software Quality through Computer Supported Collaborative Review

Philip M. Johnson
Department of Information and Computer Sciences
University of Hawaii, U.S.A.

Danu Tjahjono
Department of Information and Computer Sciences
University of Hawaii, U.S.A.

Formal technical review (FTR) is a cornerstone of software quality assurance. However, the labor-intensive and manual nature of review, along with basic unresolved questions about its process and products, means that review is typically under-utilized or inefficiently applied within the software development process. This paper introduces CSRS, a computer-supported cooperative work environment for software review that improves the efficiency of review activities and supports empirical investigation of the appropriate parameters for review. The paper presents a typical scenario of CSRS in review, its data and process model, application to process maturation, relationship to other research, current status, and future directions.

1. Introduction

Formal technical review (FTR) is a cornerstone of software quality assurance. While other techniques, such as measures of program size and complexity, or software testing can help improve quality, they cannot supplant the benefits achievable from well-executed FTR. One reason why review is essentially irreplacable is because it can be carried out early in the development process, well before formal artifacts such as source code are available for complexity analysis or testing. Another reason is because no automated process can yet provide the two-way quality improvement in both product and producers possible through review.

However, the full potential of review is rarely realized in any of its current forms. Three significant roadblocks to fully effective review are the following:

Review is extremely labor-intensive. Typical procedures for FTR involve individual study of hard-copy designs or source listings and hand-generated annotations, followed by a group meeting where the documents are paraphrased line by line, issues are individually raised, discussed, and recorded by hand, leading eventually to rework assignments and resulting changes. For one approach to FTR called *code inspection* (Fagan, 1976), published data indicates that an entire man-year of effort is needed to review a 20KLOC program by a team of four reviewers (Russel, 1991). Unfortunately, little automated support for the process and products of review is available. What support is available typically supports only a single facet of review (such as the review meeting), or is not integrated with the overall development environment.

Review is not compatible with incremental development methods. Because of their labor-intensive nature, most organizations cannot afford to review most or even many of the artifacts produced during development. Instead, review is deployed as a "hurdle" to be jumped a small number of times at strategic points during development. While this may be a reasonable tactic for development in accordance with a strict waterfall lifecycle model, more modern incremental and maintenance-intensive development methods prove problematic: there is no effective way to optimally position a small number of review hurdles in the development process.

No methods or tools exist to support the design of prescriptive review methods adapted to an organization's own culture, application area, and quality requirements. Research on review tends to fall into two categories, which we will term "descriptive" and "prescriptive". The descriptive literature describes the process and products of review abstractly, advocates that organizations must create their own individualized form of review, but provides little prescriptive support for this process (Schulmeyer, 1987; Dunn, 1990; Freedman, 1990). Such work leaves ill-defined many central questions concerning review, such as: How much should be reviewed at one time? What issues should be raised during review, and are standard issue lists effective? What is the relationship between time spent in various review activities and its productivity? How many people should be involved in a review? What artifacts should be produced and consumed during a review? The prescriptive literature, on the other hand, takes a relatively hard line stance on both the process and products of review (Fagan, 1976; Fagan, 1986; Russel, 1991). Such literature makes clear statements about the process (Meetings must last a maximum of 2 hours; each line of code must be paraphrased; lines of code must be read at rate of 150 lines per hour; etc). The data presented in this literature certainly supports the claim that this method, if followed precisely, can discover errors. However, the strict prescriptions appear to suggest that organizations must adapt to the review method, rather than that the review method adapt to the needs and characteristics of the organization.

This paper introduces CSRS[1], a computer-supported cooperative work system that is designed to address aspects of each of these three roadblocks to effective formal technical review.

First, CSRS is implemented on top of EGRET, a multi-user, distributed, hypertext-based collaborative environment (Johnson, 1992) that provides computational support for the process and products of review and inspection. This platform allows an essentially "paperless" approach to review, supports important computational services, and facilitates integration with existing development environments. In combination with an adapted review process model, CSRS provides computational support that significantly decreases the labor intensive nature of review.

Second, CSRS is designed around an incremental model of software development. While simply lowering the cost helps integrate review into incremental models, CSRS also provides an intrinsically cyclical process model that parallels the iterative nature of incremental development.

Third, CSRS exploits the use of an on-line, collaborative environment for review to collect a wide range of metrics on the process and products of review. Such metrics generate historical data about review process and products for a given organization, application, and review group that can provide quantitative answers to many of the questions concerning the basic parameters for review raised above.

The remainder of this paper illustrates our approach to FTR and the CSRS environment in more detail. Although our approach can be applied to FTR of a wide range of artifacts produced during software development, we currently concentrat on support for code review, and this paper reflects this orientation. Section 2 introduces CSRS through selected snapshots from a recent review experience. Sections 3 and 4 provide a broader perspective by detailing the CSRS data and process models. Section 5 outlines both formal and informal applications of CSRS to software process maturation. The paper concludes by comparing CSRS to other systems for review in Section 6 followed by discussing its current status and future directions in Section 7.

---

[1] An acronym for Collaborative Software Review System.

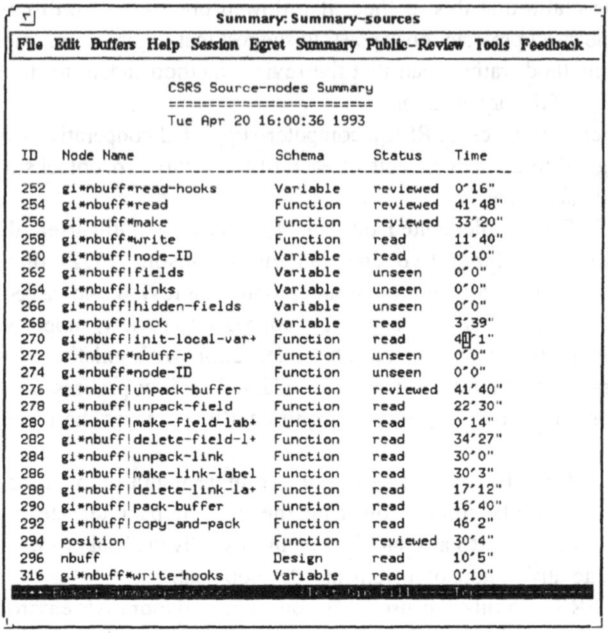

```
┌─┐                    Summary: Summary-sources                          ─┐
│ ⊽                                                                       │
├─────────────────────────────────────────────────────────────────────────┤
│ File  Edit  Buffers  Help  Session  Egret  Summary  Public-Review  Tools  Feedback │

                        CSRS Source-nodes Summary
                        ==========================
                        Tue Apr 20 16:00:36 1993

     ID   Node Name              Schema       Status     Time
    ─────────────────────────────────────────────────────────────
     252  gi*nbuff*read-hooks    Variable     reviewed   0'16"
     254  gi*nbuff*read          Function     reviewed   41'48"
     256  gi*nbuff*make          Function     reviewed   33'20"
     258  gi*nbuff*write         Function     read       11'40"
     260  gi*nbuff!node-ID       Variable     read       0'10"
     262  gi*nbuff!fields        Variable     unseen     0'0"
     264  gi*nbuff!links         Variable     unseen     0'0"
     266  gi*nbuff!hidden-fields Variable     unseen     0'0"
     268  gi*nbuff!lock          Variable     read       3'39"
     270  gi*nbuff!init-local-var+ Function   read       4 1"
     272  gi*nbuff*nbuff-p       Function     unseen     0'0"
     274  gi*nbuff*node-ID       Function     unseen     0'0"
     276  gi*nbuff!unpack-buffer Function     reviewed   41'40"
     278  gi*nbuff!unpack-field  Function     read       22'30"
     280  gi*nbuff!make-field-lab+ Function   read       0'14"
     282  gi*nbuff!delete-field-l+ Function   read       34'27"
     284  gi*nbuff!unpack-link   Function     read       30'0"
     286  gi*nbuff!make-link-label Function   read       30'3"
     288  gi*nbuff!delete-link-la+ Function   read       17'12"
     290  gi*nbuff!pack-buffer   Function     read       16'40"
     292  gi*nbuff!copy-and-pack Function     read       46'2"
     294  position              Function     reviewed   30'4"
     296  nbuff                 Design       read       10'5"
     316  gi*nbuff*write-hooks   Variable     read       0'10"
```

Figure 1. A summary window illustrating the state of review for one reviewer.

2. Review using CSRS

To get the flavor of review using CSRS, this section presents excerpts from a recent review, including illustrative screen shots and metric data. A more complete presentation of both data and process model is provided in Sections 3 and 4.

This review cycle focussed on a object-oriented class implementation called "nbuff" (short for node-buffer) in the generic-interface subsystem of EGRET. Nbuff defines an abstraction that bridges and combines the hypertext "node" abstraction provided by lower-level subsystems in EGRET and the textual "buffer" abstraction provided by higher, application-specific subsystems such as those comprising CSRS. The portion of nbuff under review consisted of approximately 500 of the 1100 lines of Lisp macros, functions, and variables in the entire nbuff class.

```
⊽                          Source: gi*nbuff*make

File  Edit  Buffers  Help  Session  Egret  Summary  Public-Review  Tools  Feedback

Name: gi*nbuff*make

Project: Project#240

Source-code:

(defun gi*nbuff*make (nschema-ID format-spec &optional hidden-p)
  "Creates and displays a new nbuff instance initialized with the
content of a new node with schema NSCHEMA-ID and node-name according
to FORMAT-SPEC.
FORMAT-SPEC is a valid format specification with one control
character %d corresponding to the new created node-ID.
If %d is not specified in the FORMAT-SPEC, the new node-name is equal
to the string FORMAT-SPEC. The new nbuff will be locked by default.
All the fields of type 'text will be initialized with one space and
two newlines characters.
If HIDDEN-P is NON-NIL, the buffer is returned without displaying it."
  (let ((node-ID (t*node-schema*instantiate nschema-ID format-spec))
        node-name)
    (when (u*error-p node-ID)
      (error "Can't instantiate node-schema-ID %d" nschema-ID))
    (setq node-name (format format-spec node-ID))
    (when (not (string-equal node-name format-spec))
      (t*node*set-name node-ID node-name))
    (gi*nbuff*read node-ID hidden-p)
    (gi*nbuff*lock)))

Issues:
[-> naming scheme for nbuffs]
[-> FORMAT-SPEC bad choice.]
[-> gi*nbuff*lock badly specified.]
[-> node-ID vs. nbuff-ID]
[-> Return value unknown]
[-> Improper use of function]
[-> redundant code]
[-> Can't call up docstring for u*error-p]

Comments:

Annotations:
```

Figure 2. A source node illustrating one of the functions under review.

In CSRS, each program object, such as a function, procedure, macro, variable or data type declaration is retrieved from a source code control system and placed into its own node in a hypertext-style database. After an orientation session to familiarize each review participant with the system under study, a *private review* phase begins. During private review, each member individually reviews the source code without access to the review commentary of others, although non-evaluative questions and answers about requirements and so forth are publically accessible. CSRS provides facilities to summarize the state of review for the reviewer, such as the window displayed in Figure 1. At this point, the reviewer has partially completed private review, as indicated by the fact that some of the source-nodes are reviewed, some have been read but have not been completely reviewed, and some have not even been seen. The total cumulative time spent on each node by this reviewer is also displayed.

Figure 3. An issue node containing an objection to an aspect of gi*nbuff*make.

By double-clicking on a line or through menu operations, the reviewer can traverse the hypertext network from this screen to a node containing a source object under review, as illustrated in Figure 2. In this case, the object under review is the operation gi*nbuff*make. Both pull-down and pop-up menus facilitate execution of the most common operations during this phase, such as creating an issue concerning the current source node under review, or proposing a specific action to address an issue. Once the reviewer is finished with a source object, he explicitly marks the node as "reviewed". Since this is the private review phase, only the issues created by this reviewer are accessible.

CSRS assumes that typical programming environment tools are available to the reviewer, such as static cross-referencing and dynamic behavior information, and thus does not attempt to duplicate that functionality. Part of the benefit of an EMACS-based platform is ease of integration with external programming environment tools (for example, the C/C++ environments XOBJECTCENTER and ENERGIZE, as well as Common Lisp environments by Lucid and Franz provide EMACS front-ends.)

A "standard_issues" menu supports an organization and/or application-specific set of specific issues to raise during private review. CSRS exploits the exploratory type system facilities provided by EGRET to allow reviewers to extend the set of issue types dynamically. In the gi*nbuff*make source node, this reviewer has generated 3 issues. One of them is illustrated in Figure 3.

Once the source nodes have been privately reviewed, the *public review* phase begins, where reviewers now read and react to the issues and actions raised by others. Each reviewer responds to the issues and actions raised by others through the creation of new issues or actions, creation of confirming or disconfirming evidence nodes to extant issues or actions, and by voting for one or more actions to be taken during the rework phase. In the nbuff review, over 100 nodes of type issue, action, and comment were created by the moderator and four reviewers during the private and public review phases.

Following public review, the moderator uses CSRS to *consolidate* the review state. Consolidation involves the condensing of information generated during review into a tightly focussed, written consolidation report that delineates the proposed actions, agreements, and unresolved issues resulting from the private and public review phases. CSRS provides automated support to the moderator in traversing the hypertext database and generating a LaTeX document containing the consolidated report.

If all issues arising from the on-line phases are satisfactorily resolved, this consolidation report constitutes the final report and rework activities based upon it can be scheduled immediately. If the consolidation process yields areas of continued debate, a face-to-face meeting is then required to resolve these issues. In the nbuff review, the total of 104 issue and comment nodes were consolidated down to 19 action proposals, of which only 6 were controversial and necessitated a group meeting to resolve. The final resolution of these issues required 35 minutes of group meeting time. (CSRS has not yet been extended to same-place same-time CSCW, and thus was not used in the group meeting.)

The consolidation report constitutes the first-order benefit of CSRS: automated, collaborative support for detection, analysis, and response to defects in a software development artifact. At least as important as this, however, is a second-order benefit of CSRS: support for analysis and improvement of the FTR process itself. CSRS supports this *process maturation* through automated collection of metric data during review. For example, Figure 4 illustrates a spreadsheet (whose data was imported directly from an ASCII file generated by CSRS) that provides just one of the many interesting perspectives on the process and products of this FTR. This important application of CSRS will be explored in more detail in Section 5. The next sections provide more detail on the data and process models of CSRS.

Source code name	Size	Reviewer 1		Reviewer 2		Reviewer 3		Reviewer 4	
		Time	Iss	Time	Iss	Time	Iss	Time	Iss
gi*nbuff*read	25		3	0:49:08	2	0:28:39	0	0:40:43	1
gi*nbuff!pack-buffer	57	0:08:59	0	0:41:33	2		0	0:08:35	1
gi*nbuff!copy-and-pack	51	0:24:18	1	0:29:07	3		0	0:02:37	0
gi*nbuff!init-local-variables	19	0:09:06	1	0:16:57	1	0:02:49	0	0:24:00	0
gi*nbuff!unpack-field	46	0:10:19	1	0:32:28	0		0	0:08:22	0
gi*nbuff*make	20		5	0:36:18	2	0:14:50	0	0:13:38	1
gi*nbuff!make-link-label	34	0:01:39	0	0:40:45	1	0:00:22	0	0:04:15	0
gi*nbuff!unpack-buffer	26		3	0:03:42	0	0:04:22	0	0:17:22	2
gi*nbuff!make-field-label	18	0:00:42	0	0:25:39	0		0	0:03:06	0
gi*nbuff*write	33	0:06:50	1	0:09:54	2	0:07:48	0	0:14:38	0
gi*nbuff!delete-field-label	18	0:00:34	0	0:25:56	1	0:03:44	1	0:02:38	0
gi*nbuff!unpack-link	12	0:20:09	1	0:00:40	0	0:01:48	0	0:06:09	1
gi*nbuff*nbuff-p	12	0:05:11	0	0:01:08	0	0:04:16	0	0:04:15	0
gi*nbuff*node-ID	12	0:00:23	0	0:02:20	0	0:04:40	0	0:08:12	0
gi*nbuff!delete-link-label	31	0:02:08	1	0:02:08	0		0	0:02:38	0
gi*nbuff*read-hooks	5	0:00:11	0	0:07:53	0	0:00:32	0	0:00:35	0
position	12	0:00:50	0	0:00:12	0	0:03:12	1		
gi*nbuff!node-ID	4	0:00:20	0	0:00:08	0	0:00:49	1	0:00:13	0
Total	435	1:31:39	17	5:25:56	15	1:17:51	3	2:41:56	6

Figure 4. An Excel spreadsheet illustrating a portion of the metric data collected during the nbuff review.

3. The CSRS Data Model

The CSRS data model consists of a set of typed nodes and links, where the nodes (in code review applications) correspond to source code under review and related artifacts generated during review, and the links represent relationships among the nodes. Source nodes are further classified into specific program objects such as function, macro, structure, etc. The exact set of program objects is language-specific: for Ada, CSRS would provide a "package" program object, for C++, a "class" object, and so forth. Review nodes are classified into issue, action, comment and evidence. Figure 5 shows the basic relationship among the CSRS nodes and links.

As illustrated in the previous section, any suspected problems or defects in the source are documented in issue nodes. Any questions about the source are recorded in comment nodes. Once issues are identified, action nodes are used to represent their resolution, either by proposing specific solutions, by proposing that the issue be ignored, or by indicating that no solution is known. Similar to source nodes, one may request clarification about issues or actions posted by others through comment nodes, and obtain responses by following respond-to links. The resulting comment may further suggest new issues or actions. Disagreement about specific issues or actions are represented through evidence nodes that disconfirm the corresponding issues or actions. Similarly, support for issues or actions is represented by following a confirming link to an evidence node.

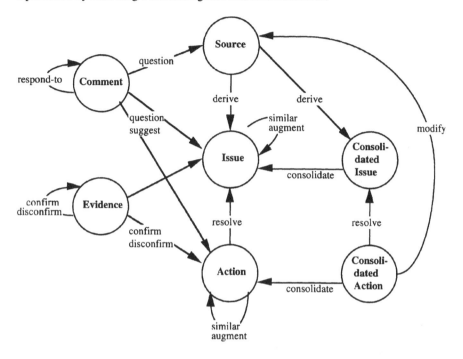

Figure 5. The CSRS data model.

Private review inevitably leads to redundant issue generation, as individuals discover the same problems. During public review, such similarities can be made explicit through the creation of similar-to links. Elaboration of issues or actions can be represented through augment links.

Finally, related issues are summarized into a single consolidated issue, and related actions into a single consolidated action. Actual rework activities are based upon a single consolidated action, rather than by reference to the individual issues and actions raised during public and private review.

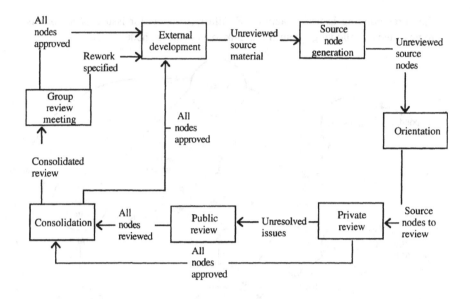

Figure 6. The CSRS process model.

4. The CSRS Process Model

The CSRS process model involves seven phases, as illustrated by the state-transition diagram in Figure 6. The process model constrains the data model by specifying what nodes and links can be legally manipulated during any given phase. The process model also defines specific participant roles similar to the ones defined in Fagan's formal inspection method (Fagan, 1976). The roles include moderator, producer, and reviewer, but eliminates the scribe role.

The next paragraphs describe the phases in CSRS process model, each of which appear as states in Figure 6. Certain administrative procedures such as calling the meeting, selecting participants, and so forth are omitted from this description. For illustrative purposes, the process model is presented in the context of code review, though review of other development artifacts follows the same general procedure.

Source node generation. In this phase, the source code producer with the assistance of the moderator generates source nodes from provided source files. The files are programmatically split into source nodes and annotated as necessary with supplemental information. When the nodes contain source code that has been previously reviewed, backlinks to the consolidated action nodes from the prior review can be created. These links help reviewers check whether prior rework requests have been properly implemented.

Orientation. In this phase, review participants are prepared for private review. Depending upon the nature of review (new review or re-review) and/or group makeup (participants' skills and familiarity with the product), this phase may range from a formal overview meeting with a presentation by the producer about the system structure and behavior, to an informal notification through e-mail noting the presence of new nodes ready for review using CSRS.

Private review. In this phase, reviewers inspect source nodes privately. They create issue, action and/or comment nodes. Issue and action nodes are not publicly available to other reviewers at this time, but comment nodes (clarification about the logic/ algorithm of source nodes) are publicly available. Normally, the producer or moderator responds to comment nodes posted by reviewers. Reviewers must explicitly mark each source node as reviewed, which allows them greater flexibility in their internal review process.

While reviewers do not have access to each other's state during private review, the moderator does. This allows the moderator to monitor the progress of private review. While private review normally terminates when all reviewers have marked all source nodes as reviewed, the moderator may move on to public review at any time.

Public review. In this phase, review participants (including the producer) react to all generated issue and action nodes. Reviewers can create new issue, action or comment nodes based upon existing nodes. They may create similar links between two issue or action nodes upon reading the content of the nodes. They may create new issues or actions that augment the existing ones. They may also post evidence nodes which confirm or disconfirm particular issue, action or other evidence nodes. They can also indicate their agreement about existing actions by voting; this information is used as a consensual indicator among participants about the most appropriate action to take on the issue. This phase normally concludes when all issue, action and evidence nodes have been marked as reviewed by all reviewers. However, control over when public review ends is ultimately in the hands of the moderator.

Consolidation. In this phase, the moderator creates a consolidated representation of the state of review thus far, oriented around the set of actions required based upon review. CSRS supports the moderator in the preparation of a written report containing this information.

Group review meeting. If the consolidated report identifes areas of continued controversy, a group meeting is required. In the meeting, the moderator presents the unresolved issues or actions and summarizes the differences of opinion. After discussion, the group may vote to decide them, or the moderator may unilaterally make the decision. The moderator notes the decision in the written report. The moderator may also declare issues unresolved if no consensus can be reached: this can either imply that informal discussion should proceed after the review or the final resolution will be decided at some later point. Finally, the moderator may also decide to reinspect some source nodes during the meeting as a group (e.g., the nodes that are difficult to understand by the majority of reviewers). The producer will lead this later activity; the reviewers raise issues and proposed actions verbally, and the recorder records only the consensual issues or actions.

External development. In this phase, actions decided upon by the review process are carried out, as well as any other development activities motivated by non-review concerns (such as changes to functional requirements, platform porting, and so forth.) This phase occurs outside the boundaries of CSRS and results in new or modified source code that has not been explicitly approved through review. External tools can be employed to automatically input non-approved source code into CSRS as required by the overall software development process model.

5. Software Process Improvement using CSRS

As illustrated in the scenario of code review in Section 2, the use of a specialized computer-supported cooperative work environment for review provides major benefits. First, it results in a richly linked repository for all artifacts of review, providing a resource that facilitates rework, project scheduling, access to design/maintenance rationale, and so forth. Second, it decreases the dependence in traditional review methods on same-time same-place group work, by providing an additional avenue for collaboration. Third, it provides automated support for the roles of producer, moderator, and reviewer, and essentially eliminates the role of scribe, thus decreasing the labor-intensive manual activities implicit in traditional review methods.

However, the use of CSRS provides an additional, equally significant benefit: the ability to easily instrument review in order to collect metrics that facilitate maturation of its process and products.

CSRS measures the review process by creating a log of each session, where timestamped events are generated by an appropriate subset of the user actions. Currently, actions such as retrieval of a CSRS node, locking and unlocking, node and link creation and deletion, and so forth are all time-stamped and spooled to a log. This logfile of events is then post-processed off-line to generate more condensed, useful information such as that illustrated in the spreadsheet in Figure 5.

Depending upon the organization, application, and group characteristics, some degree of process maturation may be possible via informal analysis of the historical values of these metrics from prior reviews. For example, an organization might find relatively simple correlations between such aggregate metrics as the number of source code lines, the amount of time spent during review, the number of issues and actions raised, and the number of participants. Such analysis can allow rough quantitative boundaries to be placed around review parameters, such as "the number of reviewers should be between 4 and 7", or "the number of lines of code to be reviewed should not exceed 800, nor should the number of source code nodes exceed 12."

On the other hand, CSRS can also be used to provide more formal and robust empirical data concerning the review process. For example, some researchers have claimed that the use of standardized checklists can improve the quality of review, by forcing reviewers to explicitly "check off" each item in a list as being satisfied by the artifact under study (Knight, 1991). This claim can be disputed by arguing that if the standardized checklist is not comprehensive, faults not covered by the checklist will be far less likely to be uncovered. CSRS provides environmental support for empirical investigation of this issue. For example, this particular question could be investigated via a simple repeated measures experimental design where a set of reviewers and a set of source nodes are split into two groups, and each participant reviews and each node is reviewed both with and without a standardized checklist. Such an experiment could also answer such questions as: Is my checklist comprehensive? Do checklists lengthen or shorten the time of review? Do checklists improve the productivity of review in terms of issues identified per unit time?

Having now discussed the CSRS environment, process and data model, and application to process maturity, the next section turns to a contrast of CSRS with other research concerning review.

6. Related Work

While the idea of facilitating review process with computer support is not a new one, we know of no other system that supports review as comprehensively as CSRS. Other computer based review systems, such as ICICLE (Brothers, 1990) support only the face-to-face group meeting by synchronizing and sharing the code window among participants; the use of hypertext technology is basically untyped, non-context sensitive, and limited to source code annotation.

CSRS provides similar benefits to those shown for other forms of computer-mediated meeting support (Nunamaker, 1991). This research indicates that activities such as private review, public review, and moderator consolidation can be more effective and efficient than traditional face-to-face meetings. Such activities decrease process losses such as attention blocking, air time fragmentation, domination, and many others. In fact, educational materials on software inspection published by Software Engineering Institute (Deimel, 1991) discuss these exact problems in the context of review meetings: the moderator dominates inspection, the producer is under attack, the reader is too fast, and so forth.

Martin and Tsai (1990) have shown that having *n* small teams inspect the same source is more effective (in the sense of generating more faults) than a single large team working together. Our past experience with traditional inspection also showed that faults detected by different reviewers overlapped very little.

Nunamaker (1991) describes this same phenomena as reduction in free-riding by individual team members. The private review phase in CSRS is designed in light of this research.

The CSRS instrumentation also helps reduce free-riding. Freedman (1990) states that a major responsibility of the review leader is to ensure that participants come prepared to the review, discusses the seriousness and frequency of insufficiently prepared review members, and suggests several ways to address the problem. For example, they suggest deliberately leaving out one page of the review artifact when distributing materials to reviewers---those who adequately prepare will notice its absence and contact the leader. CSRS supports a much less devious approach: the environment records which source nodes have been visited, how long they have been visited, and whether they have been marked as reviewed by each member. Since each member's summary window presents such information, and since this information is known to be available to the moderator, there is no point in trying to "bluff" their way through the review meeting.

On the other hand, group review has its own benefits, since participants can learn from each other, issues raised by one participant may stimulate other participants to raise new issues, and a more objective evaluation can be obtained (Nunamaker, 1991). CSRS follows the private review phase by a public review phase in order to benefit from group review as well.

The CSRS data model is similar to the one used by gIBIS (Conklin, 1988) for issues exploration and deliberation. However, the CSRS data model is specialized to review, and thus allows more specific computational support and metrics collection. Also in contrast to gIBIS, our data model is strongly tied to the process model and thus context-sensitive: most artifacts can only be manipulated at certain phases defined in the process model.

InspeQ (Knight, 1991) is a review method whose contribution primarily rests in its detailed description of a set of review phases, each of which contains an explicit checklist for reviewers to follow. CSRS can be easily tailored to the InspeQ process model. In fact, as illustrated in Section 5, CSRS can even be used to empirically determine whether or not such a tailoring is desirable.

Finally, in contrast to traditional formal inspection (Fagan, 1976), CSRS supports proposals for a course of action for each identified issue. Our experiences with traditional inspection revealed to us that if actions are prohibited from the review process, the programmer who is assigned to fix the errors often misunderstands the "real" issue. Thus, action nodes can serve as issue clarification.

7. Current Status and Future Directions

The CSRS data and process model has been under development for over a year, with refinements motivated by a variety of review experiences at both code and design level. The current implementation of CSRS employs a Unix/X windows environment, with a database server back-end written in C++ (Wiil, 1990) and a Lucid EMACS front-end interface. Such a choice of environments makes CSRS easily integrable with current development practices. For example, source code can be read from RCS or SCCS, and CSRS can automatically generate e-mail messages to inform reviewers of the state of review.

CSRS displays a property typical to most CSCW systems: introducing collaborative support into a work process dramatically changes the work process. Fagan's code inspection method, for example, is intimately tied to a work process lacking CSCW support, and we are finding that many of the concepts (such as the role of scribe) and constraints (strict prohibition of action discussion) to be irrelevent or inappropriate for a CSCW-based FTR tool.

Currently, CSRS is in active use within our research group, and we plan to release a public domain version for external evaluation within the next year. Our current work concentrates on improving the usability of the system and the precision and expressiveness of the metric information. We are beginning to build a database of review data based on our personal experience with CSRS. A primary goal of public release is to obtain data about review across a spectrum of applications, organizations, and review methods.

A long-range goal for CSRS is explicit support for learning during the review process. We believe that the greatest potential review has for improving software quality comes not from its ability to uncover faults in programs, but from its ability to uncover faults in programmers. Review holds incredible potential to teach programmers how to write correct, readable, and maintainable software, yet such a benefit is rarely recognized, much less explicitly supported. We hope to use CSRS to discover effective ways to support this aspect of software review.

Acknowledgments

We gratefully acknowledge the other members of the Collaborative Software Development Laboratory, who have contributed greatly to this research: Dadong Wan, Kiran Kavoori, and Robert Brewer. Support for this research was provided in part by the National Science Foundation Research Initiation Award CCR-9110861 and the University of Hawaii Research Council Seed Money Award R-91-867-F-728-B-270.

References

L. Brothers, V. Sembugamoorthy, and M. Muller (1990): ICICLE: Groupware for code inspection. In *Proceedings of CSCW'90*, pp. 169-181. ACM Press.

Jeff Conklin and Michael L. Begeman (1988): gIBIS: A hypertext tool for exploratory policy discussion. In *Proceedings of CSCW'88*, pp. 140-152. ACM Press.

Lionel E. Deimel (1990): *Scenes of Software Inspections: Video Dramatizations for the Classroom.* Software Engineering Institute, Carnegie Mellon University.

Robert Dunn (1990): *Software Quality: Concepts and Plans.* Prentice Hall.

Michael E. Fagan (1976): Design and code inspections to reduce errors in program development. *IBM System Journal,* 15(3):182--211.

Michael E. Fagan (1986): Advances in software inspections. *IEEE Transactions on Software Engineering,* SE-12(7), pp. 744-751.

D. P. Freedman and G. M. Weinberg (1990): Handbook of Walkthroughs, Inspections and Technical Reviews. Little, Brown.

Philip M. Johnson (1992): Supporting exploratory CSCW with the EGRET framework. In *Proceedings of CSCW'92,* ACM Press.

John C. Knight and E. Ann Myers (1991): Phased inspections and their implementation. *Software Engineering Notes,* 16(3):29-35.

Johnny Martin and W. T Tsai (1990): N-fold inspection: A requirement analysis technique. *Communications of the ACM,* 33(2):225-232.

J. F. Nunamaker, Alan R. Dennis, Joseph S. Valacich, Douglas R. Vogel, and Joey F. George (1991): Electronic meeting systems to support group work. *Communications of the ACM,* 34(7):42--61.

Glen W. Russel (1991): Experience with inspection in ultralarge-scale developments. IEEE Software, (9)1.

G. Gordon Schulmeyer and James I. McManus (1987): Handbook of Software Quality Assurance. Van Nostrand Reinhold.

U. Wiil and K. Osterbye (1990): Experiences with hyperbase-a multi-user back-end for hypertext applications with emphasis on collaboration support. *Technical Report 90-38,* Department of Mathematics and Computer Science, University of Aalborg, Denmark.

Edward Yourdon (1989): *Structured Walkthrough.* Prentice-Hall, Fourth Edition.

Proceedings of the Third European Conference on Computer-Supported Cooperative Work
13-17 September, 1993, Milan, Italy
G. De Michelis, C. Simone and K. Schmidt (Editors)

Design for Privacy in Ubiquitous Computing Environments

Victoria Bellotti* and Abigail Sellen*†
* Rank Xerox EuroPARC, Cambridge, UK
bellotti@europarc.xerox.com; sellen@europarc.xerox.com

†MRC Applied Psychology Unit, Cambridge, UK

Abstract: Current developments in information technology are leading to increasing capture and storage of information about people and their activities. This raises serious issues about the preservation of privacy. In this paper we examine why these issues are particularly important in the introduction of ubiquitous computing technology into the working environment. Certain problems with privacy are closely related to the ways in which the technology attenuates natural mechanisms of feedback and control over information released. We describe a framework for design for privacy in ubiquitous computing environments and conclude with an example of its application.

Introduction

Information technology can store, transmit and manipulate vast quantities and varieties of information. Whilst this is critical to government, public services, business and many individuals, it may also facilitate unobtrusive access, manipulation and presentation of personal data (Parker et al., 1990; Dunlop & Kling, 1991).

The term "Big Brother" in the context of computing technology, seems to imply two classes of problem. The first is due to the fact that computer technology may be put to insidious or unethical uses (e.g., Clarke, 1988). All information systems, and particularly distributed systems, are potentially vulnerable to covert subversion (Lampson et al., 1981) and, although it can be made extremely difficult to tamper with data in computing systems, protection mechanisms "are often only secure *in principle*. They are seldom secure *in practice*." (Mullender, 1989).

Deliberate or poorly considered design resulting in invasive applications and sophisticated subversion of supposedly secure systems are discouraged by cultural censure and law (although these forces trail behind the advances in sophistication of the technology). However, software must still be secure in order to reduce the risks of covert abuse of personal data and this is an important area of research. There are already a number of useful software protection models and standards which are designed to reduce the risks (see e.g., Lampson et al., 1981; and Mullender, 1989).

The second class of problem is related to very different concerns about a fast growing, less well understood set of issues. These arise from user-interface design features which interfere with social behaviour. These features may foster unethical use of the technology but, more significantly, they are also much more conducive to inadvertent intrusions on privacy (Heath & Luff, 1991).

Mediated interactions between people via technology are prone to breakdowns due to inadequate feedback about what information one is broadcasting and an inability to control one's accessibility to others. This disrupts the social norms and practices governing communication and acceptable behaviour. Our concern in this paper is tackle the latter kind of problem in the context of systems design.

In attempting to design systems which reduce perceived invasions of privacy, it would be useful to have a practical working definition of the concept. Unfortunately, although privacy is widely considered to be an important right, it is difficult to define this notion in more than an intuitive fashion (Anderson, 1991). Attitudes to what is and what is not private data vary between people in different contexts and roles (Harper et al., 1992). Codes of practice and the law offer inadequate guidance on what actually counts as violation of privacy in technologically sophisticated environments (Clarke, 1988) and it may take lengthy court proceedings to determine what the case may be (Privacy Protection Study Commission, 1991).

Any realistic definition of privacy cannot be static. With the introduction of new technology, patterns of use and social norms develop around it and what is deemed "acceptable" behaviour is subject to change. Naturally evolving social practices may interact with organisational policies for correct usage (Harper et al., 1992). In addition, people are more prepared to accept potentially invasive technology if they consider that its benefits outweigh potential risks (e.g., Ladd, 1991; Richards, 1991). In recognition of these facts we take privacy to be a personal notion shaped by culturally determined expectations and perceptions about one's environment.

The social practices and policies that determine any *rights* an individual has to privacy interact with the technical and interface design aspects of the technology they use. Technology is not neutral when it comes to privacy. It can increase or reduce the extent to which people have control over personal data. Our concern is to ensure that privacy should be a central design issue in its own right.

We present a framework for addressing the design of *control* and *feedback* of information captured by multimedia, ubiquitous computing environments. These two issues are fundamental to successful communication and collaboration amongst users as well as to maintaining privacy. We ground our examples largely in the domain of networked audio-video environments and in particular in experiences with one such environment. However, our framework may also be related to the design of CSCW systems and distributed computing environments in general.

In the following sections we first introduce the context and nature of the technology which is the focus of our interest, we then go on to outline our design framework and provide a brief example of its application.

Maintaining privacy in a media space

The need to understand and protect personal privacy in sophisticated information systems is becoming critical as computing power moves out of the box-on-the-desk into the world at large. We are entering the age of *ubiquitous computing* (e.g., Weiser, 1991; Lamming & Newman, 1991; Hindus & Schmandt, 1992) in which our environment comes to contain computing technology in a variety of forms.

Increasingly, we are seeing such systems incorporate sensors such as microphones, cameras and signal receivers for wireless communication. These sensors have the potential to transmit information such as speech, video images, or signals from portable computing devices, active badges (Want et al., 1992), electronic whiteboards (Pederson et al., 1993), and so on. These devices can be networked so that multimedia information can be stored, accessed, processed and distributed in a variety of ways. Services include audio-video (AV) interconnections, information retrieval, diary systems, document tracking and so on (e.g., Lamming & Newman, 1991; Gaver, 1992; Eldridge et al., 1992).

Ubiquitous computing usually implies embedding the technology unobtrusively within all manner of everyday objects which can potentially transmit and receive information from any other object. The aims are not only to reduce its visibility, but also to empower its users with more flexible and portable applications to support the capture, communication, recall, organisation and reuse of diverse information. The irony is that its unobtrusiveness both belies and contributes to its potential for supporting potentially invasive applications.

In light of these developments, it is dangerously complacent to assume that social and organisational controls over accessibility of personal information are sufficient, or that intrusions into privacy will ultimately become acceptable when traded against potential benefits. Such a position could leave individual users with a heavy burden of responsibility to ensure that they do not, even inadvertently, intrude on others. It also leaves them with limited control over their own privacy.

"Media spaces" (Stults, 1988) are a recent development in ubiquitous computing technology, involving audio, video and computer networking. They are the focus of an increasing amount of research and industrial interest into support for distributed collaborative work (e.g., Root, 1988; Mantei et al., 1991; Gaver et al., 1992; Fish et al., 1992). EuroPARC's RAVE environment is just one of several media spaces which have been set up in various research laboratories around the world.

In RAVE, cameras, monitors, microphones and speakers are placed in every office, to provide everyone with their own personal RAVE *node*. This allows one to communicate and work with others and to be aware of what is going on in the building without leaving one's office. Various kinds of flexible video-only and AV connections between nodes are set up and broken by central switching devices which are controlled from individual workstations.

Whilst media space technology improves the accessibility of people to one another, some may feel that their privacy is compromised. The very ubiquity of such systems means that many of the concerns with existing workstation-based information systems are aggravated. A much wider variety of information can now be captured. People are much less likely to be "off-line" (inaccessible) at any given moment. Further, the design of many of these systems is such that it may not be clear when one is off- or on-line and open to scrutiny (Mantei et al., 1991; Gaver, 1992). People also express concern about their own intrusiveness to others when they try to make contact without being able to determine others' availability (Cool et al., 1992). Concerns about such problems have strongly influenced the installation and ongoing design of RAVE, as well as the way in which people use it.

Feedback and Control in RAVE

At EuroPARC people generally do not worry much about privacy. They feel that the benefits of RAVE outweigh their concerns. This is because the design has evolved together with a culture of trust and acceptable practices relating to its use. Individual freedom was fostered to use, customise, or ignore the technology. Design was informed by studies of how collaborative work is socially organised and how such technology impacts it (e.g. Heath & Luff, 1991; 1992). Users' views and reactions were obtained via questionnaires and interviews. The varied individual feelings about privacy were accommodated by ensuring that users could decide how accessible they were to others via the media space (Dourish, 1991; Gaver et al., 1992; Dourish, 1993).

In designing for privacy in RAVE, two important principles have emerged (Gaver et al, 1992). These are *control* and *feedback*, which we define as follows:
Control: Empowering people to stipulate what information they project and who can get hold of it.
Feedback: Informing people when and what information about them is being captured and to whom the information is being made available.

RAVE users can control who may connect to them and what kind of connections each person is allowed make. If they omit to do so, automatic defaults are set to reject connections. User control via the workstation is supported by "Godard", the software infrastructure which provides the primary interface to the complex AV signal-switching and feedback mechanisms (Dourish,1991). These mechanisms comprise the kinds of connections which can be made between people, to different public areas, and to media services (e.g., video-players).

Feedback depends on the type of RAVE connection being made. Three kinds of interpersonal connection are "glance", "v-phone call" and "office-share". Glance connections are one-way, video-only connections of a few seconds' duration. V-phone and office-share connections are longer two-way AV connections. For glances, audio feedback (Gaver, 1991) alerts users to onset and termination of a connection and can even announce who is making it. For the two-way office connections, reciprocity acts as a form of feedback about the connection (if I see you, you see me) and, in the case of an attempted v-phone connection, an audio "ringing" signal is given and the caller's name is displayed on the workstation, whereupon the recipient can decide whether to accept or reject the connection. Office-shares, being very long term, do not require such a protocol.

Public areas have cameras which can be accessed by a glance or a "background" connection which is indefinite, one-way and video-only. We provide feedback about the presence of a camera in a public place in the form of a video monitor beside the camera which displays its view.

Control and feedback also figure strongly in the design of RAVE's architecture. Connection capability lists and an access control model define who can connect to whom and provide long term, static control over accessibility. Providing distinct connection types can also allow users to exercise discriminating dynamic control over their accessibility as in the v-phone call (for a fuller description of these features see Dourish, 1993). Our concern, however, is with the moment-to-moment continuous control that people exercise over how they present themselves in public as respectable, social beings (Goffman, 1963). In the next section we indicate why people, especially newcomers and visitors to places with media spaces and other kinds of ubiquitous computing technology, can feel uneasy about their ability to monitor and control their self presentation and consequently their privacy.

Disembodiment and dissociation

A number of problems with RAVE relate to the extended duration of v-phone calls and office-shares. Users tend to forget about their existence and associated implications. Even seasoned users can get confused about the nature of their connections. For example, if a colleague with whom you have an office-share switches off their camera or moves out of shot, it is easy to forget that they can still see you.

Problems in public areas include the fact that monitors next to cameras only suggest (and then only to those familiar with a media space) that a video image may be being broadcast to many people, via background connections. They cannot inform people when or to whom the image is being sent. For most EuroPARC "regulars" this is not a major concern, but for newcomers to the building, it may be.

The underlying causes of such problems lie in the fact that the technology results in *disembodiment* from the context into and from which one projects information (Heath & Luff, 1991) and *dissociation* from one's actions. These phenomena interfere with conveying information about oneself or gaining information about others.

Conveying information: In the presence of others you convey information in many ways. These include position, posture, facial expression, speech, voice level and intonation, and direction of gaze. Such cues influence the behaviour of others. For example, they can determine whether or not others will try to initiate communication with you.

In CSCW and ubiquitous computing environments disembodiment means that these resources may be attenuated. So you may not be able to present yourself as effectively to others as you can in a face-to-face setting. For example, in an AV connection, you may only be a face on a monitor (Gaver, 1992) with your voice coming out of a loudspeaker, the volume of which you may not be aware or able to control. You may only appear as a name (McCarthy et al., 1991) or a name associated with a room displayed on a screen (e.g., Harper et al., 1992). At worst (e.g., in a RAVE background connection) you may have no perceptible presence at all. On the other hand, disembodiment also means that you may be unaware of when you are convey information to others because of a lack of feedback from the technology.

Dissociation occurs in CSCW applications when only the results of actions are shared, but the actions themselves are invisible. In other words when you cannot easily determine who is doing, or did, what (e.g., ShrEdit, a shared editor with no telepointers; McGuffin & Olson, 1992).

Gaining information: In face-to-face situations, cues given by others influence your judgements about whether to attempt conversation, what to say and how to act.

In media spaces, there is usually no way to gauge how available someone else is before connecting to them (Louie et al., in press). Once connected, awareness of the person at the other end of the link or their actions is likely to be limited to the fixed and narrow field of view of a camera, and whatever a microphone picks up (Gaver, 1992). That person also has a reduced, disembodied presence. In turn, you are likely to receive fewer cues when someone is observing you, or your work.

Breakdown of Social and Behavioural Norms and Practices

The effects of disembodiment and dissociation manifest themselves in a variety of breakdowns in behavioural and social norms and practices. For example, breakdowns associated with disembodiment include a tendency for users to engage in unintentional, prolonged observation of others over AV links (Heath & Luff, 1991). Users may intrude when they make AV connections, because they cannot discern how available others are (Louie et al., in press). Furthermore, the intuitive principle that if I can't see you then you can't see me, does not necessarily apply to computer mediated situations where one person may be able to observe others' activities without themselves being observed.

A major problem related to dissociation is one's inability to respond effectively to a perceived action because one does not know who is responsible for it. A familiar example of this problem exists with telephones where it is impossible to identify nuisance callers before picking up the receiver.

Problems of disembodiment and dissociation receive far less attention in the literature than insidious exploitation of technology. This is unfortunate as they are also problems for social interaction and communication mediated by technology and likely to be much more pervasive, particularly because they often relate to purely unintentional invasions of privacy. Furthermore, by addressing these problems through careful design, we may reduce the potential impact of system abuse.

It must be pointed out that the technology itself is not inherently problematic. Resources used in face-to-face situations can be exploited, simulated, or substituted through design. For example media space systems can embody the principle "If I see your face, you see mine," which is natural in face-to-face situations (e.g., VideoTunnels; Buxton & Moran, 1989) or they can supply means to convey availability (e.g., Louie et al., 1992). Dissociation problems in CSCW systems have been reduced by means of conveying gestures, or even body posture (e.g. Minneman & Bly, 1991; Tang & Minneman, 1991).

Our ongoing research assumes that problems of interaction, communication and privacy in ubiquitous computing systems, can be reduced through technological design refinements and innovations. Disembodiment and dissociation may be reduced through the provision of enriched feedback about the state of the technology and information being projected about users. Users must also have practical mechanisms of control over that personal information. We now present a framework for systematically addressing these issues. Although it may have general use for designing CSCW technology to support social interaction and communication, we focus in particular on how it helps us confront privacy as a central design concern.

A design framework

Based on our experience with privacy issues in RAVE and other similar systems, we have developed a simple design framework aimed at counteracting the kinds of problems we have outlined.

Addressing the Problems

Much of the mutual awareness, which we normally take for granted may be reduced or lost in mediated interpersonal interactions. We may no longer know what information we are conveying, what it looks like and how permanent it is, who it is conveyed to, or what the intentions of those using that information might be. In order to counteract problems associated with this loss, our framework proposes that systems must be explicitly designed to provide feedback and control for at least the following potential user and system behaviours:

Capture: What kind of information is being picked up? Candidates include voices, actual speech, moving video or framegrabbed images (close up or not), personal identity, work activity and its products such as keypresses, applications used, files accessed, messages and documents.

Construction: What happens to information? Is it encrypted or processed at some point or combined with other information and, if so, how? Is it stored? In what form? Privacy concerns in ubiquitous computing environments are exacerbated by the fact that potential records of our activity may be kept and possibly manipulated, and used at a later date and out of their original context. This leads to numerous potential ethical problems (Mackay, 1991).

	Feedback About	Control Over
Capture	When and what information about me gets into the system.	When and when not to give out what information. I can enforce my own preferences for system behaviours with respect to each type of information I convey.
Construction	What happens to information about me once it gets inside the system.	What happens to information about me. I can set automatic default behaviours and permissions.
Accessibility	Which people and what software (e.g., daemons or servers) have access to information about me and what information they see or use.	Who and what has access to what information about me. I can set automatic default behaviours and permissions.
Purposes	What people want information about me for. Since this is outside of the system, it may only be possible to infer purpose from construction and access behaviours.	It is infeasible for me to have technical control over purposes. With appropriate feedback, however, I can exercise social control to restrict intrusion, unethical, and illegal usage.

Figure 1. A framework for designing for feedback and control in ubiquitous computing environments: Each cell contains a description of the ideal state of affairs with respect to feedback or control of each of four types of behaviour.

Accessibility: Is information public, available to particular groups, certain persons only, or just to oneself? What applications, processes, and so on utilise personal data.

Purpose: To what uses is information put? How might it be used in the future? The intentions of those who wish to use data may not be made explicit. It may only be possible to infer what these are from knowledge of the person, the context, patterns of access and construction.

We now consider each of these four classes of concerns in relation to the following two questions:

What is the appropriate feedback?

What is the appropriate control?

We thus have eight design questions which form the basis for a design framework (Figure 1) with which we can analyse existing designs and explore new ones, with respect to a range of privacy issues. This framework is a domain specific example of the QOC approach to design rationale in which design issues, couched as questions, are explicitly represented together with proposed solutions and their assessments (for more details see MacLean et al., 1991; Bellotti, 1993).

The issues in the cells within the framework are not necessarily independent of one another. For instance, in order to be fully informed about the purpose of information usage, one must know something about each of the other behaviours. Likewise, in order to appreciate access, one must know about capture and construction. Understanding construction requires knowing something about capture. Hence there is a dependency relationship for design of feedback between these behaviours. Control over each of them may, however, be relatively independently designed.

For those concerned about privacy, and the potential for subversion in particular, control over, and thus feedback about, capture is clearly the most important. Given appropriate feedback about what is being captured, users can orient themselves appropriately to the technology for collaboration or communication purposes and exercise appropriate control over their behaviour or what is captured in the knowledge of possible construction, access and purposes of information use.

Evaluating Solutions

Our framework emphasises design to a set of criteria, which may be extended through experience and evaluation. Whilst questions about what feedback and control to provide set the design agenda, criteria represent additional and sometimes competing concerns which help us to assess and distinguish potential design solutions. The set of criteria acts as a checklist helping to encourage systematic evaluation of solutions. They have been identified from our experiences with the design and use of a range of ubiquitous computing services. Particularly important in our current set are the following eleven criteria.

Trustworthiness: Systems must be technically reliable and instill confidence in users. In order to satisfy this criterion, they must be understandable by their users. The consequences of actions must be confined to situations which can be apprehended in the context in which they take place and thus appropriately controlled.

Appropriate timing: Feedback should be provided at a time when control is most likely to be required and effective.

Perceptibility: Feedback should be noticeable.

Unobtrusiveness: Feedback should not distract or annoy. It should also be selective and relevant and should not overload the recipient with information.

Minimal intrusiveness: Feedback should not involve information which compromises the privacy of others.

Fail-safety: In cases where users omit to take explicit action to protect their privacy, the system should minimise information capture, construction and access.

Flexibility: What counts as private varies according to context and interpersonal relationships. Thus mechanisms of control over user and system behaviours may need to be tailorable to some extent by the individuals concerned.

Low effort: Design solutions must be lightweight to use, requiring as few actions and as little effort on the part of the user as possible.

Meaningfulness: Feedback and control must incorporate meaningful representations of information captured and meaningful actions to control it, not just raw data and unfamiliar actions. They should be sensitive to the context of data capture and also to the contexts in which information is presented and control exercised.

Learnability: Proposed designs should not require a complex model of how the system works. They should exploit or be sensitive to natural, existing psychological and social mechanisms that allow people to perceive and control how they present themselves and their availability for potential interactions.

Low cost: Naturally, we wish to keep costs of design solutions down.

The first seven criteria are especially relevant to protection of privacy. The final four are more general design concerns. Some of these criteria have to be traded off against one another in the search for design solutions.

Applying The Framework: Feedback and Control for Video Data from a Public Area

We have begun to apply our framework to RAVE to reveal aspects of its design which can be refined. For the sake of brevity, we focus on just one aspect of this media space which involves a video connection from the Commons, a public reading and meeting area at EuroPARC.

In RAVE, people can access the camera in the Commons either in the form of short glance or indefinite, background, video-only connections. The video data can sent to devices such as a framegrabber which takes digitised video snaps. These can be used by various services such as Vepys, a video diary which takes still images of people via media space cameras, every so often, wherever they are, and stores the series of images as a browsable record of their day-to-day activity (Eldridge, 1992).

Providing feedback and control mechanisms over video data taken from this public area is a challenging problem but it is an important one, since the Commons is an area where many visitors to EuroPARC spend their time.

Our framework prompts us to ask the following questions for which we describe existing or potential design solutions (relevant criteria appear in italics):

Q: What feedback is there about when and what information about me gets into the system?

Existing Solutions:

Confidence monitor: A monitor is positioned next to the camera to inform passers by when they are within range, and what they look like. This solution fulfils the design criteria of being *trustworthy, meaningful* and *appropriately timed.*

Mannequin (the Toby): In order to alert people to the presence of the camera, a mannequin affectionately named Toby is positioned holding the camera. Toby draws people's attention because he looks like another person in the room. Originally the camera was in his head, but this concealed it and some visitors thought it was deliberately being hidden. Now Toby holds the camera on his shoulder. This feedback is *less obtrusive* than the confidence monitor (which can be distracting), however it is less *meaningful* because it doesn't tell you whether the camera is on, or if you are in its view.

Alternative Solution:

Movement Sensors: A solution which might supplement the use of confidence monitors would be to try using infra-red devices to alert people, either with an audio or visual signal, when they move into the field of view of a camera. These would provide *appropriately timed* feedback about onset of capture of video information, however they would not be *meaningful* without some other form of feedback.

Q: What feedback is there about what happens to information about me inside the system?

No Existing Solution:

The confidence monitor does not inform visitors and newcomers to the lab that the video signal is sent to a switch. This can potentially direct the signal to any number of nodes, recording devices or ubiquitous computing services in the lab. Unfortunately Toby cannot tell you whether recording or some other construction of video data is taking place. In fact the EuroPARC policy is that recording never takes place without warnings to lab members.

Proposed Solutions:

LED display: A simple design solution would be to have an LED status display by the camera, connected to the media space switch and other devices responsible for collecting, recording and distributing the video signal. This is a *low cost* proposal to give *appropriately timed* feedback about when and which services are actively collecting information. Unfortunately it might not be sufficiently *perceptible*.

Audio and video feedback: We could provide audio feedback to indicate connections and image framegrabbing but it could be *obtrusive* and *annoying* to provide repeated audio feedback to a public area at a sufficient volume to be heard all round the room. An alternative would be to superimpose the flashing word "Recording" on the screen of the confidence monitor. This would have to be refined to find a solution which draws attention whilst being *unobtrusive.*

Q: What feedback is given about who has access to information about me and what information they see?

Existing Solutions:

Textual information: In order to warn people that they might be "watched", Toby wears a sweatshirt with the message "I may be a dummy but I'm watching you!" printed on it. Together with the fact that Toby is holding a camera, the *meaning* of this is fairly clear in a general sense, but not specific enough about who is doing the watching and when.

Proposed Solutions:

Viewer display: One option is to display a list of names or pictures on the wall to indicate who can watch a public area. If we want to update the information we could adapt Portholes, an "awareness sever" which distributes images to EuroPARC and PARC media space users (Dourish & Bly, 1992). In order to be *perceptible* to passers by, the display would have to be larger than a normal monitor. We could project images of who is currently connected to the camera onto the wall. However, this would be *expensive*, and possibly *intrusive* to those who connect to a public area.

Audio feedback: In private offices audio feedback alerts occupants to onset and termination of short term glance connections. Such feedback about video connections to the Commons would be *inappropriately timed*, since they are normally of the long term background variety which outlast most visits to the room.

Q: What feedback is provided about the purposes of using information about me?

No Existing Solution

There is no technical feedback about the intentions of those who access the video signal. However, lab members are reasonably confident that their privacy is not threatened by others' uses of information, probably because, in a public area, they already behave in what they consider to be a publicly presentable and acceptable fashion.

Proposed Solution:

We cannot provide technological feedback about people's intentions. These may only be deduced from feedback about capture, access and utilisation of information, together with knowledge of the culture, context and individuals concerned.

Q: What control is there over when and when not to give out what information?
Existing Solutions:

Moving off camera: People can move on or off camera; there is a "video-free zone" in the commons for those who want to relax in private. This kind of solution is very *easy to learn.*

Covering the camera: If certain activities, such as the potentially embarrassing "weekly step-aerobics work-out," are taking place in the commons, the camera lens is covered. This is an extremely *trustworthy* solution.

Behaving appropriately: If people have to walk in front of the camera, they can orient themselves appropriately to it given the *meaningful* feedback they obtain from the confidence monitor (for example, they will probably not get too close or stare into it for fear of appearing foolish).

Control over what happens to information, who can access it and for what purposes it is used?

We do not propose to give individuals any additional technical control over the capture, construction and access of the Commons video signal because it is a *public* rather than a private information source. Technical control over purposes for which information can be used, however, is impractical with any information source, whether public or private. At EuroPARC, social control is effectively exercised. The culture of acceptable use which has evolved with RAVE dictates that certain practices are frowned upon.

Lab members are always expected to warn others that constructions and access other the normal background connection, glance and Portholes services, are occurring. For example, Vepys video diary experiments, in which subjects have their picture taken wherever they go, are announced to all lab members and the subjects wear labels to warn of potential recording of camera images in areas they enter.

Anyone who objects to this can either avoid the label wearers or ask the researchers concerned to make sure that they are not recorded.

Use of the framework

In the example, our framework serves three important purposes.
- It helps to clarify the existing state of affairs with respect to privacy problems, and social norms and practices currently in place.
- By clarifying the problems, it helps to point to possible design solutions and explore a range of possibilities.
- It is used to assess the solutions in terms of how they might reduce the existing problems as well as how they might cause new ones.

With regard to this last issue, it is important to point out that, while the framework and design criteria help us evaluate proposed solutions prospectively, it is only by implementing these solutions that we can truly judge their usefulness. A case in point is the software infrastructure, Godard, whose privacy feature allows users to select who is allowed to connect to them. Consistent with the criterion of being fail-safe, the default is that lab newcomers are automatically denied access until each person in the lab explicitly allows them access. Unfortunately, because lab members generally forget to change their settings, newcomers find that they are unable to connect to anyone. As a result, they have been known to give up trying and thus never get in the habit of using RAVE. There are simple solutions to this problem, like automatically notifying people to whom an unsuccessful attempt to connect has been made. However, many problems are not foreseen and thus evaluation through use must always be part of the design cycle.

In addition, the framework itself needs to be evaluated and refined. To do this we will be applying it to a range of existing ubiquitous computing technology at EuroPARC. In doing so we hope to identify how it needs to be enhanced or extended.

Discussion and conclusions

In this paper we have focused on technical, rather than social or policy solutions for protecting privacy in ubiquitous computing environments. We have argued that this is an important design focus, and offered a framework as guidance. That being said, it is interesting that the framework has also highlighted ways in which cultural norms and practices affect and sometimes ameliorate privacy concerns.

In spite of shortcomings which our framework highlights, RAVE is, in general, very acceptable to lab members. In part, this is because feedback and control of information capture are well attended to overall in its design, enabling people to orient themselves appropriately to the technology. Further, lab members know roughly how it works, and trust the benign culture which governs its use. Visitors have no such knowledge or trust, and one can imagine that, other contexts, a RAVE style media space could seem very sinister indeed. It is thus quite understandable that many visitors to the lab experience some trepidation.

RAVE is a research tool and is also itself the object of research, like all of the ubiquitous computing systems at EuroPARC. It is not intended to be a model for a commercial, standard media space. Rather, it is an instance of a facility which has evolved inextricably with a culture of use and is only thus acceptable to members of that culture. The problems highlighted by our framework could, however, point to design refinements which might be essential in other contexts.

Another issue which the framework helps to elucidate, is the delicate balance that exists between awareness and privacy. Providing too much awareness of other people's activity and availability may be seen as intrusive. However, too little awareness may result in inadvertent invasions of privacy such as when people cannot tell how receptive another person is to being disturbed. The aim then is to provide awareness without crossing the line into intrusiveness.

A related issue is that data which could be feedback to one person may feature someone else's personal information which they might not want to make available. For example, our proposal to display large Portholes images of people currently connected to the Commons camera may make them feel as if they are on display. This suggests that designs which solve some privacy problems may cause others. Our framework must therefore be applied not only to the systems in place, but also to the privacy solutions themselves.

It is often the case that design decisions involve trade-offs and compromises. Designing to protect privacy is extreme in this respect. There is no guarantee that features put in place to protect privacy will confer the benefits that the designer intends. We therefore aim to prototype some the design refinements we have suggested and evaluate these in use at EuroPARC in the near future.

The framework described in this paper aims to provide a systematic basis for tackling a range of user-interface design problems. The problems we have been dealing with are those that interfere with interactions between people and the exchange of personal information and that are likely to arise with CSCW systems and, in particular, media space and other ubiquitous computing systems. Perhaps more important, we have made the case that *privacy is a user-interface design issue*, and one which we hope will become an increasingly integral part of the design process of information technology in general.

Acknowledgements

We wish to thank Mike Molloy and Paul Dourish for their support in implementing some of our design ideas. We also thank Bob Anderson, Sara Bly, Graham Button, Matthew Chalmers, Paul Dourish, Bill Gaver, Steve Harrison, Mik Lamming, Paul Luff, Wendy Mackay, Allan MacLean, Scott Minneman, William Newman and Peter Robinson for interesting discussions and helpful comments on drafts of this paper.

References

Anderson, R. (1991): *The Ethics of Research into Invasive Technologies.* Technical Report, EPC-91-107, Rank Xerox EuroPARC, Cambridge, UK, 1991.

Bellotti, V. (1993): "Integrating Theoreticians' and Practitioners' Perspectives with Design Rationale" in *Proceedings of INTERCHI'93, Conference on Human Factors in Computing Systems*, Amsterdam, The Netherlands, April, 1993.

Buxton, W. and Moran, T. (1990): "EuroPARC's Integrated Interactive Intermedia Facility (IIIF): Early Experiences". *IFIP Conference on Multi-User Interfaces and Applications*, Herakleion, Crete, September 1990.

Clarke, R. (1988): "Information Technology and Dataveillance", *Communications of the ACM*, 31, 5, 1988, pp. 498-512.

Cool, C., Fish, R., Kraut, R. and Lowery, C. (1992): "Iterative Design of Video Communication Systems" in *Proc. CSCW'92. ACM Conference on Computer-Supported Cooperative Work*, Toronto, Canada, October-November, 1992, pp. 25-32.

Dourish, P. (1991): "Godard: A Flexible Architecture for A/V Services in a Media Space" Technical Report EPC-91-134, Rank Xerox EuroPARC, Cambridge, UK, 1991.

Dourish, P. and Bly, S. (1992): "Portholes: Supporting Awareness in Distributed Work Groups" in *Proc. ACM Conference on Human Factors in Computing Systems, CHI'92*, Monterey, California, May 1992. pp. 541-547.

Dourish, P. (1993): "Culture and Control in a Media Space", in *Proc. European Conference on Computer-Supported Cooperative Work ECSCW'93*, Milano, Italy, September, 1993.

Dunlop, C. and Kling, R. (1991): *Computerization and Controversy: Value Conflicts and Social Choices.* Academic Press, Inc., 1991.

Eldridge, M., Lamming, M. and Flynn, M. (1992): "Does a Video Diary Help Recall?" in *People and Computers VII, Proceedings of the HCI'92 Conference*, York, UK, September, 1992, pp. 257-269.

Fish, R., Kraut, R. and Root, R. (1992): "Evaluating Video as a Technology for Informal Communication" in *Proc. ACM Conference on Human Factors in Computing Systems, CHI '92*, Monterey, California, May, 1992, pp. 37-47.

Gaver, W. (1991): "Sound Support for Collaboration" in *Proc. European Conference on Computer-Supported Cooperative Work, ECSCW'91*, Amsterdam, The Netherlands, September, 1991, pp. 293-308.

Gaver, B., Moran, T., MacLean, A., Lövstrand, L., Dourish, P., Carter K. and Buxton, B. (1992): "Realising a Video Environment: EuroPARC's RAVE System" in *Proc. ACM Conference on Human Factors in Computing Systems, CHI '92*, Monterey, California, May 1992, pp. 27-35.

Gaver, B. (1992): "The Affordance of Media Spaces for Collaboration" in *Proc. CSCW'92. ACM Conference on Computer-Supported Cooperative Work*, Toronto, Canada, October-November, 1992, pp. 17-24.

Goffman, E., *Behaviour in Public Places.* The Free Press, 1963.

Harper, R., Lamming, M. and Newman, W. (1992): "Locating Systems at Work: Implications for the Development of Active Badge Applications", *Interacting with Computers*, 4, 3, 1992, pp.343-363.

Heath, C. and Luff, P. (1991): "Disembodied Conduct: Communication through Video in a Multi-Media Office Environment" in *Proc. ACM Conference on Human Factors in Computing Systems, CHI'91*, New Orleans, Louisiana, April-May 1991, pp. 99-103.

Heath, C. and Luff, P. (1992): "Collaboration and Control: Crisis Management and Multimedia Technology in London Underground Line Control Rooms", *Computer Supported Cooperative Work (CSCW)*, 1, 1992, 69-94.

Hindus, D. and Schmandt, C. (1992): "Ubiquitous Audio: Capturing Spontaneous Collaboration" in *Proc. ACM Conference on Computer-Supported Cooperative Work, CSCW'92*, Toronto, Canada, October-November, 1992, pp. 210-217.

Ladd, J. (1991): "Computers and Moral Responsibility: A Framework for Ethical Analysis" in C. Dunlop & R. Kling (eds.) *Computerization and Controversy: Value Conflicts and Social Choices*, Academic Press Inc., 1991, pp. 664-675.

Lamming, M. and Newman W. (1991): "Activity-Based Information Retrieval Technology in Support of Personal Memory", EuroPARC Technical Report, EPC-91-103.1, 1991.

Lampson, B., Paul, M. and Siegert, H. (1981): *Distributed Systems - Architecture and Implementation*. Springer Verlag, 1981.

Louie, G., Mantei, M. and Sellen, A. (in press) "Making Contact in a Multi-Media Environment", to appear in *Behaviour and Interaction Technology*.

Mackay, W. (1991): "Ethical Issues in the Use of Video: Is it Time to Establish Guidelines?" SIGCHI Discussion Forum in *Proc. ACM Conference on Human Factors in Computing Systems, CHI'91*, New Orleans, Louisiana, April-May 1991, pp. 403-405.

MacLean, A., Young, R., Bellotti, V. and Moran, T. (1991): "Questions, Options, and Criteria: Elements of a Design Rationale for user interfaces", *Human Computer Interaction*, vol 6 (3&4), pp. 201-250.

Mantei, M., Becker, R., Sellen. A., Buxton, W., Milligan, T. and Wellman, B. (1991): "Experiences in the Use of a Media Space" in *Proc. ACM Conference on Human Factors in Computing Systems, CHI'91*, New Orleans, Louisiana, April-May 1991, pp. 203-208.

McCarthy, J., Miles, V. and Monk, A. (1991): "An Experimental Study of Common Ground in Text-Based Communication" in *Proc. ACM Conference on Human Factors in Computing Systems, CHI'91*, New Orleans, Louisiana, April-May 1991, pp. 209-215.

McGuffin, L. and Olson, G. (1992): "ShrEdit: A Shared Electronic Workspace", CSMIL Technical Report, Cognitive Science and Machine Intelligence Laboratory, University of Michigan, 1992.

Minneman, S. and Bly, S. (1991): "Managing à Trois: A Study of a Multi-User Drawing Tool in Distributed Design Work", in *Proc. ACM Conference on Human Factors in Computing Systems, CHI'91*, New Orleans, Louisiana, April- May 1991, pp. 217-224.

Mullender, S. (1989) "Protection", in S. Mullender (ed.) *Distributed Systems*. Addison Wesley, 1989.

Parker, D., Swope, S. and Baker, B. (1990): *Ethical Conflicts in Information and Computer Science, Technology, and Business*, QED, Information Sciences Inc. Wellesley, MA, 1990.

Pedersen, E., McCall, K., Moran, T. and Halasz, F. (1993): "Tivoli: An Electronic Whiteboard for Informal Workgroup Meetings", in *Proc. INTERCHI'93, Conference on Human Factors in Computing Systems*, Amsterdam, The Netherlands, April, 1993.

Privacy Protection Study Commission (1991): "Excerpts from Personal Privacy in an Information Society" in C. Dunlop & R. Kling (eds.) *Computerization and Controversy: Value Conflicts and Social Choices*, Academic Press Inc., 1991, pp. 453-468.

Richards, E. (1991): "Proposed FBI Crime Computer System Raises Questions on Accuracy, Privacy", in C. Dunlop & R. Kling (eds.) *Computerization and Controversy: Value Conflicts and Social Choices*, Academic Press Inc., 1991, pp. 436-438.

Root, R. (1988) "Design of a Multi-Media Vehicle for Social Browsing" in *Proc. ACM Conference on Computer Supported Cooperative Work, CSCW'88*, Portland Oregon, September 26-29, 1988, pp. 25-38.

Stults, R. (1988): "The Experimental Use of Video to Support Design Activities", Xerox PARC Technical Report SSL-89-19, Palo Alto, California, 1988.

Tang, J. and Minneman, S. (1991): "VideoWhiteboard: Video Shadows to Support Remote Collaboration" in *Proc. ACM Conference on Human Factors in Computing Systems, CHI'91*, New Orleans, Louisiana, April-May 1991, pp. 315-322.

Want, R., Hopper, A., Falcco, V. and Gibbons, J.(1992): "The Active Badge Location System", *ACM Transactions on Office Information Systems*, January, 1992, 10(1), pp. 91-102.

Weiser, M. (1991): "The Computer for the 21st Century", *Scientific American*, September, 1991, pp. 94-104.

Proceedings of the Third European Conference on Computer-Supported Cooperative Work
13-17 September, 1993, Milan, Italy
G. De Michelis, C. Simone and K. Schmidt (Editors)

The Designers' Notepad: Supporting and understanding cooperative design

Michael Twidale, Tom Rodden, Ian Sommerville
Department of Computing, Lancaster University, U.K.

ABSTRACT: We describe the development of a system to support cooperative software design. An iterative development approach has been used, based upon the observation of system use in authentic design sessions. This allows us to correct interface errors, and also to learn more about the nature of collaborative design. The observations of use and the resulting refinements of the system are described. In particular we note the variability in design activity both amongst designers and according to circumstances. We also note the way in which concepts mutate over time (often involving frequent and rapid revision) leading to an evolution of structure.

1. Introduction

Supporting the work of designers has been a major focus for the developers of cooperative systems and is illustrative of one of the fundamental problems of developing CSCW systems. While we recognise that most design involves collaboration, our understanding of its nature as a cooperative process is limited. Worse, our intuitions as to the support required may themselves be flawed (Grudin 88). Consequently, tool developers must discover the nature of the design process while simultaneously developing mechanisms to support and potentially improve it. We believe this interplay between the nature of an activity and the influence of the supporting tool to be a central feature of all CSCW systems development. Over the last two years we have been developing a system which provides support for system design. This paper describes the iterative approach to systems development based upon the observation of system use in realistic design sessions. The observations of use and the various features of the system which have emerged as a result of these observations are also described. The development of co-operative systems is a problematic endeavour requiring a combination of skills often drawn from a range of different disciplines. By use of iterative development we can make use of the results of an ongoing ethnographic study of collaborative design (Button & King 92) as these results become available.

2. Supporting the work of designers

Design is an essential part of the systems development process and has consequently attracted considerable interest from the software development community. This has resulted in a range of different methods including JSD (Jackson 83) and OOD (Booch 91). These approaches prescribe a particular design model and require designers to adopt that perspective. The methods have been increasingly supported by the use of CASE tools (CASE 89). However, while CASE tools have provided techniques to support the enforcement of the approaches suggested by different methods, they have provided very little support for the creative process of design, as distinct from solution structuring, refinement and documentation.

The design process is often viewed by designers themselves as a creative and personal activity (Lawson 80). It involves the development and normalisation of concepts relating to the artefact being constructed. Designers tend to adopt flexible and personal notations to express these concepts. These take the form of diagrams, sketches and personal notes. These design notes form an integral part of the activity of design. However, they are viewed as personal resources and consequently are not intended to be interpreted by others.

The reality of modern design is that the work is shared both between different designers and across different phases of the development process. This communication and sharing of designs requires the adoption of some standard notation or formalism. To date these notations have been provided by different design methods. The methodological approach adopted by design methods and CASE tools have proven problematic, so that designers tend to design 'away from the tool' and use the tool to document designs after the event. Thus little tool support is actually provided for the creative design process.

A number of tensions exist in the design process which need to be addressed to allow support for design as a creative activity. Most notably two tensions which we intend to address are:

The private v communal nature of design
Although taking place within a cooperative setting many aspects of design are essentially a personal endeavour. The interplay between public and private design is a significant portion of design.

Freedom of expression v formalisation of shared understanding
Initial design concepts require a high degree of freedom in the notation used to express them. However, subsequent activities within the design and development process require a greater degree of formality to alleviate problems of misunderstanding across a community of designers and developers.

Our approach involves the development of techniques to directly address these tensions. We believe these tensions to be central not only to design but to many cooperative activities within real organisational settings. Consequently, the approach we have adopted to development is of interest to the CSCW community in general.

2.1 Previous approaches to design support

Within the domain of cooperative work, research in design support has generally followed one of two approaches. The first focuses on uncovering and recording the *rationale* used to arrive at different designs. The second concentrates on providing a *shared surface* for expressing designs and reflecting upon how these surfaces are used by designers. Our aim is to draw from the experiences of both these groups.
The intent of design rationale is documentation of the sequence of decisions made in realising a design. Some systems have adapted existing paper-based methods of externalising rationales. The most notable of these are gIBIS (Conklin 88) and rIBIS (Rein 91). Other representations have been proposed (Carroll & Kellogg 89, Fischer & Girgensohn 90, Lee 90 and MacLean et al. 89).

A number of problems have been noted with design rationale systems: they may have problems of acceptability (Yakemovik & Conklin 91) and difficulties with forcing users to decide at an early stage on the nature of each piece of information. This can be difficult to do, particularly where collaborators have to agree on the classification (Shipman & Marshall 92, Conklin & Bergman 88). Much of the motivation of current research is in the development of an appropriate theoretical base for the representation of design rationales and on the cognitive process of design. Little consideration has been given to the development of techniques and tools to support the creation of design rational within the early creative portion of the design process.

The research on *shared space* (for example Bly 90, Greenberg 91 and Ishii 91) adopts a contrasting approach to information capture. These systems provide a space upon which designers can collectively express and structure their ideas in a relatively unconstrained way. They have often focused on drawing as the primary means of expression and have studied how users interact with and through the shared surface. The Cognoter tool (Stefik et al. 87) is an example of this group. It provided facilities to allow ideas to be expressed, collected and commented upon by other users. However, later studies of its use revealed communication breakdowns and suggested that these were a consequence of various assumptions in its design which did not relate to actual tool use (Tatar 91).

The NoteCards approach uses hypertext as a kind of shared surface. Although offering many advantages, classification problems similar to that for gIBIS have been observed (Shipman & Marshall 92, Monty 90). Users had difficulty chunking information into cards, naming cards and filing cards. Typed links were rarely used (and then, inconsistently). Link direction and link semantics also proved to be problematic. Many of these difficulties again spring from design assumptions which did not match actual systems usage.

3. Developing the DNP: an iterative approach

Our work builds upon the experiences of these previous approaches to design support and aims to tackle the difficulties that they unearthed. While we recognise the need to represent and record design information in a form which may ultimately be useful during later parts of the development process, we also acknowledge the problems of requiring designers to commit to a particular interpretation too early in the design process. Indeed, an overriding criterion for any system must be acceptability (Grudin 88). Therefore our main focus is on the development of an interface that users find easy to operate and which is appropriate for the early stages of design. We do not have a theory of design that we wish to impose or test on designers, but rather a desire to discover their requirements. This has led us to an approach to tool development based upon rapid prototyping.

We support the notion that idea representation tools such as Cognoter or more general design surfaces provide a medium of representation within the conversation surrounding the design process (Tatar et al. 91). Previous studies have examined the use of traditional whiteboards and shared drawing media in the design process (Suchman 88, Tang 89). However electronic drawing surfaces are different from these traditional media (Tatar et al. 91) and gaining a clear understanding of how these are exploited to express design concepts is a crucial part of our approach. Our central problem is that the medium of expression plays a central role in the representations. In fact, we would argue that the possibilities offered by electronic systems to represent designs and the nature of these representations are sufficiently intertwined that neither can be adequately addressed in isolation. Thus, not only is little known about the software design process, whether by one or many people, but the development of computer systems to support the process makes some features necessarily unknowable. This is because the computerised design tool is likely to change the nature of the design process as the word processor has changed the nature of writing (Haas 89). Therefore we have adopted an iterative approach to development based upon developing facilities in close cooperation with the designers using the system.

We started by providing an initial set of core facilities which allowed designs to be expressed. These facilities were then used by designers over a prolonged period to support a variety of real design tasks. This usage was observed and videotaped and the participants invited to comment on their experience with the system. The aim of the sessions was:-.

1. To isolate problems caused by features of the user interface.

2. To examine the use made of the system and to highlight additional functionality required by designers.

3. To assess the usefulness of existing functionality before adding to the system.

4. To provide information about the process of design itself.

The prototyping approach is shown diagrammatically in Figure 1.

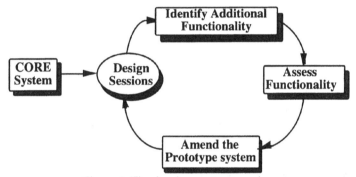

Figure 1. The development approach.

Our approach has links with participatory design (Bodker 91) and is similar to the approach proposed by (Tang 91). It also borrows from other domains including HCI (Hartson 91) and AI and Education (Twidale, in press). The latter domain has many similarities with CSCW in that both focus on the use made by people of computer systems and concern the support of human activities (learning and work respectively) that are imperfectly understood. In AI&ED it has been observed that a single flaw in an interface can have a substantial negative effect in learning outcomes, but also that a feature of the interface intended for one purpose can have additional beneficial purposes (Twidale 91). Thus features of the interface have the potential of swamping the effects of deeper, more interesting and sophisticated modules of a system.

An iterative approach to development can help to alleviate this problem. By testing basic versions of the system in simple circumstances, (such as with a single designer, two designers sitting at the same terminal or two designers with a terminal each sitting next to each other), we can eliminate the grosser interface errors. This can inform the design when it is extended to the necessarily more complex cases (such as many designers separated in space and with limited bandwidth communication). For this approach to work, we need to focus more on the interface difficulties rather than the successes. We can be confident that the difficulties will scale up to the more complex cases if nothing were done about them, while the successes may not.

3.1 The Software Design Process

Rather than considering all aspects of design as an abstract process, we are primarily concerned with the software development process. This allows us to make particular assumptions about the design setting within which any development systems will be applied. In particular, the software design process is characterised by:

The development of structure

Software design is closely concerned with the transition from partially-defined, loosely structured ideas and concepts to fully defined and structured design descriptions. These descriptions form the basic plans for subsequent development. The majority of these design descriptions are specified diagrammatically using some form of network diagram. These diagrams show a number of software entities which are linked to describe corresponding relationships.

The work of groups

Any design of a significant size is the endeavour of a number of designers. A team of software designers will work together in a variety of different ways over a substantial time period to realise a completed design. The patterns of work involved and the different forms of cooperation which take place are only partially understood by the participants in the design process.

This view of the design process forms the context for our construction of the DNP. It is important to note that software design forms only the initial phase of the overall development process and some benefits of supporting design activities may only be realised much later in the software lifecycle. To reap these benefits though, the design tool must be *used* by software designers. Meeting the needs of designers by meshing with their work practice becomes an issue of paramount importance.

3.2 Design Sessions

When investigating a domain so poorly understood as collaborative software design it is vital to be in contact with designers as early as possible. A tool that designers find unusable or even just awkward to use will not be adopted.

Given that our development of a system to support software design is necessarily exploratory, it is inevitable that we will make mistakes. The aim of our approach is to increase the speed and ease of identifying and correcting these mistakes. Considerable attention is given to mistakes relating to the interface. It is clear that the interface to any system has a substantial effect on its use. If care is not taken over the interface, problems of use may not be due to some feature of the support for CSCW that is counterproductive or missing but merely to an interface problem. It is possible to identify many of these issues when the system is being used by a single user, even though it is intended for collaborative work: difficulties that a single user has are more than likely to be also experienced with multiple users.

It is for this reason of simplicity that we chose to start by concentrating on a system for multiple simultaneous use of a single workstation by two or three people. A distributed version for two workstations has been developed and tested, but the bulk of the work has been on the single version. In the case of the distributed version we had the workstations side by side. We chose this in order to maximise the potential communication bandwidth between the participants. In this way any problems observed could not be ascribed to bandwidth limitations and so would scale up to true distributed usage if not remedied. The approach is intended to be complementary to ongoing research addressing the challenging technological and social implications of the more complex forms of collaboration such as synchronous working over long distances (Clark & Scrivener 92).

3.3 The Mini-DNP

Our starting point for providing support for designers was the development of a minimal system with a set of simple core facilities called the mini-DNP. This system was influenced by a previous system to support design by a single user (Sommerville et al. 1990) and the experiences gained from developing and using that system. The essence of mini-DNP is a means of creating entities and links between them (Figure 2).

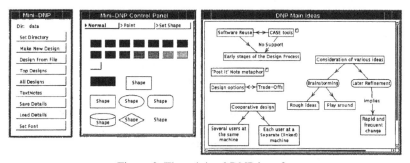

Figure 2. The minimal DNP interface.

The user creates an entity by typing in a design window. He or she may then move it with the mouse. Linking is done by selecting one entity and then clicking on the entity one wants to link to with the shift key down. This linking of entities forms the diagrams ultimately needed to specify design descriptions. We also provided textnotes which are based on the Post-It Note metaphor (see figure 5) and allow designers to attach one or more notes to an entity. These can be used by design teams for more textual comments, ideas, opinions, code fragments, references etc. A variety of textnote types are provided and users may define their own (including form structures). An entity with textnotes has an icon attached (eg. the entity 'CASE tools' in figure 2) and the notes can be examined by clicking on the icon. Designs can be saved and loaded from a file and a paper report may be created containing a screendump of the design and a list of the entities and their textnotes. Each entity may itself be expanded to become a subdesign. A new window is opened and entities and links created in the normal way. Subdesigns may contain entities that are themselves subdesigns. A loose form of typing for entities and links is provided using colour, shape and labels. The user controls the degree to which s/he wants to use typing. The type of an entity or link can easily be changed at any time.

The initial system has certain characteristics which make it suitable for supporting the design process:

1. A fast, easy-to-use interface which supports the creation of directed graphs. These may be created at any number of levels with simple navigation from one level to another.

2. Untyped entities and relations. This is critically important in the early stages of an analysis where it is unrealistic to fit an entity into a type hierarchy.

3. Extensive annotation facilities which allow system entities and relations to be annotated with structured and unstructured text.

4. Post-creation type attribution. These facilities also allow the type of an entity to be easily changed.

5. Report generation facilities.

3.4 Assessment

We have used a variety of users to assess the system. Given that the aim is continual refinement, one can initially use members of the development team to test the system. At first sight it may seem a problem that they will be more motivated than most to use the system and consider it in a favourable light. Nevertheless, provided that they have genuine tasks (such as the ongoing design of the system itself) they are likely to discover some of the grosser interface errors. We can be confident that such errors will scale out: a feature that a developer finds hard to use will certainly be difficult for an outsider (and of course if the developers don't like using the tool on a regular basis it is unlikely anyone will). Later we tried the system on users not involved in its development in order to discover any hidden assumptions in the developer community about ease of use and needed features.

The system has been simultaneously subject to use and under development for approximately two years. During this time a substantial community of users have exploited the system. Table 1 summarises the variety of system use.

By designer:	Single designer
	Two designers at one workstation
	Three designers at one workstation
	Two designers at two adjacent workstations
By task:	Software design
	Information organisation and browsing
	Project management
	Lecture course design
	Designing papers (including this one)
	Designing talks
By user:	System developer
	Project members
	PhD students
	Sociology colleagues
	Visiting academics
	Undergraduates

Table 1. Nature of usage of the system in tests.

In all cases of use, whether by individuals or groups, we asked our volunteers to bring along a task that they had to undertake anyway. We believe it is important to develop the system on real-world tasks as these have features that are very hard to replicate in contrived tasks. These features include ambiguity, open-endedness, history and engagement of the user, who ideally will be focussing more on the problem than the tool. Our instructions to the user were to try and use the tool, asking where necessary how to achieve anything they want to do. Our assumption is that the tool will be usable up to some point when it becomes frustrating because it prevents the user doing something s/he wants. We can identify what s/he wants to do and then can assess what sort of functionality should be added to the system.

Given the desire to use authentic tasks we are somewhat at the mercy of the needs of our volunteers. Fortunately a tool intended to support the very early stages of software development is equally useful for many other creative design tasks such as project management, making ethnographic notes and the design of papers and reports (Sommerville et al. 93). Indeed the initial structure and elements of this paper were collaboratively developed using DNP.

Some of the system use has been in one-off design sessions, others have continued over a number of sessions and yet others (particularly those involving project management and the design and management of research activities) are ongoing over many months. The system is now accessible from an number of different locations on campus. In particular, two users have access to the DNP from their office and use it on a day to day basis. These latter forms of use are beginning to reveal the nature of the requirements for management of the complexity of designs over time.

4. Design Support in the DNP

The intent of the design sessions was to discover the various patterns of use of the DNP (including difficulties) for different designers. Our observations of use informed the development of appropriate support facilities. This section briefly highlights the results of this process.

4.1 Variability of use

Our studies have confirmed the great variability in design activities both between users and by the same users over time and circumstance (see figures 3, 4, 5 & 6). For example, some designers use very terse entity names with textnotes to contain details, whereas others use phrase- or sentence-like names. Some designers use many links to indicate connectedness whilest others use two-dimensional proximity (Marshall & Rogers 92). Some use a great deal of colour and many different shapes, whilst others use black rectangles all the time. As examples of variability over time, we have observed cycles involving bouts of entity creation and rough positioning. These involve very rapid and intense activity where the minimum of options are employed. After such a bout there is a recovery period where the display is 'tidied up'. Links are created and the entities rearranged to convey additional meanings by their proximity to other entities as well as to reduce the clutter of areas of great activity.

This variability confirms the need for flexibility and ease of revision in the DNP. Much of this flexibility comes from our decision to avoid associating semantics with entities, links and subdesigns and to allow these to be used primarily as a means of expression by users. The meaning of these initial design graphs are left to the interpretation of different designers. The intense 'bursts' of activity surrounding the generation of entities caused us to focus on supporting the rapid entry of entities (just typing and hitting return between entities generates entries positioned in a list format). Once entered these entities can be tidied by altering their position, colour and shape. For example, contrast the design in figure 3 showing the early stages of the design with a later stage shown in figure 5.

4.2 The Evolution of structure

The elements of a design that are added to the Notepad in the form of entities are necessarily ambiguous; they consist of a label of a few words referring to a concept. However, not only is that label capable of misinterpretation by anyone other than its creator, but even for the creator it seems that deliberately ambiguous

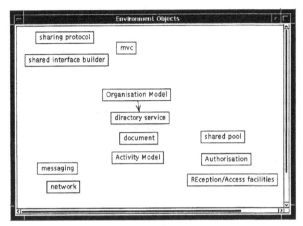

Figure 3. An initial design in the DNP.

terms are chosen (for example, entities were often called "object" or "user"). This is an instance of postponing decisions about details in order to deal with overview concepts. Later on in the design process, the meaning of the initial concepts will be refined. This can involve qualifying the entity by editing its name (including completely changing the name), creating more entities for the constituent concepts in an ambiguous description, adding more information by attaching textnotes, creating a subdesign for the entity, or completely replacing the entity.

It would seem that designers need to have a certain degree of ambiguity during design so as to not get too held down by details. Gradually these ambiguities are addressed and refined. This has been observed in other situations (Marshall & Rogers 92) and reasons proposed for why users wish to avoid formalisation (Shipman & Marshall 92). In a similar manner, the meaning of a link can change over time. Initially its meaning may be 'these entities are in some way connected'. Eventually this is refined into a more precise meaning. The gradual evolution of precision is often associated with the usage of link typing; links with a similar meaning are now given the same colour or label.

The attributes of entities and links are used within the DNP as a mechanism to support the evolution of structure. The use of colour and shape as a means of typing both entities and links is directly supported by the DNP. Once created these different attributes of entities and links can be modified by users over time from the control panel shown in figure 2. This freedom allows appropriate structure to emerge within the design after the entities have been created and allows the type of entities to change after the creation of the entity. Figures 3 and 5 illustrate this migration. This is in contrast to previous systems which supported the definition of a set of types but required the designer to select the type for each entity as it is created.

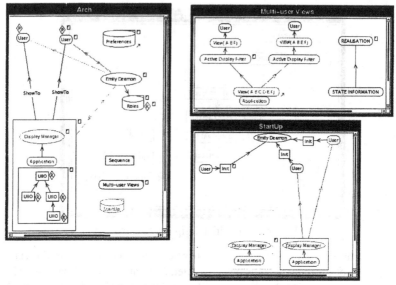

Figure 4. The arrangement, framing and grouping of entities.
The two designs on the right are subdesigns of the one on the left.
11 colours were used in this design

The relationship of entities within any non trivial design is extremely complex. In addition to links, space is often used to distinguish this relationship as appropriate entities are clustered (Marshall & Rogers 92). Users expressed a need to abstract from these groupings once they were made. Subdesigns were used to facilitate this. The user can frame entities to form a group. S/he may then 'push down' the group into a subdesign to be replaced by a single entity (figure 4).

4.3 Cooperative and Single use

The most visible difference between cooperative and single use is speed; single designers enter, refine and revise items far more quickly than do groups. This is mainly due to the need of group participants to justify and explain their actions to others. No action is completely unambiguous and the degree to which features can be left implicit by a single user are naturally far less than when ideas have to be shared. Not only is greater explanation and elaboration required, but actions such as revisions and additions have to be negotiated, leading to a debate about the appropriateness of the activity. By contrast, single designers create entities and links and rearrange them with at times almost bewildering speed. We take this as evidence for the need for the tool to support frequent and rapid revision of designs provided by the DNP.

The sharing of a keyboard and mouse on the whole did not appear to cause great difficulties, with users taking turns to enter text or rearrange entities. Control of the keyboard can involve either a position of power, temporarily controlling the collaboration, or it can involve a secretarial function, minuting the deliberations of the others. In the distributed version of the DNP, despite the close proximity of the machines involved, users exploited the shared view of the design to quickly partition the design activity and work independently upon different portions of the overall design. Substantial use was made of textnotes to annotate features of the other user's design (figure 5).

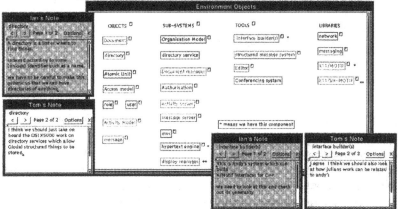

Figure 5. The use of textnotes to comment on a design.
7 colours were used in this design.

An interesting feature of cooperative use in both settings was how entities were moved and highlighted for emphasis, as part of a debate. The user currently controlling the mouse would select an entity s/he wished to discuss, causing it to be highlighted. S/he might move this entity slightly (from side to side or in small circles) as a means of emphasis. This activity of moving entities for emphasis can be contrasted with occasions when the move was more substantial, indicating some semantic feature, by positioning an entity closer to another entity. This could be permanent, or merely a continuous movement as a suggestion. Besides the use of the mouse, more direct interaction was observed, namely users pointing at the screen with their fingers. The cooperative situation also saw another use of the DNP's ability to support the evolution of meaning. Often participants in a group design activity would use an entity as an argument placeholder and use this accepted design entity to refer back to a previous debate.

As a result of our observation of groups, the facilities associated with the placement of textnotes were extended to allow users to easily exploit textnotes as a method of annotation. These extensions allow facilities for the definition of new note types which can be associated with different users and/or purposes. Figure 6 shows the tool to create a new pad of notes with a user-defined structure, and another created notepad. Facilities are provided to filter and highlight the presence of notes from different designers.

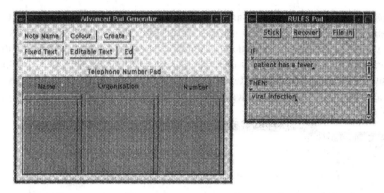

Figure 6. The generator for creating a structured note and a user defined notepad.

5. Conclusions

An iterative development approach is appropriate for CSCW systems development because it facilitates our need to learn more about the nature of cooperative activity while simultaneously developing the system. The testing of the early versions of the Designers' Notepad have emphasised the variability in design activity both amongst designers and according to circumstances. We also noted the way in which concepts mutate over time leading to an evolution of structure. This can lead to frequent and rapid revision. Ease of revision is important in encouraging the brainstorming of concepts that are necessarily incomplete. Systems to support the early stages of design need to support these features of the process. By means of an iterative development we are able to correct the grosser interface errors that have the potential to swamp the effect of deeper issues concerning design and cooperative work in general. The methodology also enables us to profit by the stream of results that an ethnographic study produces. In its current state the Designers' Notepad is as much a tool for acquiring information about design activity as it is a tool for supporting that activity.

6. Acknowledgements

Michael Twidale is a Science and Engineering Research Council Junior Research Fellow. The development of the Designers' Notepad was funded partialy by the Joint Council Initiative in Cognitive Science and COMIC (Esprit basic research project 6225). The authors would like to thank their colleagues in the Sociology department; John Hughes and Val King for their support and advice throughout this project.

7. References

Bly, S.A. & S.L. Minneman, S.L. (1990). Commune: A shared drawing surface. *Proceedings of the Conference on Office Information Systems,* Boston, April 25-27. pp 184-192.

Bodker, S., & Gronbaek, K. (1991). Cooperative prototyping: Users and designers in mutual activity. *International Journal of Man Machine Studies,* 34(3) 453-478.

Booch, G. (1991). *Object Oriented Design with applications.* Menlo Park CA: Benjamin Cummings.

Button, G. & King, V. (1992). Hanging around is not the point: calling ethnography to account. Paper presented at the Workshop on Ethnography and CSCW system design, CSCW '92, Toronto.

Carroll, J.M., & Kellogg, W.A. (1989). Artifact as Theory-Nexus: Hermeneutics Meet Theory-Based Design. *Proceedings of ACM CHI'89 Conference on Human Factors in Computing Systems.* pp 7-14.

CASE (1989). The CASE experience, *Byte,* April 1989, pp 206-246.

Conklin, J. (1988). gIBIS: A hypertext tool for exploratory policy discussion. *Proceedings of the Conference on Computer-Supported Cooperative Work (CSCW '88),* Portland, Oregon. ACM Press, pp 140-152.

Fischer, G., & Girgensohn, A. (1990). End-User Modifiability in Design Environments. *Proceedings of ACM CHI'90 Conference on Human Factors in Computing Systems.* pp 183-191.

Greenberg, S., and R. Bohnet, R. (1991). GroupSketch: A multi-user sketchpad for geographically-distributed small groups. *Proceedings of Graphics Interface '91,* Calgary, Alberta, June 5-7.

Grudin, J. (1988). Why CSCW applications fail: problems in the design and evaluation of organizational interfaces. In *Proceedings of the Conference on Computer Support Cooperative Work (CSCW '88),* (pp 85-93). Portland, Oregon: ACM Press.

Haas, C. (1989). How the writing medium shapes the writing process: effects of word processing on planning. *Research in the Teaching of English,* 23(2) 181-207.

Hartson, H.R., & E.C. Smith, E.C. (1991). Rapid Prototyping in Human-Computer Interface Development. *Interacting with Computers,* 3 (1) 51-91.

Ishii, H., & Arita, K. (1991). ClearFace: Translucent multiuser interface for TeamWorkstation; *Research report* NTT Human Interface Laboratories. January.

Jackson M.A. (1983). *System Development.* Prentice-Hall, New Jersey.

Lawson, B. (1980). *How designers think.* Chatham: W & J Mackay.

Lee, J. (1990). SIBYL: A tool for sharing knowledge in group decision making. *Proceedings of the Conference on Computer Supported Cooperative Work (CSCW '90),* Los Angeles, California. ACM Press, pp 79-92.

Marshall, C.C. & Rogers, R.A. (1992). Two years before the mist: experiences with Aquanet. Proceedings *ECHT '92.* Milan.

MacLean, A., Young, R.M., & Moran, T.P. (1989). Design Rationale: The Argument Behind the Artifact. *Proceedings of ACM CHI'89 Conference on Human Factors in Computing Systems.* Issues in Interface Design Methods. pp 247-252.

Monty, M. L. (1990). *Issues for supporting notetaking and note using in the computer environment.* Unpublished Dissertation, Department of Psychology, University of California, San Diego.

Rein, G.L., & Ellis, C.A. (1991). rIBIS: A real-time group hypertext system. *International Journal of Man Machine Studies* 34 (3) 349-368.

Shipman, F. M. & Marshall, C.C. (1992). Formality considered harmful: experiences, emerging themes and directions. Submitted to *InterCHI '93*.

Sommerville, I., Haddley, N., Mariani, J.A. & Thomson, R. (1990). The designer's notepad - a hypertext system tailored for design. In McAleese, R. & Green, C. (Eds.), *Hypertext: state of the art* (pp 260-266). Oxford: Intellect.

Sommerville, I., Rodden, T., Sawyer, P., Bentley, R. & Twidale, M. B. (1993). Integrating ethnography into the requirements engineering process. *Proceedings, 1st International Conference on Requirements Engineering,* San Diego, January 1993, IEEE Press.

Stefik, M., Bobrow, D. G., Foster, G., Lanning, S., & Tatar, D. (1987). WYSIWIS revised: Early experiences with multiuser interfaces. *ACM Transactions on Office Information Systems,* 5(2) 147-167.

Suchman, L. (1988). Representing practice in cognitive science. *Human Studies,* 11, 305-325.

Tang, J. C. (1989) *Listing, drawing, and gesturing in design: A study of the use of shared workspaces by design teams.* PhD thesis, Department of Mechanical Engineering, Stanford University.

Tatar, D.G., Foster, G. & Bobrow, D.G. (1991). Design for conversation: Lessons from Cognoter. *International Journal of Man Machine Studies* 34 (2) 185-210.

Twidale, M. B. (1992). Student activity in an Intelligent Learning Environment, *Intelligent Tutoring Media,* 2(3/4) 113-127.

Twidale, M. B. (in press). Redressing the balance: the advantages of informal evaluation techniques for Intelligent Learning Environments. *Journal of Artificial Intelligence In Education.*

Yakemovic, K.C.B. & Conklin, E.J. (1990). Report on a development project use of an issue-based information system. *Proceedings of the Conference on Computer Supported Cooperative Work (CSCW '90),* Los Angeles, California. ACM Press.

Proceedings of the Third European Conference on Computer-Supported Cooperative Work
13-17 September, 1993, Milan, Italy
G. De Michelis, C. Simone and K. Schmidt (Editors)

A Spatial Model of Interaction in Large Virtual Environments

Steve Benford

The University of Nottingham, UK.

Lennart Fahlén

The Swedish Institute of Computer Science (SICS), Sweden.

Abstract: We present a spatial model of group interaction in virtual environments. The model aims to provide flexible and natural support for managing conversations among large groups gathered in virtual space. However, it can also be used to control more general interactions among other kinds of objects inhabiting such spaces. The model defines the key abstractions of object aura, nimbus, focus and adapters to control mutual levels of awareness. Furthermore, these are defined in a sufficiently general way so as to apply to any CSCW system where a spatial metric can be identified - i.e. a way of measuring position and direction. Several examples are discussed, including virtual reality and text conferencing applications. Finally, the paper provides a more formal computational architecture for the spatial model by relating it to the object oriented modelling approach for distributed systems.

1. Introduction

Our paper presents a model for supporting group interaction in large-scale virtual worlds[1]. The model provides generic techniques for managing interactions between various objects in such environments including humans and computer artefacts. Furthermore, the model is intended to be sufficiently flexible to apply to any system

---

[1] This work is part of the COMIC project, a European ESPRIT Basic Research Action to develop theories and techniques to support the development of future large scale CSCW systems.

where a spatial metric can be identified (i.e. a way of measuring distance and orientation). Such applications might range from the obvious example of multi-user virtual reality through conferencing systems, collaborative hypermedia and even databases and information spaces. Where the interacting objects are humans, the model provides mechanisms for conversation management. These contrast with existing floor control and workflow modelling techniques by adopting a "spatial" approach where people employ the affordances of virtual computer space as a means of control. In so doing, our underlying philosophy has been to encourage individual autonomy of action, freedom to communicate and minimal hard-wired computer constraints. Where the interacting objects are artefacts, the model provides mechanisms for constructing highly reactive environments where objects dynamically react to the presence of others (e.g. you may activate a tool simply by approaching it).

2. Rooms and virtual spaces

We have chosen to base our work around the metaphor of interaction within virtual worlds. Under this metaphor, a computer system can be viewed as a set of spaces through which people move, interacting with each other and with various objects which they find there. The use of such spatial metaphors to structure work environments is not particularly new, having previously been explored in areas such as user interface design, virtual meeting rooms, media spaces, CSCW environments and virtual reality. Xerox used a rooms metaphor to structure graphical interfaces (Henderson 85, Clarkson 91) and this was later followed up with VROOMS (Borning 91). Audio Windows applied a spatial metaphor to audio interfaces (Cohen 91). Multi-media virtual meeting rooms have been demonstrated in a variety of projects (Leevers 92, Cooke 91). The CRUISER system explored social browsing in larger scale virtual environments (Root 88) and multi-user recreational environments have been available for some time (e.g. MUD (Smith 92) and Lucasfilm's HABITAT (Morningstar 91)). Spatial metaphors also feature heavily in discussions of Virtual Reality (VR) (Benedikt 91) including early collaborative VR systems (Codella 92, Takemura 92, Fahlén 92). In contrast to virtual reality, media-spaces explore the role of space in providing more embedded support for cooperative work (Gaver 92a, Gaver 92b). Finally, spatial metaphors have been adopted as an integrating theme for large scale CSCW environments (Michelitsch 91, Navarro 92).

In short, spatial approaches to collaborative systems have become increasingly popular. One reason for this is their strong relation to physical reality and therefore their highly intuitive nature. However, from a more abstract standpoint, space affords a number of important facilities for collaboration including awareness at a glance; support for ad-hoc as well as planned interaction; use of body language and other social conventions in conversation management; flexible negotiation of access to resources (e.g. queuing, scrumming and hovering), and structuring, navigation, exploration and mapping of large-scale work environments.

However, we believe that current spatially-oriented systems will not effectively scale to heavily populated spaces. More specifically, as the number of occupants in a virtual space increases beyond a few people, the need to effectively manage interactions will become critical. One example, is the need for conversation management. As a starting point, we might consider borrowing the conversation management and coordination mechanisms developed in other areas of CSCW. Previous conferencing systems have introduced a range of floor control mechanisms such as chairpeople, reservations and token-passing (Crowley 90, Sarin 91, Cook 92). Alternatively, the work-flow and process oriented techniques from asynchronous systems also represent a form of conversation management (e.g. THE COORDINATOR (Winograd 86), DOMINO (Victor 91), CHAOS (Bignoli 91), COSMOS (Bowers 88) and AMIGO (Pankoke 89)). However, we believe that these approaches are generally too rigid and unnatural to be applied to spatial settings. As an example, a real-world implementation of explicit floor control would be tantamount to gagging everyone at a meeting and then allowing them to speak by removing the gags at specific times. New techniques are needed which support natural social conventions for managing interactions. One approach might be to take advantage of the highly fluid and dynamic nature of space. The following section introduces a *spatial model* of interaction which aims to meet these goals. Furthermore, although we base our discussion on a consideration of three dimensional space, the model is intended to be sufficiently generic to apply to any system where a spatial metric can be identified, including possible higher dimensional *information terrains*.

3. The spatial model

Virtual spaces can be created in any system in which position and direction, and hence distance, can be measured. Virtual spaces might have any number of dimensions. For the purposes of discussion we will consider three. The objects inhabiting virtual spaces might represent people and also other artefacts (e.g. tools and documents). Our model has been driven by a number of objectives including ensuring individual autonomy; maintaining a power balance between "speakers" and "listeners" in any conversation; minimising hard-wired constraints and replacing them with a model of increasing effort; and starting with support for free mingling and only adding more formal mechanisms later if needed.

The spatial model, as its name suggests, uses the properties of space as the basis for mediating interaction. Thus, objects can navigate space in order to form dynamic sub-groups and manage conversations within these sub-groups. Next, we introduce the key abstractions of **MEDIUM, AURA, AWARENESS, FOCUS, NIMBUS** and **ADAPTERS** which define our model.

Any interaction between objects occurs through some **medium.** A medium might represent a typical communication medium (e.g. audio, visual or text) or perhaps some other kind of object specific interface. Each object might be capable of interacting through a combination of media/interfaces and objects may negotiate compatible media whenever they meet.

The first problem in any large-scale environment is determining which objects are capable of interacting with which others at a given time (simultaneous interaction between all objects is not computationally scaleable). **Aura** is defined to be a sub-space which effectively bounds the presence of an object within a given medium and which acts as an enabler of potential interaction (Fahlén 92). Objects carry their auras with them when they move through space and when two auras collide, interaction between the objects in the medium becomes a possibility. Note that an object typically has different auras (e.g. size and shape) for different media. For example, as I approach you across a space, you may be able to see me before you can hear me because my visual aura is larger than my audio aura. Also note that it is the surrounding environment that monitors for aura collisions between objects.

Once aura has been used to determine the potential for object interactions, the objects themselves are subsequently responsible for controlling these interactions. This is achieved on the basis of quantifiable *levels* of awareness between them (Benford 92). The measure of awareness between two objects need not be mutually symmetrical. As with aura, awareness levels are medium specific. Awareness between objects in a given medium is manipulated via **focus** and **nimbus**, further subspaces within which an object chooses to direct either its presence or its attention. More specifically, the more an object is within your focus, the more aware you are of it and the more an object is within your nimbus, the more aware it is of you. Objects therefore negotiate levels of awareness by using their foci and nimbi in order to try to make others more aware of them or to make themselves more aware of others. We deliberately use the word negotiate to convey an image of objects positioning themselves in space in much the same way as people mingle in a room or jostle to get access to some physical resource. Awareness levels are calculated from a combination of nimbus and focus. More specifically, given that interaction has first been enabled through aura,

The level of awareness that object A has of object B in medium M is some function of A's focus on B in M and B's nimbus on A in M.

The resulting quantified awareness levels between two objects can then used as the basis for managing their interaction. Exactly how this is achieved depends upon the particular application. One approach might be to use awareness levels to directly control the medium (e.g. controlling the volume of an audio channel between two objects). Another might be allowing objects to actively react to each others presence depending on specified awareness thresholds (e.g. I might automatically receive text messages from you once a certain threshold had been passed). Notice that the use of both focus and nimbus allows both objects in an interaction to influence their awareness of each other. More specifically, they support our stated goals of autonomy and also power balance between "speakers" and "listeners".

Now we consider how much of this apparent complexity the user needs to understand. The answer is very little, because a person need not be explicitly aware that they are using aura, focus and nimbus. First, aura, focus and nimbus may often be invisible or may be implied through "natural" mechanisms such as the use of eyes to provide gaze awareness and hence convey visual focus. Second they will be manipulated in natural ways which are associated with basic human actions in space. To be more specific, we envisage three primary ways of manipulating aura, focus and nimbus and hence controlling interaction:

1. Implicitly through movement and orientation. Thus, as I move or turn, my aura, focus and nimbus will automatically follow me. A number of novel interface devices are emerging to support this kind of movement. These are generally known as six dimensional devices (three for position and three for orientation) and include space-balls, body-trackers, wands and gloves.

2. Explicitly through a few key parameters. A user interface might provide a few simple parameters to change aura, focus and nimbus. I might change the shape of a focus by focusing in or out (i.e. changing a focal length). This might be achieved by simply moving a mouse or joystick.

3. Implicitly by using various **adapter** objects which modify my aura, focus or nimbus. These can be represented in terms of natural metaphors such as picking up a tool.

Adapters support interaction styles beyond basic mingling. In essence, an adapter is an object which, when picked up, amplifies or attenuates aura, focus or nimbus. For example, a user might conceive of picking up a "microphone". In terms of the spatial model, a microphone adapter object would then amplify their audio aura and nimbus As a second example, the user might sit at a virtual "table". Behind the scenes, an adapter object would fold their aura, foci and nimbi for several media into a common space with other people already seated at the table, thus allowing a semi-private discussion within in a space. In effect, the introduction of adapter objects provides for a more extensible model.

To summarise, our spatial model defines key concepts for allowing objects to establish and subsequently control interactions. Aura is used to establish the potential for interaction across a given medium. Focus and nimbus are then used to negotiate the mutual and possibly non-symmetrical levels of awareness between two objects which in turn drives the behaviour of the interactions. Finally, adapter objects can be used to further influence aura, focus and nimbus and so add a degree of extendibility to the model.

4. Applying the spatial model

The spatial model is intended to be applicable to any system where a spatial metric can be identified. We now briefly describe some example applications of the spatial model including the multi-user virtual reality and text conferencing systems currently being prototyped at SICS and Nottingham respectively.

4.1. Multi-user virtual reality - the DIVE system

Perhaps the most obvious application of the spatial model is to virtual reality systems. A prototype multi-user Virtual Reality (VR) system, DIVE (Distributed Interactive Virtual Environment) (Fahlén 91) (Carlsson 92) has been developed as part of the MultiG program (a Swedish national research effort on high speed networks and distributed applications (Pehrson 92)). DIVE is a UNIX-based, multi-platform software framework for creating multi-user, multi-application, three-dimensional distributed user environments. There is support for multiple co-existing "worlds" with gateways between them to enable inter-world movement. Users are represented by unique graphical 3D-bodies or icons whose position, orientation, movements and identity are easily visible to other participants. In this first realisation, aura is implemented as a volume or sphere around each user's icon which is usually invisible. Aura handling is achieved through a special collision manager process. When a collision between auras occurs, this manager sends a message containing information such as the id's of the objects involved, positions, angles and so on, to other processes within the DIVE environment. These processes (e.g. the owners of the objects involved) then carry out appropriate focus, nimbus and awareness computations. It is possible to have support for a multiple users, objects, media and service specific aura types with associated collision managers mapped onto separate processing nodes in a network. Focus and nimbus handling can be mapped in a similar way. Further details on the aura implementation in DIVE can be found in (Ståhl 92b). Figure 1 shows a screen dump from DIVE of an aura collision, with the auras made specially visible.

Figure 1: Body Images with Colliding Auras

A more general toolkit has been developed as a first step towards constructing a distributed collaborative environment and for experimentation with the concepts of aura, focus, nimbus and awareness. Presently it consists of four major components, the whiteboard, the document, the conference table and the podium.

The whiteboard (Ståhl 92a) is a drawing tool similar in appearance to it's real world counterpart. Several users can work together simultaneously around the whiteboard. There can also be groups of whiteboards, with the contents being duplicated across the group. That is, the actions performed by one user on one whiteboard are immediately replicated by the other whiteboards in the same group. The aura surrounding the whiteboard is used to enable whiteboard access and use (e.g. by automatically assigning a pen to a user when their aura collides with that of the whiteboard).The content of a whiteboard can be copied into something called a document that a user can pick up and carry away. Apart from being "single user", documents have the same functionality as a whiteboard. More specifically, when document auras intersect, their contents are copied to other users documents and onto whiteboards.

The conference table detects participants presence, and establishes communication channels (video, voice and document links) between them via aura. The auras, foci and nimbi of the conference participants around the table are then extended to cover everyone in attendance. So, by having a very long table, people can form larger collaborative groups than "direct" aura/focus/nimbus functionality makes possible. Users can come and go as they please and it is easy to obtain an overview of who is present. The conference table can also distribute documents to conference participants and to whiteboards. To do this a user simply places a document in the centre of the table and then the aura collision manager initiates the distribution. Figure 2 shows a screen dump of a meeting in Cyberspace involving the whiteboard and conference table.

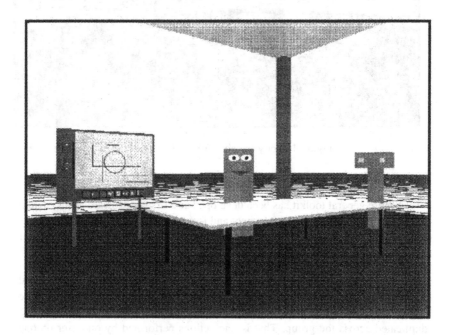

Figure 2: A Conference in Cyberspace

A participant can enter a podium and is thereby allowed to be "heard" (or seen) by a dispersed group of users that "normally" (e.g. without the podium) are not within communication distance of the "speaker". The aura and nimbus of the participant on the podium are enlarged to cover, for example, a lecture hall or town square. The podium is an example of an aura/nimbus adapter and it is asymmetric, i.e. the "listeners" can't individually communicate back to the "speaker" without special provisions.

A teleconferencing subsystem is also under construction and will be integrated into DIVE in the near future (Eriksson 92) . Apart from the CSCW toolkit, some other concept demonstrators have also been developed within the DIVE environment, including control of a real-world robot, a 3D customisable graph editor for drawing and editing graphs in 3D space, a 3D-sound renderer allowing objects or events to have sounds and for these sounds to have a position and direction and finally a computer network visualiser and surveillance tool.

4.2. Text conferencing - the CyCo system

We can also apply the spatial model to less sophisticated technology. For example, several text conferencing systems have been produced over recent years. Such systems support communication through the medium of text messages and often introduce a floor control mechanism for managing conversations in groups of more than a few people. Consider, instead, the application of the spatial model to such a system. We might define rooms to be two dimensional spaces which could be readily mapped in a window on a typical workstation screen. Aura might be circular in shape and focus and nimbus might be modelled as segments of a circle projecting from a person's current position that could be manipulated both by moving and turning. In the simplest case, these areas might provide for discrete values of focus and nimbus (i.e. if an object is inside the area, then it is in focus/nimbus; if it is outside, then it is not). Considering two people, A and B, we can now evaluate three possible levels of awareness (see figure 3) :-

- A is fully aware of B if B is within A's focus and A is within B's nimbus. In this case, A would receive text messages from B.

- A is not aware of B if B is not within A's focus and A is not within B's nimbus. In this case A sees no messages from B.

- A is semi-aware from B if either B is within A's focus or A is within B's nimbus, but not both. In this case A wouldn't receive messages from B, but would be notified that B was speaking near by.

Even with such a relatively crude application of the spatial model (i.e. using simple discrete valued foci/nimbi), some interesting and novel effects come into play. In particular, there is a semi-aware state in which I am notified that you are trying to speak (perhaps in a separate window) without hearing what you say. Notice also that there is a power balance between A and B in terms of their abilities to influence the conversation and also that their levels of awareness may be asymmetrical. A prototype application of the spatial model to a text conferencing system is being realised in the *CyCo (Cyberspace for Cooperation)* system at Nottingham University (Benford 92). CyCo provides a large environment of connected virtual rooms and is implemented on top of the ANSA Distributed

Processing Platform (ANSA 89). The current prototype supports two user interfaces, an X Windows interface using the Motif widget set and a teletype interface based on the UNIX Curses C library. CyCo can be configured to support specific world designs by creating new room descriptions and topology information and also provides inbuilt mapping facilities to aid navigation.

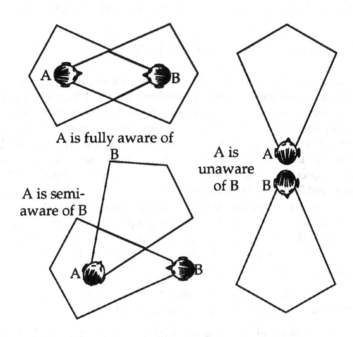

Figure 3 - Levels of Awareness in Text Conferencing.

4.3 Other applications

We can also envisage the application of the spatial model to a range of other CSCW systems. One interesting example might be that of collaborative hypermedia. A hypermedia document can be considered as a one dimensional space where the spatial metric is the number of links between two nodes. Simple aura, focus and nimbus might then convey a sense of awareness between people browsing through such a space. Hypermedia browsers could use measures of awareness to take actions such as notifying people of the presence of others or automatically opening up communication channels.

To go a stage further, it may be possible to spatially organise more general information domains, classification schemes and taxonomies. One approach to the spatial visualisation of large databases is given in (Mariani 92). As a second example, work has been carried out into the spatial mapping and classification of scientific disciplines based on a statistical analysis of the co-occurrence of keywords in academic papers. More specifically, the analysis resulted in measures of *inclusion* and *proximity* between keywords and these were used to automatically draw maps of scientific areas (Callon). The spatial model could be applied to manage interactions across such a space. Similar techniques might have applications in areas such news systems, bulletin boards and shared databases. Perhaps in the future, we will see collaboration taking place across large *populated information terrains* of spatially arranged data.

5. Distributed support for the spatial model

This section outlines a more formal computational framework for the spatial model by relating it to current object-based approaches for building distributed systems. This process also highlights a number of key requirements for future distributed systems support for collaborative virtual environments.

5.1. Object-based models of distributed systems

Much effort has been invested in to the development of platforms for building large scale distributed systems including the Open Distributed Processing framework (ODP) (ISO 91a); the work of the Object Management Group (OMG) (OMG 90); OSF's Distributed Computing Environment (DCE) (OSF 92) and systems such as ISIS (Birman 91). Although not identical, these emerging platforms share much in common; particularly the use of an object-based modelling approach. The following discussion uses terminology from the ODP work. However, the underlying principles are generally applicable to other emerging platforms.

A distributed system can be modelled as a set of *objects* which interact through well defined *interfaces*. An interface groups together a set of related *operations* which are invoked by one object on another. A distributed platform provides some mechanism for establishing contact between objects, negotiating the use of interfaces and invoking operations. In the Open Distributed Processing model, this is supported through the process of *trading*, probably one of the most important concepts to emerge from distributed systems work in recent years (ISO 91b). In order to trade, a provider object exports its interfaces by registering them with a well known system object called the trader. The trader notes the *type* of each interface and also the *context* in which it is provided (effectively the name of the service provided). A consumer object that wishes to use an interface queries the trader, supplying both the desired interface type and also target contexts. The trader looks for a match and, if one exists, returns an *interface reference* to the consumer. This interface reference can then be used by the consumer to invoke operations on the provider. Notice that, in current trading models, it is the consumer who decides when to request an interface reference from the trader and that, in effect, the trader is a passive service. The main advantage of trading is that it provides a high degree of transparency for object interactions. The concepts of objects, interface, operations and trading are summarised by figure 4. Other distributed platforms define similar mechanisms (e.g. the Common Object Request Broker (CORBA) in the OMG work).

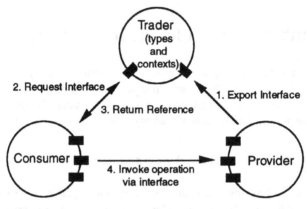

Figure 4: Trading

5.2 Requirements of trading in virtual environments

We expect that collaborative virtual environments will be characterised by a number of features which will impact on the nature of object interactions and on fundamental ideas such as trading. First, they will include objects which represent human beings. Human beings are intelligent and autonomous, often liking to explore their environments. Interaction between objects will therefore often be ad-hoc and opportunistic. Objects will not always know in advance which interfaces they require and so the passive trading model will not be sufficient. Instead, objects will require the trader to actively inform them of new services that become available as they move about (i.e. services that come into range). Second, in addition to interface type and context, trading will be based on the spatial proximity of objects. In other words, as objects get closer to each other, they will become more aware of each other and will able to invoke new operations on each other. In this way the environment becomes more reactive (i.e. objects react to each other's presence). A good example might be moving up to a bulletin board. At a great distance you don't see it. Closer to, you see it is there. Even closer and you can read messages. Even closer and you can write on the board. In summary, trading in collaborative virtual worlds will be active as well as passive and will be based on a notion of spatial proximity, and hence awareness, between objects. Finally, large distributed systems will contain many traders, each of which is responsible for a specific set of objects. In this case, we say that each trader manages a local *trading domain*. Furthermore, traders may federate together in order to exchange information about trading domains and so achieve a distributed trading service.

5.3 Extending object interfaces and trading

Next, we outline key extensions to the distributed object model to support the spatial model. At the same time, this provides a more computational and general definition of the spatial model itself. First we consider a general mapping of terms. People and artefacts are represented as objects. Communication media are mapped onto different interfaces (e.g. "audio" or "text") allowing interaction between these objects. A single virtual space containing many objects maps onto a trading domain managed by a given trader. Now we can introduce the idea of managing object interactions through inter-object awareness. We can associate an aura with each interface. When two auras collide, the relevant interfaces are enabled - in other words, the objects mutually acquire interface references. It is the role of the trader to detect aura collisions and to actively pass out interface references. Next, we associate focus and nimbus with an interface. This time it is the objects themselves, not the trader, that negotiate awareness levels. These levels can then be used in two ways. Operations within an interface can be associated with an awareness threshold at which they become available to other objects. Also, objects can decide to invoke operations on others once certain thresholds are passed. This ability for objects to determine levels of mutual awareness requires support from standard operations to return values of focus and nimbus from a given interface. Notice that, in terms of where computation takes place, the trader is concerned with supporting aura whereas the objects themselves deal with the use of focus and nimbus. These key extensions of aura, focus and nimbus in object interfaces are shown in figure 5. We also need to consider how aura, focus and nimbus are formally represented and computed. Given that we require a quantitative measure of awareness, we can model them as mathematical functions which map from spatial properties of objects such as position and orientation into real number values. This is similar to the way in which functions can be used to describe properties of surfaces in surface modelling. We then combine values of aura, focus and nimbus through a separate awareness function. A more detailed mathematical treatment of focus and nimbus is given in (Benford 92).

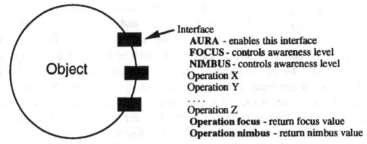

Figure 5: Spatial model extensions to object interfaces

As a final comment, by considering general object interfaces, we need not only use awareness to control conversation across communication media; it can also be used to govern any kind of interaction between objects in distributed systems. Thus, the spatial model might eventually provide a more generic platform for building a variety of virtual environments.

6. Summary

Our paper has described a spatial model of group interaction in large-scale virtual environments. The model provides mechanisms for managing conversations between people, as well as interactions with other kinds of objects, in spatial settings. The notion of awareness is used as the basis for controlling interaction and the model provides mechanisms for calculating awareness levels from the spatial properties of objects (e.g. position and orientation). This allows objects to manage interactions through natural mechanisms such as movement and orientation in space. The model defines the key concepts of aura, focus, nimbus and adapter objects all of which contribute to awareness. Furthermore, these concepts are defined in a sufficiently general way so as to apply to any system where a spatial metric can be identified. The paper then considered several example applications including virtual reality and text conferencing, both of which are currently being prototyped. Finally, we outlined a more computational definition of the spatial model by relating it to recent work on distributed systems; in particular, to the notions of objects, interfaces, operations and trading. Much work remains to be done. The current prototypes require extension and eventually proper evaluation. Additional applications also need to be modelled and demonstrated. However, at this stage, we are optimistic that spatial models of interaction such as the one described in this paper, will form an important aspect of support for CSCW, particularly as new technologies such as virtual reality become more widespread in the next few years.

References

(ANSA 89) *The ANSA Reference Manual*, Architecture Projects Management Ltd, Poseiden House, Castle Park, Cambridge CB3 PRD, UK, 1989.

(Benedikt 91) Michael Benedikt, *Cyberspace: Some Proposals*, in Cyberspace: First Steps, Michael Benedikt (ed), MIT Press, 1991, pp 273-302.

(Benford 92) Steve Benford, Adrian Bullock, Neil Cook, Paul Harvey, Rob Ingram and Ok Ki Lee, *From Rooms to Cyberspace: Models of Interaction in Large Virtual Computer Spaces*, The University of Nottingham, Nottingham, UK (to appear in the Butterworth-Heinmann journal, Interacting With Computers in 1993).

(Benford 92) Steve Benford, Wolfgang Prinz, John Mariani, Tom Rodden, Leandro Navarro, Elsa Bignoli, Charles Grant Brown and Torbjørn Naslund, *MOCCA - A Distributed Environment For Collaboration*, Available from the MOCCA Working Group of Co-Tech.

(Borning 91) A. Borning and M. Travers, *Two Approaches to Casual Interaction over Computer and Video Networks*, In Proc. CHI'91, New Orleans, April 27-May 2, 1991, pp13-19.

(Bignoli 91) C. Bignoli and C. Simone, *AI Techniques to Support Human to Human Communication in CHAOS*, in Studies in Computer Supported Cooperative Work: Theory, Practice and Design, J. Bowers and S. Benford (eds), Elsevier Science Publishers, 1991.

(Bowers 88) J. Bowers and J Churcher, *Local and Global Structuring of Computer Mediated Communication: Developing Linguistic Perspectives on CSCW in COSMOS*, In Proc. CSCW'88, Portland, Oregon, September 26-28, 1988.

(Callon) Michel Callon, John Law and Arie Rip (eds), *Mapping the Dynamics of Science and Technology*, Macmillan press, ISBN 0-333-37223-9.

(Carlsson 92) Carlsson, C. and Hagsand, O. *The MultiG Distributed Interactive Virtual Environment*, In Proc. 5th MultiG Workshop, Stockholm, December 18, 1992.

(Clarkson 91) Mark A. Clarkson, *An Easier Interface*, BYTE, February 1991, pp227-282.

(Codella 92) Christopher Codella, Reza Jalili, Lawrence Koved, J. Bryan Lewis, Daniel T. Ling, James S. Lipscomb, Favid A. Rabenhorst, Chu P. Wang, Alan Norton, Paula Sweeney, Greg Turk, *Interactive Simulation in a Multi-Person Virtual World*, In Proc. CHI'92, ACM, 1992.

(Cohen 91) Michael Cohen and Lester F. Ludwig, *Multidimensional Audio Window Management*, in Computer Supported Cooperative Work and Groupware, Saul Greenberg (ed), Harcourt Brace Jovanovich, 1991, ISBN 0-12-299220-2.

(Cook 91) Cook,S., Birch,G., Murphy, A., and Woolsey, J., *Modelling Groupware in the Electronic Office*, in Computer-supported Cooperative Work and Groupware, Saul Greenberg (ed), Harcourt Brace Jovanovich, 1991, ISBN 0-12-299220-2.

(Cook 92) Neil Cook and Graeme Lunt, *XT-Confer: Dynamic Desktop Conferencing*, In Proc. European X User Group Fourth Annual Conference, September, 1992

(Crowley 90) Crowley, T., Milazzo, P., Baker, E., Forsdick, H. and Tomlinson, R., *MM Conf: An Infrastructure for Building Shared Multi-media Applications*, In Proc. CSCW'90, October 1990, ACM Press.

(Eriksson 92) Eriksson H., Frecon E., Carlsson C., *Audio and Video Communication in Distributed Virtual Environments*, In Proc. 5th MultiG Workshop, Stockholm, Dec. 1992.

(Fahlén 91) Fahlén, L. E. *The MultiG TelePresence System*, In Proc. 3rd MultiG Workshop, Stockholm, December 1991, pp. 33-57.

(Fahlén 92) Fahlén, L. E. and Brown, C.G., *The Use of a 3D Aura Metaphor for Compter Based Conferencing and Teleworking*, In Proc. 4th Multi-G Workshop, Stockholm-Kista, May 1992, pp 69-74.

(Fahlén 93) Lennart E. Fahlén, Charles Grant Brown, Olov Stahl, Christer Carlsson, *A Space Based Model for User Interaction in Shared Synthetic Environments*, The Swedish Institute of Computer Science (SICS) (to appear in Proc.InterCHI'93).

(Gaver 92a) Gaver W., *The Affordances of Media Spaces for Collaboration*, In Proc. CSCW'92, Toronto, November 1992, ACM Press.

(Gaver 92b) Gaver, W., Moran, T., MacLean, A.,Lovstrand, L., Dourish,P., Carter, K. and Buxton W., *Realising a Video Environment: EuroPARC's RAVE System*, In Proc. CHI '92 Human Factors in Computing Systems, Monterey, Ca., USA, May 1992.

(Henderson 85) Henderson and Card, *Rooms: The Use of Multiple Virtual Workspaces to Reduce Space Contention*, ACM Transactions on Graphics, Vol. 5, No. 3, July 1985.

(ISO 91a) ISO/IEC, *Basic Reference Model of Open Distributed Processing, Working Document RM-ODP - Part 1: Overview, December 1991*, Available through national standards bodies.

(ISO 91b) ISO/IEC, *Basic Reference Model of Open Distributed Processing, Working Document on topic 9.1 - ODP Trader, December 1991*, Available through national standards bodies.

(Leevers 92) David Leevers, *Prototyping Multimedia Communications for Manufacturing SME's*, Presented at the CI Europe Seminar, 2-3rd July 1992, and also an internal report of BICC Central Development, Maylands Avenue, Hemel Hempstead, UK.

(Mariani 92) J. Mariani, Lougher, *TripleSpace: an Experiment in a 3D Graphical Interface to a Binary Relational Database*, Interacting with Computers, Vol 4, No. 2, 1992, pp147-162.

(Michelitsch 91) Georg Michelitsch, *Providing a Shared Environment to Distributed Work Groups*, In Proc. GLOBECOM'91, Pheonix, Arizona, December 2-5th, 1991.

(Morningstar 91) Chip Morningstar and F. Randall Farmer, *The Lessons of Lucasfilm's Habitat*, in Cyberspace: First Steps, Michael Benedikt (ed), MIT Press, 1991, pp 273-302.

(Navarro 92) L. Navarro, M. Medina and T. Rodden, *Environment Support for Cooperative Working*, In Proc. IFIP 6.5 ULPAA'92 Conference, Vancouver, Canada, May 1992, North-Holland.

(OMG 90) The Object Management Group (OMG), *Object Management Architecture Guide*, OMG Document Number 90.5.4, Available through the Object Management Group, 1990.

(OSF 92) OSF, *Distributed Computing Environment: An Overview*, Available from the OSF January 1992.

(Pankoke 89) Uta Pankoke-Babatz (ed), *Computer Based Group Communication - The Amigo Activity Model*, Ellis-Horwood, 1989.

(Pehrson 92) Pehrson, B., Gunningberg, P. and Pink, S. *MultiG-A research Programme on Distributed MultiMedia Applications and Gigabits Networks*, IEEE Network Magazine vol 6, 1 (January 1992), pp. 26-35.

(Root 88) R.W. Root, *Design of a Multi-Media Vehicle for Social Browsing*, In Proc. CSCW'88, Portland, Oregon, Spetember 26-28 1988, pp25-38.

(Sarin 91) Sunil Sarin and Irene Greif, *Computer-Based Real-Time Conferencing Systems*, in Computer Supported Cooperative Work: A Book of Readings, Irene Greiff (ed), Morgan Kaufmann, 1988, pp397-421.

(Sarkar 92) Manojit Sarkar and Marc H. Brown, *Graphical Fisheye Views of Graphs*, In Proc. ACM SIGCHI'92 Conference on Human Factors in Computing Systems, May 3-7 1992, pp 83-91, ACM Press.

(Smith 92) Jennifer Smith (ed), *Frequently Asked Questions: Basic Information about MUDs and MUDing*, Posting to the alt.mud USENET News Group, July 1992.

(Ståhl 92a) Olov Ståhl, *Mdraw - A Tool for Cooperative Work in the MultiG TelePresence Environment*, Technical Report T92:05, SICS, 1992.

(Ståhl 92b) Olov Ståhl, *Implementation Issues of Aura Based Tools*, In Proc. 5th MultiG Workshop, Stockholm, December 18, 1992.

(Takemura 92) Haruo Takemure and Fumio Kishino, *Cooperative Work Environment Using Virtual Workspace*, In Proc. CSCW'92, Toronto, Nov 1992, ACM Press.

(Victor 91) F. Victor and E. Sommer, *Supporting the Design of Office Procedures in the Domino System*, in Studies in Computer Supported Cooperative Work: Theory, Practice and Design, J. Bowers and S. Benford (eds), Elsevier Science Publishers, 1991.

(Winograd 86) T. Winograd and F. Flores, *Understanding Computers and Cognition: A New Foundation for Design*, Norwood, New Jersey, Ablex 1986 and Addison-Wesley 1987.

Proceedings of the Third European Conference on Computer-Supported Cooperative Work
13-17 September, 1993, Milan, Italy
G. De Michelis, C. Simone and K. Schmidt (Editors)

Culture and Control in a Media Space

Paul Dourish
Rank Xerox EuroPARC, Cambridge, UK
dourish@europarc.xerox.com

Abstract: Media spaces integrate audio, video and computer networking technology in order to provide a rich communicative environment for collaboration. The connectivity which they provide brings with it important concerns regarding privacy, protection and control. In order to derive the fullest benefit from this technology, it is essential that these issues be addressed. As part of our investigation of media space systems, we developed a computational infrastructure addressing these problems our own working environment. A key aspect of this work is the relationship between two aspects of this control system—the *technological* components which determine how the system will behave, and the *social* components which determine acceptable use and behaviour.

This paper discusses our experiences with the privacy and control aspects of our RAVE media space environment, specifically with regard to connection management, and compares them to the experiences of other research groups. We discuss the nature of the relationship between technological and social elements in using this technology, and discuss the consequences for the design of such systems.

Introduction: Media Spaces

One focus for research into workgroup communication and collaboration is the investigation of media space technology. A media space is formed by the combination of audio, video and computer networking technologies to provide a flexible, dynamic interconnection environment for collaborative work groups. Our "RAVE" media space (Buxton and Moran (1990); Gaver *et al* (1991)) is one of a number of systems which have been used in investigations into issues of workgroup support and collaboration (*e.g.* Root (1988); Stults (1989); Abel *et al* (1990); Mantei *et al* (1991)).

At its most basic, the media space provides a means for setting up multi-media communication channels between individuals and groups; beyond that, it supports collaborations, both formal and informal, providing a communication infrastructure which is amenable to rapid reconfiguration and connection. This element of *flexible* and *dynamic* control by individuals is at the heart of what we mean by media space; a media space is more than simply point-to-point audio and video connections. While fixed video links can provide communication between remote individuals, the easy reconfiguration and control of connections is critical in exploring the means by which the technology can create a space in itself, rather than being simply a restructuring of the physical space.

Clearly, the provision of this sort of media infrastructure is a useful means towards contact and direct collaboration between individuals who are not co-located in time or space. The media space is not just a desktop video-conferencing system; our research (*e.g.* Dourish and Bly (1992)) has pointed to other, less formal mechanisms which can be built in media space environments to support a variety of work groups.

On the other hand, it is equally clear that the introduction and use of media space technology raises a host of issues concerning the protection of individual privacy and access control. This is particularly true in environments such as RAVE which are used not only by research staff involved in the development of the technology, but also by other office workers throughout our lab. Even within our own environment, then, it was critical that these issues be addressed if our work was to be successful. The result is a software component called "Godard" (Dourish, 1991) which provides inhabitants of the media space with flexible control over the degree of access they grant to others, and dynamic information on connections and connectivity.

However, control and accessibility in the RAVE environment is not purely based on a technological infrastructure, but also on the culture which has developed around this system. We would claim that any technological control system like Godard sits within a culture which determines aspects of its use; and that this relationship between technological and social control must be considered as part of the design process. In essence, the relation between the technology and its use is *coadaptive*, and must be analysed as such (Mackay, 1990). This relationship is the central focus of this paper.

In the rest of this paper, we will first discuss aspects of the Godard system in more detail, and describe the way in which its introduction changed aspects of media space use within RAVE. We will then consider the design of some other media space environments and aspects of privacy control and usage culture in those systems. Finally, we will talk more generally about the relationship between technological and social control and its importance in designing such systems.

The RAVE Media Space Environment

The Ravenscroft Audio-Video Environment is a media space being developed and used at Rank Xerox EuroPARC. It comprises switchable analogue video and audio networking technology, workstation software to control connections among individuals and public spaces, and other systems which provide facilities for coordination, informal interaction and focussed collaboration. RAVE extends these with computer-based systems which augment the power of the media space for collaboration. Multi-user drawing surfaces (e.g. ShrEdit (McGuffin and Olson, 1992) and shdr (Dourish, *to appear*)), a shared active calendar (Lövstrand, 1991) and other tools for collaboration in a number of computational domains are all important parts of the system as a whole.

One critical aspect of the RAVE system is its ubiquity within our work place. Rather than being restricted to a small group of individuals who are involved in the development of the technology, RAVE connections are provided to *all* members of the lab, including research, technical and administrative staff. Although there is no obligation to make use of the technology, the hardware and associated software systems are made available by default. Furthermore, users are encouraged to "adopt" the technology and make it their own. For instance, there is no obligation to have cameras pointed directly at work areas. Pointing the camera out of a window for privacy during a meeting or conversation is quite common.

Clearly, the ubiquity of our system raises a number of issues concerning privacy and protection for individuals. Being deployed through our lab, the RAVE system does not require the "sign-up" process observed in some other environments, where an individual must explicitly request membership of the media space, and accept whichever norms govern its use. Hence it was extremely important for us to explicitly address issues of privacy and control in the development of our system. It was critical to the success of our experimentation that the participants could maintain the level of privacy they desired, maintain control over the ways in which others could connect to their offices, and have flexible control over feedback indicating the state of the media space and their visibility within it. At the same time, it was also important that we maximise the flexibility and utility of our media space, in order to investigate the range of ways it could support collaborative work in our environment. RAVE is, after all, a research tool.

These requirements led us to develop a solution based on people's styles of interaction in the real world (Anderson and Moran, 1990). This is realised primarily in a system component called Godard.

Godard

Godard is a software infrastructure which provides the primary interface for users of the RAVE media space. It encompasses subsystems which are responsible for making connections and controlling the media space, as well as for controlling access from other individuals and connection status feedback.

There are two concepts which underlie the design of Godard. The first is the notion of a *service*. A service is the basic "unit of interaction" in the RAVE media space. The network offers a range of services to users of the system, and these services are encapsulations of stereotypical user behaviours in a physical office environment. Some examples will give the flavour of what we mean by a service:

1. The glance service provides the media space equivalent of glancing into a colleague's office as you walk by their door. In the media space, this takes the form of a one-way video connection of a few seconds' duration.

2. The vphone service is the media space equivalent of a telephone call. A two-way audio and video connection is set up between two individuals after the "recipient" of the connection has answered a ring signal.

3. The office-share service is the media space equivalent of sharing an office with a colleague. A two-way audio and video connection links individuals and can be maintained for as long as both parties agree (some office-share connections have been in place almost continuously for over a year). The individuals can choose to use open ("hands-off") audio, or to control it with a foot-pedal.

4. The background service is the media-space equivalent of the view out an office door or window. It is a video connection from an office to a public area such as a corridor, the coffee room or even a view out of a window towards the park behind our building. This view will generally be shown on a monitor when it is not engaged in any other activity. It is automatically disconnected when other connections are made, and reconnected after they are over.

The difference between the vphone and office-share connections is particularly interesting, and illustrates the orientation of these services around *user behaviours* rather than technical descriptions of system activity. Both vphone and office-share link offices with two-way audio-and-video connections; they are technologically almost identical. However, their mode of use is very different. Whereas a video phone call will typically be short and directed (another property it has in common with "real" phone calls), an office-share connection between two individuals is normally of much longer duration and much less continuously attended.

This definition of services around stereotypical real-world behaviours, then, gives us a useful way to partition the space of possible connections. By tagging a video connection with some notion of an analogous real-world behaviour, we can provide a way for users to discriminate between connections. For example, users may choose to accept glance connections but not office-share ones. This discrimination is based on an understanding of the kind of connection being made (the service). Technically, it happens through the action of the other principal Godard component, a RAVE *agent*.

The agent is essentially a gatekeeper, which responds semi-autonomously to requests for audio or video connections made by other users. The agent, then, embodies individual privacy within the system. RAVE participants cannot be glanced at unless to appropriate agent has been consulted. The agent decides whether or not to accept a particular connection by consulting a set of individual preferences supplied by the user. These record the details of which connections should be accepted, which should be rejected, and which should cause the agent to interrupt the user for confirmation.

As well as providing a basic level of protection, we can also use this mechanism to provide *feedback* to users on the state of connections. Thus, for instance, a user can control three feedback parameters for the glance service:

1. the Before parameter specifies some action which should take place before the actual video connection is made;
2. the After parameter specifies a behaviour which should take place when the video connection is broken;
3. the Inform parameter specifies a way that the system should inform the user of the *identity* of the individual making the connection.

Typically, this feedback takes the form of non-speech audio cues (Gaver, 1991), or, less often, pop-up messages on the workstation screen. Thus, the before action might generate the sound of an opening door, and the after action may sound like the door closing again. Since these actions are stored individually for each user in a particular agent process, a user has complete control over what form these feedback messages should take, or of they should be used at all, for their own node. Parameter settings for various services remain private, and inaccessible to other users of the system except through their externally-observable result. Since the introduction of our system, the audio cues have proved to be the most popular—probably because they do not require that the user is attending to the screen when a connection is made.

Introducing Godard

A natural question at this point is, in what ways did the introduction of these mechanisms change the nature of the media space, and why? The first answer is that, as had been hoped, privacy protection *made the system more open*. Many more people were prepared to make themselves accessible to their colleagues via the media space for three main reasons:

1. They now trusted that a system was in place to protect their privacy if they wanted, which reduced the cost of changing accessibility. It was possible to make oneself accessible without the worries about how one could undo that again.
2. The presence of feedback in the system meant that users felt they could be part of the system without the original feeling that they didn't know what was going on. Feedback made the status of media space actions much more immediate.

3. The use of different services to delimit the space meant that users could make themselves *selectively accessible*. They could be accessible for short-term connections (glance) without being available for longer-term connections (vphone or office-share), or even long-term one-way connections (watch connections, which are generally only offered for public areas). This gave them a much finer degree of control than had previously been available.

It might be regarded as curious that a system designed to enforce privacy and protection results in a more open communicative environment and increases access. However, this is really quite natural. The openness and accessibility of an environment is not purely a function of the technology, but of the culture of use which arises around it. Godard enabled a different culture of use to emerge. We will consider the point in more detail later, after a brief look at other media space systems and their approaches to these issues.

Other Systems

In the introduction, we referred to a variety of research projects investigating media space technologies. Each of these environments has some means for controlling access, whether by technological or social means. In this section, we discuss some other systems in more detail, with emphasis on the ways in which they control access and availability of participants.

Xerox PARC: Media Space

The system at Xerox's Palo Alto Research Center was probably the earliest example of a media space (in fact, it's called "Media Space"). The use of media space technology at PARC has its roots in a split-site experiment, when part of the System Concepts Laboratory was divided between Palo Alto, California, and Portland, Oregon. The group was linked with a digital audio and video connection, initially between two public areas, but later between two local switching hubs, giving them the opportunity to make inter-office connections between sites (Olson and Bly, 1991). Although the Portland lab has now closed, the Media Space continues as an active research area centered in the Information Sciences and Technologies Laboratory in Palo Alto, and links around 16 offices as well as public areas and shared resources.

The PARC media space operates on a "sign-up" basis. New users wishing to join the media space approach the existing group and must explicitly request access. Part of the process of "signing up" is an acceptance of the social practices and norms which govern acceptable media space use.

There is a minimal technological protection system, which protects inter-node connections already in place from being broken by others, rather than protecting nodes. However, this "locking" mechanism is rarely used. The result is that any

Media Space user can make an audio and/or video connection to any other, and disconnect most ongoing connections. Privacy can be maintained by pointing the camera out of a window, or turning off the microphone.

PARC's protection model, then, is largely a cultural one. While the technology makes it possible for individuals to "misuse" the technology, there are social pressures which prevent them from doing so, and these can be preserved through the "sign-up" model. Within a small community, the result is a stable situation, comfortable and acceptable to participants, without direct need for a more technological solution.

University of Toronto: CAVECAT

The CAVECAT system is a media space under development at the University of Toronto. Experiences of the use of this media space have been reported elsewhere (Mantei *et al*, 1991), but here we concentrate in particular on some of the privacy and accessibility concerns, especially with reference to the other systems under discussion.

The basis of the CAVECAT system is the IIIF connection management system (Milligan, 1991), which is the same system as underpins RAVE. Extensions to manage accessibility and resource contention, which RAVE encapsulates in Godard, are realised at Toronto by extensions to IIIF and intelligent clients, which together form the CAVECAT system (Louie *et al*, to appear).

CAVECAT users can create rules for connections, similar in spirit to the service access lists which Godard maintains. However, these rules are managed differently in practice, since they are based on *explicit properties* of the underlying media connections, rather than on distinguished services. A rule in the CAVECAT system might say:

> **If** one of the users [*tom, marilyn, bill, gifford*] requests a
> connection with properties [*short-term, one-way, video*] to
> my node, **then** accept with notification [*audio, knock*]

This rule refers to glance-type behaviour. Certain common rule patterns are reified as accessibility states presented to users through an iconic interface which draws on the metaphor of office doors. Full accessibility is suggested by an open door; a door which is ajar makes me less accessible, requiring my permission for some sorts of connections; a closed door requires more permission again, and a locked or barred door indicates that the user is completely inaccessible.

The connection properties are superficially similar to Godard's services, but differ in the degree to which they can be distinguished. Godard's services are based on descriptions of real-world behaviour; CAVECAT's are based on technological descriptions of the underlying media connections. This means that Godard can distinguish between connections which are technologically identical but have different modes of use; this is not available in CAVECAT. On the other hand, the CAVECAT rules generalise to new connection types in a way in which Godard's cannot.

One characterisation of this distinction is in terms of the assignment of responsibility which the systems imply. In Godard, the burden of responsibility for declaring the connection type (the service or "context" of connection) lies with the initiator, who has to select the service being requested. In CAVECAT, on the other hand, discrimination takes place on properties of the connection itself; there is no declaration of intent on the basis of the initiating party. Recipients must configure their own rules so as to correctly intuit the mode of use of the system based on properties of the underlying connections. It must be recognised that a long term, two-way video connection from a particular person, for instance, implies a particular mode of use, and hence is to be dealt with in a particular way. The burden of responsibility is on the recipient to form the appropriate generalisations and then structure these into rules.

So, CAVECAT strives to manage protection and control largely through technological measures. In their rules, users create embodiments of the social conventions which mediate their interactions, describing them in terms of connection properties; but however much the rules are a formal technical system, they still record socially-derived preferences for initiating and managing interactions. However, the formal structure of the rules distances users from the social situations they are describing; and the orientation of the rule system puts the burden on responsibility for connection interpretation on the recipient. Managing the social nature of media space interaction in a framework such as this can be difficult, as it attempts to use the technological mechanisms to replace, rather than augment and preserve, the social components which are the essence of media space use.

Bellcore: CRUISER

Another workplace media space is that developed at Bellcore, called "Cruiser" (Root, 1988). Cruiser is designed to provide a mechanism for "social browsing", encouraging informal interactions between work group members, including those separated by distance. The original Cruiser design was based on a hallway metaphor; initiating a "cruise" would cause brief connections to a number of individuals in succession, similar to walking down a hallway and looking into the offices. Either party in a connection could halt the cruise and engage the other in conversation. Later versions of Cruiser added a specific "glance" facility, rather like a one-stop cruise.

In terms of protection mechanisms and privacy control, two aspects of Cruiser are of interest to us here. The first is that all connections in Cruiser are *reciprocal*; that is, when I see another media space participant, she sees me at the same time. It is simply not possible to make a one-way connection with the Cruiser system. The second point is that the members of the Cruiser media space have a simple way of indicating their level of accessibility through the use of computer-generated bars which appear on their video image. The bars obscure the video image of the participant, indicating to the remote observer that this individual is not accessible for conversation.

Cultural aspects of Cruiser use are embodied in its strong "corridor browsing" metaphor, and are carried across from those real-world behaviours. Certain behaviours are "anti-social" (*e.g.* repeatedly "cruising" the same individual), and reciprocity in Cruiser serves something of the same role as feedback in RAVE by making aspects of the system-internal behaviour accessible in the real world and amenable to social control. A price is paid in terms of the potentially increased intrusion of a two-way connection. In fact, a major privacy concern expressed by users focussed not so much on the violation of privacy through connection, but through the imprecise and unpredictable nature of the technology (Fish *et al*, 1992).

A number of technological features of Cruiser, such as reciprocity, essentially serve to support a socially-controlled mechanism for interaction and initiating of conversations. To an extent, then, reciprocality and a strong face-to-face metaphor make it very easy to carry across behaviours from real-world social interaction into Cruiser; but on the other hand, it makes it much more difficult to have new behaviours develop within the media space, since the modes of interaction are strictly limited.

The Social-Technical Continuum

The preceding sections have discussed a number of experimental experiences with the use of media space technologies in work group collaboration. We have shown the way in which different groups have addressed issues of privacy and control, using both social and technological mechanisms to regulate access and accessibility.

One characterisation which we can make of the various privacy controls is their position along a posited "social-technical continuum". At one end, we might place PARC's system in which control is largely social; the technology provides many facilities which are not allowed by the social norms which determine its use. RAVE's Godard solution is close to the other end, in that control (at least on a per-connection basis) is largely technical; far fewer "misuses" are allowed by the technology.

But to what extent is the Godard mechanism purely based in technology? In fact, it would be false to claim that Godard implements a purely technical model of "correct video behaviour" which obviates the need for social controls. For instance, if I grant only glance access to other users, I clearly intend this to provide short-term views into my office; the technology will ensure that requests for long-term connections are denied. However, what is to stop another user from making repeated glance connections to my office and thus watching me over a much longer period of time?

In the RAVE environment, the use of the feedback mechanism deters this type of misuse. Making repeated glance connections in the media space becomes rather like pressing your ear to a colleague's closed door in an office; while the technology does not prevent it, it is easily discovered and clearly against the prevailing culture. So, one of the roles of connection feedback in Godard is to "lift" aspects of control from the technical domain to the social one. The feedback from repeated glance connections means that this form of misuse is amenable to social, rather than technological, control. This relationship between the two modes of control is critical to Godard's success, and a fundamental aspect of its design.

We would claim that even those media space control systems which based themselves strongly in technology are also subject to the culture of use which emerges from them. There are both positive and negative aspects of this cultural embedding. On the positive side, we would simply point out that media space technologies do not necessarily impinge upon and nullify the social conventions which regulate workplace behaviours; the media space is just as amenable to such forces as are physical spaces. The negative side is that the negative aspects of cultural embedding are still present; social pressures may mitigate against, for instance, refusing video access to superiors. (In Godard, one user cannot examine another's agent preferences; however, a superior can still *demand* access as much as before.)

This is not a question of exchanging one evil for another, however; it is merely another example of the way in which social controls still matter in media spaces. In our research environment, Godard is not proposed as *the* way to manage privacy and control issues; rather, it is our particular embodiment in a technical system of the controls which we choose for our workplace. On a more general level, it points towards the importance of the balance between technical and social constraints in these systems.

The raising of control issues into the social domain may also change the way the technology is used. The use of audio feedback in Godard's glance service provides an example of this. Within our environment, it is typical to allow anyone to glance as long as full feedback is enabled. This convention has allowed a different use of glance to arise, in which users may initiate glance connections when they arrive in the morning to say "hello" to their colleagues; they are making use of the cultural convention that a glance connection is announced at the other end.

These cultural phenomena arise every day in normal workplaces. A mundane example is to be found in the conventions that give meaning to open and closed office doors. We are all familiar with the conventions of our own workspaces, and the messages that open and closed office doors send to passers-by about the accessibility of the individual within. One door at EuroPARC, although typically closed, carries a notice which reads "this door is OPEN"; the owner of that office wishes to distinguish between the physical state of the door and the statement of a closed door in our office culture. Similar conventions surround the use of phones, answering machines, voice mail and forwarding mechanisms; letting my phone calls forward to a receptionist has a different meaning from letting them forward to an answering machine.

In other words, the tension between the technological and social barriers which ensure individual privacy and control over access is something which we deal with regularly. It is a tension which is natural to us in our everyday lives. It seems only natural, then, that we should capitalise upon this tension in the design of media space environments. Indeed, it is a contention of this paper that it is impossible not to; technological systems cannot be designed which are not then subject to the influences of social factors in their use.

The social factors which influenced the design of Godard continue to be an important aspect of further design within our environment. In particular, some colleagues are currently investigating the way that low-level information about the connection status of the media space and the use of equipment can be provided in order to reduce the problem of disembodiment of the individual from the communicative environment which characterises aspects of media space interaction (Bellotti and Sellen, 1993). This work pursues the theme of the relationship between social and technical control over privacy and accessibility in media space environments.

Summary

The use of multimedia communication environments, or media spaces, is of increasing interest to research groups studying various forms of collaborative and group working. One critical aspect of these systems is the extent to which individual privacy is maintained and accessibility controlled. If this technology is to be successful in supporting collaboration, it is first essential that means are provided allowing people to control the extent to which they are accessible, preferably without a steep learning curve.

A variety of mechanisms, technological and social in nature, can be used to make the media space a comfortable place to live and work. By discussing mechanisms that various systems use and the ways in which they differ, we suggest that a purely technical notion of protection and control is not only inappropriate, but impossible. Interaction in a media space is by its very nature a social activity, and the technological systems we might use to manage media space connectivity are embedded within social and cultural contexts.

We would argue that an acknowledgment of these social and evolving elements surrounding interaction in media spaces is a critical element in the design of a system to manage privacy and accessibility. This can greatly benefit the technological designer, since it serves, to an extent, to delimit the scope of any technological control; and it allows us to integrate media space interaction much more easily into everyday behaviour by exploiting our everyday understanding of the cultural elements of workplace interaction.

ACKNOWLEDGEMENTS

The development of the RAVE media space has involved contributions from many individuals. I would like to acknowledge Sara Bly, Alan Borning, Bill Buxton, Kathy Carter, Ian Daniel, Mik Lamming, Lennart Lövstrand, Hugh Messenger, Wendy Mackay, Allan MacLean, Tom Milligan, Mike Molloy, Tom Moran, Mike Travers and Alex Zbyslaw for their help and contributions.

The ideas expressed in this paper, and the form of the paper itself, have similarly benefitted from discussions with a number of colleagues, including Bob Anderson, Victoria Bellotti, Sara Bly, Bill Gaver, Steve Harrison, Rachel Jones, Wendy Mackay and Abigail Sellen.

References

Abel, M., Corey, D., Bulick, S., Schmidt, J. and Coffin, S. (1990): "The US West Advanced Technologies TeleCollaboration Research Project", in Wagner (ed.), *"Computer Augmented Teamwork"*, Van Nostrand Reinhold.

Anderson, R. and Moran, T. (1990): "The Workaday World as a Paradigm for CSCW Design", in *Proc. ACM Conference on Computer-Supported Cooperative Work CSCW'90*, Los Angeles, Ca., October 1990.

Bellotti, V. and Sellen, A. (1993): "Designing for Privacy in Ubiquitous Computing Environments", in *Proc. European Conference on Comuter-Supported Cooperative Work ECSCW'93*, Milano, Italy.

Buxton, W. and Moran, T. (1990): *"EuroPARC's Integrated Interactive Intermedia Facility (IIIF): Early Experiences"*, in *Proc. IFIP Conference on Multi-User Interfaces and Applications*, Herakleion, Crete, September 1990.

Dourish, P. (1991): "Godard: A Flexible Architecture for A/V Services in a Media Space", EuroPARC Technical Report EPC-91-134, Rank Xerox EuroPARC, Cambridge, UK.

Dourish, P. and Bly, S. (1992): "Portholes: Supporting Awareness in Distributed Work Groups", in *Proc. ACM Conference on Human Factors in Computer Systems CHI '92*, Monterey, Ca., May 1992.

Dourish, P. (to appear):, "Anatomy of a Shared Workspace: Dissecting Shdr", to appear in Dourish (ed.), *"Implementation Perspectives in CSCW Design"*, Springer-Verlag, in preparation.

Fish, R., Kraut, R., Root, R. and Rice, R. (1992): "Evaluating Video as a Technology for Informal Communication", in *Proc. ACM Conf. Human Factors in Computing Systems CHI '92*, Monterey, Ca., May 1992.

Gaver, W. (1991): "Sound Support for Collaboration", in *Proc. European Conference on Computer-Supported Cooperative Work ECSCW '91*, Amsterdam, September 1991.

Gaver, W., Moran, T., MacLean, A., Lövstrand, L., Dourish, P., Carter, K.and Buxton, W. (1992): "Realising a Video Environment: EuroPARC's RAVE System", in *Proc. ACM Conference on Human Factors in Computing Systems CHI '92*, Monterey, Ca., May 1992.

Louie, G., Mantei, M. and Sellen, A. (to appear): "Making Contact in a Multi-media Environment", to appear in Behaviour and Information Technology.

Lövstrand, L. (1991): "Being Selectively Aware with the Khronika System", in *Proc. European Conference on Computer-Supported Cooperative Work ECSCW-91*, Amsterdam, Netherlands, October 1991.

Mackay, W. (1990): *"Users and Customisable Software: A Co-Adaptive Phenomenon"*, PhD Thesis, Sloan School of Management, MIT, Cambridge, Mass.

McGuffin, L. and Olson, G. (1992): "ShrEdit: A Shared Electronic Workspace", CSMIL Technical Report, Cognitive Science and Machine Intelligence Laboratory, University of Michigan.

Mantei, M., Baecker, R., Sellen, A., Buxton, W., Milligan, T., and Wellman, B. (1991): "Experiences in the Use of a Media Space", in *Proc. ACM Conf. Human Factors in Computer Systems CHI '91*, New Orleans, Louisiana.

Milligan, T. (1991): "The IIIF Design Report", University of Toronto, 1991.

Root, R. (1988): "Design of a Multi-Media Vehicle for Social Browsing", in *Proc. ACM Conf. Computer Support for Cooperative Work CSCW '88*, Portland, Oregon.

Stults, R. (1989): "The Experimental Use of Video to Support Design Activity", Xerox PARC Technical Report SSL-89-19, Palo Alto, Ca.

Proceedings of the Third European Conference on Computer-Supported Cooperative Work
13-17 September, 1993, Milan, Italy
G. De Michelis, C. Simone and K. Schmidt (Editors)

TOSCA
Providing organisational information to CSCW applications

Wolfgang Prinz

GMD - German National Research Centre for Computer Science, Germany

Abstract: Most cooperation support systems require information about the organisational context in which they are used. This is particularly required when systems are used in a large organisation or for the support of inter-organisational cooperation.

Following from this requirement, this paper presents the design and functionality of the organisational information system TOSCA for cooperation support systems. TOSCA is composed of two major components: an organisational information base server, which provides services to applications and an organisational information browser, which provides user access.

The paper describes the motivation for an organisational information system, the object oriented data model that is used for the information representation, the architecture of the overall system, and the design of the user interface that presents and provides access to the multimedia information. It concludes with the description of how this system supports a task management system and the role it would play in a CSCW environment.

1. Introduction & Motivation

The overall aim of TOSCA[1] is the representation of knowledge about organisations and their resources which are relevant for the support of communication and cooperation. Major issues of the system are:

• provision of organisational context information

Cooperation in teams and organisations is always embedded in an organisational framework. This requires the provision of information about the organisational context in which users work which helps to choose the right patterns for

---

[1] The organisational information system for CSCW applications
The work described in this paper has been partly supported by the CoTech project MOCCA and the ESPRIT Basic research action COMIC.

communication and cooperation. Information must be provided to answer questions such as: Who is responsible for carrying out a specific task? Whom can I ask for help? Furthermore the system should provide information as to how particular tasks are handled in the organisation. What are the organisational rules one has to consider? Whom do I have to ask first? Which document type do I have to use? All this information belongs to the knowledge which is normally not or only very implicitly provided by CSCW applications, although it plays a significant role in cooperation. TOSCA provides this information to users and applications. Thus, not for every application which requires this information an own information base must be developed and managed.

• **distributed provision of directory information**

Communication requires reachability information about the cooperating partners. This includes communication addresses as well as information about reachability and preferred communication methods. Most applications tackle this by providing simple address directories, which are often not distributed and furthermore can not be shared between different applications. So, in the worst case, each user manages his own directory for each cooperation support application he is using. It is one of the aims of the organisational information system presented here to overcome this problem by providing and integrating a distributed directory service to applications and users.

• **integration of standardised external resources**

An approach chosen in (Hennessy et al., 1993), which we also have investigated (Prinz and Pennelli, 1992), is the application of the X.500 Directory. X.500 is a CCITT and ISO standard for an electronic address book (X.500, 1992). With its potentially world-wide distribution, its methods for distributed management, and its standardised service interface, it fulfils the requirements for a distributed address directory and scalability. However, shortcomings arise when the directory is applied to a more detailed modelling and administration of organisational information. Major problems deal with the representation and modelling of organisational relationships and data integrity. Nevertheless, in order to benefit from the existence of X.500, we found it important that TOSCA integrates access to the X.500 world.

• **integration of cooperation resources**

Comprehensive cooperation support benefits when the resources for cooperation support such as documents, calendars, structured message types (Pankoke-Babatz, 1989; Borenstein, 1992; Malone et al., 1992) can be integrated with the context in which they are used. The advantage of TOSCA is that it is more than a storage server for this information. It allows the association of this information to its organisational context, i.e. by linking it to the projects, departments, etc. where they are used or to the people who use it.

- **support for scalability**

Organisational information is of particular importance in large geographically distributed organisations and for the support of inter-organisational cooperation (Engelbart, 1990). This raises the aspect of scalability which we see as a crucial issue for the success of CSCW applications. From the administrative viewpoint it must be easily possible to extend the number of users of an application. This requires an underlying distributed service environment which provides a set of common services needed by cooperation support service. The organisational information service presented here is one fundamental component in such an environment. As a support service it simplifies the introduction and use of new applications into the working environment and this may increase the acceptance of these services (Markus and Connolly, 1990).

- **visible and user tailorable model**

We aimed to develop a flexible data model that allows an adaptation of our system to various organisations. This is required, because organisations change and it is impossible to develop a single representation that fits all considerable organisations. For that reason an object oriented approach has been chosen. Together with the provision of an object modelling tool TOSCA provides visibility of the concepts and allows users and groups to tailor the object model to their specific need.

This paper is organised as follows. First we will present the data model for the representation of organisational information. The design of an organisational browser is described afterwards, showing three different scenarios of use. Then, the architecture of the system is presented followed by an examination how the system is integrated into a larger CSCW environment. The paper concludes with a brief description of future plans and a summary.

2. A Data Model for the representation of organisational information

2.1. General considerations

Before we explain our data model we should define what we understand by organisational information. We consider organisational information to be information about the entities of an organisation that determine and describe the working context of users. This includes information about the employees, projects, roles, committees, departments, locations, etc. of an organisation. Furthermore, the resources of cooperation such as documents, calendars and other kinds of commonly used data must be considered. In order to provide helpful information on how to perform tasks in an organisation, the system needs to represent guidelines which can be used as resources for planning and carrying out a cooperative activity.

All these discrete bits of information become expressive only when they can be related to each other. Therefore we need ways to describe organisational relationships such as: who is member or leader of a project, which projects are undertaken by a particular department, who is the projects secretary, who is occupying the role of the technical administrator of a special file-server, or who supports which task, or which forms do I need to apply for an organisational procedure? It is also necessary that these relationships can be defined in a dynamic way according to the organisational rules. For example, if a committee consists of the members of the projects of a department, we do not want to list all these people explicitly as would be required in X.500, but we want to express this by an appropriate rule. This reduces redundancy, management overhead and increases consistency when the information is changed.

These requirements and the fact that we wanted to develop a system that is extendible and tailorable to different organisational settings led to the decision to choose an object oriented model for the representation of the organisational information.

The meta object model distinguishes between organisational components and relationships between these entities. Two different basic object types are defined for the representation of organisational objects and organisational relationships. Based on these basic object types a comprehensive set of subtypes for the specific representation of organisational information is defined. The definition of a type requires the specification of several properties each instance of the type must fulfil.

All organisational objects and relationships inherit from basic types which implement the required methods to access and manage object instances. Additional methods can be added for subtypes if needed, but this requires programming which is not expected to be done by end users. Therefore we will focus only on the structural and not on the functional issues of the object model.

2.2. Model of an organisational object type

Organisational object types are used to define a schema for the representation of organisational components. Such a type is specified as follows:

- type name & super type
- corresponding X.500 object class name
- scope of type definition
- textual description of the type
- user friendly name construction rule
- graph layout description
- mandatory and optional attributes
- mandatory and optional relationships

The **type name** is a unique identifier which should describe the semantics of the type. The model provides single inheritance, i.e. one **super type** must be identified.

If available, the name of the corresponding **X.500 object class**[2] can be provided This information is used to map X.500 entries which have been retrieved from the Directory onto the appropriate object type in the organisational data model.

Assigning a **scope** to a type restricts its use to a special organisational context, e.g. a project or group. For example, the usage of a type can be restricted to the context of a group which avoid type clashes and a proliferation of types throughout the whole distributed system. However, users must be aware that it might also hinder cooperation.

The name of an object is often not expressive or user friendly enough for its use in a user interface. Therefore a construction rule for a **user friendly name** can be supplied for an object type. This name can be built by a combination of attributes as well as by retrieving information from objects that this object is related to.

To supply a description of the context in which an object is embedded it is very helpful to provide a graphical view. A **graph layout description** is used for the creation of organisational charts which describe the organisational context of a focused object.

The object model distinguishes between **mandatory and optional attributes** of an object type. Attributes can be basic data types but they might also contain picture, audio or video information (see the section on the user interface). Furthermore attributes can contain expressions which are evaluated on access. These expressions are used to refer to other objects, to express general rules, or to generate a value from others.

Relationships between organisational objects are represented by objects of a special relationship object type. Like attributes, relationships can be either mandatory or optional.

In the past, approaches to model organisations were mainly undertaken in the context of organisational science for the analysis of organisations (Heilmann et al., 1988), or for the planning and support of office procedures (Rupietta, 1990; Victor and Sommer, 1991). Although these systems do not address all the specific issues of TOSCA, our object model has been influenced by their investigations in organisation modelling.

We have developed an object model for GMD. During this exercise we found it very useful to be able to change the object model on the fly. This allowed us to react immediately to new requirements which where raised during data acquisition. The same experience was made when the system was used as a demonstrator for other organisational settings. A full description of all object types that have been defined for our prototype system is not possible in the framework of this paper.

---

[2] The notation X.500 object class corresponds to the notation of an object type in our object model.

2.3. Model of an organisational relationship type

The organisational relation object type has the following characteristics:
- type name & super type
- corresponding X.500 attribute name
- relation identifiers
- value set attributes

Type name & super type are same as for the organisational object type.

If available the name of the corresponding **X.500 attribute type name**, is used to map X.500 attributes which have a distinguished name syntax, i.e. which point to another entry onto the appropriate relation object type and vice versa.

A relation object describes a relationship between two organisational objects. Depending from which entity the relationship is viewed, it needs to be denoted differently. For example a project membership relation between a project and an employee object is called "has members" from the project view, but "is a member of" from the employees view. These identifiers are called **relation identifiers**.

Relationship objects include two **value set attributes** (source and destination) which contain the description of the related organisational objects. These objects can be described by naming them or by expressions which allow for a dynamic description of the relationships. These expressions allow the description of organisational rules such as: voting members of this committee are the project leaders of all projects of the department. Also, they can be used to reduce redundancy by describing rules such as: employees of this institute are the members of all projects of this institute. Furthermore it is possible to define user dependent rules. This is needed for example, when the person who is responsible for a task, depends on the users membership in a project. In this case the actual user identity is needed to answer a request.

2.4. The object model designer - creating and extending the object model

The meta object model was designed to be tailorable to various organisational settings. For that purpose, a window-based object model designer has been realised. This tool allows administrators to create and modify the object types which are used to represent the basic organisational components such as project, department, etc., i.e. which are needed for the structural modelling. Users are allowed to extend the model by definition or subtyping of types which are relevant for their local or cooperative work. For example these are types for the storage of addresses, or for the representation of shared working resources such as texts or notes.

An interesting application of that functionality is the definition of message type objects similar to the approach of semi-structured messages presented in (Pankoke-Babatz, 1989). Members of a project might define their own message types which are used to exchange meeting dates, automatic generated notes, etc. To support such applications the object model defines some basic message object types which can be subtyped for further purposes. Although this approach is comparable to the one taken by the Oval system (Malone et al., 1992), the difference lies in the fact that our system allows the association of these message types to an organisational context, e.g. a project or a committee. This scoping of object types helps to avoid a proliferation of types throughout the whole system. Supplementary solutions for that problem can be found in (Lee and Malone, 1990; Johnson, 1992).

Although the system has not been primarily designed for that purpose, the facility of a user tailorable object model combined with automatically generated forms, makes the system applicable for a simple emulation of cooperative hypermedia applications (Haake and Wilson, 1992). The additional advantage is that our system allows an association of such documents into their organisational context, e.g. a hypermedia document can be easily linked to the appropriate project in which it was produced. Thus, organisational context information is augmented with working resources, and vice versa the resources are linked to their originating context. This provides access to the information via different associations and from different context.

3. The Organisational Information Browser

3.1. Introduction

The organisational information browser provides user access to organisational information. Three major patterns of cooperative work are supported. First, it allows access to and multimedia presentation of organisational information Second, the interface integrates different communication media to support ad-hoc communication. Third, in combination with a task management system, it provides means for the planning, instantiation and coordination of cooperative tasks.

3.2. Querying and presenting organisational information

Cooperation requires information about the cooperating partners. This ranges from simple address and technical reachability information to their organisational context which helps to choose the right patterns for communication and cooperation. It is furthermore very comfortable, when the resources of communication are integrated and can be accessed in the same way. This section describes how that information is presented by the interface and how it can be accessed.

The interface allows browsing and searching for organisational information and tracing of organisational relations via a graphical window interface. As well as text information the interface is able to present different media which is represented in the information base: graphics used for maps and the presentation of organisational hierarchies, relations, procedures and rules; photos (people, groups, buildings, rooms), audio (explanatory text) and video (video demonstrations of software, presentation of public services, etc.).

Normal user interaction starts with a window that provides browsing and querying functionality, as well as means for an easy switching between both search methods (Figure 1).

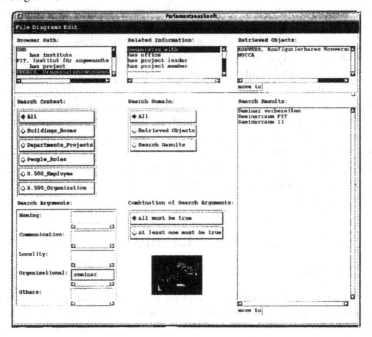

Figure 1. The browser and search window

A set of predefined windows for the display of particular object types and their organisational interrelations has been implemented. In addition, for those which don't have a special presentation a generic window is displayed that is automatically generated from the object's type information. This reacts flexible on model extensions done with the object model designer presented above.

The whole system is realised as a hypermedia interface. Thus, whenever information is displayed which refers to another information object, this can be immediately retrieved by a user action. That allows manifold ways to access and browse through the organisational information, but it also expresses the various relationships which exist.

Using the mapping information provided as type information for each object the user interface is also able to display objects which have been read from X.500 directory. This is useful for example, when an international project description contains references to members which are not stored locally but represented as entries in the X.500 directory. Thus, the administration of that information is done remotely by that person, while we still have access to it. This reduces redundancy and guarantees actuality. This external information object is viewed like an internal one. Of course, the user sees a difference in the richness of the data, because X.500 doesn't provide the same amount of data and relations as our system.

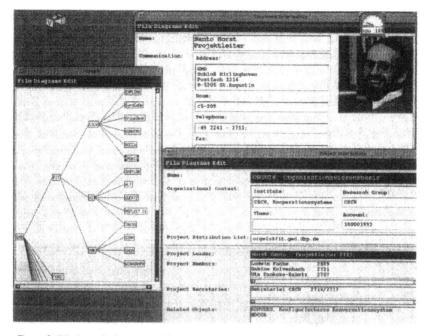

Figure 2. Windows displaying partial information about a project , an employee and a graph that displays the organigram for the project and its supervising institute.

For getting an overview on an organisational object and its relationships a graph can be displayed. This is typically an organigram that shows an object in its organisational context. Figure 2 shows a graph for an institute. The graph shows the research groups and projects of this institute, as well as the other institutes of the organisation. It is generated interpreting the object types graph description. The graph can be used for further browsing, i.e. by selecting any of its entries the appropriate object is displayed.

When pictures or maps are used to represent information, they can be used for browsing, too. Linking a picture object by special relationship objects to other objects, areas of a picture become sensitive, so that additional information, e.g. a more detailed map, or text information is displayed when this area is selected. Audio information can be used to give additional online description.

Cooperation support systems and their user interfaces can not be treated as closed applications. Integration and interworking with other applications must be possible (Engelbart, 1990). In our system this has been achieved via object adapters for external applications or data. By that technique we have integrated calendars, document editing systems, etc. into our organisation browser. This allowed us to turn the information system into a kind of general desktop interface that groups the working resources of a user according to his organisational context (private and project calendars, project papers and documents, etc.).

3.3. Support for ad-hoc communication

For the support of immediate communication with partners or about resources that have been identified it is very important to integrate communication support applications. Currently we have integrated mail and a broad-band video-conferencing tool that has been implemented locally. So, when appropriate, a user can send mail to a person he has just retrieved, or start a video conference with a partner without launching another application first. The system provides information about the communication partners preferences as well as their technical infrastructure. This helps to avoid unsuccessful contact approaches and delays. Obviously, this will not replace the standalone communication applications, but the idea is to provide a stronger integration of these applications also into other applications which deal either with resources that can be communicated or with communication partners.

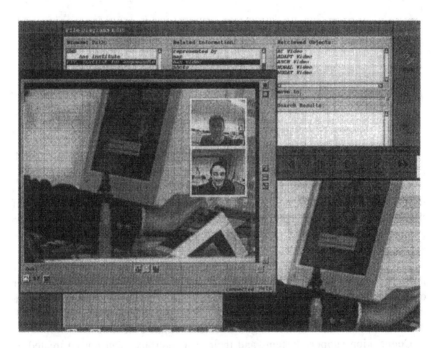

Figure 3 A video conferenced has been launched in which a video retieved from TOSCA is shown to the communication partner.

Figure 3 gives an example for a scenario which illustrates the integration of video-conferencing with the browser's ability to manage and present video clips. A user has started a video-conference using our locally developed video-conferncing system LIVE (Fuchs, 1993), with a partner he retrieved using the browser (upper left window). Then, he selected a project video from a project entry (lower right window), which he is now transmitting in the conference. The video is retrieved from a video tape which contains a set of video clips. It is controlled remotely by our application using time coordinates which are stored for each clip in a video entry. This scenario exemplifies the benefits received by the integration and support of a video-communication tool with the organisational information system.

For each object that is displayed a simple white board functionality is provided. This allows users to communicate on information they have found in the system. For that purpose, comments can be patched on each object (similar to yellow post-it notes). These comments can be viewed, added and modified by all users. It can be used to leave useful experiences or to express problems for other users who lookup the same information. It can also be used as by a group of users who start a discussion about an information object, e.g. about possible extensions on a service that is described, or about informal work-arounds for organisational procedures. With that functionality a communication and discussion tool is directly integrated with the context of discussion, i.e. with the information and its organisational context that caused the discussion.

3.4. Support for cooperative tasks - application by a task management system

TOSCA provides means to describe how tasks or procedures can be carried out in an organisation or in a group. This is represented in task template objects according to a model that has been developed by our local partner project at GMD (Kreifelts et al., 1993). A task is described in an outliner format. This allows the description of major and subordinate tasks. For each single task it can be specified who can support that task or who is responsible to carry it out. Furthermore, resources can be associated to each task, such as documents, forms, calendars, etc. This is done by appropriate relationship objects. These are described user specific. Each user gets individual information about the people who are responsible or the forms which are valid for him. Thus, TOSCA represents abstract templates which are interpreted and individualised on retrieval.

We would like to stress that the task templates are understood as resources for users to develop their own plan. They are not intended as a prescription how a cooperative task must be carried out (Robinson and Bannon, 1991).

Task lists can be interrelated, so that users are informed about alternatives or related templates. This increases the visibility of organisational procedures (Schmidt, 1991). The white board functionality can be used to comment on work-arounds or experiences one has had in carrying out a task.

Although this information is already very useful as a resource to initiate and carry out a cooperative task, it becomes more useful when it can be transferred into a system that supports its coordination. That integration has been realised with the task management system in the framework of the ASCW prototype (Hoschka, 1991; Kreifelts et al., 1993). Users can export a task template from TOSCA and then import it into their personal task list. This is convenient for routine task descriptions and it helps when the user carries out a task for the first time. Then the distributed execution of that task is supported by the task manager. In the further process TOSCA is used for address lookup, to resolve role descriptions when administrative offices are involved, or to look for substitutes, etc.

4. Architecture & Implementation

TOSCA consists of two major components, an organisational information server and the organisation information browser. The server stores and manages the organisational information objects and relations.

The server is realised on top of a distributed object oriented database (ONTOS). Access to the X.500 world is provided by an integrated directory user agent. All requests for external information are forwarded to the X.500 service. References from the organisational information to X.500 information are automatically resolved. Entries retrieved from X.500 are translated into the internal object schema.

The server provides a data and a schema management application interface to applications. These interfaces are used by the organisational information browser, the object model designer, by communication and cooperation support services.

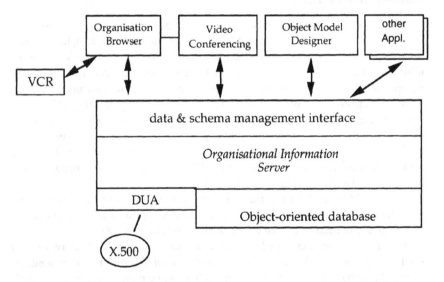

Figure 4. Architecture of TOSCA

The whole system has been implemented in C++, using GINA (Spenke and Beilken, 1991) as an interface toolkit, and Quipu (Kille, 1989) for the X.500 directory components. The server contains currently appr. 750 organisational objects and 600 organisational relationships which are used to represent parts of GMD.

5. Integration with a CSCW environment

With TOSCA, we have developed a system for the support of CSCW applications. However, a comprehensive support requires the provision of additional underlying services among which an organisational information service plays an important role. This is illustrated by figure 5 which outlines the relationships between the developments from e-mail services to CSCW systems and the required supportive services starting from a directory service and ending with a CSCW environment in a simplified way.

As a member of CO-TECH[3] project Mocca (Navarro et al., 1993) we are working on the requirements and design of a CSCW environment. That environment aims to provide a platform for the support, integration and interworking of CSCW applications. Five views on cooperative work have been identified: information, organisation, workspace, distributed architecture, and a rooms metaphor. For the first three views models have been developed while the others lead to the design of an architecture and a virtual world. The organisational model presented in this paper has been chosen as the model for the organisational view.

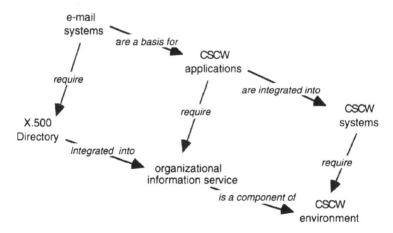

Fig. 5: Relationships between cooperation support applications and supportive systems

Integrated into a CSCW environment, the organisational information service provides a set of services to the other components. To list the major ones:

- Distributed environments require a unique naming and addressing scheme that allows the identification of objects. This naming scheme is provided by the organisational information base for the other environment components.
- Workspaces are used to model shared working areas for groups of people. The definition of a workspace includes the specification of its relation to the organisational context in which the work takes places, e.g. the members of the

---

[3] CO-TECH is a basic research action aimed at establishing a Europe wide CSCW community.

workspace, a project for which the workspace is created, etc. Since all that information is already present in the organisational information server, no additional information needs to be provided and furthermore access rights or other organisational rules can be automatically derived from the policies described for the members context.

- The virtual world user interface requires an underlying system that provides information about the topology of rooms, access and constraints on rooms, the tools and resources available in rooms, etc. This information is represented in TOSCA. It comprises both, the representation of real rooms, buildings and locations and of virtual ones.

6.   Open aspects and future work

Our first prototype will be extended by a more powerful user interface for the distributed administration of the organisational information. Our concept for future developments will allow a distributed administration of the information by users and administrators, since it would be wrong to assume that the whole information base is administered by a single organisation expert. This will be based on the description of access rights and responsibilities. Using these rules, objects will automatically request update-information from the appropriate administrator when they are newly created or when inconsistencies are detected.

Another interesting aspect is the provision of awareness about changes in the organisation. This will be realised using an eventing concept. Modification of objects which reflect changes in the organisation will produce events of different types. Based on the event type an event is then forwarded along appropriate organisational relationships to other objects which then can react on this. For example: The creation of a new employee object in a department produces an event that is forwarded as an informal notification mail to all other employees related to that department while it will also produce a request for the e-mail administrator to install a new account. Or, changing a task template description leads to a notification of all people who are involved.

This work will be partly carried out in the framework of the Esprit Basic Research project COMIC[4]. In the long term, our aim is to extend the organisational information service to a general CSCW object service in the context of the Polikom programme (Hoschka et al., 1993).

7.   Summary

This paper presents the motivation, design and realisation of an organisational information service for the support of CSCW applications. We believe that such a service is a fundamental service in a CSCW environment which provides common

---

[4] Computer-based Mechanisms of Interaction in Cooperative work.

services to other applications and serves as a helpful information service for users in their cooperative work. To summarise:

- the system allows the representation of the organisational context for the support of:
  - applications for cooperation support
  - users as an information and cooperation support service
- it provides and integrates different communication media and facilitates ad hoc communication
- it represents task descriptions as resources for cooperation support of users and applications
- it provides a visible and user tailorable object model and thus allows an adaptation to various organisational settings.
- it provides an integrated access to the internationally standardised X.500 directory service
- in order to provide the best possible representation of information, the system is capable of handling multimedia data

The application domain for such a service are larger organisations as well as the support for inter-organisational cooperation which becomes more relevant for CSCW in the future. That requires scalable systems on the underlying support and application level. Our design decisions to realise a tailorable, flexible object model, to integrate X.500 access, and to base our implementation on a distributed system makes the system scalable to a large extend. In addition its use by other applications will also simplify their scalability and technical integration into an organisational setting.

8. Acknowledgements

The system presented in this paper has been realised within the Orgwis project at GMD. Many thanks to all its members for their ideas and implementation work. Special thanks to M. Busch, J. Mariani, U. Pankoke-Babatz, and H. Santo for their comments on this paper.

9. References

Borenstein, Nathanial. 1992. Computational Mail as Network Infrastructure for Computer-Supported Cooperative Work. In *CSCW '92, Toronto, Canada*, 67-74. ACM.

Engelbart, Douglas. 1990. Knowledge-Domain interoperability and an open hyperdocument system. In *CSCW '90, Los Angeles, USA*, 143-156. ACM.

Fuchs, Ludwin. 1993. *LIVE - Videokonferenz auf der Sun SPARCstation*. GMD, Februar 1993.

Haake, Jörg and Brian Wilson. 1992. Supporting Collaborative Writing of Hyperdocuments in SEPIA. In *CSCW '92, Toronto, Canada*, 138-146. ACM.

Heilmann, Heidi, W. Sach, and M. Simon. 1988. Organisationsdatenbank und Organisationsinformationssystem. *Handbuch der Modernen Datenverarbeitung* : 119-129.

Hennessy, Pippa, Thomas Kreifelts, and Ute Ehrlich. 1993. Distributed work management: Activity coordination in the EuroCoOp project. *Computer Communications* 15 (8): 477-488.

Hoschka, Peter. 1991. Assisting Computer - A New Generation of Support Systems. In *Verteilte Künstliche Intelligenz und kooperatives Arbeiten, 4. Int. GI Kongress, München*, ed. Brauer and Hernandez, 219-230. Springer.

Hoschka, Peter, Berthold Butscher, and Norbert Streitz. 1993. Telecooperation and Telepresence: Technical challenges of a government distributed between Bonn and Berlin. *Informatization and the Public Sector* to appear.

Johnson, P. 1992. Supporting Exploratory CSCW with the EGRET Framework. In *CSCW'92, Toronto, Canada*, 298-305. ACM.

Kille, Steve. 1989. The Quipu Directory Service. In *Message Handling Systems and Distributed Applications, IFIP 6.5 Int. Working Conference, Costa Mesa, USA*, ed. Einar Stefferud, Ole J. Jacobson, and Peter Schicker, 173-186. North-Holland.

Kreifelts, Thomas, Elke Hinrichs, and Gerd Woetzel. 1993. Sharing ToDo List with a distributed Task Manager. In *ECSCW '93: Third European Conference on Computer Supported Cooperative Work, Milan*. to be presented.

Lee, J. and Thomas Malone. 1990. Partially Shared Views: A Scheme for Communicating among Groups that Use Different Type Hierarchies. *ACM Transactions on Office Information Systems* 8 (1): 1-26.

Malone, Thomas, Ch. Fry, and K.-Y. Lai. 1992. Experiments with Oval: A Radically Tailorable Tool for Cooperative Work. In *CSCW '92, Toronto, Canada*, 289-297. ACM.

Markus, K. and T. Connolly. 1990. Why CSCW Applications Fail: Problems in the Adoption of Interdependent Work Tools. In *CSCW '90, Los Angeles, USA*, 371-380. ACM.

Navarro, Leandro, Wolfgang Prinz, and Tom Rodden. 1993. CSCW requires Open Systems. *Computer Communications, Special Issue "Selected Papers of the Third IEEE Workshop "Future Trends of Distributed Computing Systems"* to appear.

Pankoke-Babatz, Uta. 1989. *Computer Based Group Communication. the AMIGO Activity Model.* Information Technology, Chichester: Ellis Horwood.

Prinz, Wolfgang and Paola Pennelli. 1992. Relevance of the X.500 Directory to CSCW Applications. In *Groupware: Software for computer supported cooperative work*, ed. Dave Marca and Geoffrey Bock, 209-225. IEEE Computer Society Press.

Robinson, Mike and Liam Bannon. 1991. Questioning Representations. In *ECSCW '91, Amsterdam, Netherlands*, ed. Liam Bannon, Mike Robinson, and Kjeld Schmidt, 219-234. Kluwer.

Rupietta, W. 1990. An Organisation and Resource Model for Adapting Office Systems to Organisational Structures. In *Database and Expert Systems Applications*, ed. Tjoa and Wagner, 346-350. Springer.

Schmidt, Kjeld. 1991. Riding a Tiger, or Computer Supported Cooperative Work. In *ECSCW '91, Amsterdam, Netherlands*, ed. Liam Bannon, Mike Robinson, and Kjeld Schmidt, 1-16. Kluwer.

Spenke, Mike and Christian Beilken. 1991. An Overview of Gina - The Generic Interface Application. In *Workshop on User Interface Management Systems and Environment, Lisbon, Portugal*, ed. Duce and et. al, 273-293. Springer.

Victor, Frank and Edgar Sommer. 1991. Supporting the Design of Office Procedures in the DOMINO System. In *Studies in Computer Supported Cooperative Work*, ed. John Bowers and Steve Benford, 119-130. North-Holland.

X.500. 1992. *The Directory.* Information Technology - Open Systems Interconnection, ed. CCITT and ISO /IEC 9594-1.

Proceedings of the Third European Conference on Computer-Supported Cooperative Work
13-17 September, 1993, Milan, Italy
G. De Michelis, C. Simone and K. Schmidt (Editors)

Unpacking Collaboration: the Interactional Organisation of Trading in a City Dealing Room

Christian Heath, Marina Jirotka, Paul Luff and Jon Hindmarsh
University of Surrey, University of Oxford and Cambridge EuroPARC, UK

Abstract: It is increasingly recognised that whilst CSCW has led to a number of impressive technological developments, examples of successful applications remain few. In part, this may be due to our relative ignorance of the organisation of real world, cooperative activity. Focusing on share trading in a securities house in the City of London, we explore the interactional organisation of particular tasks and the ways in which dealers interweave individual and collaborative activity. These observations suggest ways in which we might reconsider a number of central concepts in CSCW and begin to draw design implications from naturalistic studies of work and interaction.

1. Introduction

Despite impressive technological developments in CSCW, it is widely recognised that there are relatively few examples of successful applications in real world settings. In part, this is due to the innovative character of many of the systems and their relative fragility. More seriously however, it is suggested that the lack of success of CSCW systems derives not so much from their technological limitations, but more from their insensitivity to the organisation of work and communication in real world environments (e.g. Grudin 1988, Orlikowski 1992). Galegher and Kraut (1990) suggest, for example that the design and application of CSCW systems could learn a great deal from 'what we know about social interaction in groups and organisations'. In this light, we have recently witnessed a growing interest in delineating some basic distinctions concerning the organisation of 'cooperative work' and exploring their implications for the design of particular tools and technologies. Whilst many of these distinctions are indeed fundamental to the organisation of cooperative work and the design of relevant technologies, including co-present verse physically distributed, synchronous verse asynchronous, symmetrical verse asymmetrical, the idea of 'cooperation' or perhaps more specifically 'collaboration' remains ambiguous and largely unexplicated (cf. Schmidt and Bannon 1992). If this apparent ambiguity were merely a matter of sociological relevance, then it would be of little importance to CSCW, however, our relative ignorance of the organisation of cooperative and collaborative activities in work settings may have profound implications for the success of the technologies we are attempting to develop.

In this brief essay, we wish to explore a few aspects of the organisation of collaborative work in a real world setting, namely the dealing room of an international securities house in the City of London. By examining the ways in which dealers coordinate their actions with colleagues and participate in each other's conduct, we wish to provide a sense of the delicacy and complexity of collaborative work, and show how apparently individual tasks are systematically, yet unobtrusively, coordinated with the actions of colleagues. In the light of these observations, we will consider not only the relevance of proposed technological support for market trading, but also discuss their more general implications for the design of systems to support cooperative work.

2. The Setting

There are many different types of trading that take place on dealing room floors, for example, there are markets in foreign exchange, bonds and derivatives ('forwards', 'futures' and options), and combinations of these vary from one dealing floor to another. However, much of this trading tends to focus around the notion of making 'deals' that is, the buying and selling of shares and bonds in order to make a profit.

Our study focuses on market makers on the equities desk of one dealing floor of a securities house, who deal in stocks on both the US and UK markets. These dealers have a continuous responsibility to buy shares at their published bid price or to sell shares at their offered price, whether or not they actually hold the shares. In this way market makers make a profit on the difference between the prices at which they buy and those at which they sell.

Our study is gathering materials from the 'number one' position on the equities desk which deals in the top ten stocks (for example, Hanson, ICI and Wellcome). Dealers currently work the stock collaboratively, and at present, this position is managed by two dealers; one (John) being mainly responsible for dealing in registered stocks, those which are listed on the UK Stock Exchange, and the other (Robert) for American Depository Receipts (ADR's), which are certificates traded in the US backed by registered holdings of shares in UK companies. As these dealers can effectively trade and hold stock in both sterling and dollars, they have to keep track of changes in the exchange rate and the current state of both markets. They also must ensure that the bank has enough of the appropriate currency to cover any deals done in ADR's (figure 1 is a rough plan of the local area of the dealing room where John and Robert are located).

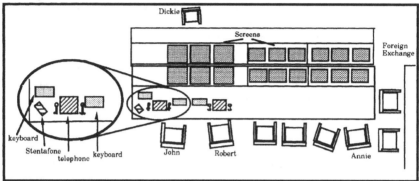

Figure 1. The 'number one' desk in the dealing room

Primarily, dealing in shares takes place over the telephone between different market makers' dealing rooms. But other deals occur within the dealing room either through the stentafone (an intercom system), face-to-face or shouted across the dealing floor and usually occur between market makers and salespeople with or without consulting foreign currency dealers. Dealers have a range of technology to assist them in understanding the current state of the market. Figure 2 is a diagram of the displays for various systems that John and Robert have available to them.

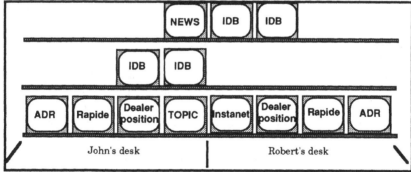

Figure 2. The displays available to the 'number one' desk

These systems include: TOPIC, for screen based price and market news; Instanet for American wide information on stocks and prices; IDB systems which provide a facility for displaying anonymous prices from Inter-dealer brokers (i.e. Cedar Street Ltd, Tullet and Tokyo, Garban Equities and First Equity); and Rapide, the security house's own system which, by presenting a restricted amount of information, allows dealers to see 'at a glance' which competing market makers are 'on the strip', that is, offering the best prices on a particular stock. This is also the only system, on which dealers can input information, enabling them to change their bid and offer prices on stock according to the current state of the market. ADR screens show the equivalent information on ADR's along with conversions from registered stocks to ADR's. Finally, each dealer has a screen which displays their current position, that is, the dealer's current holdings in stocks in which they are dealing. Thus, from all these resources, dealers must be able to discriminate what is relevant for them in order to make a deal.

After a deal is made, whether through the telephone to another market-maker or within the dealing room itself, it is required to be recorded and transferred to the Stock Exchange centralised database. As at peak times a dealer may make deals anywhere from every five to thirty seconds, great effort is spent in ensuring that these records are accurate. At present, this activity, called 'deal capture' is done on 'tickets'. Each dealer has a book which holds the tickets on which he or she writes a record of the deal. The ticket itself is then removed from the book and picked up by 'deal input' staff.

3. Coordinating collaboration with activity completion

Each dealer is responsible for a number of stocks or ADR's and is accountable for the profits and losses made through their sale or purchase. So, whilst dealers need to remain aware of the work of their colleagues, they frequently make deals themselves without direct reference to others within the local milieu. Within the dealing room, we do find instances of the forms of sequential, collaborative activity one finds in other settings, such as Control Rooms, medical consultations or more conventional office environments. In these cases, the activity of one individual, is coordinated with the completion of the activity of another, so that we can find sequences or trajectories of conduct which allow separate individuals within a relatively circumscribed division of labour, accomplishing collaboratively, step by step, a particular task or activity. In general, the form of collaborative activity supported by many CSCW applications, is designed to support this cumulative, sequential collaboration, characteristic of many organisational settings.

Whilst such sequential collaboration is perhaps less prominent within the dealing room than within the other environments, at least between dealers themselves, we do find that individuals frequently orient to the potential completion of a colleague's activity, prior to initiating collaboration. Their reluctance to 'interrupt' an activity of a colleague is hardly surprising, not simply because it might infringe conventional etiquette, but by virtue of the fact that to some extent a colleague's current activity is only partially 'visible' or available to others, even within the local vicinity. The relative inaccessibility of many of the activities of one's colleagues within the local milieu, especially those undertaken on the telephone, coupled with one's inability to access the relative importance of particular actions, however seemingly trivial, encourage personnel to be sensitive to when and where they should attempt to initiate collaboration. Notwithstanding the etiquette in question, it is likely that an individual will stand a far greater chance of establishing mutually focused collaboration with a colleague, if he coordinates his initiating action with the completion of an activity in which the other has been involved.

So for example, in each of the following instances, a dealer produces an utterance which demands a reply from a colleague, just as the other completes an activity.

Fragment 1. 14:40:47

```
      R:     Thanks very mu:ch.{on the 'phone}
             (2.3) {R replaces receiver on console}
  →   J:     Do you want to take the B.P. in New York?
      (R):   Yes:::
      J:     An then run em up (.) a bit.
```

Fragment 2 14:27:26

```
      R:     DICKIE:{outloud, having taken an incoming call}
             (1.2)
      R:     Cedar Street
             (2.2) {R replaces receiver on console}
  →   H:     I've put some Shell (an) sell at fifty six and three
             quarters...
```

Fragment 3 14:24:02

```
      R:     {Lifts hand from keyboard and flicks calculator to
             one side}
  →   J:     Wh-what are Hansons, they're twenty: o five offered?
             (0.4)
      R:     Yeah.
             (0.2)
      J:     Ninety two o five I'd say.{picks up 'phone}
```

In fragment 1, John initiates a query concerning whether they should buy B.P. shares which immediately develops into buying stock on the New York Market. In the second instance, Robert tells Dickie that Cedar Street (an Inter-Dealer Broker) is on the phone and then replaces his receiver. Harold then turns and informs Robert that he has put out some Shell for sale. Harold then proceeds to detail the various shares and their prices that he has put out on the New York Market. In fragment 3, John asks a question concerning the price of Hanson, precisely at the point at which Robert marks the completion of typing with an exaggerated press of the key and the movement of his calculator to one side.

In each instance a dealer successfully initiates collaboration with a colleague by producing an utterance, such as a query or an informing, as his colleague completes an activity in which he has been engaged. By positioning the utterance in this way, dealers not only preserve the integrity of the activities in which their colleagues may be engaged, avoiding interrupting a potentially important business which is being undertaken, but also initiate collaboration at a juncture at which they are more likely secure the cooperation of colleagues.

4. Monitoring potential boundaries within a colleague's activities

In the instances mentioned above, the initiation of collaboration by a colleague is coordinated with relatively gross, visible features of a co-participant's conduct, such as closing a telephone conversation, or removing one's hands from a keyboard. Even so, it is interesting to note that in these and other cases, a dealer does not necessarily have to wait for actual completion of the activity before successfully initiating mutual engagement with a colleague. In the cases at hand, a colleague can be aware of the upcoming completion of a particular activity, even before the last few moves are actually accomplished. On a telephone call for example, well before the actual receiver is placed on the console, a colleague can monitor the talk and know, unambiguously, that it is drawing to completion. More interesting perhaps, individuals can assess a physical action or activity undertaken by another, within the course of its production, and prospectively envisage its completion. So for example, it is not unusual in the dealing room for individuals to time, with precision, an utterance which engenders collaboration, so that it coincides with a colleague finishing writing out a ticket or swallowing a mouthful of lunch. By monitoring the course of action in this way and by prospectively identifying its upcoming boundaries, individuals can successfully initiate collaboration so that it does not interrupt an activity in which a colleague is engaged.

In these instances, an individual initiates one activity immediately following the potential completion of another. In some cases, the subsequent activity is relevant to the prior, and is directed towards the accomplishment of a task, such as collaboratively selling some stock. In other cases, the activity is juxtaposed with the prior, simply to avoid interrupting an action in which a colleague is engaged. Either way, we find that individual tasks are temporally coordinated, activity by activity. However, collaboration within the dealing room often involves the mutual overlapping of multiple activities, where a dealer will not await the completion of an activity prior to initiating collaboration, but interject an utterance at a 'natural juncture' within the course of the activity. Consider, for example, the following instance in which Robert positions an utterance at a potential boundary point within the developing course of one of Harold's current activities.

Fragment 4   14:26:07

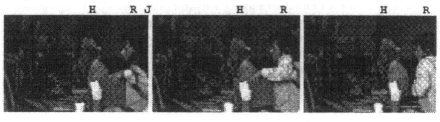

```
H: {Writing notes}

                              R: Things: like Han:son
                              Trust ┌Har old we want
                                    └
                              H:     Errrr
                                    R: ou:t there:,
                                       (1.0)
                                    R: I wan:t ter::
                                       (.) B.P. out
                                       there,
```

Harold is waiting for someone to answer a call. Whilst he waits he is making some notes on a piece of paper. He momentarily lifts his pen from paper, not so much completing the activity, but beginning a new line or section. As his hand breaks from the trajectory of writing, Robert produces an utterance which mentions the sorts of things that his colleague should be 'putting out' in New York. Harold briefly orients towards Robert while the initial part of the utterance is being delivered, and then turns away, producing a loud "Errrr" into the mouthpiece of the telephone, as if both to display to Robert that he is engaged on the telephone and simultaneously to respond to the caller. Despite his colleague's seeming difficulty in participating in the talk, Robert continues to list relevant stocks.

It is worth noting that in this case, Robert's interjection is not so much attempting to initiate a new activity between himself and Harold, but rather contributing to an activity in which he and his colleague are engaged and which has been the subject of an earlier discussion. The delicate design of Robert's utterance(s) does not demand mutually focused engagement and talk, but rather preserves Harold's primary commitment to the telephone conversation, whilst providing some potentially relevant information. The utterance(s) exploits Harold's ability to be participate in one activity, whilst 'peripherally monitoring' another.

5. Stepwise progression into collaborative activity

Whilst dealers may successfully initiate collaborative activity by coordinating an utterance with the completion of, or a boundary within, a colleague's activity, in many instances the actual initiation of mutual engagement is foreshadowed by non-verbal, or better, non-vocal behaviour through which the participants progressively enter into collaboration. In the following instance, Robert's utterance, through which he initiates a discussion concerning stocks they are trying to purchase, is immediately preceded by his turning from the right hand side of his desk towards a monitor on the nearside of his colleague's desk. As he appears to complete the turn, John who is sitting on his left, turns and appears to look at the same monitor (picture 5.2). The moment John begins to realign his gaze, Robert moves posturally and facially so that his bodily orientation, as well as his gaze is in parallel with his colleague.

Fragment 5   14:42:48

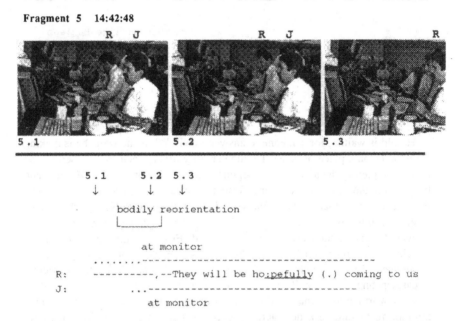

```
             5.1      5.2 5.3
              ↓        ↓   ↓
           bodily reorientation
           L_____J

                   at monitor
      . . . . . . . _____
 R:        ----------,--They will be ho:pefully (.) coming to us
 J:             . . . _____
                   at monitor
```

John's response to the initial realignment of gaze, and in particular his turning towards the same focal point, appears to encourage Robert to align himself further with John (picture 5.3), and provide an environment for the delivery of the utterance. By placing himself alongside his colleague and adopting a parallel alignment towards the same focal point, Robert builds an environment of mutual orientation which may not simply provide a mutually established display of commitment to collaboration prior to the delivery of the initiating utterance, but actually inform both the design and interpretation of the utterance. It may be the case that the pronoun "they" invokes and refers to an object at which they are simultaneously looking; namely a bid which they have submitted for a particular stock that is being displayed on the monitor.

In eliciting a realignment of gaze from John towards the 'relevant' focal domain, Robert secures his cooperation to enter into mutually focused collaboration, prior to the delivery of the initiating utterance.

Unlike face to face interaction, where participants successively establish a bodily framework in which they are physically oriented towards each other in the dealing room, mutually focused activity is often foreshadowed by one individual bringing his visual and bodily alignment in parallel with a colleague and in particular orientating towards the focal area of the other's attention. Dealers, in initiating collaboration, rarely turn and directly look at the other as one might in face to face interaction, to do so would demand rather than encourage co-participation; (cf. Heath 1986). Rather by looking into the physical domain of a colleague, and aligning towards the objects and artefacts of their attention (the focal point(s) of their activity), dealers display their orientation to their colleague's activity, and preserve the integrity of the other's conduct. It allows a dealer to discern more accurately when it might be opportune to initiate collaboration and have the other see that their current activity is being attended to, but does demand the immediate involvement of the other. Such monitoring is potentially accountable, and the initiation itself, reflexively provides an explanation for the attention the other's activity is receiving. The ability to exploit a look, particularly aligning towards the focal object of another's activity to foreshadow mutual engagement, necessarily relies upon the participant's orientation within the dealing room to specific physical areas, monitors, and artefacts, belonging to particular individuals. The glance at the monitor, for example, is accountable by virtue of it not simply being the focal area of a current activity, but by being located within the immediate horizon of a colleague's work domain. The spatial distribution of personal work domains within the dealing room is momentarily exploited for the purpose of initiating collaboration.

6. Outlouds and recipient sensitivity

The data begin to suggest therefore, that though dealers may be engaged in a particular, individual, task they remain sensitive to the conduct of colleagues and the possibility of collaboration. As in other settings, such as London Underground Control Rooms (Heath and Luff 1992) and Air Traffic Control (Harper et al. 1991), individuals appear to remain sensitive to, and monitor, activities within the local milieu, whilst participating in relatively distinct activities and tasks. 'Peripheral' monitoring or participation, appears to be an essential feature of both individual and collaborative work within these environments.

The ability of dealers to remain sensitive to goings on within the local milieu whilst engaged in particular tasks also forms the foundation to the delivery and receipt of more general information within the dealing room; information which can serve to encourage focused collaboration between dealers.

Prior to the large-scale introduction of new technologies into stock exchange dealing rooms, dealing took place on an open floor. This 'open cry' aspect of floor trading and recent representations of trading rooms on film and television suggests an image of dealers in a continual state of over excitement, shouting figures and stocks at each other in order to secure deals. Whilst this image reflects only short periods of activity, a visitor to a dealing room is immediately struck by the trader's practice, when necessary, of shouting names and calling numbers without either waiting for, or apparently expecting, a reply. In many cases, as in fragment 2, "DICKIE: (1.2) <u>Cedar Street</u>", names are shouted across the floor to have a trader answer a call which has been taken by a colleague at another desk. Whilst such information may be relevant for others who overhear the shouting, in large part, such public utterances are simply to have another take a telephone call. Other sorts of information which are shouted across the trading room floor are of more general relevance, and may be heard and acted upon by one or more dealers. These 'outlouds' are not necessarily, indeed rarely, designed for any particular dealer, but are available for and likely to be picked out by, any trader, who at that moment has, or can generate an interest in using the information. Such 'outlouds' can engender collaboration, and can lead, as in the following example, to traders deciding on whether they should buy or sell particular stocks.

Fragment 6 14:29:10

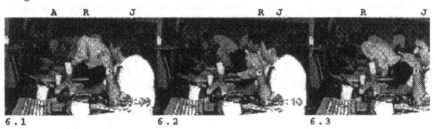

6.1   6.2   6.3

```
A: HAN:SON. TWENTY OF AN
   EIGHTH, FORTY BY
   FIFTEEN:, (SHEARSON)
   ON THE BI:D
R: ((Sitting down))
   (0.2)
                     J: Are we going to hit
                        'em?
                        (2.3)
                     R: ((Peers at screen))
                     R: Erm::^ (.) YES::,
                                        R: (0.9) WHO'S: THAT
                                           (1.0)
                                        R: Bernie? ((Picks ι
                                           phone))
                                           (3.0)
                                        R: We want to sell
                                           (forty:) .......
```

In fragment 6, Annie who is sitting at one end of the ADR desk, shouts across the room that Shearson is on the bid (picture 6.1). Robert is in the process of sitting down and makes no indication that he has heard the utterance. As Robert lands in his chair, John turns momentarily towards his domain and asks whether they should try to 'hit the bid' (i.e. sell Hanson shares - picture 6.2). John's question assumes that Robert has both heard the utterance and may be prepared to collaborate in selling the stock. The utterance appeals to, and invokes a mutual orientation towards, selling stock and initiates collaboration with John. A second or so later, Robert grabs the telephone and shouts to Annie, asking who is actually on the phone (picture 6.3). A little later a substantial amount of stock is sold.

Whilst Annie's utterance is shouted outloud, as if potentially relevant for anyone within the local vicinity, it is perhaps only two or three traders who might have an interest in the information. Shouting outloud, rather than specifically telling certain colleagues, is not only a relatively economic way of informing a number of recipients, but also delivers the information in a way that does not necessarily demand that anyone responds. So, whilst shouting across the room might be thought relatively incursive, potentially interrupting activities being undertaken by various traders in the room, it is perhaps less obtrusive than actually informing specific recipients. Annie's utterance does not demand that anyone respond; it allows them to overhear and receive the information without necessarily abandoning the activity in which they are currently engaged. It also provides a basis for collaboration, since one dealer, like John, can presuppose that others for whom the information might be potentially relevant will have heard the utterance.

Many 'outlouds' within the dealing room have this sort of character. They are designed to have a number of potential recipients hear the information, without demanding that all, or even any, of them actually respond. Even at the more local level, we find dealers delicately designing particular talk, including utterances which 'on the surface' are addressed to a particular recipient, to encourage another also to participate in the activity, if he or she so desires.

7. Individual and Collaborative Conduct

Within a working environment such as a dealing room therefore, as within other organisational settings, we can see the ways in which collaboration, as a delimited form of cooperative work, is simply a gloss to capture a complex configuration of momentary arrangements through which two or more individuals, sequentially or simultaneously participate in particular tasks or activities. Not only is collaboration initiated through a variety of interactional procedures and practices, but the form of cooperation which actually arises, is contingent and continually subject to rearrangement and reorganisation as it emerges step by step, within the activity(ies) in which the participants are engaged. Moreover, to characterise the cooperative arrangement of the number one position on the equities desk as a 'group', provides no firm anchor with which to secure a technologically relevant description. Even a prief glance at the domain reveals that the various tasks rely upon an socio-interactional organisation allowing dealers to co-produce, and co-participate in, particular activities in highly variable and contingent ways.

The analysis above has not only revealed the complex set of arrangements which might reasonably constitute 'collaboration' within the environment, but also the difficulties of demarcating individual activities or tasks. For example, we find that whilst a dealer may be engaged in an apparently individual task such as making a deal, he will simultaneously monitor the local environment, including the activities of colleagues and the changes to his own computer screens and to those of others. Moreover, his production of the tasks or activities in which he is engaged is sensitive to the concurrent activities of colleagues, and may be altered, during the course of their production, in the light of some information he receives or overhears. Such 'peripheral monitoring' is an integral feature of the proper accomplishment of tasks within the dealing room, and dealers would be called to account if they failed to follow the array of concurrent 'goings on' within the local milieu. Indeed, a missed remark, an undetected screen change, or even an unnoticed sale or purchase by a colleague, can, during the course of deal, greatly effect a dealer's position in the market and have costly results for the bank. Individual work within the dealing room, relies upon a dealer's ability to monitor the action of his colleagues and changes within the local environment, even though he may be engaged in a potentially unrelated activity.

Dealers, however, are not simply expected to remain sensitive to the local environment of action and to discriminate what may, or may not, be relevant. Rather, work within the dealing room demands that whilst they are engaged in one activity they may have to participate simultaneously in the activities of colleagues. So, for example, we find dealers who are apparently engaged on the telephone, making recommendations to a colleague as to what he should buy or sell. Indeed, a dealer may design a single utterance in such a way that it not only secures a sale on the telephone, but simultaneously publicises the purchase within the dealing room itself, encouraging a colleague to make the necessary currency arrangements. More complex still, are the ways in which dealers simultaneously sustain and participate in multiple activities with their colleagues, so that a number of deals will be built alongside each other, and at the right moment, a substantial amount of stock will be sold as it is being purchased, maximising profit and keeping the books balanced. Within the dealing room therefore, we not only find a myriad of ways in which dealers collaborate with their colleagues, but it is difficult, if not impossible, to delineate the 'individual' from the 'collaborative', since personnel are continually participating in multiple activities which more or less involve their colleagues, and are produced with respect to the emergent conduct of others.

Through an examination of collaborative activity in the dealing room we have begun to reveal in more detail the nature of these forms of collaboration and the ways in which individuals move into and achieve collaborative activities. Ever from this preliminary analysis it appears that the conventional distinction between 'individual' and 'collaborative' work requires further refinement, and it may be that such relatively restrictive conceptions of work have confined the nature of the technology that has been intended to support it. Furthermore, unpacking the notion of 'collaboration' may have implications for the design of technology that is not normally conceived of as being intended to support the work of several individuals. This respecification has consequences not only for technologies to support activities in the dealing room, but also for computer systems to support 'collaborative work' in general.

8. Collaboration and Technological Innovation

The technological failure of certain systems for dealing rooms has been one of the motivations for suggesting 'radical' alternatives for transforming the work of dealers. For example, it has been claimed that as the process of writing 'tickets' to record deals is time-consuming and prone to error, computational technology could be developed to automate the process known as 'deal capture'. Particular suggestions to support this process have included the addition of headphones to current systems, the use of touch screens to input the details of transactions and voice recognition technology to record the deal directly from the dealers' phone conversations (e.g. Howells and Crowley-Clough 1991). The analysis above may reveal why some of these solutions have encountered difficulties in their design and introduction into the workplace. For example, touch screens, not only reduce the visibility of particular items from the dealer who is using them, but also the dealer's 'interaction' with the screen may become too undifferentiated, making it difficult for others to identify boundaries and thereby coordinate their own activities. Similarly, headphones introduced to eliminate the 'negative effects' of noise, impede the dealer's ability to monitor for junctures in a colleague's activities and, more importantly, restrict the dealer's sensitivity to potentially relevant utterances, such as outlouds. At present, activities such as ripping a ticket from the book and placing it in a pot are often utilised as a display of 'completing a deal' and recognised as such by others for assessing a dealer's engagement in his or her work. Such activities have been viewed as archaic by some system designers and are obviated by automating the entire process of deal capture through the use of voice recognition technology. However, these innovations may also reduce the opportunities for dealers to monitor potential boundaries within a colleague's activities and thus hinder the stepwise transition into more focused collaborative work.

It is interesting to note that many of the justifications for the use of voice recognition systems in this domain arise from the constraints of the current state of the technology. It has been argued the limitations on the size of the vocabulary that such systems are able to recognise is matched by the limited amount of information that the system needs to record and the small number of words and jargon that dealers use (e.g. thirty words plus numbers). In addition, the predominant use of the phone for dealing and the apparent limited movement of dealers around their local environment should make it possible to train these systems on individual dealer's voices using specific phones. However, even preliminary observations of the materials gathered from dealing rooms shows that these assumptions appear to be optimistic and to overlook the interactional and collaborative nature of dealing. In particular, dealers' vocabulary does not appear to be as restricted as originally envisaged, but more importantly dealers make sense of the details of transactions, without necessarily making them explicit, by utilising a range of resources which include: the information on the screens in front of them; news broadcasts and outlouds occurring in the local environment; and their co-participants' contributions to deals on the phone. Furthermore, deals are also made over the stentafone and across the floor; dealers 'cover' for each other often when just passing by an empty desk; and deals are collaboratively achieved not just between buyer and seller but also co-produced between dealers (see Jirotka et al. 1993).

An alternative focus for the design of deal capture systems may be to consider supporting the interactional nature of the activities. Thus, for example pen-based, 'mobile' systems with 'gestural interfaces' may allow deals to be recorded while preserving opportunities for others, non-intrusively, to monitor the activity for potential boundaries and make use of these to initiate more focused collaboration. One suggestion may be actually to design 'gestures' that make particular activities on the screen available or visible to others in the local environment, for example, it has been proposed that the gesture required for completing a transaction could be an exaggerated 'sweeping' gesture similar to 'ripping off' a ticket from the book. Whether such developments are considered as 'conservative', by attempting to maintain existing work practices, or as 'innovative' because they utilise novel technological devices, both adopt 'radical' ways of reconceiving the relationship between participants in the workplace and their interactions with and through technology.

Such an orientation to the design for systems to support collaborative work in the dealing room may also have implications for other, more conventional 'technologies' in the setting. For example, at present, the loudspeakers attached to the telephone and other audio devices are designed for individual use. Considering the ways in which others overhear and monitor deals undertaken using this technology, may inform ways of redesigning or reorienting the audio devices that allow for multiple forms of participation in such activities (cf. Gaver 1991). Similarly, the design and positioning of the various monitors are organised around the desks of individual dealers, and yet the instances above reveal how dealers make use of another's displays in order to move progressively towards more focused collaboration. The space surrounding the participants, and the configuration and design of technology used within it, could be reconsidered to take into account how dealers make use of particular 'domains of interest'.

Analysis of the ways in which dealers coordinate their actions with colleagues and participate in each other's conduct may also have implications for the design of systems to support collaborative work in general. For example, the development of systems to support shared editing, shared drawing and other focused activities has led to a range of possible solutions to the problem of 'floor control', including particular users being able to take pre-emptive control of devices, waiting for pauses in activities or in queues, and having and open and free floor (Greenberg 1991). In addition, there has been recent emphasis on supporting the 'seamless' movement from individual to collaborative activity (Ishii 1990). However, even these notions appear too restrictive when we consider the delicate ways in real world settings in which individuals move into focused activities, are sensitive to the activities of others and the range of ways co-participants engage in collaborative work. For example, we have revealed how a dealer can monitor a range of activities performed by a colleague, such as their use of a keyboard or a calculator, for boundaries in which to initiate more focused, collaborative work.

In this environment as in others, we find that the use of computer systems which were primarily designed to support 'single users' undertaking individual tasks, is embedded in the users' 'ongoing' interaction with colleagues within the local milieu. Indeed, the system, and the visibility of its use, provides an essential resource in the co-production and collaborative organisation of seemingly individual tasks. Although, some recent research has begun to investigate technological support for such aspects of collaborative work, even when the co-participants are physically distributed (e.g. Ishii et al. 1992, Gaver et al. 1993), it would be unfortunate if the emergence of CSCW detracted attention away from the collaborative organisation of many individual tasks. It may well be important for the development of suitable systems to design particular tools to support the more tacit, yet nonetheless essential, interactional practices which underpin the use of systems by single users in settings not conventionally seen as relevant to CSCW. However, when considering the methods, techniques and representations developed in HCI, it is perhaps not surprising that such aspects have also been overlooked for 'single-user' systems. For example, the concept of 'task' in task analyses is often restricted to work undertaken by an 'individual' and the particular representations utilised seem to impose a structuring which fails to account for the interactional and interleaved nature of activities in real world settings.

It may be the case, that we not only need to learn more about the social organisation of collaboration in order to develop requirements for systems to support cooperative work, but that it might be useful to reconsider some of the basic presuppositions which underlie empirical research and technological design in HCI. Indeed, we are beginning to respecify some of the key concepts, such as 'task', 'user', 'collaboration' and 'information' that inform many current methods and techniques for the analysis of requirements and system design.

Acknowledgements

We are grateful to Joseph Goguen, Matthew Bickerton and others members of the Centre for Requirements and Foundations at the University of Oxford for discussions relating to the issues raised in this paper. We would also to thank Graham Button, David Greatbatch and Eric Livingston for helpful comments concerning the dealing room materials. The work reported in this paper is jointly supported by BT, EuroPARC and the EC RACE MITS Project. Finally, we are indebted to the individual dealers and management in the trading room for all their kindness and patience while we were undertaking this study.

References

Galegher, J. and Kraut, R. E. (1990): "Technology for Intellectual Teamwork: Perspectives on Research and Design", in J. Galegher, R. E. Kraut, and C. Egido (eds):*Intellectual Teamwork*, Lawrence Erlbaum Associates, Hillsdale, New Jersey, pp.1-20.

Gaver, W. W. (1991): "Sound Support for Collaboration", in *Proceedings of E-CSCW 1991*, Amsterdam, 1991. pp. 293-324.

Gaver, W. W., Sellen, A., Heath, C. C. and Luff, P. (1993): "One is not enough: Multiple Views in a Media Space", in*Proceedings of INTERCHI '93*, Amsterdam, Apr. 24-29.

Greenberg, S. (1991): "Personalisable Groupware: Accommodating Individual Roles and Group Differences" in *Proceedings of the ECSCW '91*, Amsterdam, 1991. pp. 17-32.

Grudin, J., (1988): "Why CSCW Applications Fail: Problems in the Design and Evaluation of Organizational Interfaces" in *Proceedings of CSCW '88*, 26th-28th Sept., Portland, Oregon, pp. 85-93.

Harper, R., Hughes, J. and Shapiro, D. (1991): "Harmonious Working and CSCW: Computer Technology and Air Traffic Control," in J. Bowers and S. D Benford (eds.): *Studies in CSCW. Theory, Practice and Design*, North-Holland, Amsterdam.

Heath, C.C. (1986): *Body movement and speech in medical interaction*, Cambridge University Press, Cambridge.

Heath, C. C. and Luff. P (1992): "Collaboration and control: Crisis Management and Multimedia Technology in London Underground Line Control Rooms", *Computer Supported Cooperative Work*, Vol. 1, Nos. 1-2, pp. 69-94.

Howells, P. and Crowley-Clough, J. (1991): "Practical Applications of Voice Data Capture in Trading Environments" paper Prepared for *Computers in The City*, London, 12-13 Nov. 1991.

Ishii, H. (1990): "TeamWorkStation: Towards a Seamless Shared Workspace", in *Proceedings of CSCW '90*, Los Angeles, 1990. pp. 13-26.

Ishii, H., Kobayashi, M. and Grudin, J. (1992): "Integration of Inter-Personal Space and Shared Workspace: Clearboard Design and Experiments", in *Proceedings of CSCW 92*. Toronto, Oct. 31 - Nov. 4, pp. 33-42.

Jirotka, M., Luff, P. and Heath, C, C. (1993 a): "Requirements Engineering and Interactions in the Workplace: a case study in City dealing rooms" in *Proceedings of the Workshop on Social Science, Technical Systems and Cooperative Work*, CNRS Paris, March 8-10.

Orlikowski, W. J. (1992): "Learning from Notes: Organizational Issues in Groupware Implementation", in *Proceedings of CSCW 92*, Toronto, Oct. 31-Nov. 4, pp. 362-369.

Schmidt, K. and Bannon, L. (1992): "Taking CSCW Seriously Supporting Articulation Work", *Computer Supported Cooperative Work*, Vol. 1, Nos. 1-2, pp. 7-40.

Proceedings of the Third European Conference on Computer-Supported Cooperative Work
13-17 September, 1993, Milan, Italy
G. De Michelis, C. Simone and K. Schmidt (Editors)

Analyzing Cooperative Work in an Urban Traffic Control Room for the Design of a Coordination Support System.

Geneviève Filippi   Jacques Theureau
France

Abstract: A recent approach to computer technology aims the design of support systems as opposed to tools conceived as prostheses. However, most studies developping this new design paradigm consider the interaction between a stand-alone user and his technological environment. Focussing on an Urban Traffic Control Room, we explicate how work analysis should take into account the course of action of individuals and their interrelation. The design proposal sketched in this paper illustrates how a *coordination support system* should be capable of simultaneously supporting individual and cooperative work to meet the needs of complex and crisis-prone work situation.

Introduction

Recent advances in computerizing of work environments renew the methodological and theoretical issues traditionnally treated by ergonomics in French-speaking countries. The design of these situations must take into account the technical environment as a whole, i.e. not only the computer system but also other sources of information on the situation, communication devices, documentation, organization and training. Similarly, while ergonomic design was mainly concerned by the individuals up to now, the need to study work environments in all its complexity leads to studies taking into account cooperative work.

The investigation which we will be discussing here is part of a programme aimed at the design of computer systems in terms of *support systems for users.* Since Norman (1986) showed the need to develop a "user centered system design", many authors (Pinsky &Theureau, 1987; De Keyser 1988; Falzon 1989;

Haradji 1993) agree that the success of the introduction of an expert system depends on its capability to provide good advice rather than technological capacity to solve a problem.

Most computer systems are designed as "cognitive prostheses" (Woods & Roth, 1988; Visetti,), insofar as they are supposed to concentrate the intelligence of experts. The user is considered as the system's "servant": he supplies data which the computer system is unable to acquire in other ways and he is supposed to follow the system's instructions. However when the system fails, the user must manage on his own. Paradoxically, the user is assigned a passive role under ordinary circumstances, whereas he is suddenly called upon to play the role of a super-expert in troubleshooting circumstances, where he has to actively contribute to a diagnosis process. An alternative approach is to consider computer technology as support system helping the user increase his understanding of the situation while letting him manage by himself the problem solving process.

In order to actually support activity in complex process control settings, the developments of technology must take into account the preponderance of the cooperative aspects of work. This paper shows how the analysis of a particular cooperative setting, a Paris underground Control Room, orients the design of devices supporting both individual and collective activity.

Background of the study

This investigation is part of a wider research[1] which links public announcement to the analysis of traffic control in order to study the complete chain of traffic supervision, starting from the Control Room and ending up with the passenger.

It concerned the Control Room of the RER[2] A line which was, at the time of the study, undergoing important changes. On the one hand, computerization was progressing: it concerned the rolling stock follow up, new functions of signalling and automatic calculation of train delays at each station. On the other hand, the Control Room was moving to a larger room because of the line's extension towards Eurodisneyland, which was the occasion to modify it's general layout.

With 70 000 passengers per hour at peak hours, the RER A Line has one of the world's heaviest trafic density in urban rail transport. It's operating is relatively complicated because of two forks at both ends of the line and of it's connexion with the French railway company (SNCF) and the two different kind of rolling stock incompatible with each other it entails. Every train is identified by a name which indicates its itinerary (such as NAGA 12).

---

[1] M. Grosjean and I. Joseph studied other aspects of this work setting.

[2] The Reseau Express Regional is a high speed suburban branch of the Paris metro

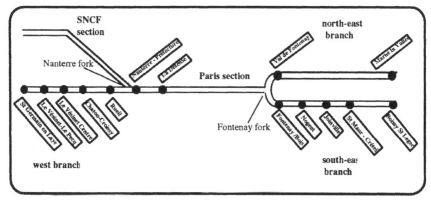

Figure 1: The RER A Line

Technical facilities available in the Control Room have been added gradually with traffic growth and were not designed as a coherent apparatus. This includes means of communication (telephone and radio), a *fix-line diagram* representing traffic movement in real-time, *computer consoles* showing the same kind of information but in greater detail, and working documents, including the *graph of train movements*, the duty roster for drivers, etc.

Controlling the RER's traffic is a collective activity which involves about a dozen operators in the room: a team of three Controllers in charge of the different geographic sectors of the line: West, South-east and North-east., each having two Signal Assistants under their responsability, an Information Assistant and, in the event of disruptions, the managerial staff of the line. (Figure 2) The *Controllers* are responsible for ensuring the smooth running of the trains in case of disruptions (small and moderate disruptions are usual during peak hours), implementing actions to control traffic by taking into account the supervision of drivers, following the rolling stock and handling their entry into the depots (maintenance and repair). The *Signal Assistants* establish the itineraries, check the times the trains passing through their sectors and inform the Controllers of any delays, they control the movement of the rolling stock by carrying out the instructions for the trains to be shunted in or out of the sheds and by keeping an accurate account of the shunting positions. They also check the time-tables posted in the stations and make amendments when necessary.

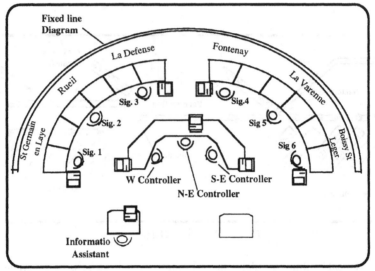

Figure 2: The RER A Line Control Room

We therefore have a work environment with teamwork considered as fundamental, which is immediately reflected by the importance, on the one hand, of the verbal communication between the various Control Room officials, and on the other hand, of the radio and telephone links with persons external to the Control Room, such as train drivers, station masters, depot managers and other operators.

Work analysis to understand activity

Wether one is concerned by its individual aspects or it's collaborative aspects, traffic control is an extremely complex activity. Giving a full account of the entire reality as such would be an utopian view and would turn out to be useless. What knowledge is required to design a good support system? The classic knowledge of "human factors" is useful but insufficient. It consists of generalities on persons divided into segments: cognition (itself divided into planning and problem solving, in turn sub-divided into diagnosis and solution, etc.), action, perception (itself divided into hearing, sight, etc.), reactions to separate elements of the environment (lighting, ventilation, etc.).

To obtain a full view of an actor taken as a whole, one must analyze his global activity in its own specific work situation. For instance, the identification of what should be assisted by computers requires a previous understanding of the activity of users in their non-computerized (or unsatisfactorily computerized assistance) work environnement as well as knowledge on the global activity of users in other similar situations with a more satisfactory computer support.

With the theoretical and methodological framework developped by Pinsky and Theureau (1987) it is possible to approach these global activities by studying the *course of action* of users i.e. to determine what in the activity of one or several actors belonging to a specific culture and engaged in a specific situation, is significant for the latter, i.e. that can be related or commented by him (or them) at any moment..

Activity in work situation is creative and is continuously constructed anew: a person's action is not merely a response to the constraints of the environment. Likewise, no action is completely isolated from other actions, but is incuded in groups of actions or units which are organised in a way that is meaningful to the actor.

The study of the course of action produces two kinds of descriptions: the first one concerns the *intrinsic organization of activity*, i.e. the description of action and communication here and now representing an inside view of cognition; the second one shows how the work environnement (procedures, rules, etc..) and the actor's culture (training, past experiences) are *extrinsic constraints* to his activity. Analyzing an actor's behavior only the basis of the extrinsic description, in other words on the basis of what we, observers, see of the situation, we are liable to attribute improperly to an actor an organization of processes which does not belong to him, for instance in terms of deviation from what we, observers, consider as being required by the situation. As in fact demonstrated by various ergonomic studies (Montmollin, 1972), the identification of an actor's "abilities" outside his work activity is limited and leads to scientific errors with negative practical consequences. To show an "error" in reasonning is useless if we don't know the cognitif process of production of this error.

Studying the course of action helps consider essential issues for the design of computerizedwork settings but it is not sufficient for the understanding of cooperative work environments which requires complementary contributions of other theories.

Analyzing cooperative work

Distributed cognition and analysis of human interaction

There is a recent trend in micro-sociology and andthropology to study the collaborative aspects of working with computer environments. One approach consists in considering the group, rather than individuals, as the unit of analysis, that is to say, a functional cultural unit. Thus, to describe how the crew of a large ship "fixes" it's position, or how pilots xxxxan aircraft, Hutchins (1988) traces the movement of information through the joint cognitive system composed of the team and technical artefacts. The notion of "distributed cognition" he proposes offers a promising approach to study large groups, but it deliberately does not cope with the individuals participating to the collective activity.

Another approach is inspired by the detailed analysis of human interactions provided mainly by Goffman's (1974) work and by conversation analysis (Sacks

& all, 1974; Goodwin, 1981). The studies of Suchman (1991) and Goodwin & Goodwin (1991) describing commmunications in an airline operations room or Heath & Luff's study of coordination in London underground control rooms (1991) stress on the construction of context by the partners, the importance of verbal and body language in the coordination between individuals. These investigations, systematizing the use of video recordings as a methodological principle, explore the way participants show one another the meaning of what they are doing or saying. Yet, emphasizing the role of communication as if the whole of cognition was included in the communicative interaction itself may lead, in some cases, to neglect the fact that individuals interact during their global course of action in order to acheive specific objectives constrained by the work environnement. This may explain that most of these researches tend to focus only on relatively short periods of interaction (about 5 mn), leaving aside the global dynamics of longer and more complex incidents.

The interrelation of courses of action

The study we are presenting here, emphasizing a rather different conceptual point of view, is concerned, on the one hand, with the activity of each individual, and on the other hand, with the collaborative activity itself.

The analysis of individuals brings out the extent of cooperation in terms of a *social course of action:* the action of each person depends on the action of the others, it is linked to and can have a bearing upon that of the others. The analysis of the *interrelation of multiple courses of action* underscores the nature and the components of the coordinated collective activity. This deliberate choice of a simultaneous and integrated approach to the working group and to its indivdual members directly serves the practical ergonomic objective: designing the physical setting of workstations and technical devices to meet both individual and collective working needs.

Thus, as a first stage, we carried out a detailed analysis of the individual activity of the various staff members in the Control Room, mainly Controllers and Signalmen. The purpose was to clearly show the reasoning of each person concerning the activity of traffic control on their line, while seeking to understand what the action of the other means to a given operator. This first stage tackles the collaborative issue through the point of view of each individual.

In a second stage, we have considered collaborative work pratices as such, i.e. as several individual practices which take place simultaneously so as to see how they are linked to each other to constitute a coordinated collective activity whose characteristics were then defined. This second stage takes on collective activity as a whole on its own, i.e. which can not be considered as the mere addition of the individual activities making it up.

However, we are not postulating the primacy of individual on the group, even though we start with the analysis of individuals. But, following methodological considerations, to understand a complex collective work setting such as the metropolitan traffic control room, it is easier to study individual courses of action before dealing with their articulation.

Method of collecting and analyzing data

A specific method was developped to study the course of action to collect in natural situations, the data required for the description of the dynamic organisation of actions and communications, allowing a reconstruction of the operator's reasonning process. The data collected covered:

- *continuous observations* of the behaviour of action and communication in a work situation which consisted of recordings (by tape recorder and video camera), with a wealth of communications completed by notes on the events taken into account by the operator and the actions of the others when related to his course of action;

- different kinds of *instigated verbalizations* from the actors, in particular those arising in self-confrontation interviews: the operator is shown a video recording of his activity and he is asked to comment on very specific aspects of his behaviour. The purpose of such an exchange is not only to obtain a description of the operator's activity from his own point of view, thereby eliminating the risk of the observer making erroneous interpretations, but also to probe more deeply into the problems encountered by the actor..

Two stages of data collection

During the first stage, with a view to analyzing the courses of action of each individual, we made several observations, with a camera focussed on a Controller and a microphone in the middle of the team of Controllers.

Likewise, during the second stage, in order to perceive the synchronic linkage between individual activities, we collected systematic data on "subsets of cooperation":

- three Controllers belonging to the same team who are constantly coordinating their actions in order to control the line's total traffic (Figure 3, subset A),

- a traffic Controller and the Signal assistants of his geographical sector, who have tio work together concerning their part of the line. (Figure 3, subset B),

These observations were made with two video cameras and two tape recorders.

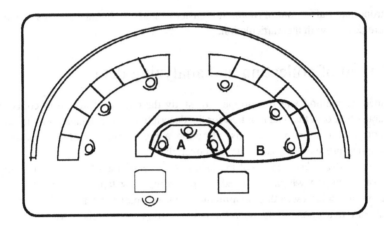

**Figure 3: The subsets of cooperation defined for data collection
on the articulation of courses of action**

Specific methodological aspects

Video recordings

Because of our desire to understand the collective nature of the work, and the complexity of the situation, we had to face specific methodological problems. With respect to the use of the video, the time/space and organizational constraints of the work situation prevented the installation of several cameras which would have produced different kinds of images, such as images focused on the behaviour of the operator, precise images of the contents of the screens and the fix-line diagram, images of the other operators. We therefore chose to install a camera in a fixed position, placed in such a way that its field of vision was a little wider than the post of the person under observation, in order to have data on the interactions with his immediate neighbours while retaining a fairly clear picture of the person himself, as well as an idea of the technical apparatus at his disposal without having the exact content. The data collected with the camera were always completed by the tape recordings described above.

Self- confrontation verbalizations

It should be noted that if in one respect the fundamentally collective nature of work makes the gathering of data more difficult, it is also endowed with a methodological interest for the researcher: in fact, many actions and telephone communications are spontaneously related and justified by the operators for the others who need these for their own courses of action. However,this cannot take the place of self-confrontation vebalizations because these verbal communications only partly give access to the signification of actions and events for the actor:

In the case of the process of complex work, the self-confrontations based on transcriptions, either of an audio tape or a video film, were of definite relevance: the researcher, having himself assimilated the incident during the transcription, had time to spot the critical moments that merited closer questioning. Thus, self-confrontation does not serve principally to create an understanding of the work process for the researcher who is unfamiliar with the situation, this would be lengthy and could tire the operator. In addition, the written transcription gives temporal reference points to the operator during the self-confrontation sessions whereas watching the video tape does not always enable an accurate chronological reconstruction of the actions and events.

Data analysis

The analysis of data in *significant units* for the actor provides a particular description of the incidental situations observed. It is a matter of dividing the continuous development of the course of action into significant units by replying to the question: "What is this about, from the point of view of the controller?" By naming each of these units, an account is built up which gives meaning to the untreated data. This analysis clarifies the temporal organization of the actions and events and provides a few elements on their sequence. Thus, the insertion of significant units reflects work carried out in divided time during which several preoccupations are handled simultaneously by the officials.

Handling disruptions

The detailed analysis of data collected during the first stage gives prominence to the complex planning of their actions by the Controllers, required to handle disruptions in the Control Room's collective context. An important part of the Controller's activity while dealing with an incident consists in *defining the situation as the events occur* rather than finding immediately an adequate solution. Likewise, there is *not one best solution* nor a precise or complete procedure to follow in order to solve an incident, even though there are bits of procedures, most often expressed in the form of safety regulations. Consider the example of the NAGA 12's disrupted situation to understand the individual course of action of Controllers.

NAGA 12 a train running in the direction of Boissy St Leger, breaks down at the exit of Joinville's station stopping all trains eastbound. As soon as the S-E Controller, in charge of the Joinville sector, understands there is a beakdown concerning platform 1, he directs the next train, RUDY 12, onto platform A, letting it wait in the station. The solution viewed by S-E Controller is to ask NAGA 12 to back a hundred meters in order to free the station's exit point (see figure 4). This solution allows trains following behind to pass NAGA 12 by platform A. But its implementation is rather risky because the Controller cannot communicate directly with NAGA 12's driver, who is busy trying to repair his train and is therefore not in the front cabin: the S-E Controller has to pass on his message to RUDY 12's driver.

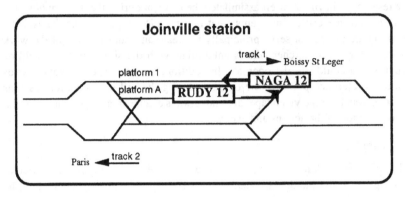

Figure 4: NAGA 12 blocking Joinville's station

Considering the uncertainty of a rapid outcome of this solution, the Controller launches another solution which is more costly to put up insofar as it implies to run trains on the opposite track. But, eventually, NAGA 12's driver succeds in reversing his train and the Controller is able to cancel the second solution.

Once the core of the problem (i.e. NAGA 12 blocking the Joinville station) is solved, the Controller has to deal with the other problems resulting from this disruption such as using RUDY 12 to ensure the rest of NAGA 12's journey up to Boissy St Leger, and also finding replacement trains and standby drivers for the return journey of these two trains.

The *implementation of a decision is gradual and shifted in time*, that is to say that the handling of the incident is dependent upon the time needed to manoeuvre the trains as well as the possibility of communicating with the drivers. In the meantime many other problems have cropped up and some have already been solved.

The relatively long time - about twenty minutes - needed to sort out the breakdown makes it very difficult to turn back once a decision is launched. Consequences of the decision must, therefore, be evaluated in advance. Furthermore, this type of relatively long process time leads to solve overlapping problems: other incidents are tied with that of the NAGA 12 breakdown and must be handled simultaneously.

The analysis of the handling of incidents also reflect the importance of colleagues for each Controller's activity. A *high number of persons involved in an incident* (drivers, station masters, Signalmen, other Controllers) are to be informed. This creates an additional difficulty for planning the actions of the Controller, for he must ensure that everyone has completely understood what it is about and what has to be done.

The coordination of Controllers activities during a disruption

Data on the interrelation of courses of action show *various forms of cooperation* emerging during disrupted situations.

Synchronical interrelating courses of action

While a Controller solves the core of an important incident, the other Controllers and Signal Assistants often carry out secondary jobs to help their colleague, such as holding back, in a station, the trains following behind a defective train to avoid jamming them under a tunnel; or informing station masters of a breakdown; or searching for a line manager to ask him to the train's driver.

They also participate in the background to the solving of an incident by giving advice to their colleague in charge of it and by showing him aspects of the problem he may have overlooked. In this sense, they play a role of guardians of the smooth handling of an incident. When the Controller's attention is focused on a specific problem, the intervention of others makes it possible to "de-focus" on the general context when this is necessary. Or else, when a breakdown occurs at peak hours, the urgent nature of the situation immediately generates an implicit sharing of the work: the Controller concerned by the core of the incident tries to solve it with the driver, while the other Controllers handle the upstream and downstream traffic.

However, when the general situation in the Control Room is too disturbed because of the accumulation of incidents, every body tends to focus on his own problem solving, and nobody can play the role of collective guard anymore. The result is often a lack of coordination in the passing on of information towards colleagues outside the Control Room.

Diachronical interrelating courses of action

Part of the Controllers' competence consists in their ability to actively listen and pay attention to the details of the solving of an incident by their colleagues, to be able to anticipate delays and amendments which they will have on their own sector. The repercussion of the "NAGA 12's brekdown" for the W Controller ilustrates how his courses of action is diachronically linked to the S-E Controller's course of action.

About an hour after the stopping of NAGA 12 in Joinville station, i.e. quite a long time after this incident had been settled by the S-E Controler, a problerm appears concerning track 2 at the other end of the line: three ZHAN (return journey of the RUDY) and three XILO (return journey of the NAGA) are following each other without their usual spacing. The consequences are important for passengers because the XILOs stop in all stations up to Le Pecq whereas the ZHAN are semi-direct to St Germain en Laye. (See Figure 1)

The origin of this erroneous sequence of trains is an error of the Signal Assistant in charge of the Joinville sector who had updated the computer system cancelling RUDY 12's return journey. The many manipulations of trains made by the S-E Controller to make up lost time after NAGA 12's breakdown, and in particular the change of decision concerning ZHAN 23 (the return journey of RUDY 12) which had first been cancelled and eventually had been rescheduled, misled the Signal Assistant.

The W Controller is immediateley able to connect together the sequence of three ZHAN and three XILO with NAGA 12's breakdown which happened an hour earlier, for he had kept up with its management by the S-E Controller, in particular when the latter had found a replacement train for ZHAN 23, which consequently was running behind schedule.

The two logics of work sharing

The sharing of the handling of a disruption between Controllers follows two logics which may be contradictory in certain cases. The *first logic*, which corresponds to the prescribed allocation of roles, is *geographic*: each Controller manages the disruptions occuring in his own sector, even though, the sectors' borders are loose and giving a hand is a tacit rule. The *second logic* which follows the dynamics of train movement postulates that the person who starts handling a disruption is responsible for it during its entire course, because he knows all the surrounding circumstances and the consequences of his own decisions.

The co-existence of theses two logics is implicit to the coordination of the Controller's action, the choice of one or another depends of how each person is involved in the situation: a Controller may make way for his colleagues depending on their receptiveness at the moment and on the fact that they have participated in the background to the beginning of the incident's solving.

In the case of the repercussion of the NAGA 12's breakdown, the Signal Assistant who mixed up the trains is in charge of the junction, which is at the border of the N-E sector and the S-E sector. Following the geographical logic, both Controllers were liable to supervise what was happening at the junction. But, at that time, the N-E Controller happened to be dealing with another incident on the North-east branch and had not paid attention to the details of the arrangement made by his colleague in relation to NAGA 12's return journey. The S-E Controller was busy evacuating the defective NAGA 12 out of Joinville station and he didn't consider there could be a problem for the Signal Assistants to follow through the return journey of the trains.

From this evidence, it is clear that multi-disrupted situations, when Controllers and Signal Assistants are busy with several incidents at the same time, affect functionning of the group because neither of these two logics may be efficiently followed.

Directions for design

To be of real help to the activity of the Control Room staff , modernization of the traffic regulation apparatus must take into account the importance of the collective nature of the job. It is then essential to conceive the whole technical environment of the Control Room as *a support system for the coordination of actions,* even it has not been thought as such. In reality, all the tools used by the staff (the fix-line diagram representing the trains, the paper documents and computer terminal) indirectly support cooperation: each person regularly looks at the fix-line diagram, certain sheets of paper pass from one to person to another, etc.

In this paper, we briefly present one of the proposals for the design of tools supporting coordination we have put forward after the analysis of the interrelation of courses of action during traffic control work. It is a device, to enhance the present computer system, liable to support the individual handling of an incident, but also, the collaborative supervision of train movements.

We have first to consider the present means of handling an incident. Three main devices are of permanent use: the fix line diagram, the consoles' images and the graph of train movements are different maps representing the same territory, the RER A Line.

The graph of train movements is a reference document indicating the journeys of every train. Its graphic presentation makes it possible to follow a given train (where does he come from? what was his previous journey? where does he go? what will be his future journey?). It also allows a comparison between several trains.

Contrary to the fix-line diagram, or to the computer consoles, the graph of train movements, is not a representation of what is going on "here and now", but is the basis to which Controllers permanently refer, as a tool to evaluate the present situation. In this sense, it is a map of a "normal" situation, from which modifications are defined (for example: the amendment made on a train's itinerary). When perturbations occur, information given by the computer system is meaningfull only in reference to its discrepancies with the normal situation seen on the graph of train movements.

However, it is not easy to draw a correlation between these two information sources, because they are not related to the same level of information. From one side, the graphic is about the dynamics of the *theoretical* traffic, as a whole. It is a very rich tool, which adresses many aspects:

- *diachronical*: each train has it's past and future route;
- *synchronical:* at a given time, the location of all the trains is defined. What the Controllers are actually interested in is a combination of the *synchronical/diachronical* aspects: on a given portion of the line, there is a set of trains going in the same direction but having different itinerary. By comparing this set of trains, it is possible to replace a deffective train by another train with a similar journey.

- chronological: at a given location, one has all the trains passing from the beginning of the day.

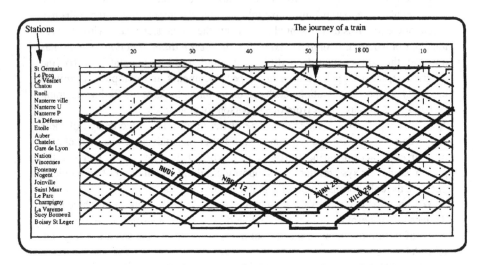

Figure 4: The synchronical/diachronical aspect of the graph of train movements

The computer consoles give in real time, a precise view of all trains at a given moment, in other words, the *synchronical aspect:* it operates like a succession of snapshots.

Our design proposal is optimizing the current computer system for the follow-up of train movements which should give *the historical background* of all the trains by providing equivalent information to those of the graph of train movements, but applied to the real running of trains. Hence, this dynamic tool would hold concurrently the synchronical/diachronical and the chronological aspect of train movements which is now lacking.

When the computer system is updated, this tool would also support the coordination of actions between the staff by rendering the amendments made on trains more visible than it currently is. For instance, a changed intinerary should be displayed one way or the other on the consoles so that any member of the staff knows immediately of modifications of the traffic even if he is unaware of the details of the handling of the incident.

The research reported here is an exploratory study: It primarily served to understand the global work practice of the RER Traffic Controllers, and it was not integrated in a specific design process even though some of its findings are being implemented to optimize the RER Control Room.

Other directions for design were concerned with the use of the fixed line diagram in connection with the problem of information sharing, communication devices, and additional functions for the computer system. These directions should be worked out for specific design projects with users and computer scientists.

Aknowledgements

The study on which this paper is based benefited from discussions with our research partners, Michèle Grosjean and Issac Joseph, and also with Christian Heath and Michèle Lacoste. We also thank the members of the "Ergonomics and Cognitive Antthropology" seminar for their comments.

References

De Keyser V. (1988): " De la compétence à la complexité: l'évolution des idées dans l'étude des processus continus. Quelques étapes clés." *Le Travail Humain*, 51, n° 1, pp. 1-18.

Falzon P. (1989): "Analyser l'activté pour l'assister."*Actes du Congrès de la Société d'Ergonomie de Langue Française*, Lyon, pp. 167-174.

Garfinkel H. (1967): *Studies in Ethnomethodology*, Englewood Cliffs, N.J. Prentice Hall.

Goffman E.(1974): *Forms of talk*, Blackwell, Oxford.

Goodwin C. (1981): *Conversational organization: interaction between speakers and hearers*. New York: Academic Press.

Goodwin C. & Goodwin M. (1991): "Formulating planes: seeing as a situated activity" in Y. Engestrom and D. Middleton (eds.): *Cognition and Communication at work*, Sage , in preparation.

Haradji Y. (1993): *De l'analyse de l'aide humaine à la conception d'une aide informatique à l'utilisation de logiciel*, Thèse de Doctorat d'Ergonomie, Conservatoire National des Arts et Métiers, Paris.

Heath C., Luff P. (1991): "Collaboration and activity and technical design; task coordination in London Underground Control Rooms," *Proceedings of the Second European Conference on Computer-Suported Cooperative Work*, September 24-27 . 1991, Amsterdam.

Hutchins E. L. (1988): "The Technology of Team Navigation", in J. Galagner, R.E. Kraut, and C. Egido (eds): *IntellectualkTeamwork: the Social and Technological Foundations of Cooperative Work* , 1991-221. Lawrence Erlbaum Associates, Hillsdale, New Jersey.

Montmollin M. de (1972): *Les psychopitres*, PUF, Paris.

Norman D. A. (1986): "Cognitive Engineering" in D.A. Norman and S. W. Draper (eds): *User Centered Design System*. New perspectives o Human-Computer Interaction, London, pp. 31-62.

Pinsky L and Theureau J. (1987): *L'Etude du Cours d'Action. Analyse du travail et conception ergonomique*. Collection d'Ergonomie et de Physiologie du Travail n° 88, Conservatoire National des Arts et Métiers, Paris.

Sacks H, Schegloff E. & Jefferson G. (1974): "A simplest sytematics for the organization of turn-taking for conversation." *Language* 50: pp.696-735.

Suchman L. (1991): Constituting Shared Workspaces in Y. Engestrom and D. Middleton (eds). *Cognition and Communication at work,* Sage , in preparation.

Theureau J. (1992): *Le cours d'action: analyse sémio-logique,* collection Sciences de la Communication, Peter Lang, Berne.

Visetti Y-M. (1991): "Des systèmes experts aux systèmes à base de connaissances: à la recherche d'un nouveau scéma régulateur", *Intellectica,* 2, 12, pp. 221-279.

Woods D.D. and Roth E.M. (1988): "Cognitive systems engineering" in Helander M. (ed): *Handbook of Human - Computer Interaction,* Elsevier Science Publishers.

Proceedings of the Third European Conference on Computer-Supported Cooperative Work
13-17 September, 1993, Milan, Italy
G. De Michelis, C. Simone and K. Schmidt (Editors)

Design for unanticipated use.....

Mike Robinson[1]
University of Århus, Denmark

Abstract: Support for work practice is better conceptualised as support for activity taking place in a multidimensional space than as prescription of temporal task sequences. The notion of "common artefact" is introduced to illustrate, unify, and summarise recent research that identifies significant dimensions of cooperative work. Common artefacts may be mundane, everyday objects like hotel keyracks or sophisticated computer tools. Both are multidimensional, in that they provide orthogonal features. They are predictable; help people see at a glance what others are doing (peripheral awareness); support implicit communications through the material being worked on; provide a focus for discussion of difficulties and negotiation of compromises (double level language); and afford an overview of the work process that would not otherwise be available. It is argued that CSCW should support these dimensions of work, rather than trying to anticipate its specific sequentiality.

Introduction

Computer systems and applications that mediate work between people are increasingly discovered to be used in ways that were not anticipated by their designers. The paper highlights themes that emerge from the last decade of work in CSCW that help explain this, and which provide a framework of sensitizing concepts for the design and evaluation of future systems. Failure to anticipate sequences of action is explained by recent ethnography, e.g. Button (1993), that demonstrate order — and hence sequence — to be an ongoing product of people's work. Work is thus best supported by the provision of resources. The search for abstracted optimum sequences is understandable given the successes of "scientific management"

---

[1]The author would like to thank the COMIC ESPRIT Basic Research Project for supporting this work, and the COST 11 COTECH Working Group IV (CSCW Design) for discussion and comment on many of the ideas.

(Taylor, 1947), and the sequential nature of most computing machinery and programming representations. The following three examples illustrate support for specific activities is best designed to avoid the anticipation of sequence.

Information Lens (Malone et al., 1987a; Malone et al., 1987b) was initially designed to provide an "intelligent" agent, an automatic secretary, to filter electronic mail. One well publicised function was to get rid of junk mail before it was read, or even seen. In a field study, Mackay (1988; 1990) noted that several people were unwilling to use this function. They felt a need to be aware of messages, and to view everything, at least at a cursory level. Of the many modes of use devised and shared by users, the one of special interest here is an innovation where users ran the rules (the way in which Information Lens sorted e-mail) on their messages *after* they had read or scanned them. Users needed to impose their own sequence: deciding between a secretary-filter to sort mail on the way in, or a secretary-archiver to put mail in appropriate folders after it was read.

Second, in a large field study of a number of "groupware" products, Bullen and Bennett (1990) noted many "fancy" functions of these packages were ignored. In particular, the sequentially structured conversational model and message categories in The Coordinator (Version 1) was largely by-passed. Many of those interviewed reported they ignored the choices, and just "hit enter" to send a message. They found messaging and selective archiving useful, but needed to create their own messaging sequences.

A third interesting example is given by Schmidt and Robinson (1993), citing Kaavé (1990). In a company with 50% of the world market in specialised optical equipment, production was controlled by a Manufacturing Resource Planning system (MRP). The system "knew" about all the products, sub-assemblies, and components down to the last nut and washer. It "knew" about the route each product took through the various production shops, and the number and breakdown of labour hours. From this, and other information, it calculated a production master schedule. As Schmidt observes, such a system is only feasible under conditions of limited product range in a stable market, so deviations in sales can be countered by inventories of products. Shortly after the MRP was introduced, the factory changed from large scale manufacture of a limited product range to order-driven production of a wide range of customised products. Production was driven by local plans based on current orders, not the master schedule. Yet the MRP system continued to be used. The workers found out that by using it 'backwards', it gave them an invaluable overview of the whole work process — letting them see, for instance, whether parts they would need shortly were scheduled.

These examples illustrate unanticipated use. In each case the designers had specific sequences of operations in mind. In each case the users appropriated the functions, while drastically reconstructing the planned sequences to match their actual work. This does not mean that CSCW systems design cannot be informed by analysis of practice: only that the practice is better conceptualised in a multi-dimensional space rather than as temporal task sequences. In the following sections, current understanding of the nature of work will be briefly summarised; "common artefact" characterised as a multi-dimensional support system consistent with this understanding; and several relevant dimensions of work practice illustrated. It will be concluded that, in CSCW, the search for common artefacts is a better starting point for analysis and design than a search for work sequences.

The nature of work...

Unanticipated use of computer artefacts reflects the fact that work itself is underdetermined until realised in situ. Empirical and theoretical work over the past few decades has shown that there are severe limits to the "programmability" of work, and to the project of precise "Scientific Management" [2].As Suchman (1983) put it:

> "While for computer scientists "procedure" has a very definite technical sense, for practitioners of office work the term has some other more loosely formulated meaning and usefulness. The distinction is something like that of a predetermined and reliable sequence of step-like operations versus an unelaborated, partial inventory of available courses and desired outcomes."

Suchman (1987) later used the term "situated action" to underscore the view that every course of action is essentially *ad hoc,* and depends on material and social circumstances. The function of plans and other abstract representations

> ".... is not to serve as specifications for the local interactions, but rather to orient or position us in a way that will allow us, through local interactions, to exploit some contingencies of our environment, and to avoid others."

Gerson and Star (1986) made a similar point with the notion of "articulation work"

> "*Without an understanding of articulation, the gap between requirements and the actual work process in the office will remain inaccessible to analysis.* ...... It will always be the case that in any local situation actors "fiddle" or shift requirements in order to get their work done in the face of local contingencies. We argue here that *such articulation* is not extraneous to requirements analysis, but *central to it.*"

None of this means that organisational procedures, structures, roles, workplans, objectives, and so on, are without value. Local flexibility, articulation work, and the shifting of requirements all happen in order to get the work done, within a framework of plans and objectives. It is simply that no procedure, no anticipated sequence of events, will ever match the rich, concrete detail of an actual situation. Procedures are more like advice than algorithms. For most purposes, such forms of organisational memory help make good choices and avoid pitfalls. But, as March (1976) points out, the ability to forget and overlook is essential.

Other factors in the nature of work impinge on attempts to anticipate use of artefacts. Schmidt and Bannon (1992) point out that working relationships are embedded within larger ensembles. They may be transient, and where they are not, patterns of interaction change with the requirements and constraints of the situation. Membership is not stable, and may even be non-determinable. Putting this in other words, there is no way of telling in advance exactly who will be needed where or

---

[2]See, inter alia, March and Olsen, 1976; Mintzberg, 1979; Salaman, 1979; Winograd and Flores, 1986; Anderson et al., 1987; Bjerknes et al., 1987; Suchman, 1987; Galegher et al., 1990; Schmidt, 1990; Robinson and Bannon, 1991

when... The consequence for CSCW design is that neither sequences of action, nor specific actors are pre-determinable. What can be known in advance is summarised in the phrase *"fluid transitions"* ..... There will be fluid transitions between individual and cooperative work (Hughes et al., 1991), between formal and informal interactions, between different tasks (Reder and Schwab, 1990), and between different media and tools (Bignoli et al., 1991; Ishii and Arita, 1991). Specific work is often an attempt to link required activities, to prevent the needs of one task from disrupting another, or to replace or repair a missing resource. Workflow diagrams and other types of formal representation may be a resource, or a frame for understanding work. They cannot predict or prescribe such specifics.

"Common artefacts" neither anticipate sequences of actions, nor attempt to enforce procedures. Like a Common in a traditional village, they allow many patterns of use without needing to anticipate specific actions or people. Common artefact has its origin in an attempt to understand the role of language in CSCW applications (Robinson, 1991a). It was noted that "successful" applications seemed to allow two modalities of communication: natural, fairly unrestricted conversation and communication via a system where actions were constrained by formation and transformation rules. A good example is an outliner, used in collective authoring (Ellis et al., 1991). Here it is clear that participants need to create and change a structure using rules, and also need to discuss their work. Both modalities of communication are necessary, and together are termed "double level language". "Common artefact" is an elaboration of the dimensions of communication that take place through, and are supported by a system.

Common artefacts

"The altitude of a technology might not be measured only in terms of the sophistication of the inner workings of the hardware device, but also in terms of the extent to which the device renders an important problem easy to solve"
(Hutchins, 1990)

Mundane everyday life provides many examples of common artefacts. Many of them work so well that they are taken for granted, inconspicuous, and appear trivial. Most of them are not considered to have any great "technological altitude" or sophistication. Yet they contain important lessons on the dimensions of computer applications to support people working together.

The keyrack behind the reception desk in a hotel is an example. Guests can leave and collect their keys; can see which other guests are in or out, and leave messages in the pigeonholes. Hotel staff use it to communicate with their colleagues, and place bills, faxes, etc. to be given out to guests. The presence of keys, or the contents of pigeonholes, conveys information, and may be the subject of questions or discussion. Some operations are considered legitimate, while others are not: usually only the receptionist can place keys or messages; keys have to be hung over appropriate numbers; etc. The keyrack is a model of the hotel, mapping the rooms. A glance at the it in the late evening gives an overview of the hotel occupancy.

Yet this keyrack is not foolproof, nor is it "active". There is nothing to prevent keys being hung in the wrong places, or lost. It can be used in many idiosyncratic ways — probably violating the recognised procedures. Conversely, there are certain things about a keyrack that are fixed, like the positions of the hooks. It is simply not possible to hang a key between two hooks, as there is nothing to hang it on. So potential uses are a result of physical properties, local conventions and rules, and situated activities.

It is argued that the mundane, old fashioned keyrack summarises the dimensionality necessary for Computer Supported Cooperative Work. It has a further advantage of being comprehensible to designers and users alike. The following sections will explore generic dimensions of common artefacts that appeared in the example.

Characteristics of common artefacts

Predictability

Common artefacts need to be predictable (and hence dependable) to the people using them. At this level, they are simply a tool for getting the job done — the keyrack stores keys. Examples in CSCW change train times, negotiate wages, move passengers and baggage between planes, steer large ships, coordinate air traffic, and schedule the prescription of medicines in hospitals.

In order to function as a tool at all, an artefact needs structure and operational predictability (the two notions are not independent). Hooks that did not stick out would be troublesome. Spreadsheets that did not enforce a grid structure would be useless. Even the universal tool[3] (Bannon, 1989) depends on structure for its multiplicity of uses. No-one wants an unpredictable artefact, whether it is a machine or a computer program. Predictability is probably the best understood aspect of system design, in terms of functions to be provided, consistency and compatibility between them, and appropriate human interfaces.

It should not be forgotten that there are many designs for tools to do any particular job. The particular form of any given artefact is a consequence of processes of competition, persuasion, selection, evolution, and diffusion. There is no Platonic Blueprint for a keyrack. Its general form has evolved because it makes an important problem "easy to solve". The important problem is not just storing keys — there are ways of storing small bits of metal that do not take up several square metres of space. Understanding the nature and dimensions of the "important problem" that everyday common artefacts resolve can reveal areas that CSCW applications need to address if they are to achieve equal success.

---

[3] An old fridge handle that was used as bottle opener, hammer, tea stirrer, etc.

Predictability (function, dependability, appropriate interface) is a crucial part of CSCW application design. But there is a danger of over-concentration on this, to the exclusion and detriment of other dimensions of cooperative working.

Peripheral Awareness

Implementing basic functionality alone can lead to disruption of the work. A good example is the French Nuclear Power Station (Kasbi and Montmollin, 1991) where old-fashioned dials were to be replaced with better tools — more sophisticated computerised displays. These were easier to read for each operator individually. It was forgotten that the power station operatives, collectively, needed to be aware of what the others were paying attention to, and what they were doing. It was easy to see which part of the system was of concern when someone went over to a dial and stared at, or tapped it. It was easy to read the context of any action that might subsequently be taken. This would have been lost with the "better" individual displays, which were fortunately not implemented.

Hotel keyracks and the power station setup allow experienced people to see what others are doing "*at a glance*" (Goodwin and Goodwin, 1993). This is possible because both artefacts and operations on them can be seen easily. "Peripheral awareness", and its importance for collaboration is illustrated by several studies ranging from libraries (Anderson and Crocca, 1992) to Air Traffic Control Rooms (Bentley et al., 1992). A good example is provided by Heath and Luff (1991):

A London Underground Control Room

The Bakerloo Line control room can house several staff. Two main actors are the Line Controller and the Divisional Information Assistant (DIA). The latter, amongst other things, provides information to passengers via a PA system, and to Station Managers by touch-screen phone. Both are able to see the state of Bakerloo line traffic on a real-time display which runs the length of the room. There is a radio system for contract with drivers, a PA control panel, and closed circuit television for viewing platforms. In addition, a paper timetable specifies train numbers, times, and routes; crew allocations, shifts, and travel; vehicle storage and maintenance; etc. The timetable is actively used by all control room staff to identify difficulties with, and manage the service.

> "Controller and DIA cover their paper timetables with collophane sheets which allows them to mark changes and add details with a felt pen and later to remove the various arrows, figures, and notes. ...... the various changes undertaken by the Controller are rarely explicitly told to DIA or to others (who) pick up the various changes (and) sketch in the reformations and adjustments on their own timetable."

(Heath and Luff, 1991)

The layout and the evolved constellation of common artefacts support peripheral awareness. This facilitates some near-telepathic coordination between Controller and DIA. For instance, to keep trains running at regular intervals, the Controller was observed to ask a driver on the Charing Cross Southbound line to delay for a couple of minutes. The DIA, glancing at the real-time display, aware of the timetable, and overhearing the controller's first attempt to contact the driver, is announcing the delay to passengers before the controller has finished his request to the driver.

Such situations illustrate that, in addition to predictability and functionality, a dimension of peripheral awareness will often need to be taken into account in the design of common artefacts. If this is not supported, damage to coordination may easily outstrip any gains.

Implicit Communication

Another dimension of common artefacts is implicit communication, though as will be seen later, this is inextricably bound up with double level language. Hotel staff use keyracks to communicate with their colleagues, for instance by leaving bills. In other words, they communicate without (necessarily) exchanging words. They communicate *implicitly* through their actions on the common artefact. This feature of work was first noticed by Pål Sørgaard, who used the term "shared material".

> "A simple example is the way two people carry a table. A part of the co-ordination may take place as explicit communication, for example in a discussion of how to get a table through a door. When the table is carried, however, the two people can follow each others actions because the actions get mediated through the shared material. This co-ordination is not necessarily explicit."

(Sørgaard, 1988)

Carrying a table through a door is an excellent but limited way to illustrate *implicit communication*. When people carry out a joint activity, conversation is only the tip of an iceberg. Much communication is mediated by the material they work on, whether it is physical like the table, or symbolic, like accounts or portfolios. Schmidt (1993) noted potential disadvantages of this as a sole means of coordination:

(1) The bandwidth is usually very restricted.

(2) The turn-around time of the interaction is determined by the frequency of state changes in the artefact.

(3) The act is embodied in the state change in the field of work.

On the other hand, the restricted nature of implicit communication through an artefact has advantages — if other means, like talking, are not prevented. It augments the number and type of channels available, allowing parallelism and delayed responses not available in simple speech. The changes marked by felt pen on the cellophane timetable cover in the London Underground Control Room are one example. Implicit communication, reading states of work objects as signs, becomes more powerful, and less open to misreading, when accompanied by local convention. This is well illustrated by the following example.

Flight Strips in Air Traffic Control: An example of convention in implicit communication

A long term study on cooperative work in air traffic control has provided interesting insights into the delicate balance between the characteristics of artifacts and cooperative work practices (Harper et al., 1989; Harper et al., 1991; Bentley et al., 1992). Civilian flights over England and Wales are controlled from a center near London. Airspace is divided into 16 sectors, each of which is controlled from a "suite", equipped with radar screens, TV monitors, telephones and other communication facilities, maps, computers etc. Typically, a suite is staffed by two air traffic controllers, two assistants, and one sector chief. Controllers have three main artifacts to aid them. Radar displays show a trail of 'blips' representing a particular flight, with a data block alongside showing the flight number and flight level. Telephone and radiotelephone links enable controllers to talk to pilots, other controllers, and neighboring airspaces. Flight progress "strips" contain information on each flight. These latter items are the focus of this investigation into the nature of common artefacts.

The strips are made of card, approximately 200 by 25 mm, and are divided into fields. Information in the fields comes from a database holding the flight plan filed by the pilot prior to departure, sometimes modified by inputs keyed in by controllers or assistants. It includes the aircraft's callsign, flight level, heading, planned flight path, navigation points on its route, estimated time of arrival, departure and destination airports, and the aircraft's type. Strips are arranged in racks immediately above the radar screens. The collection of strips enables a controller to gauge how many aircraft are due in the sector, where they are bound and when, and the strip can be used to record any instructions given to the aircraft.

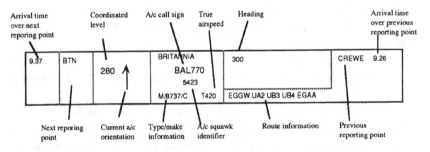

A flight progress strip.

When a controller gives an instruction to a pilot, for example to ascend to flight level 220, he or she marks this on the strip. In this case, the mark is an upwards arrow and the number 220. When the pilot acknowledges, the controller crosses through the old flight level on the strip. When the new flight level is attained, the controller marks a check beside it. Changes in heading, estimated time of arrival, route, call sign etc. are dealt with in similar ways.

"This means that *this* information, and any subsequent revisions, is 'ready at hand' as the 'current state of affairs'. As a controller aptly remarked, the strips 'are like your memory, everything is there'. Important to this functionality are the conventional notations on a known-in-common format and a known sequential organisation of the strips themselves. They are note pads, but not personal ones."

(Harper, 1889)

Each team member uses a differently coloured pen so the source of the annotations is immediately apparent. The changes in state of the common artefact are *conventional and formalised* (upward arrows, numbers, check marks, crosses through numbers). Any old mark or annotation will not do. The signs have to be immediately readable and comprehensible. This is a clear example of how convention supports implicit communication.

In similar vein, anyone who notices a problem with a strip or pair of strips — perhaps two flights due at the same navigation point at a similar time and at the same height — can "cock out" the strips, i.e., move them noticeably out of alignment in the racks. This makes it immediately obvious that, when it becomes time to deal with those flights, a problem will need to be considered, and to the practiced eye it will be obvious from a glance at the strips what the problem is. The vocabulary and syntax of annotation and ordering the strips are a language through which the members of the team communicate with each other and create a 'common statement' about the state of the flight and of the sector (Hughes et al., 1992).

Changing flight levels and "cocking out" strips are both cases where a common artefact becomes articulate because its state can be "read" according to convention. The artefacts support this since they are predictable; can be taken in at a glance; and additionally, by providing a set of symbols for which there are formation and transformation rules, they support conventionalised implicit communication. This is the further dimension of cooperative work that needs to be taken into consideration.

Double Level Language

Implicit communication can only happen when the participating actors are able to *maintain* an evolving set of rules, understandings, and expectations about the meanings of actions, signs, and changes of the common artefact — in other words, when the *participants can also communicate directly using the fullness of their natural language to interpret the concrete situation in front of them*. This is a further dimension of cooperative working that needs to be facilitated, and certainly not prevented, by any common artefact.

The achievement of mutual learning, coordination, negotiated conventions, accident recovery, and misunderstanding repair has been examined by Gerson and Star (1986) and by Suchman (1987) with the important concepts of articulation work and situated action. Neither concept implies that coordination can be accomplished by speech *alone*. The concrete work situation and its common artefacts are critical in grounding conversation and spoken exchanges. They provide essential context for explicit communication.[4] "Double Level Language" is a phrase intended to catch the idea that implicit, often indirect communication (through artefacts) and explicit communication (speech, ad hoc notes) are not alternatives, but complementary and mutually supportive.

In general it can be said that any non-trivial collective activity requires effective communication at both levels. 'Computer support' is valuable insofar as it facilitates the separation and interaction between them. Applications that support one level at the expense of the other tend to fail. The dimension of implicit, formal or conventionally readable "states" is essential as it provides a common reference point for participants. A sort of 'external world' that can be pointed at, and whose behaviour is rule-governed and predictable. But this 'world' is meaningless without interpretation, without the talking that maintains its meaning. Conversely, dialogue is almost vacuous unless it is grounded (Robinson, 1991a: 43).

The Wage Bargainer is an example of the symbiotic relation between these two types of communication. It provides an 'external world' that can be pointed at, whose behaviour is rule-governed and predictable, and that facilitates and grounds dialogue and negotiation.

The Wage Bargainer[5]

The problem was two hundred people in a dozen or so workgroups, with a wage structure that had "evolved" over 19 years. During this time, the organisation had increased in size six fold, and many new specialisms and functions had developed. The wage structure had become so complicated that it was almost incomprehensible. Anomalies and discontent abounded. The organisation was a co-operative, so there was no external owner, or separate management to bargain with. No single group could *impose* a new structure. In practice, and in some way, the workers had to bargain with each other.

An Open University team, in consultation with co-op members, created a distributed spreadsheet. Each group could change any of the factors that directly affected it (wage scale and range, increments, overtime rate, number of workers, etc.). Although any group could make any change, what the co-op *could* pay was determined by the relation of the aggregated "claims" to total (budgeted) income. Finally it was agreed that the reality of the budget income was such that a 3% across-the-board increase was the minimum everyone would accept, and the most that could be paid. Anomalies remained, but the problem they were causing was resolved. The final agreement could not have been deduced from the original claims. It was necessary to have the iterative, dialectical movement between the formalised 'world' of the spreadsheet and the negotiations and discussions.

---

4 Ethnomethodology and Conversation Analysis have demonstrated the *indexical* character of spoken exchanges. "This" and "that" are obvious examples of words that do not have meaning outside specific contexts. It now appears that the majority of human interchanges need an awareness of the particular situation in which they are happening in order to be comprehensible.

5 developed in 1987 by the Open University as part of the WISDOM Project to explore collective uses of new technology (Robinson, 1988; Robinson, 1991b)

In CSCW, such reciprocity can be ignored. Some applications try to support conventional (formal) operations on the common artefact, while others concentrate on providing additional channels for dialogue. The success of either will depend on whether or not the people who use the system can *maintain both modalities* of communication.[6] Cooperative work needs to be both *discursive* (setting rules and conventions, achieving agreements) and *indexical* (grounded in the objects of work). Communication happens at both levels. The combination of implicit and explicit communication is "double level language". This is supported by mundane artefacts like keyracks, timetables, and flight strips. Computer applications may ignore this lesson. They may make it difficult to access the object of work, and disrupt indexicality and implicit communication. Alternatively, they may simply assume formal communications (signs on an artefact of some sort) are enough, and attempt to disallow discussion, resolution of ambiguity, further elaboration of context or detail. In both cases, the systems are generally disliked, not used, and, in the end, fail commercially (Ehrlich, 1987b; Ehrlich, 1987a; Grudin, 1989; Markus, 1990). Alternatively, as with the undoubtedly successful e-mail (Bannon, 1985), the application may support just one level of language, provided that the participants have an established and trusted method of communicating on the other level.

Overview

Common artefacts afford an overview on the work-world *which would not otherwise be available.* As an extra dimension, overview has greater spatio-temporal scope than peripheral awareness, and need not have the conversational qualities of a double level language. Artefacts that afford overviews have a long history. The usefulness of maps, photographs from the air, watchtowers, exploded diagrams, keyracks showing room occupancy, etc. does not need to be argued. Computers graphics are a powerful way of gaining overview on social trends and phenomena that would otherwise be "mere numbers". The appearance and importance of "overview" in computer-based artefacts that were designed to do something else is an exciting discovery of CSCW research, and well illustrated in the following study.[7]

Overview of the Ward in a Norwegian Hospital

Bjerknes and Bratteteig (1988) tell a story of the design and implementation of a system to support nurses in their daily work — "The Florence Project". The researchers implemented a "work sheet system" based on scraps of paper used in the short-stay cardiological ward. The nurses had previously used these scraps to make notes of the most important patient information at the beginning, update during, and

---

[6] The controversy over whether electronic mail is a CSCW application or not is related to this distinction. E-mail allows conversation-like exchanges, but does not support access (peripheral, implicit, or otherwise) to the object or context of the conversation.

[7] See also Schneider and Wagner (1992) for a similar overview effect in a study of information systems and collaborative work in four French hospitals.

pass on at the end of their shift. In a previous paper (Robinson, 1991a) it was noted that the work-sheets provide an example of double level language. They "fix" information that the nursing group has decided to be relevant, and facilitate discussion of it. This helped nurses to a "new competence" in dealing with their role of "information exchange" in hospitals.

The worksheets were modeled on the beds (or rooms) of the patients. They were printed out with basic patient information: name, year of birth, diagnosis, observations, investigation results, medicines, and tests. There was space for notes and comments to be added on each patient. An area in the middle was reserved for information of nurses' tasks and duties. Critically:

> "The information in the Work Sheets is presented in a way that gives the nurses overview of the patients in the ward. It is this overview that is the basis of the decisions made by the nurses during a shift."
>
> (Bjerknes and Bratteteig, 1988: 171)

"Overview" was a notion that originated from the nurses themselves. The researchers note that the

> "nurses use 'lack of overview' to explain the rejection of different suggestions for changes. Overview seems to relate to the nurses' 'inner' picture of the ward. This 'inner picture' has to be in common (to some extent) to the nurses in a ward, and it seems to be the basis for their cooperation. The nurses are not able to explicate what gives overview, but they are quick to tell if something is not useful for getting an overview." (ibid.: 176)

The authors noted a lack of strict division of labour in updating the worksheets and producing the reports. Sometimes this was done by the team leader, sometimes by others, especially the night shift to help them "keep awake". A perspective of seeing the worksheets as common artefacts suggests that the nurses were doing more than keeping awake in a physical sense when they shared the updating and printing work. They were also "keeping awake" to the common 'inner picture' or overview of the ward.

The value of overview was emphasised in the appropriation of worksheets by other groups on the ward. One "kernel group" of nurses had refused the computer system. But they produced worksheets nonetheless. They found out how to print 'empty' worksheets, and filled them in themselves. Most surprising was when the doctors asked for the worksheets — which they had originally complained didn't suit their needs or contain 'useful information'.

Conclusion

Multidimensionality

Multidimensionality is the most basic characteristic of common artefacts: they are implicated in and support many facets of work. They are not *just* tools. The dimensions of predictability, peripheral awareness, implicit and explicit communication, double level language, and overview have been examined. In isolation, each can appear accidental, or contingent on the ingenuity of workers in specific situations. Taken together, under the generic label of common artefact, they provide a design space to support cooperative work in all its fluid transitions — yet without the need to prescribe or anticipate activity and task sequences.

Routine Trouble.....

.... and its resolution is the nature of most cooperative work. Suchman and Trigg (1991) tell the story of ground control, the "Ops Room" at an airport for one airline. There are schedules to be kept, but planes may be unpredictably delayed; gates may have to be changed; ramp crews have to know which baggage to transfer where, and quickly; ticket agents on the gates have to know which passengers to expect; recording and control formats, on paper or computers, may get out of synch with the reality, and so on. These "routine troubles" easily translate into other office and factory contexts. Suchman and Trigg (1991) give an account of a paper based common artefact ("the complex sheet") that was a key resource in managing the situation. Their categories do not map exactly onto the dimensions used here, but several overlap. The complex sheet is a medium for peripheral awareness, and for implicit communication about "irregular or problematic sub-events". As "transparent artefact" and "reproducible representation" it gives overview, and provides an indexical focus for discussion of particular "troubles". The complexity of work practice is matched by the dimensionality of the artefact supporting it.

Common artefact summarised

Common artefact is a label for a set of work dimensions that need to be reflected in CSCW applications. Specific artefacts are considered common artefacts when they span the dimensions of

- predictability
- peripheral awareness
- double level language (implicit conventionalised communication and open dialogue with an indexical focus)
- overview

The design space of a common artefact can support cooperative working in all its routine troubles without a need to anticipate particular contingencies, or the order in which they might arise.

References

Anderson, Bob J., Wes W. Sharrock, and John A. Hughes. 1987. The Division of Labour. In *Action Analysis and Conversation Analysis, Maison des Sciences de l'Homme, Paris, September 1987.*

Anderson, William and William Crocca. 1992. Experiences in Reflective Engineering Practice: Co-Development of Product Prototypes. In *PDC '92 (Participatory Design Conference), Cambridge. MA.,* ed. M. Muller Kuhn,S., & Meskill,J. CPSR.

Bannon, L. & Bødker, S. 1989. "Beyond the Interface: Encountering Artefacts in Use". In *IBM Workshop of Cognitive Theory in Human Computer Interaction. June 20-22., New York.*

Bannon, L.J. 1985. *Extending the Design Boundaries of Human-Computer Interaction.* Institute for Cognitive Science, University of California San Diego, 1985.

Bentley, R., T. Rodden, P. Sawyer, I. Sommerville, J. Hughes, D. Randall, and D. Shapiro. 1992. Ethnographically-informed systems design for air traffic control. In *CSCW '92, Toronto.* ACM.

Bignoli, Celsina, Giorgio De Michelis, and Renata Tinini. 1991. UTUCS: A support for synchronous and asynchronous communication. In *International Workshop on CSCW, Berlin, April 9-11, 1991,* ed. K. Gorling and C. Sattler, 74-84. Institut für Informatik und Rechentechnik.

Bjerknes, G. and T. Bratteteig. 1988. "The Memoirs of Two Survivors: or The Evaluation of a Computer System for Co-operative Work". In *Conf. on Computer Supported Co-operative Work Sept.26-28, Portland, Oregon,* ed. D. Tatar, 167-177. ACM.

Bjerknes, G., P. Ehn, and M. Kyng, ed. 1987. *Computers and Democracy: A Scandinavian Challenge.* England: Avebury.

Bullen, C. and J. Bennett. 1990. *Groupware in practice: An interpretation of work experience.* MIT Center for Information Systems Research, Cambridge MA 02139, March 1990.

Button, Graham, ed. 1993. *Technology in Working Order: Studies of Work, Interaction, and Technology.* London & New York: Routledge.

Ehrlich, S.F. 1987a. Social and psychological Factors influencing the design of office communication systems. In *CHI+GI '87 Human Factors in Computing Systems, Toronto, 5 - 9 April '87.*

Ehrlich, S.F. 1987b. Strategies for encouraging successful adoption of office communication systems. *ACM TOOIS* (5).

Ellis, C. A., S. J. Gibbs, and G. L. Rein. 1991. Groupware: Some issues and experiences. *Communications of the ACM* 34 (1): 38-58.

Galegher, J., R.E. Kraut, and C. Egido, ed. 1990. *Intellectual Teamwork: Social and Technological Foundations of Cooperative Work.* New Jersey: Lawrence Erlbaum.

Gerson, Elihu M. and Susan Leigh Star. 1986. Analyzing Due Process in the Workplace. *ACM Transactions on Office Information Systems* 4 (3): 257-270.

Goodwin, Charles and Marjorie Goodwin. 1993. Formulating Planes: Seeing as a situated activity. In *Communication and Cognition at Work,* ed. Y. Engestrom & Middleton, D., N.Y.: Cambridge University Press (in press).

Grudin, Jonathan. 1989. Why groupware applications fail: problems in design and evaluation. *Office: Technology and People* 4 (3): 245-264.

Harper, R. R., J. A. Hughes, and D. Z. Shapiro. 1989. Working in harmony: An examination of computer technology in air traffic control. In *EC-CSCW '89. Proceedings of the First European Conference on Computer Supported Cooperative Work, Gatwick, London, 13-15 September, 1989,* 73-86.

Harper, R. R., J. A. Hughes, and D. Z. Shapiro. 1991. Harmonious Working and CSCW: Computer technology and air traffic control. In *Studies in Computer Supported Cooperative Work. Theory, Practice and Design*, ed. John M. Bowers and Steve D. Benford, 225-234. Amsterdam etc.: North-Holland.

Heath, Christian and Paul Luff. 1991. Collaborative Activity and Technological Design: Task Coordination in London Underground Control Rooms. In *ECSCW '91. Proceedings of the Second European Conference on Computer-Supported Cooperative Work*, ed. Liam Bannon, Mike Robinson, and Kjeld Schmidt, 65-80. Amsterdam: Kluwer Academic Publishers.

Hughes, John, Dave Randall, and Dan Shapiro. 1991. CSCW: Discipline or Paradigm? A sociological perspective. In *ECSCW '91. Proceedings of the Second European Conference on Computer-Supported Cooperative Work*, ed. Liam Bannon, Mike Robinson, and Kjeld Schmidt, 309-323. Amsterdam: Kluwer Academic Publishers.

Hughes, John A., David Randall, and Dan Shapiro. 1992. Faltering from Ethnography to Design. In *Proceedings of ACM CSCW'92 Conference on Computer-Supported Cooperative Work*, 115-122. ACM.

Hutchins, Edwin. 1990. The Technology of Team Navigation. In *Intellectual Teamwork: Social and Technological Foundations of Cooperative Work*, ed. J. Galegher Kraut,R.E. & Egido,C., 191-220. New Jersey: Lawrence Erlbaum.

Ishii, Hiroshi and Kazuho Arita. 1991. ClearFace: Translucent Multiuser Interface for TeamWorkStation. In *ECSCW '91. Proceedings of the Second European Conference on Computer-Supported Cooperative Work*, ed. Liam Bannon, Mike Robinson, and Kjeld Schmidt, Amsterdam: Kluwer Academic Publishers.

Kaavé, Bjarne. 1990. *Undersøgelse af brugersamspil i system til produktionsstyring.* MSc. diss., Technical University of Denmark, 1990.

Kasbi, Catherine and Maurice de Montmollin. 1991. Activity Without Decision and Responsibility: The Case of Nuclear Power Plants. In *Distributed Decision Making. Cognitive Models for Cooperative Work*, ed. B. Brehmer J. Rasmussen J. Leplat, 275-283. Chichester: John Wiley & Sons.

Mackay, W. 1988. *More than Just a Communication System: Diversity in the Use of Electronic Mail.* Working Paper Sloan School of Management, MIT, 1988.

Mackay, W. 1990. *Users and Customizable Software: A Co-Adaptive Phenomenon.* Doctoral dissertation, Sloan School of Management, MIT, 1990.

Malone, T. W., K. R. Grant, K. -Y. Lai, R. Rao, and D. Rosenblitt. 1987a. Semistructured messages are surprisingly useful for computer-supported coordination. *ACM Transactions on Office Information Systems* 5 (2): 115-131.

Malone, T. W., K. R. Grant, K. R. Turbak, F. A. Brobst, and M. D. Cohen. 1987b. Intelligent information sharing systems. *Communications of the ACM* 30: 390-402.

March, J.G. and J.P. Olsen. 1976. *Ambiguity and Choice in Organizations.* Universitetsforlaget.

Markus, M.L. 1990. Why CSCW applications fail: Problems in the adoption of interdependent work tools. In *CSCW 90, Proceedings of the Conference on Computer-Supported Cooperative Work, Los Angeles, CA, October 7-10, 1990*, N.Y.: ACM.

Mintzberg, Henry. 1979. *The Structuring of Organizations. A Synthesis of the Research.* Englewood Cliffs, New Jersey: Prentice-Hall.

Reder, Stephen and Robert Schwab. 1990. The temporal structure of cooperative activity. In *CSCW 90, Proceedings of the Conference on Computer-Supported Cooperative Work, Los Angeles, CA, October 7-10, 1990*, 303-316. New York: ACM Press.

Robinson, Mike. 1988. Computer Assisted Meetings: Modelling and Mirroring in Organisational Systems. In *EURINFO '88: First European Conf. on Inf. Tech. for Org. Systems., Athens,16-20 May 1988*, 81-88. North Holland.

Robinson, Mike. 1991a. Double-Level Languages and Co-operative Working. *AI & Society* 5: 34-60.

Robinson, Mike. 1991b. Pay Bargaining in a Shared Information Space. In *Studies in Computer Supported Cooperative Work: Theory, Practice, and Design*, ed. J. Bowers and S. Benford, Amsterdam & New York: North Holland.

Robinson, Mike and Liam Bannon. 1991. Questioning Representations. In *ECSCW '91. Proceedings of the Second European Conference on Computer-Supported Cooperative Work*, ed. Liam Bannon, Mike Robinson, and Kjeld Schmidt, 219-233. Amsterdam: Kluwer Academic Publishers.

Salaman, Graeme. 1979. *Work Organisations: resistance and control*. London: Longman.

Schmidt, Kjeld. 1990. *Analysis of Cooperative Work. A Conceptual Framework*. Risø-M-2890. Risø National Laboratory, DK-4000 Roskilde, Denmark, June 1990. 87-550-1668-5.

Schmidt, Kjeld and Liam Bannon. 1992. Taking CSCW Seriously: Supporting Articulation Work. *Computer Supported Cooperative Work (CSCW). An International Journal* 1 (1): 7-40.

Schmidt, Kjeld and Mike Robinson. 1993. *Developing CSCW Systems: Design Concepts*

EC COST11 Report of CoTech WG4. Risø National Laboratory,Cognitive Systems Group, PO BOX 49, Roskilde 4000, Denmark, 1993.

Schneider, Karin and Ina Wagner. 1992. Constructing the 'Dossier Representatif'. draft.

Sørgaard, Pål. 1988. Object Oriented Programming and Computerised Shared Material. In *Second European Conference on Object Oriented Programming (ECOOP '88)*, ed. S. & Nygaard Gjessing K., 319-334. Springer Verlag, Heidelberg.

Suchman, Lucy. 1987. *Plans and situated actions. The problem of human-machine communication*. Cambridge: Cambridge University Press.

Suchman, Lucy A. 1983. Office Procedures as Practical Action: Models of Work and System Design. *ACM Transactions on Office Information Systems* 1 (4): 320-328.

Suchman, L.A. and R.H. Trigg. 1991. "Understanding Practice: Video as a Medium for Reflection and Design". In *Design at Work*, ed. J. & Kyng.M Greenbaum, 65-89. London and New Jersey: Lawrence Erlbaum.

Taylor, F. 1947. *Scientific Management*. Harper & Row.

Winograd, Terry and Fernando Flores. 1986. *Understanding Computers and Cognition: A New Foundation for Design*. Norwood, New Jersey: Ablex Publishing Corp.

Proceedings of the Third European Conference on Computer-Supported Cooperative Work
13-17 September, 1993, Milan, Italy
G. De Michelis, C. Simone and K. Schmidt (Editors)

Low overhead, loosely coupled communication channels in collaboration

Dorab Patel and Scott D. Kalter
Twin Sun, Inc., USA

Abstract: Communication and coupling are two central aspects of systems developed for computer-supported cooperative work. Synchronous communication usually implies tight coupling while asynchronous communication is often used with loose coupling. This paper explores the previously neglected role of loosely coupled channels in synchronous communication by providing some example channels and evaluating their tradeoffs.

Such loosely coupled channels efficiently meet specialized communication needs that often arise in spontaneous, short-lived collaborations. They can also augment existing channels in specific domains.

These channels impose few requirements on their host applications and hence can be easily integrated into tools familiar to most users. Our implementation is built over an inter-application communication framework that provides flexible high-level communication abstractions for the rapid prototyping, implementing, and experimenting with these channels.

1   Introduction

There is increasing interest in developing computer-based tools to promote collaboration. One important aspect of collaboration is the communication of information. This communication may be synchronous (all participants are present at the same time) or asynchronous (all participants need not be present simultaneously). In both of these cases, the coupling between the participants can be loose, tight, or intermediate. Tight coupling, as in shared whiteboards, involves each participant knowing continuously about changes made by the others. The application state may be distributed, but all the copies are kept consistent continuously. Loose coupling means that the participants use independent applications which use one-shot, application-initiated information exchanges to copy state among one another. No attempt is made to keep the copies consistent after the state transfer. Previously, the emphasis in synchronous collaborative systems has been on tight coupling. This paper explores the role of loosely coupled communication channels in synchronous collaboration.

One can imagine a world without single-user applications. All applications would be tightly coupled and group aware. Users would not need to do anything different to share their work with others. But, we do not live in such a world. Existing tightly coupled systems usually incur a cognitive overhead for collaboration. By "cognitive overhead" we mean the extra mental effort required to set up a collaboration and to establish a shared context, over and above the actual collaboration. Also, tightly coupled systems are often too slow or too expensive to implement. Since most popular applications today are written with a single-user mind-set, it is difficult to convert them to multi-user use. Hence many group-aware applications are unfamiliar to users who are reluctant to give up their comfortable single-user tools. This tendency retards the spread of collaborative applications.

In a tightly coupled system, users have to be aware of others. They do not have the flexibility of decoupled use and might inadvertently do something with adverse effects on the others. Also, users might be inhibited if everything they do is visible to others. These problems can be solved by having a separate private data space that can be used in these circumstances. The data location, rather than the multi-user application, would control the data sharability.

Though a tightly coupled system is useful for situations that require a continuous and highly coherent sharing of context (e.g., meetings), there are other situations for which it is not as appropriate. Human collaborations are often spontaneous, unstructured, and have short lifetimes. For example, you ask someone a quick question; or you solicit an opinion on some of your work. A loosely coupled communication channel accurately models this situation and hence is familiar to users. This type of collaboration only works if setup and shutdown are a small fraction of the total collaborative session. A low cognitive overhead for collaboration makes it more likely that the system will be used for short-lived spontaneous collaborations. A low implementation overhead makes it easier to insert these features into existing applications, increasing the likelihood of making such systems widely available. By implementing shared multi-writer environments, a tightly coupled system provides facilities that are beyond those normally available. The availability of such features is one reason why tightly coupled systems have received more attention. However, a loosely coupled channel with limited benefits may still be desirable if its costs are sufficiently low.

To use an analogy with network protocols, loosely coupled communication channels are similar to datagram communication, and tightly coupled channels are similar to virtual circuits. Like loosely coupled channels, datagrams are suited to short, low overhead communications. Virtual circuits, like tightly coupled channels, require the overhead of setting up and tearing down a connection, but provide efficient long term communications.

Channels at different levels of coupling will be suited to different collaborative situations. The benefit provided by a particular channel has to be evaluated with respect to its implementation and cognitive costs. Some provide lots of functionality

Type		Examples
Video		VIDEODRAW, VIDEOWINDOW, CLEARBOARD
Asynchronous	loosely coupled	Email, USENET
	annotations	PREP, FOR COMMENT
Synchronous	application sharers	SHAREDX, XTV, SHOWME
	toolkits	GROUPKIT, SUITE, RENDEZVOUS, DISTEDIT, COEX
	tightly coupled	WSCRAWL, GROUPDESIGN, SHREDIT, ASPECTS

Table 1. Existing channels

at a high cost. Others provide less functionality but at a much reduced cost. Choosing the right one depends on the application. We focus on loosely coupled channels that incur minimal costs and have proven to be useful in our environment.

This paper begins with a survey of existing communication channels for collaboration, followed by examples of new, low cost, and useful channels. A taxonomy of communication channels provides a basis for comparison of various alternatives. We touch on our implementation environment which allows us to experiment with new channels easily, and application functionality necessary to permit integration of such channels. We conclude with lessons learned in building and using low cost loosely coupled communication channels for synchronous collaboration.

2 Existing communication channels

Before collaborating, participants must develop a shared context. This context is created by the exchange of information across communication channels. Each channel has its own characteristics and affordances (Gaver, 1992). Channels may or may not be computer-supported. Channels such as paper, whiteboards, phone, fax, and video are usually not well integrated with the workstation. Paper and whiteboards are convenient, ubiquitous, and familiar, but require co-location of participants. Phone, fax and video require more session setup but can be used remotely. The rest of the paper concentrates on computer-supported channels.

Computer-supported channels can support and augment collaborations. The more channels that are available to the participants, the better, so they can choose the channel appropriate to the task at hand. We survey some existing channels, provide examples of each, and review their characteristics.

Video channels (e.g., VIDEODRAW (Tang & Minneman, 1990), CLEARBOARD (Ishii, Kobayashi & Grudin, 1992), and VIDEOWINDOW (Fish, Kraut & Chalfonte, 1990)) allow free-form interactions among participants. These systems use data that is external to the computer, though CLEARBOARD-2 includes a sketching tool called TEAMPAINT. This lack of integration limits the ability to manipulate the data and eliminates the possibility of maintaining semantic relationships with other stored computer data.

Asynchronous, loosely coupled channels such as email and USENET are passive systems, limited to a single writer for each document. However, they allow participants to communicate when convenient, rather than being present simultaneously in order to communicate.

Asynchronous annotation systems like PREP (Neuwirth, Kaufer, Chandhok & Morris, 1990) and FOR COMMENT allow participants to work at different times, and allow multiple writers to annotate the same document. PREP even provides a computer-maintained relationship from the annotations to the underlying document.

Synchronous application multiplexers such as SHOWME, XTV (Abdel-Wahab & Feit, 1991), and SHAREDX (Garfinkel, Gust, Lemon & Lowder, 1989), allow any application to be shared in a strict WYSIWIS (Stefik, Bobrow, Foster, Lanning & Tatar, 1987) manner. This can be beneficial in certain situations such as teaching or presentations. However, these applications require premeditation—users must know, before starting an application, whether they are going to be sharing it or not. Strict WYSIWIS can be a hindrance in situations where participants require independent views of shared data. SHOWME shares dynamic annotations over a static snapshot of an application. The others allow continuous sharing of the underlying application.

Toolkits (e.g., RENDEZVOUS (Hill, Brinck, Patterson, Rohall & Wilner, 1993), GROUPKIT (Roseman & Greenberg, 1992), COEX (Patel & Kalter, 1993), DISTEDIT (Knister & Prakash, 1990), and SUITE (Dewan & Choudhary, 1991)) for developing tightly coupled applications that share their data among application instances, have been developed recently. They provide fine grained sharing among participants, but require modification of existing applications. RENDEZVOUS uses a centralized state architecture, whereas all the others use a decentralized state approach.

Tightly coupled synchronous applications like SHREDIT (McGuffin & Olson, 1992), WSCRAWL (Wilson, 1992), ASPECTS (Group Technologies, Inc., 1990), and GROUPDESIGN (Beaudouin-Lafon & Karsenty, 1992), share the characteristics of the toolkits mentioned previously. Since these applications are new, they are unfamiliar to users who resist converting to using these applications. WSCRAWL uses a centralized state approach. All the others use a distributed state approach.

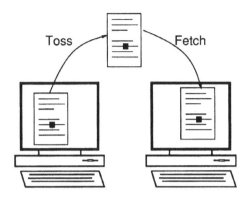

Figure 1. TOSS/FETCH

3 New communication channels

This section introduces some new computer-mediated communication channels. These channels are similar to some common, existing channels and thus are familiar. Each channel is designed to be unobtrusive to the communicators, so they can concentrate on the substance rather than the method of their collaboration. The primary goal of a new channel is either to enrich an existing communication channel, or to replace an existing channel with one that is less cumbersome. These channels were motivated by our own daily needs in designing systems, developing code, and writing papers. Our work style is such that we often work closely together, often at the same desk, and were hampered by the lack of collaborative tools.

3.1 Toss/fetch

A common need is to show a colleague what text file we are examining, from our own point of view. This is usually to establish a context for further discussion. Typically, we would walk into their office or call them and ask them to look at the relevant part of a file. The problem with this is that the conversation may deviate from the substance of the discussion to describing how to establish the context. For example, the file might be accessed via a different path on the colleague's host, it might be read protected, or locating the relevant region of the text might be tedious.

One solution would be to take a snapshot of our window and display it on their screen,[1] but this results in a static view. Another possibility is to use either SHAREDX or XTV. These are rather heavyweight solutions that require premeditation of the need to share, and different modes of use while sharing (floor-passing and session management).

A lightweight system, that provides one user's point of view (POV) within an application to another user within their own application context, is more appropriate. The received view is read-only, thereby avoiding complex consistency issues,

---

[1] A trivial implementation using X: xwd | xwud -display host:display.

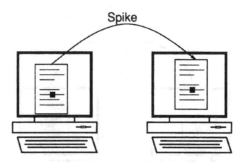

Figure 2. SPIKE

keeping the channel loosely coupled, and its implementation simple. This provides recipients with a dynamic, rather than static, view—one they can scroll or otherwise manipulate independently. Furthermore, although they cannot modify the original document, they can modify their copy normally.

Given these constraints, we developed a channel called TOSS/FETCH (see Figure 1). One user can toss the point of view within their own application and another user can then fetch this POV. The POV consists of the file being viewed, the cursor location, and, if the editor supports it, where the "mark" is. Our experience indicates that this definition of a POV includes sufficient information to establish a context for collaboration involving text editors..

There are many benefits to the TOSS/FETCH mechanism. Since the tossed POVs are globally visible, the communication is undirected, as in USENET. The undirected communication leads to a very simple user interface. It requires only one keystroke to toss or fetch a POV. There is no automatic notification associated with this channel. The sender is expected to inform the receiver, through other channels, that there is something to fetch. Typically, the participants will already be conversing at this point, so informing the receiver is not a problem. The modest requirements of the TOSS/FETCH mechanism impose very few demands on the host application. Hence it is easy to implement TOSS/FETCH in familiar applications preferred by users. To demonstrate the ease of implementation, we implemented TOSS/FETCH for EMACS (Stallman, 1987) (no C changes, only ELISP (Lewis, LaLiberte & the GNU Manual Group, 1990) additions), VI (no changes, addition of two macros), and STED (less than 200 lines of C++ added; all but 4 in a new file). The TOSS/FETCH concept can be extended to different media (e.g., video) or differently structured information (e.g., hypertext).

The channels described next provide added functionality at the cost of imposing greater demands on the application.

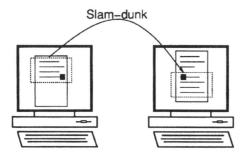

Figure 3. SLAM-DUNK

3.2 Spike

There are a few problems with TOSS/FETCH.

- The recipient has to be notified about a toss via an alternate channel.

- The tossed POV is visible to all users and hence may not be suitable for private communications.

- The recipient has to take action to fetch a POV.

- Since a fetch retrieves the last tossed POV, if multiple users are tossing and fetching simultaneously, they may interfere with each other.

SPIKE (see Figure 2) was developed to address these problems. SPIKE is a directed communication channel for transmitting POVs directly to the intended user. SPIKE requires the ability of applications to exchange messages, leading to a more complex implementation than for TOSS/FETCH. To spike a POV the sender activates SPIKE with a single keystroke and then specifies the recipients. The recipients of the SPIKE will be presented with the POV on their display.

The sender's cognitive overhead is increased since a target must now be specified. However, the recipient's overhead is reduced since the POV is directly deposited into a distinguished buffer of their application. The notification is now active and the recipient does not need to take any action to retrieve a POV. Since the communication is directed, multiple users can use this channel without interfering with each other, and only the intended recipient sees the POV.

3.3 Slam-dunk

Sometimes there is a need to take a text fragment from one user's buffer and insert it into the buffer of another. This situation occurs often when two people work together in close proximity, but only one of them is directly editing the object of collaboration. The other writes some text that must be transferred into the buffer of the first.

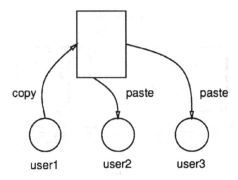

Figure 4. A global clipboard

One way of transferring the data is to write out the text fragment into a file and have the primary author read the file in at the appropriate location. This approach suffers from the same security and path name problems mentioned earlier. Alternatively, email, TOSS/FETCH, or SPIKE could be used to transfer the fragment. The recipient must then explicitly copy the fragment over to the desired location.

We developed a channel, SLAM-DUNK (see Figure 3), that allows the sender to select a region of text and send it to a specified user. The recipient's application automatically places the received text at the current location of the cursor. SLAM-DUNK requires some external coordination to prepare the recipient to receive the fragment. This coordination could be eliminated by complicating the user interface. The recipient could simply be notified that data had arrived in a distinguished buffer. The data could then be inserted wherever necessary with a single keystroke. Our experience is that leaving the coordination outside the system seems quite natural in this situation.

3.4 Clipboards

A multi-user clipboard is a reasonable generalization of the previous channels. However, this generality can make the clipboard more cumbersome to use. Where the data is stored and how it is accessed defines the clipboard design space. We assume that a single clipboard contains a single object and manages cut, copy, and paste operations.

3.4.1 Global clipboard

In the simplest case there is one global clipboard that everyone can copy to and paste from (see Figure 4). This is similar to TOSS/FETCH since it is undirected. The advantage to this clipboard is that the interface is exactly like that of a standard clipboard, making it familiar. However, a potent disadvantage is that the probability of interference is high. Many users copying to the same clipboard will overwrite each others' information. This may be acceptable in a small user community, but

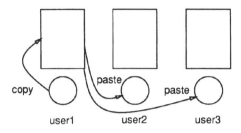

Figure 5. A public clipboard

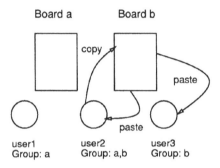

Figure 6. Group clipboards

not in a large one.

3.4.2 Public clipboard

A variation is to make a separate public clipboard (see Figure 5) for each user that is stored in the user's own application memory. Operating on a user's own clipboard is the default. A user also can copy to or paste from another's public clipboard. This directed communication greatly reduces the problem of interference as the user community grows, at the cost of only a minor complication of the interface. However, the clipboard has to be public so that another user can cut to or paste from one's clipboard. Adding security would alleviate this problem at the expense of unduly complicating the interface.

3.4.3 Group clipboard

An intermediate variation between the global clipboard and public clipboards is to have a clipboard for every group (see Figure 6). Only members of a particular group would be able to access the group's clipboard, thus reducing privacy concerns. Group clipboards also alleviate the interference problems caused by a large user community. The overhead of specifying the target of a cut or paste can be reduced by choosing the last target as the default.

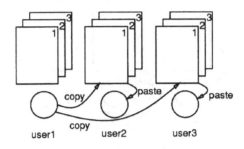

Figure 7. Private clipboards

3.4.4 Private clipboard

The final variation is to provide each user with a separate, private clipboard (see Figure 7) to communicate with other users. This provides each pair of users with two distinct privately shared clipboards (a local one and a remote one). Each user also has a private clipboard for their own use. This scheme provides flexibility in communication and security, at the cost of making the model and interface more complicated. The target clipboard is normally specified by a user identifier. Depending on the design of the system, additional information may be necessary to disambiguate between the user's local and remote clipboards. As the communication is directed, no special security mechanisms are necessary. For two users to communicate information with this channel, two directed operations must be used. The first user copies explicitly to the second user who then pastes from the first.

The channels that we have described are just examples. Other variations are conceivable. These channels are important because they are simple and they either enrich existing communication channels, or make some forms of communication less cumbersome, or both. Their simplicity makes it easy to understand what they will do under different circumstances and allows for easy integration into a system or application design. We have found them to be reasonably useful and powerful in our own collaborative tasks.

4 A taxonomy of communication channels

This section provides a taxonomy of various communication channels based on selected attributes. The cognitive overhead of each attribute highlights the tradeoffs in choosing a particular channel over another for a given situation. A channel involves communication from a sender to one or more receivers. The attributes listed below are in chronological order of occurrence during a communication. Not all the attributes are orthogonal to each other. Table 2 summarizes the channels described in this paper. Synchronous applications are included to provide a point of comparison.

	TOSS/FETCH	SPIKE	SLAM-DUNK	clipboards	sync apps
User interface	snapshot	snapshot	snapshot	snapshot	continuous
Source data	both	both	region	region	both
Target	undirected	directed	directed	either	directed
Recipient	broadcast	unicast	unicast	unicast	multicast
Transport	async	sync	sync	either	sync
Notification	passive	active	active	both	active
Destination data	buffer	buffer	point	point	NA
Recipient action	yes	no	no	yes	no

Table 2. Channel taxonomy

4.1 Interface type

What kind of interface does the channel provide to the sender? Is it similar to a datagram, involving minimal specification of the collaborative session; or is it similar to a virtual circuit, which involves setting up the channel?

In a datagram-like situation, the communication is either undirected or uses easily specifiable addresses with good use of defaults. Thus, there is little cognitive overhead for a sender. The low overhead makes this type of channel appropriate for quick, short-lived communications. Examples include TOSS/FETCH, SLAM-DUNK, and SPIKE.

Longer communications can benefit from expending effort in setting up a session, since there is an expectation of a larger number of longer communication events. The user has to set up the application and collaboration participants before the collaboration can occur. Examples include XTV, WSCRAWL, and SHOWME.

4.2 Source data

What does the source data include? The data sent as part of the communication may be a whole buffer, a region in a buffer, or both. In the case of a buffer, the sender requires less specification since the buffer can be assumed to be the one containing the current location by default. Sending a region at least involves specifying its extent. SPIKE uses a whole buffer, SLAM-DUNK uses a region, and TOSS/FETCH uses both a buffer and a region.

4.3 Targets

Is the target of the communication directed or undirected? Directed communication involves a greater cognitive overhead than undirected communication because the targets require extra specification. This overhead may be reduced by the use of good default schemes. This attribute has some overlap with the interface type attribute. For example, email is usually directed, whereas USENET is relatively undirected communication.

4.4 Recipients

Can multiple recipients receive the communications? Some communications are point-to-point or unicast; others are multicast or broadcast. This attribute is similar to the previous one except that the target is from the sender's point of view whereas the recipient is from the receiver's point of view. Unicast requires more specification than broadcast and hence more overhead. TOSS/FETCH is an example of broadcast, whereas SPIKE exemplifies unicast.

4.5 Transport

Is the transport asynchronous or synchronous? This attribute does not have direct impact on user overhead, except that asynchronous transports usually imply loosely coupled systems like email, while synchronous transports are usually used for tightly coupled systems like XTV.

4.6 Notification

Is the notification active or passive? On the receiving side of the communication, the receipt of a message can either be actively notified to the recipient or have the recipient check for the message. Passive notification puts a greater burden on the user. SLAM-DUNK can be considered to have active notification, while USENET typically has passive notification.

4.7 Destination data

Where does the received data go? Most often, the destination of the communicated data is a new or existing buffer or file. However, as in the case of SLAM-DUNK, the destination may be a location in an existing buffer. The latter incurs an overhead for the recipient since the cursor has to be positioned at the correct location.

4.8 Recipient action

Does the recipient have to take any action on the receipt of a communication? This is similar to notification, but focuses on the actions the recipient takes after notification. For example, email usually has active notification, but requires the receiving user to read in the new message using a mail user agent. On the other hand, SPIKE requires no recipient action since the message is automatically delivered into a new buffer.

5 Implementing communication channels

Most of the channel prototypes were built in a environment that we developed to experiment with communicating applications and to explore both loosely coupled and tightly coupled groupware. The environment allows EMACS processes to communicate data between one another. We use an EMACS process as a server and other EMACS processes as clients which led to the name ESC (Emacs Server Client).

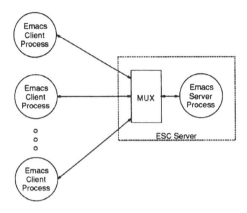

Figure 8. ESC Process Architecture

We implemented the environment in EMACS using an object-oriented extension to ELISP called EOOPS (Houser & Kalter, 1992).

The ESC server is actually two processes, an EMACS running ESC server code and an additional process called the ESC-mux which is used to listen on ports and do non-blocking writes (see Figure 8). Performing these operations in a single EMACS process would have required low-level modifications to EMACS, which we wanted to avoid.

ESC provides reusable classes that solve many low level problems in communication, resource identification, and session management so that experimenters can concentrate on higher level issues. The class library provides support for creating and maintaining connections with the server, managing client registration information, sending and receiving messages, notifying applications of events, and writing user interfaces. ESC is not meant for production systems but to provide extremely flexible and high level primitives with which to experiment. It also provides a basis with which to modify these primitives to seek better abstractions, and to improve functionality and performance.

Implementing channels in this environment limits their availability to applications written in the ESC framework. The advantage of ESC is that it provides high level primitives to prototype and experiment with working versions of an experimental channel quickly. For instance, with ESC support, the classes that implement SPIKE and SLAM-DUNK are about 50 lines of EOOPS code each. The first version of SLAM-DUNK was completed within a couple of hours of recognizing its potential usefulness.

These mechanisms could be implemented using USENET or email as a transport mechanism. This would certainly be possible, but a notification mechanism, API, and user-interface would also have to be developed in order to integrate the communication into actual applications.

6 Necessary application characteristics

A significant benefit of loosely coupled communication channels is that they require minimal support from the application. Hence it is easy to implement such channels for almost any application. This means that users can continue to use familiar applications, increasing the likelihood that these channels will be used. These requirements are listed below.

Command loop modifications Most interactive applications have a command or event loop. It is usually trivial to add a new command to such applications.

Read/write document fragments The ability to read data from a section of the document and write to a section of the document without disturbing the rest of the application state is required.

Get/set the current point and mark The ability to retrieve and set the current cursor location is required. If the application supports the notion of a mark, retrieving and setting the mark is useful too.

Communication support Low-level communication system support is required for ESC-supported applications, like SPIKE and SLAM-DUNK, which do not require recipient intervention. The communication is required for active notification so that the application can perform some action upon certain events without user interaction.

Fortunately, most interactive applications support the first three requirements with very little effort. Event-driven applications also support the last requirement trivially, by allowing additional communication channels to be hooked into their event loop. The low-level communication facility is important. ESC provides this for EMACS. Other applications can use other inter-application communication frameworks such as TOOLTALK (SunSoft, 1991), ISIS (Birman & Joseph, 1986), COEX (Patel & Kalter, 1993), and SOFTBENCH (Cagan, 1990).

7 Future work

The communication channels mentioned earlier are examples of loosely-coupled channels that are useful during collaboration. Many more variations on this theme need to be tried out to determine their value in practice. We have used these communication channels within our group and found them to be useful. Systematic external user testing of promising channels is required before the usability claims can have more general validity. Our ESC development environment was instrumental in allowing us to explore alternatives rapidly. As a result, most of our experimentation has used EMACS. Adapting these channels for use in other applications will help evaluate the applicability of this approach to other domains.

8 Conclusion

Our experience, as reported in this paper, has shown that loosely coupled communication channels are easy to implement and are useful in providing low-overhead channels for meeting specific communication requirements during a collaboration. Existing applications can integrate these channels with ease since the application requirements are moderate.

Low cost, loosely coupled channels for specialized communication, or for augmenting existing channels, are useful in limited domains. The ability to implement and experiment with such a channel quickly is important. Inter-application communication frameworks, like ESC, provide flexible, high-level communication abstractions that greatly facilitate rapid experimentation with various loosely coupled channels.

References

Abdel-Wahab, H. M. & Feit, M. A. (1991). "XTV: A framework for sharing X window clients in remote synchronous collaboration". In *Proceedings of the IEEE TriComm'91: Communications for Distributed Applications and Systems*, April 1991, pp. 159–167, Chapel Hill, North Carolina.

Beaudouin-Lafon, M. & Karsenty, A. (1992). "Transparency and awareness in a real-time groupware system". In *Proceedings of the ACM Symposium on User Interface Software and Technology UIST'92*, November 1992, pp. 171–180, Monterey, CA. ACM Press.

Birman, K. P. & Joseph, T. A. (1986). "Communication support for reliable distributed computing". Technical Report TR 86-753, Computer Science Department, Cornell University, Ithaca, NY.

Cagan, M. R. (1990). "The HP SoftBench environment: An architecture for a new generation of software". *Hewlett-Packard Journal, 41*(3), 36–47.

Dewan, P. & Choudhary, R. (1991). "Primitives for programming multi-user interfaces". In *Proceedings of the ACM Symposium on User Interface Software and Technology UIST'91*, November 11–13 1991, pp. 69–78, Hilton Head, South Carolina. ACM Press.

Fish, R. S., Kraut, R. E., & Chalfonte, B. L. (1990). "The VideoWindow System in informal communication". In Halasz, F. (Ed.), *CSCW90: Proceedings of the Conference on Computer-Supported Cooperative Work*, October 7–10 1990, pp. 1–11, Los Angeles, California.

Garfinkel, D., Gust, P., Lemon, M., & Lowder, S. (1989). "The SharedX multi-user interface user's guide, version 2.0". Technical Report STL-TM-89-07, Hewlett Packard Laboratories, Palo Alto, California.

Gaver, W. W. (1992). "The affordances of media spaces for collaboration". In Turner, J. & Kraut, R. (Eds.), *CSCW92: Proceedings of the Conference on Computer-Supported Cooperative Work*, October 31–November 4 1992, pp. 17–24, Toronto, Canada.

Group Technologies, Inc. (1990). *Aspects User Manual*. Arlington, Virginia: Group Technologies, Inc.

Hill, R. D., Brinck, T., Patterson, J. F., Rohall, S. L., & Wilner, W. T. (1993). "The Rendezvous language and architecture". *Communications of the ACM, 36*(1), 62–67.

Houser, C. & Kalter, S. D. (1992). "Eoops: An object-oriented programming system for Emacs-Lisp". *LISP Pointers, 5*(3), 25–33.

Ishii, H., Kobayashi, M., & Grudin, J. (1992). "Integration of inter-personal space and shared workspace: ClearBoard design and experiments". In Turner, J. & Kraut, R. (Eds.), *CSCW92: Proceedings of the Conference on Computer-Supported Cooperative Work*, October 31–November 4 1992, pp. 33–42, Toronto, Canada.

Knister, M. J. & Prakash, A. (1990). "DistEdit: A distributed toolkit for supporting multiple group editors". In Halasz, F. (Ed.), *CSCW90: Proceedings of the Conference on Computer-Supported Cooperative Work*, October 7–10 1990, pp. 343–355, Los Angeles, California.

Lewis, B., LaLiberte, D., & the GNU Manual Group (1990). *The GNU Emacs Lisp Reference Manual* (1.02 ed.). Cambridge, Massachusetts: Free Software Foundation.

McGuffin, L. & Olson, G. M. (1992). "ShrEdit: A shared electronic workspace". CSMIL Technical Report 45, Univeristy of Michigan, Ann Arbor, Michigan.

Neuwirth, C. M., Kaufer, D. S., Chandhok, R., & Morris, J. H. (1990). "Issues in the design of computer support for co-authoring and commenting". In Halasz, F. (Ed.), *CSCW90: Proceedings of the Conference on Computer-Supported Cooperative Work*, October 7–10 1990, pp. 183–195, Los Angeles, California.

Patel, D. & Kalter, S. D. (1993). "A UNIX toolkit for distributed synchronous collaborative applications". *Computing Systems*, 6(2). To appear.

Roseman, M. & Greenberg, S. (1992). "GroupKit: A groupware toolkit for building real-time conferencing applications". In Turner, J. & Kraut, R. (Eds.), *CSCW92: Proceedings of the Conference on Computer-Supported Cooperative Work*, October 31–November 4 1992, pp. 43–50, Toronto, Canada.

Stallman, R. (1987). *GNU Emacs Manual* (Sixth ed.). Cambridge, Massachusetts: Free Software Foundation.

Stefik, M., Bobrow, D. G., Foster, G., Lanning, S., & Tatar, D. (1987). "WYSIWIS revised: Early experiences with multiuser interfaces". *ACM Transactions on Office Information Systems*, 5(2), 147–167.

SunSoft (1991). *ToolTalk 1.0 Programmer's Guide*. Mountain View, California: SunSoft.

Tang, J. C. & Minneman, S. L. (1990). "VideoDraw: A video interface for collaborative drawing". In Chew, J. C. & Whiteside, J. (Eds.), *CHI'90: Proceedings of the Conference on Human Factors in Computing Systems*, April 1–5 1990, pp. 313–320, Seattle, Washington. ACM, Addison Wesley.

Wilson, B. (1992). "WSCRAWL 2.0: A shared whiteboard based on X-Windows". Technical Report 33, Apple Computer Library, Cupertino, California.

Proceedings of the Third European Conference on Computer-Supported Cooperative Work
13-17 September, 1993, Milan, Italy
G. De Michelis, C. Simone and K. Schmidt (Editors)

A Model for Semi-(a)Synchronous Collaborative Editing

Sten Minör & Boris Magnusson
Department of Computer Science, Lund University, Sweden

Abstract: This paper presents a new model for semi-synchronous collaborative editing. It fills the gap between asynchronous and synchronous editing styles. The model is based on hierarchically partitioned documents, fine-grained version control, and a mechanism called active diffs for supplying collaboration awareness. The aim of the model is to provide an editing style that better suits the way people actually are working when editing a document or program together, using different writing strategies during different activities.

1. Introduction

During the last couple of years, a number of collaborative editors have been developed. The aim of the different systems vary, some are specifically supporting collaborative authoring, some are general purpose text editors, some support collaborative sketching or drawing, and some provide a framework for integrating existing editors into a collaborative environment. Furthermore, different systems are based on different architectures, provide sharing at different levels, and use different strategies for distribution. Despite the different goals and architectures the systems support two main editing styles: synchronous and asynchronous editing.

1.1 Synchronous editors

Up till now, work on synchronous editing has been dominating within the area of collaborative editing. A synchronous editor allows multiple users to access and edit a document (a text, picture, drawing, etc.) simultaneously. Since simultaneous editing operations performed on shared material by different users may conflict, most editors have a protocol to ensure consistency. This may either be done by some locking mechanism where a user explicitly locks an object before editing it to avoid conflicts, implicit locking where the system locks an object edited by a user, or by ordering editing events ensuring consistent updating at the different sites. Some synchronous editors support shared views and telepointers. A shared view allows different users to see a part of a document in exactly the same manner using the WYSIWIS (What You See Is What I See) metaphor. The user interfaces are here tightly coupled and if one user scrolls a window, for instance, the same window will be scrolled at the other sites. Telepointers allow multiple cursors, one for each user, which are shown at all sites and are updated in real time. Furthermore, some systems provide support for "meta work", i.e. communication about the work the system primarily supports, e.g. in the form of shared workspaces for text and drawings and support for speech and image communication. Examples of different kinds of collaborative editors supporting synchronous editing are: GroupSketch (Greenberg and Bohnet, 1991), a shared workspace for sketching, GROVE (Ellis, Gibbs, and Rein, 1991), a textual multi-user outlining tool, ShrEdit (McGuffin and Olson, 1992), a multi-user text editor, and DistEdit (Knister and Prakash, 1990), a toolkit for implementing distributed group editors.

1.2 Asynchronous editors

Conventional text editors and drawing tools are typically asynchronous. Even though they may run in a distributed environment with a shared file system they do not support collaboration by multiple users. Prep (Neuwirth, Kaufer, Chandhok, and Morris, 1990) is an example of an asynchronous editor supporting collaboration. It allows only one user to edit a document at a time, but has specialized support for commenting a document. A document is organized as a number of columns. The author may create the document contents in one column and a reviewer, for instance, may create a new column for his/her comments and bind the different comments to places in the author's column. The Prep editor thus mainly supports asynchronous collaboration for authoring in form of reviewing and commenting.

1.3 Synchronous or asynchronous editing?

An interesting question is if the separation into synchronous and asynchronous editing is for good. Does an editor of one of these categories really meet the users' needs in different tasks and different situations? We believe not.

Asynchronous editors may be useful for some tasks, e.g. when one person is commenting the work of another. This is intrinsically an asynchronous task where the reviewer typically finishes the work and returns it to the author. However, asynchronous editors do not allow people to work simultaneously on the same document. If this shall be achieved the document has to be partitioned and later joined manually by the users. While working on their own fragment, the users are not aware of what other users are doing meanwhile. Another option is to serialize the work, which, of course, is not desirable.

Synchronous editors support sharing of a document and awareness about other users' work, but they do not support the asynchronous working style. Synchronous editing may be very useful in the brainstorming phase of authoring a paper or in initial design of a program. It may also be useful when discussing the contents of the document with other users. However, it assumes the collaborating users to be *present*. If, for instance, two persons are co-authoring a paper, they do not work simultaneously all the time. One person may be away for some time (an hour, a day, a week). When the work is continued by that person he/she is not primarily interested in what the other person is doing right now, but rather what has happened in the document since the last time.

The fact that different situations demand different editing styles has been acknowledged before. Dourish and Belotti (1992) calls for an editing model which supports both synchronous and asynchronous work and a smooth transition between them. The SEPIA hypertext authoring system (Haake and Wilson, 1992) allows work in modes called: *individual, loosely coupled,* and *tightly coupled* respectively and switching between them. The *individual* mode works like traditional asynchronous editing. In *loosely coupled* mode a node may be edited by one user at a time while other users may see the changes, i.e. synchronous editing based on locking. Finally, *tightly coupled* mode adds shared views, telepointers, and audio communication.

An empirical study of how people actually are collaborating in writing is presented by Posner and Baecker (1992). A number of different writing strategies used in different phases of the authoring of a document are identified. They conclude that both synchronous and asynchronous strategies are used in different phases of a collaborative writing project and that a system must support both styles and a smooth transition between them. An interesting result of the study is that most collaborative writing projects used the "separate writers strategy", i.e. an asynchronous style of authoring, extensively.

In our own experience from software development, several of the observations by Posner and Baecker are valid also for explorative software development. A synchronous style of work is often used in the initial phases of development, e.g. brainstorming and initial design. For more detailed design and implementation the work is often split up and the work is mostly done asynchronously on a separate fragment of the design. When it comes to integration, testing, and debugging the work style turns to be more synchronous again. The situation seems to be similar to authoring. Collaborative software environments thus have to support both synchronous and asynchronous working strategies and smooth transitions between them.

In the next section we present a model which supports semi-synchronous editing. It is a general editing model which may be used as a basis both for authoring and software development. In section 3 the properties of the model is discussed. In section 4 some notes on the implementation and future work is given followed by conclusions in section 5.

2. A semi-synchronous editing model

The editing model presented here has been developed as a part of an ongoing project on collaborative software development environments. It is based on previous work in the Mjølner project, a project on object-oriented software development (Knudsen, Löfgren, Madsen, and Magnusson (1993), (Magnusson, Minör, and Hedin, 1990). However, we believe the basic editing model is more widely applicable. Thus we present it in more general terms. In our view the editing model is a general technique for semi-synchronous editing which may be the basis for application specific environments, e.g. authoring systems or software development environments.

First we present the notion of hierarchical documents and hierarchical browsing which is fundamental in our model. We then describe the fine-grained version control functionality, which automatically keeps track of the modifications of a document and supports simultaneous editing by different users and merging. Finally, we present active diffs which are used for continuously making the users aware of changes done by other users thus giving the editor a synchronous appearance.

2.1 Hierarchical documents

A document is organized as a hierarchical structure. The hierarchy corresponds to chapters, sections and paragraphs in a book or to blocks, classes, and procedures in programming languages. This hierarchy is fundamental in our model. A document is displayed using this hierarchy, it is edited in terms of the hierarchy, all elements in the hierarchy are version controlled, and the database server stores documents in terms of the hierarchy.

Figure 1 shows an example of the users view of a document. In the figure there are two main objects, the hierarchical document at the top and an evolution graph below, explained later. The document "ECSCW'93" contains a number of parts: the title, an abstract, section 1-4, and a references part. All these parts are shown and manipulated by a hierarchical browser, which allows parts at one level to overlap but not to be moved outside its parent window. Subparts are added and removed in the browser by selecting entries from a menu, e.g. "new Section". The parts in the figure contain text which is edited by a text editor.

The subdivision into particular parts is not built into the system but is described in a grammar specifying the hierarchy. The example in figure 1 shows a rather flat hierarchy. Using another grammar, the sections may contain subsections, which in turn may contain paragraphs and sub-paragraphs, etc. This is a matter of tailoring the system, which can be different for different groups or projects. Furthermore, by

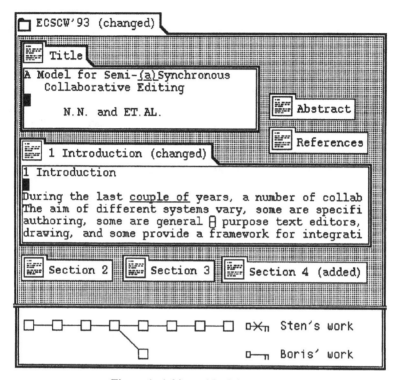

Figure 1 A hierarchical document

supplying different grammars, the browser may be tailored for different application areas, e.g. software development where the sub-parts may consist of classes, modules, procedures, functions, and methods, as long as the document forms a hierarchy.

The approach for hierarchical browsing initially was developed in the Mjølner Orm software environment (Hedin and Magnusson, 1988) where it turned out to be a useful and "intuitive" way of viewing and editing program structures. The explicit view of the logical structure of a document can in a collaborative environment be used as a means for organizing the work, where the users share the same partitioning of the document.

2.2 Fine-grained version control

Our editing model heavily relies on version control. In software engineering, version control is an established technique for dealing with complex systems developed by a team of system developers (Tichy, 1988), (Gustavsson, 1990). In our view, version control is a crucial technique for all collaborative design environments and editors. In such systems we do not only have to deal with potentially complex designs or documents but also with modifications of a document performed by a possibly large group of users simultaneously or at different times. Version control is important for several purposes. One is to keep track of the evolution history of a document. Another is to maintain consistent configurations of a complex design. It may also be used as a means for coordinating activities between several project members. All these aspects are important for collaborative systems.

In our editing model, hierarchical documents are version controlled. The lower part of figure 1 shows an evolution graph of the document "ECSCW'93". A graph contains three different evolution steps: versions, alternatives and alternative merging as depicted in figure 2.

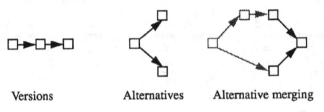

Versions   Alternatives   Alternative merging

Figure 2 Evolution steps in an evolution graph

A version[1] is one step in the evolution of a document. It may contain arbitrary changes compared to its predecessor. Typically it may contain new chapters or paragraphs, parts may have been removed, or it may contain minor modifications such as corrections of spelling errors. A version is never changed once it has been established. The only way of modifying a document is to create a new version (or alternative) with the desired modifications.

An alternative (sometimes called variant) serves two main purposes. One is to split up the evolution into two (similar) documents with different purposes. A document may, for instance, be modified into two alternatives for two groups of readers, novices and experts, but with a core of common contents. The other purpose is to support simultaneous development among multiple users. If one user wants to edit a version that is edited by another user, an alternative is created instead of a version. The users edit their own alternatives and merge them into one version when ready.

Merge is taking place between alternatives which always have a common root, one or several steps away as shown in figure 2. All the concatenated changes in the alternatives (starting from the root version) are candidates for inclusion in the

---

1. Usually a distinction is made between versions and revisions. We do not do that distinction here, but use the term *version* in a generic fashion.

merged version. If there are conflicting changes the decision on what to include has to be made by the person doing the merge who can also do any other changes to the document at the same time. Conflicts might occur on the lexical, syntactical or semantic levels and automatic detection of such conflicts can be perceived at least at the primitive level. This schema can be used when merging two or more alternatives although it might be practical to merge two alternatives at the time.

In our model, all subparts of a hierarchical document are subjected to version control. If, for instance, the "Section1" subpart of the document in figure 1 is edited resulting in a new version, a new version of the document "ECSCW'93" is automatically created. The new version will contain the new version of "Section1" but will share unchanged parts with the old version of "ECSCW'93". Furthermore, the version control keeps track of and stores the deltas between the two versions of "Section1", i.e. the editing operations performed by the user for creating the new version from the old one.

This hierarchical fine-grained version control functionality is implemented as a basic functionality of the database server for hierarchical documents. A more elaborate description of the approach can be found in (Magnusson, Asklund, and Minör, 1993). Since it is fundamental in our editing model, it is also integrated into the other parts of the system, the hierarchical browser and the text editor. One reason is to support collaboration awareness, which we will expand on in the next section.

2.3 Collaboration awareness

In addition to handling versions and alternatives, our model supports collaborative editing by means of collaboration awareness. It is based on the hierarchical organization and the hierarchical version control functionality. Collaboration awareness is available in two ways in the system: by the evolution graph which is shared among all users and by the presentation of *active diffs*.

When a user enters the system to edit a document, the evolution graph gives a hint of the status of the document. The user can see who is editing it at the moment and what has happened since last time. In figure 1, for instance, one can see that there are two alternatives of the document and that the "Sten's work" alternative is edited at the moment (the editing key of this alternative is crossed over). If no other user is present when entering, the user can select his/her latest version for editing and use the system as any asynchronous editor. The system will automatically create a new version of the changed parts (and of the document) when the user starts editing them. It does not impose any overhead for dealing with versions compared to a conventional editor.

If other users are present one can still choose to asynchronously edit a version which is not in use by any other user. However, it is also possible to open a version currently edited by another user. In this case the system will create an alternative of the parts of the document the user edits. This alternative is edited independently of other alternatives of the same part. The alternatives may at a later time be merged. Since parts unchanged by any of the users still are shared between the alternatives, merging only has to take place for changed subparts of the document.

In order to make users aware of what other users actually are doing in the document, e.g. in two alternatives of a document part simultaneously edited by two users, the system provides active diffs. An active diff is showing the difference between two versions (or alternatives) of the document. The diffs are based on the actual edit operations performed, which are stored by the version/database handler as differences between versions. In this way fine-grained and accurate differences that reflect what modifications actually have been performed by the user can be presented. The diffs are presented in a semi-graphical form, at the presentation level quite similar to the presentation of diffs in Prep (Neuwirth, Chandhok, Kaufer, et al., 1992).

The "Section1" window in figure 1 shows a small example. The differences between the current and the previous versions are shown in the window used for editing. All insertions appear as underlined text and all deletions as "-" markers. The "-" markers may be expanded interactively in order to see the actual deletions. In the same way the underlined insertions may be collapsed to "+" markers. By collapsing all markers the user can see the text common to the two versions, by collapsing the minus markers and expanding the plus markers the text is viewed as the new version (as in figure 1), and finally by expanding the minus markers and collapsing the plus markers the text is viewed as the old version. Differences between parts of the document are shown in a similar way with the icons in the window titles marked as additions, deletions, and changes within a part (or one of its subparts).

By default the diff between the current version and its predecessor is shown. However, diffs between arbitrary versions and alternatives can be shown. This is done by selecting the versions (alternatives) in the evolution graph. In this way it is possible to see what has happened in the document since a certain version or in what way different alternatives differ. A view used in the merge situation shows the difference from the root version following the different alternatives (say A, B, etc.) with different markers. Diffs can also be shown for different alternatives currently being edited. If a user A sets up a diff between the alternative currently edited and an alternative edited by B simultaneously, the differences between the two versions will be shown continuously, i.e. all modifications performed by B will appear as markers in A's window. Notice that these diffs are shown on A's demand and A is free to turn off the diffs whenever wanted. The diff markers cannot be edited by A, A can only edit his/her own alternative. However, the markers make A aware of what B is doing and may contribute to avoiding conflicting changes which result in unnecessary resolving of conflicts during alternative merges at a later stage. The example with two users can be generalized to several users, e.g. using color coding of the markers in order to visualize who has changed what. Active alternative diffs may in this way be used for giving a "synchronous editing" view of the document, presenting a "what-if-I-merged" situation, useful for discussions, initial design, or brainstorming.

3. Properties of the model

The model for semi-synchronous editing we propose is based on the observation that a high degree of collaboration awareness can be obtained without actually sharing the document in the way synchronous collaborative editors usually do. Our model is basically based on an asynchronous style of editing using a traditional split-edit-merge approach for simultaneous editing. However, the fine-grained version control combined with the technique for active diffs adds collaboration awareness which comes close to pure synchronous editing. The fact that the user may choose the editing style from pure asynchronous editing to almost synchronous editing makes the approach very flexible. By selecting diffs the user may choose a style of editing which is in-between asynchronous and synchronous editing. The style can be changed while editing which allows several styles to be used within an editing session and a smooth transition between them.

The fact that simultaneous modifications of the same part of a document always are done in different alternatives and that changes made by other users merely are reflected by the active diffs have several technical consequences. One is that operations such as undo/redo of editing operations always are well defined. They may be applied to the local alternative in the same manner as in any asynchronous text editor. Another (more important) consequence is that no floor control is necessary. Neither locking, explicit or implicit, nor any turn-taking protocol to avoid conflicting operations is needed. If conflicting modifications are introduced they have to be resolved at merge-time. However, we expect that the use of active diffs will reduce the number of conflicts even though we do not have any empirical evidence for that at present. This expectation is supported by experience from the use of GROVE (Ellis, Gibbs, and Rein, 1991), which shows that conflicts are infrequent as a result of awareness of others' activities. Furthermore, we believe that this kind of "maximally lazy" consistency approach has the advantage that users need not be distracted by consistency issues, such as locking objects before editing or handling the floor between users, while performing the task.

Except for producing documents, the editing model can be used for commenting or reviewing. A reviewer can create an alternative of the document and add the comments. The author can at a later time (or actually at the same time if desired) set up an active diff to the reviewer's alternative and obtain the comments as markers in his/her own alternative. The author may then choose between just reading the markers as the document is revised in his/her own alternative and merging the two alternatives to a version containing the comments for further revisions.

The model is fairly robust against network failures. In case of a network failure during editing a user can continue editing. The collaboration awareness is lost and the editing has to continue asynchronously until the failure is repaired. We are also optimistic about that space and time requirements will scale up. The version/database manager is based on a backwards delta technique for storing versions which allows versions to be stored without maintaining multiple copies of the document. The time requirements are modest since the editing model does not rely on immediate distribution of editing operations among different users or the fact that they arrive at the different sites in a certain order. The active diffs are, of course, dependent on changes arriving within some reasonable time. The order of magnitude required is, however, seconds rather than fractions of a second.

A restriction of our model is that a document is hierarchically organized. This is due to the functionality of the database/version server which explicitly supports fine-grained version handling of hierarchical structures. In (Haake and Haake, 1993) version control for hypertexts in a cooperative system is described. Hypertexts put special demands on the version control server since it handles a general graph structure rather than a tree, which is not supported in our model. The main purpose of our model has been editing of hierarchical structures such as programs and documents. Based on our experience from the Mjølner project we do, however, believe that it may be applicable for other hierarchical structures, such as file-systems, mail-tools, spreadsheets, language grammars, and application-oriented languages.

4. Implementation status and future work

The editing model is the basic editing model in a tool for collaborative software development, which currently is developed within the object-oriented software development group at our department. The implementation is at the time of writing a fairly rudimentary prototype. It supports only editing of a program (or document) according to a grammar using the model presented in this paper. Some crucial parts still remain to be implemented in order to get a usable system. One is merging of alternatives based on the editing deltas maintained by the version server. Another is showing active diffs between several (more than two) alternatives which is necessary when several users are editing alternatives simultaneously.

Other areas we find interesting for future work are different kinds of merging. A merge can be made using an optimistic strategy, i.e. all changes made by any user, which is not in conflict with a change made by some other user, will be present in the version that is the result of the merge. A merge of documents not containing conflicting changes can be merged automatically using this strategy. However, modifications that are not in conflict in a technical sense may be in conflict semantically. A sentence added by one user may, for instance, contradict a sentence added by another user. A pessimistic strategy for merging should prompt the user for changes to the same document part (chapter, paragraph, sentence). It should also allow the user to control the result of the merge in case of a potential semantic conflict. Another reason for pessimistic merging is that the user may want to select different parts from different alternatives to the resulting merged version.

An area we have not yet dealt with is access control. This is particularly interesting for the active diffs. Since one user sees an active diff based on another user's editing operation deltas, it should be possible for the other user to work in a "private mode" where the editing deltas are not distributed to other users. Maybe it also should be possible to create versions and alternatives that are invisible to other users in the evolution graph.

Furthermore, the architecture of the distribution aspects of the system is a subject for further studies. At present the architecture is based on the client-server approach. The editors are replicated at each site and communicate with a central database/version server over a local area network. For collaborative editing over larger distances with unreliable communication this will not be sufficient.

Finally, we are interested in developing domain-specific support for software development where the editing model presented in this paper is included. This includes areas such as collaborative language-based editing, incremental compilation issues for collaborative systems, and collaborative debugging.

5. Conclusions

We have presented a model for semi-synchronous collaborative editing. The model relies on three fundamental concepts: hierarchical organization of documents, fine-grained version control, and presentation of active diffs. The hierarchical organization allows a document to be partitioned into separate parts, such as chapters, sections, and paragraphs, while the connection between the parts is maintained. The fine-grained version control mechanism maintains versions and alternatives of the document parts and the document itself. It supports collaboration using the split-edit-merge approach rather than sharing of the same material. Finally, the active diffs provide group awareness by showing differences between versions and alternatives as markers. In particular, the active diffs allow presentation of diffs between alternatives while different users edit the alternatives, resulting in a continuous updating of the diff presentation.

By integrating the above functionality, an editor that fills the gap between asynchronous and synchronous editing is obtained. The editor may be used asynchronously, synchronously, or in a mode in-between. The mode can easily be changed during an editing session and may be different for different users working simultaneously.

The aim has been to obtain an editing model that support the way groups actually work in collaborative editing, using different writing strategies during different activities and phases of a project. In order to obtain a usable system for some application area, it has to be extended with domain-specific support, e.g. for authoring or software development.

Acknowledgements

The authors wants to thank all the members of the software development research group at Department of Computer Science, Lund University, for stimulating discussions which have contributed substantially to the work presented in this paper. In particular, we want to thank Ulf Asklund and Torsten Olsson, who are involved in designing and implementing the fine-granular version/database server, the text editor, and the active diffs.

The work presented in this paper was supported in part by NUTEK, the Swedish National Board for Industrial and Technical Development.

References

Dourish, P. and Belotti, V. (1992): "Awareness and Collaboration in Shared Workspaces", *Proceedings of CSCW'92, ACM 1992 Conference on Computer-Supported Cooperative Work*, Toronto, 1992

Ellis, C.A., Gibbs, S.J., and Rein, G.L. (1991): "Groupware: Some Issues and Experiences", *Communications of the ACM*, 34(1), January, 1991

Greenberg, S. and Bohnet, R. (1991): "GroupSketch: A Multi-User Sketchpad for Geographically Distributed Small Groups", *Proceedings of Graphical Interface '91*, Calgary, 1991

Gustavsson, A. (1990): *Software Configuration Management in an Integrated Environment*, Licentiate thesis, Dept. of Computer Science, Lund University, Lund, 1990

Haake, A. and Haake, J. (1993): "Take CoVer: Exploiting Version Support in Cooperative Systems", *Proceedings of INTERCHI'93, 1993 Conference on Human Factors in Computing Systems*, Amsterdam, 1993

Hedin, G. and Magnusson, B. (1988): "The Mjølner Environment: Direct Interaction with Abstractions", *Proceedings of ECOOP'88, 2nd European Conference on Object-Oriented Programming, Lecture Notes in Computer Science*, vol. 322, Springer-Verlag, 1988

Haake, J.M. and Wilson, B. (1992): "Supporting Collaborative Writing of Hyperdocuments in SEPIA", *Proceedings of CSCW'92, ACM 1992 Conference on Computer-Supported Cooperative Work*, Toronto, 1992

Knudsen, J.L., Löfgren, M., Madsen, O.L. and Magnusson, B. (1993): *Object-Oriented Development - The Mjølner Approach*, Prentice-Hall, 1993, to appear

Knister, M.J. and Prakash, A. (1990): "DistEdit: A Distributed Toolkit for Supporting Multiple Group Editors", *Proceedings of CSCW'90, ACM 1990 Conference on Computer Supported Cooperative Work*, Los-Angeles, 1990

Magnusson, B., Asklund, U., and Minör, S. (1993): "Fine-Grained Revision Control for Collaborative Software Development", Tech. Report LU-CS-TR:93-112, Dept. of Computer Science, Lund University, Lund, Sweden, 1993

Magnusson, B., Minör, S., Hedin, G., Bengtsson, M., Dahlin, L., Fries, G., Gustavsson, A., Oscarsson, D., Taube, M. (1990): "An Overview of the Mjølner Orm Environment", *Proceedings of the 2nd International Conference TOOLS (Technology of Object-Oriented*

Languages and Systems), Paris, 1990

McGuffin, L.J. and Olson, G.M. (1992): "ShrEdit: A Shared Electronic Workspace", Cognitive Science and Machine Intelligence Laboratory, Tech. report #45, University of Michigan, Ann Arbor, 1992

Neuwirth, C.M., Chandhok, R., Kaufer, D.S., Erion, P., Morris, J. and Miller, D. (1992): "Flexible Diff-ing In a Collaborative Writing System", *Proceedings of CSCW'92, ACM 1992 Conference on Computer-Supported Cooperative Work*, Toronto, 1992

Neuwirth, C.M, Kaufer, D.S., Chandhok, R. and Morris, J. (1990): "Issues in the Design of Computer Support for Co-Authoring and Commenting", *Proceedings of CSCW'90, ACM 1990 Conference on Computer Supported Cooperative Work*, Los-Angeles, 1990

Posner, I.R. and Baecker, R.M. (1992): "How People Write Together", *Proceedings of the Twenty-Fifth Hawaii International Conference on System Sciences*, Vol. 4, Hawaii, 1992.

Tichy, W.F. (1988): "Tools for Software Configuration Management", *Proceedings of the International Workshop on Software version and Configuration Control*, Grassau, Germany, 1988

Proceedings of the Third European Conference on Computer-Supported Cooperative Work
13-17 September, 1993, Milan, Italy
G. De Michelis, C. Simone and K. Schmidt (Editors)

Informed Opportunism as Strategy: Supporting Coordination in Distributed Collaborative Writing

Eevi E. Beck [†][*]
[†]University of Sussex, UK

Victoria M. E. Bellotti [*]
[*]Rank Xerox Cambridge EuroPARC, UK

Abstract: There is little understanding of how distributed writing groups manage their collaboration and what kinds of support are most useful. The paper presents three case studies of distributed collaborative writing groups in academia. The process evolves over time, constantly adapting to changing circumstances. Co-authors offer and make use of a range of information. Their subsequent opportunistic use of this information to make appropriate ad hoc decisions in new circumstances, appears to be essential to achieve flexibility and coordination. We call this *informed opportunism*. We identify design implications for support tools for distributed collaborative writing.

1 Introduction

The rapid development of communications technology is making it easier and more cost effective for many people to communicate with others over a wider area than ever before. Some find it convenient or necessary to work closely with colleagues who are great distances away, and to collaborate on documents with them. The chances are increasingly that co-authors of documents are distributed over a wide area and must use that same telecommunications technology to support communication and management of writing activity.

Research on co-authoring is increasing in the humanities (Lunsford and Ede 1990; Forman 1992) as well as in CSCW. An increasing number of interview studies (*e.g.* Posner 1991; Rimmershaw 1992) and surveys (*e.g.* Lunsford and Ede 1990;

Couture and Rymer 1991; Chandler 1992; Beck 1993) are becoming available. Few longitudinal studies of the process of collaborative writing exist (although see Law and Williams 1982; Riley 1983; Couture and Rymer 1991; and Plowman 1992; and a growing number of self-reports of the experience of co-authoring). Co-authoring can be defined in many ways (Lunsford and Ede 1990), giving different perspectives on what the practices of co-authoring are (Couture and Rymer 1991). The assigning of authorship to academic papers is in itself a subject of study (*e.g.* Trimbur and Braun 1992).

We are interested in 'close' co-authoring, as opposed to, for example, editing, and define this as the writing of documents by two or more persons, where the names appearing in the author list are those of people who considered themselves involved in the writing of that document. We feel that for distributed co-authoring groups, *i.e.* those working together across geographic distance, there is a particular potential for appropriately designed computer-based tools being helpful.

Over the past few years there has been a rapid growth in the number of collaborative writing tools, *e.g.* QUILT (Leland, Fish, and Kraut 1988), GROVE (Ellis, Gibbs, and Rein 1990), SHREDIT (McGuffin and Olson 1992), and PREP (Neuwirth, Chandhok, Kaufer, Erion, Morris, and Miller 1992); and hypermedia co-authoring tools, *e.g.* COAUTHOR (Hahn, Jarke, Eherer, and Kreplin 1991). Some are designed to support writing together both at the same time and at different times, *e.g.* SASSE (Baecker, Nastos, Posner, and Mawby 1993). Few are designed for distributed co-authoring, an exception being MESSIE (Sasse, Chuang, and Handley 1993).

We have studied co-authoring in academia and have, however, found no evidence of use of special collaborative writing tools, except among those close to the development teams. Instead, face-to-face meetings, conventional workstation and printing technology, telephone, facsimile (fax), and post appear to be the means by which information is exchanged and activities managed. This is consistent with a general concern, *e.g.* with Kling (1991), that the use of CSCW tools has not proliferated at a rate corresponding to the increasingly sophisticated range of systems available. This problem has been attributed to a poor understanding of the way in which groups collaborate (Kraemer and Pinsonneault 1990; Grudin 1991).

An early indication that a distinction between discussion and annotation may not be useful for all co-authors (see Mhashi, Rada, Beck, Zeb, and Michailidis 1992), prompted our interest in whether other distinctions proposed in the analysis of writing make sense to users of the systems[1], or whether inappropriate assumptions are finding their way into collaborative writing systems. Does co-authoring proceed through 'stages' which it is meaningful to design to? COAUTHOR is one of several systems which has a strong separation of idea generation from text writing. Here, despite "no rigid phase model [being] intended" (p. 81), strong assumptions of what

---

1. Our concern here is not with whether such distinctions are appropriate in the analysis of writing or collaborative writing, nor with whether they provide useful frameworks for thinking about writing support, but, rather, with whether wholesale application of analytical and theoretical distinctions into support tools; distinctions such as those based on Flower and Hayes' influential cognitive model of writing (*e.g.* Flower and Hayes 1980); encourage a task oriented approach which may prove unnecessarily restrictive to users. Note that Flower herself in a later paper calls for writing research now to "explain how context cues cognition" (Flower 1989, p.1).

the phases are, and the order in which work should be done, are evident: "The first phase of *idea processing* determines the issues (...). During the second phase of *document design* a *formal* document structure has to be set up and associated with the conceptual items from the idea processing phase." (Hahn *et al.* 1991, pp. 80-81, orig. italics). Explicit role support has been called for *e.g.* in Baecker *et al.* 1993. But do co-authors allocate responsibilities *pre hoc* and stick with those decisions so that choosing and enforcing 'roles' is useful? The co-author roles arrived at in Posner 1991 from interviews with co-authors, were derived from *post hoc* analysis of what activities the co-authors had spent most of their time on and were not necessarily what they would have chosen initially (indeed, the final role had changed from initial expectations in one of the cases), whereas explicit role support presumably would require co-authors to commit to roles early. In what sense do writing groups devise 'strategies'? Sharples 1992 gives as pre-existing 'strategies for distributed collaborative writing' patterns of task distribution ('parallel', 'sequential', 'reciprocal') which have little empirical basis. Our concern is that unhelpful assumptions about co-authoring may become reified and find their way into system design, repeating the problem identified by Tatar, Foster and Bobrow (1991): in examining reasons for failures of the COGNOTER system, Tatar *et al.* found that incorrect assumptions about human communication had become enshrined in the design. They concluded that "[i]n a field that is as new and as complex as computer-supported cooperative work, [...] highly directed studies need to be augmented by other approaches such as undirected observation" (Tatar *et al.* 1991, p. 207).

The aim of this paper is to document practices in distributed co-authoring groups which we have observed in academia which do not support the above assumptions: salient features are not the carrying out of tidy agreements, but great flexibility and context sensitivity with which co-authors interpret information and situations and come to decisions about appropriate courses of action, even to the extent of unilaterally **contradicting** agreements. We call this strategy *Informed Opportunism*[2].

Below, we summarise the findings of two preliminary studies which looked at organisational aspects of co-authoring. These studies provided the impetus for the subsequent longitudinal case-studies. Then we present the case-studies themselves, examining in more detail the dynamic changes in the co-authoring process, with a particular emphasis on two basic questions about the nature of and support requirements for the coordination of individual activity within distributed co-authoring groups. Finally, we present design recommendations based on our findings.

2 Preliminary studies

Two studies of group organisation and collaboration aspects of co-authoring practices were undertaken. Initially, semi-structured interviews of 1-2 hours length were conducted with about ten co-authors. Issues which appeared to be the most impor-

---

2. 'Opportunism' is intended in the sense of "being guided by what seems possible, or by circumstances, in determining policy; preferring what can be done to what should be done" (Oxford Advanced Learner's Dictionary of Current English, 1974 edition). We refer to this as a 'strategy' only in the sense of "skill in managing any affair" (Oxford Adv. L.'s Dict. of Curr. Eng., *ibid.*), not *e.g.* the systematic making and execution of plans.

tant to the interviewees were reshaped into an exploratory questionnaire survey which was distributed to 23 academic researchers.

The respondents answered 24 multiple choice and rating questions, as well as supplementary open ended questions, with respect to one instance of co-authoring they had experienced. The questions addressed aspects of co-authoring practices ranging from distribution of responsibilities and discussions of the organization of the group, to membership changes, relative contributions by co-authors, motivation, perceptions of success and notions of collaborative writing.

Examples of questions asked are: Except for right at the beginning, were you at any point ever unsure about who were going to be the co-authors? (Replies allowed: Yes/No/Don't know; elaboration requested for yes-answers). What is, to you personally, the purpose of taking part in collaborative writing? (open-ended question). The main findings of the interview studies and survey are summarised in the following sections (for further details on the survey, see Beck 1993).

2.1 Group membership and roles

One third of the survey respondents indicated that membership of their writing group had changed while writing. Five respondents (23%) reported being unsure at some point who the co-authors were going to be. Thus group membership in the general case cannot be taken to be static, but is in many groups dynamically changing. Group leadership was attributed in equal proportions to a self-appointed leader or facilitator; an agreed leader/facilitator/project manager, and 'no-one'. This suggests that a system designer would be unjustified in assuming the presence of an agreed 'leader' in an academic collaborative writing group. The extent to which responsibilities were clearly divided between co-authors appeared to vary, with some evidence that it was more common for there to be overlapping areas of responsibility than not. Co-authors in the interview study reported frequent departures from agreed areas of responsibility in response to the progress of the joint writing.

2.2 Plans and goals

All survey respondents indicated that a very important measure of success was that the resulting document was acceptable to themselves. There was less agreement on quality, good communications, and getting on well with each other being important, although these also scored high mans. The contents and structure of the documents were not reported planned in advance so much as discussed during the writing. The question of the importance of 'Close adherence to an initial plan' received extremely varied ratings, with a medium to low mean.

2.3 Implications

The preliminary studies indicated that academic co-authoring groups may be subject to a complex mix of environmental influences, to the extent that roles, goals, and strategies must be regarded as subject to unpredictable change at any time. One interesting issue is, if there is such unpredictability, how do co-authors achieve the necessary coordination of activities to produce a document together? This is what our case studies set out to explore. We shall see how this suggests approaches to answering the question of appropriate system support. For example, the observation that the nature of the group and its mode of operation evolves dynamically in response to a multitude of factors relating to both group and individual member's contexts, gives an indication that a tool which is to fit in with this must incorporate great flexibility to accommodate the adapting process.

2.4 Communication and coordination: the research questions

A crucial point, we feel, is the manner in which individual work is related to the group as a whole. Co-authors make autonomous decisions when working alone, under changing and unpredictable conditions, which the group cannot foresee or plan for. However, in close collaboration each author must maintain awareness of and offer information about the current state of affairs to others, so that work is coordinated and appropriate contributions are made.

Communication mechanisms would seem critical to coordination of the collaborative writing endeavour. For distributed authors it is these mechanisms which are most likely to be particularly problematic. We would like to understand more about:

- How a document comes to exist and evolve into its final version.
- How co-authors manage access to the document.
- How co-authors decide what and when to write.

In each case we focus on information exchange and ask what co-authors inform each other of, and how.

In the following section we describe our investigation of these issues. Section 4 addresses the design implications.

3 Three case studies

Three observational case studies were conducted of *in vivo* distributed collaborative writing, *i.e.* as it was taking place in everyday work. The co-authors were employed in research in academia and industry. The completed documents were to be papers presenting research findings for publication in academic journals or conferences. The length of the joint writing ranged from three weeks (plus a post-review, final camera-ready copy preparation effort) to over a year.

3.1 The groups

Group A

Context, document and members: There were three co-authors, here referred to as A1, A2, and A3. Co-authors A2 and A3 were in the same building, whereas A1 was at a different institution 2-3 hours' drive away. The three formed the core of a research group which had already published one journal article. The document followed in this case study was another journal paper reporting on further research findings. There was no deadline. A1 and A2 were working on two other papers as well as a book concurrently with this paper.

Communication and supporting technology: A3 had been anticipated fully involved, but rarely took part in meetings, even at his own institution. Instead, A1 and A2 produced most of the paper without him. A1 and A2 were in regular contact, travelling to meet face-to-face 1-2 times per month, and telephoning 1-2 times per week. They made use of stand-alone text editors, diskettes, and occasionally fax transmission (3-4 times over four months). Other technologies available included electronic mail (email), which was viewed as potentially useful but never used.

Group B

Context, document and members: There were two co-authors, B1 and B2, separated by great distance and an 8 hour time difference. They had done research together, partly while in the same place, but mainly at a distance. The paper was to describe the results of their joint work and was to be submitted, in camera-ready format, to a conference. During the three weeks while most of the writing was done, there was considerable time pressure to meet the main deadline for dispatch (after the paper was accepted, further modifications were made).

Communication and supporting technology: B1 and B2 met face-to-face very early on, before the writing really started, but not while writing. There were daily email exchanges. Telephone calls were 1-2 per week during the busiest 3 weeks. Fax was used once, to send publishers' formatting instructions. Both authors used a sophisticated single-user text editing package. They transferred the entire document between them up to three times per 24-hr period, using electronic file exchange on networked workstations. This was by far the most intensive of the three groups.

Group C

Context, document and members: Two co-authors, C1 and C2, worked in the same department while developing the first draft, but were then separated by significant geographic distance (5 hours time difference). There was no deadline.

Communication and supporting technology: Prior to separating, printouts of the entire document were transferred twice. At separation, C2 took a copy of the file on a diskette. After separation, email was the only means of communication until a visit by C2 to C1 (for purposes other than this paper). The cost of telephoning was considered prohibitive. The writing is ongoing, and only the group's initial work is considered in this paper.

3.2 Method

In each case-study, interviews were conducted with the co-authors as soon as possible after their decision to write a paper, and after the completion of the writing. There were frequent follow-up interviews, mainly over the telephone. Interviews were audio recorded, and conducted with co-authors on their own. In addition, some

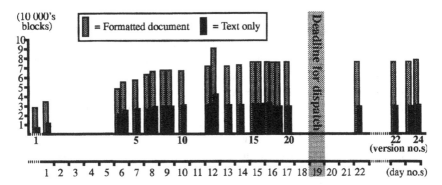

Figure 1. Growth in group B's document size over time. The horizontal axis represents time in days at which a version of the document was exchanged from co-author B1 to co-author B2 and vice versa. Dashed lines indicate a compressed timescale. The vertical axis indicates size of the document in blocks (one block is approximately 1000 characters' worth of data). Each version is represented by two bar heights to indicate the size of the text-only document file and the formatted document file. (Note that the formatted sizes exclude a large figure in the original versions (about 30 000 blocks) which the coauthors inserted into version 2, removed again (because it was slowing down their system) for version 6, and reinstated for version 18.) Two gaps in time are indicated by broken lines: between versions 1 and 2 (one week), and between versions 21 and 22 (approximately 4 months).

observation of co-authors working together was possible. Email messages, as well as notes on and intermediate versions of the document, were stored. In group B, all communication between the co-authors about the paper was recorded.

In the following three sections we report on our findings on what and how distribution of information took place. We then summarise our findings and address the question of desirable features of support tools for distributed co-authoring.

3.3 Document creation and evolution into its final version

Creation

In both groups A and B, an explicit decision to start writing a paper existed before writing started. Group B met to discuss the topic and content of their document before they began writing it. In group C, on the other hand, there was a gradual process by which an initial note was developed into a long enough document that the authors decided to turn it into a full-length publication. For all three case-studies the shared document coming into existence was a gradual realisation; it was not an event which even in retrospect could be clearly determined.

Evolution

For group B, we were able to store a complete set of versions of the document exchanged between the co-authors. Figure 1 shows the development of the paper in terms of the sizes of each of the 24 versions they exchanged.

The bulk of the writing took place over 22 days. The gaps between versions 2 and 3, and 18 and 22, were due to absence of B1 or B2; in each case, the other one went on writing. So, although the last exchange before the deadline was day 17 when B1 went away on a trip, B2 continued writing up to day 19. On day 11 the network connection was not working and thus no exchanges were possible.

A high level of activity was evident until B1's departure, with a peak at three exchanges of drafts on day 16. The deadline for sending off the document was day 19, when co-author B2 submitted version 21. (In Figure 1, version 21 is shown on day 22, when B1 returned and saw a copy). After notification of paper acceptance, versions 22-24 were produced as a final revision before publication. These were exchanged over two days approximately four months after initial submission.

Figure 1 shows that in group B, the document reached its full size early: already version 7 was of a similar size to the last versions. Examination of the actual version changes revealed that much of the total effort went into rearranging and rephrasing existing text, as opposed to generating new text.

Concern about formatting emerged early in B1's and B2's communications. They put in headers, some with mock section contents, which helped organize existing text and apparently acted as placeholders and reminders of actions to be completed in the future. Headers were also important aides in communicating summaries of changes, where they were extensively used as coordination points or shorthand references to the section contents: "[The new version] *has the* [required] *format (hopefully), the figure moved to the last page (since it looks like it will require manual placement), a rewrite of the* [section name] *stuff, and various other small modifications.*" (email message accompanying version 6).

Some formatting changes also show up in the graph: between versions 5 and 6, the document was re-formatted from single-column to double-column, resulting in an increase in the formatted size but not the text size.

In producing group B's document, no significant restructuring was done from version 13 onwards. Interestingly, most other changes—additions, deletions, and rewordings—occurred throughout. The volume of changes trailed off after version 18.

For group A, the process of writing was closely intertwined with other work including writing of other publications. Their way of working together was diverse, changing throughout the process. At face-to-face meetings, they would often sit down by the word processor and compose or review parts of the document together. Twice, an electronic file was exchanged by storing it on a floppy disk and handing this over at face-to-face meetings. Between meetings, they would normally work on separate sections, which one of them (usually A2, who was more experienced with the word processor) would incorporate into the current version. During the three months of writing, the document evolved largely through parts being passed between A1 and A2 (rarely the whole document), typically every week or two.

The rate of communication in group C was the lowest of the three case-studies. Over one year the document was expanded from an initial 3-4 page version written by C2 without a view to producing a full-length paper, to an expansion by C1 into 20-odd pages; in retrospect referred to as the first draft. C2 had done related writing for other purposes and incorporated this into a second draft, which was discussed when they met six months later. After one meeting discussing the paper, C2 made amendments and left the paper with C1 to review, which C2 did after some months. Currently the paper is back with C2, for what was hoped would be a final revision.

3.4 Managing Access to the Document

Changing membership and contributions

Group membership means access to the document. In these case-studies, there was evidence of tacit expectations existing of levels of contribution from co-authors (all groups), and of dissatisfaction (group B) or slowdown in progress (groups A and C) when expectations were not met. In group B, the expectation that both co-authors work enough was an issue that kept being referred to in email messages, *e.g.* "*you would've noticed that I've actually done some work*" (in reference to an email message that went missing).

We did not see evidence of specific roles being allocated. However, in group A, the two main co-authors initially split the sections fairly strictly on expertise. But gradually this specialization broke down; each co-author, instead, opportunistically doing what they could, often taking into account how busy the other co-author was.

Timing and organisation of document access

The available technology and the respective work rhythms (such as determined by time zone differences or other work commitments) seem to be important factors in choosing access strategies, as well as time available, or urgency of the writing. In groups B and C, explicit agreements on how to access the document were followed most of the time, whereas in group A, no such general agreement on document access was observed.

Opportunistic decisions on document control were most evident in group A. For example, one version of a document was exchanged between co-authors by handing over a diskette when the co-authors were meeting for other reasons (a seminar).

In group B, an alternative document control strategy of parallel work and later merging emerged to allow both co-authors to work despite a technical communications problem. Furthermore, B2 once changed the document despite B1 "having" control. B2 knew B1 was tied up with other work, and that there was no system enforcement of the control. This opportunistic breach of agreement caused no problem to B1 when told; he knew B2 had had the knowledge to make a good decision.

In group C, the document was initially passed between the two co-authors in its entirety, such that each had complete control. This strategy was later changed to a plan for C2 to be in charge of combining sections, as indicated above, and still later readjusted in response to slower progress than anticipated.

3.5 Deciding What and When to Write

Co-authors may agree on writing strategies, but these are not necessarily adhered to. None of the groups had an evident leader; instead individuals made agreements as

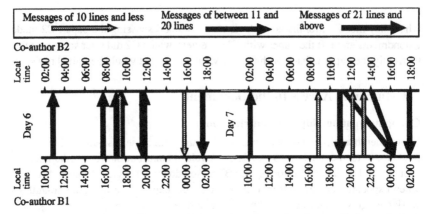

Figure 2. A sample of the email exchanges between the two co-authors in group B. Arrows indicate directions and relative sizes of email messages. (Sizes are given as numbers of text lines in the message, excluding header lines).

required, and made autonomous decisions and took opportunistic action in response to unforeseen developments. Agreements on who does what, when, were made and broken in all three groups, without necessarily causing problems.

Communicating editing and organisational information

In group B, the process was characterised by periods of intense communication when possible (using email, file exchanges and telephone calls), interspersed with longer periods of individual, autonomous work when one co-author was away.

Figure 2 shows an example of group B's email exchanges during days 6 and 7, a time when the document size was rapidly expanding, and with the highest rate of messages. Sending and reception times are indicated in the local time of each co-author. It should be clear that transmission time was usually almost instantaneous. Two messages from B2 on day 7 were held up, and crossed with other messages, which went undetected for a while, but in this case caused no problem. Once, however, a missing message did cause problems and subsequently some double-checking was done on the 'phone of whether email had got through. This suggests that the unreliability of email may cause problems for even experienced email users.

It is interesting to note, in Figure 2, that each co-author would send several messages apparently without waiting for a response. This was a typical pattern of exchanges in group B. Specific coordination information not requiring a reply was often contained in short messages: *e.g.* that a new version of the document was ready for handing over. This information was important, as it marked transfer of responsibility for the document—of who "had" it. Note also that the email messages are relatively short—two-thirds of the messages have less than 20 lines of text. This was fairly typical for the email exchanges in group B[3].

In group A, towards the end of writing, A1 and A2 had agreed that A1 should look over the near-final version and provide A2 with final changes. But after waiting

---

3. This contradicts a claim in Sharples 1992 that long communication is required for intense collaboration.

for a while without any notification of changes, and being aware that A1 was particularly busy in that period, A2 opportunistically made the last changes himself, in order to get the paper submitted sooner. It is interesting to note that both A2, and B2, in the similar situation above, were able to do this because access restrictions were not technically enforced; only socially. A1 or B1 were only notified after the event, but no disquiet about this breach of agreed control strategy was evident.

Changes were not always communicated and this sometimes lead to problems. Communication failures could result in co-authors becoming disgruntled with one another, and could mean that precious effort went to waste. On one occasion an important email message from B2 failed to get to B1. It set out a proposed structure and some contents for the paper and was sent off just before a week's absence by B2. Despite regular communication in the intervening period, it took a few weeks to discover the loss, by which time the message and the effort that went into it was largely wasted. On discovery of the loss of the message, B2 was clearly disappointed: *"(Jeez), B1, and I worked so hard to get this out before I left"*.

Group C had a different problem, in that an expectation of no feedback in case of progress meant that at one point, C1, having heard nothing, was half waiting for a second draft to turn up at any time when, in fact, there had been no progress.

Making changes visible

In group B, co-authors made their own changes visible to their co-author in a number of ways: telling them explicitly in summaries; putting in devices to attract attention in the text itself (comments in italics and square brackets), and by the removal of such devices.

Both co-authors would, at times, make comments in the text of the document itself. There might be replies to such statements or queries, and a dialogue would take place through the document versions. The ability to attach a comment to the point in the text it referred to, allowed efficient use of deictic references. This was extensively used, *e.g.* in version 14, in mid-paragraph: "... is a common activity. *[B2: Why? I don't think this is intuitively obvious. There are implications in the next paragraph but maybe something would be useful here?]*" (orig. brackets and italics). Ideas could be suggested: "Based on *[B1: something or other]*, we have ..." (in versions 12 and 13; orig. brackets and italics).

Comments were status indicators; a sign that further work was needed. Comments would remain until a solution was implemented. Thus *e.g.* the second comment above remained for two versions until replaced by "Based on [our experiences], we have ..." (version 14, our brackets). Another way of making changes visible was employed when B2 had made changes to sections of the document while B1 "had control" over the document (see above). B1, having made other changes to the same sections, left the old version of the sections in question at the end of the document for B2 to see, as a historical trace of where the new version had come from. (This shows up in Figure 1 as version 12 being significantly longer than 11. Note that this was deleted for version 13 by B2.) Finally, both co-authors would, in email messages, regularly summarise the changes they had made to the document.

We thus see how these co-authors achieved compact communication of changes by employing both a textual and historical context to carry part of the meaning.

Balancing work on the document with other activities

The co-authors were continuously having to balance work on the joint document with other activities. In group B, where the effort to produce the paper was most concentrated, there was an expectation of very high prioritising of work on the paper. In group A, the writing took place over a longer period and more other work was done in parallel. In group C, the proportion of time spent on activities unrelated to the collaborative writing was very high for both co-authors.

Co-authors made efforts to find out about and inform others about competing activities, and continuously made adjustments to expectations of the other's work. The exchange of detailed information about each others' program was particularly evident in group B. But also in group A, co-authors A1 and A2 knew a lot about each other's program (*i.e.* they had told/asked each other). *E.g.* A1 knew that A2 would be having a small operation one week and did not expect him to make any changes to the paper. In group C, C1 carried on with other work while remaining ready to prioritise the joint work, should C2 send him a new version of the document, showing great flexibility in adjusting to C2's pace of work. However, **lacking** the information that C2 was busy with other work, caused C1 to be unsure whether to set time aside from other work for this paper. Note that C1 initiated communication with C2 at a point when other work was causing less pressure on him.

4. Summary of findings and design recommendations based on case studies

In this section we summarise our case-study findings and address the design implications of the work reported above. Our data does not allow us to generalize, but does provide some pointers to issues to address. In particular, our observations of great variety in writing practices, a finding consistent with those of Rimmershaw in her interview studies (Rimmershaw 1992), we feel poses a particular requirement for designing for **flexibility**. Agreed protocols may be adapted, or individual authors may make autonomous decisions as to whether it is appropriate to break agreements. This is not done in an irresponsible fashion; rather, it is in response to continuously changing circumstances, unforeseen events, technological breakdowns, and so on. Awareness by the designer that groups may change over their lifetime, might mean, for example, allowing the way that document versions are managed, any access restrictions are enforced, and how annotations are done, to be dynamically changed by users. Designing for this kind of flexibility will, we believe, prove crucial to highly usable co-authoring tools.

The design recommendations presented below are an initial attempt at addressing what such flexibility might mean in terms of design issues. These are primarily intended to pose questions, not answers, about academic and similar co-authoring.

4.1 Coordination of editing activity

Integration with standard platforms

Shared documents may evolve from private documents, files from electronic communications and so on. Thus, support tools which allow existing text in other forms to be easily incorporated, may be useful. (Many systems currently do this.)

Formatting

Co-authors may want to make formatting changes throughout. Easy-to-change formatting can be used in a flexible way not only to help visualize the final document, but can also support a range of signals among co-authors about interpretive context, *e.g.* by making parts which are **not** intended to be in the final version stand out. Computer-based tools could support flexibility by allowing exchange of the document in a formatted form throughout the writing process.

Grounding communication in the document

It appears that for some changes it is important to communicate their rationale. Tools might usefully support linkage of communication about the document to changes in the document. Such linkage should foster common grounding of communication between authors, improving the comprehensibility of discussion about the document and allowing efficient use of deictic references.

Communicating changes

The co-authors regularly drew others' attention to some of their changes by commenting on the location, and, frequently, their nature. Co-authors also communicated an intended incompleteness of what had been written through various cues (such as bracketed comments). This may be important in indicating a willingness to have changes made. Support tools could reduce overheads of highlighting selected changes by providing easy means of referring to change locations and optionally allowing notes about the changes to be attached. PREP's "flexible diff" (*ibid.*) highlights changes of specified sizes (sentence, word, paragraph).

Author information

Decisions about when and what changes to make to a section were at times influenced by who had written it. A co-authoring tool might provide lightweight support for knowing who did what, which a user group may turn on and off. Several systems, including SASSE (*ibid.*), provide author information automatically.

History information

Editing may take place over a brief or extended period. Tools could incorporate lightweight support for making judgements about the completeness of, and confidence in, parts of the document. For example, an editing history may be presented as a quick replay of changes. This might cue co-authors about the context of particular changes, and might conceivably reduce the problem of information overload.

4.2 Coordination of responsibility

Planning and status information

Authors must decide which part of the document they can most usefully work on and what to contribute in order to best fulfil goals and avoid duplications or omissions. No individual 'leader' can be assumed to take the lead in this. Also, plans are not necessarily carried out even if explicitly agreed. Tools may be of more benefit to co-authors by supporting general exchange of information about future expectations; about goals achieved or attempted, *etc.*, than by requiring users to follow plans previously made. For a structuring and planning tool, such as GROVE (*ibid.*), particular attention may need to be paid to making previous work easy to change.

Information about ongoing activity and progress

Co-authors may be engaged in a range of other unrelated activities which make demands on their time and attention. To organize their own activities and set time aside for making contributions, they are dependent upon knowing about each others' activities. Support tools could help foster group awareness of progress, *e.g.* by broadcasting automatic notifications as to when particular authors begin editing activity, and perhaps about what part of the document is being edited. Such automatic information must be possible to turn on and off easily. SASSE (*ibid.*) provides a document overview tool which indicates who is working on the document and where.

Control of access

At times, for maintaining consistency or ensuring that the best qualified person carries out certain tasks, it can be useful for one author to have exclusive access to part or all of the document. This may be successfully socially enforced, but support tools may feature facilities to alert co-authors to the status of document parts with respect to currently agreed access rights. MESSIE (*ibid.*) permits one user at a time to have editing access to the document and sends an email message with information about who is editing it to anyone else attempting to change it. This, however, removes from the group the possibility of working on parallel versions and merging them later, and may discourage short or intermittent working.

Roles vs. responsibilities: Inform, rather than constrain

Social control can be, it would seem, highly effectively used to manage the rights and responsibilities of each participant in a writing project. It allows areas of responsibility to be in continuous change without overheads, and avoids the problem that desired access restrictions may not coincide with predefined roles (Dourish and Bellotti, 1992). We therefore believe that rather than providing generic co-author roles for tools to support, designers might usefully seek to support co-authors' exchange of information to help them make their own judgements about appropriate contributions. Some such information may be appropriate to collect and make available automatically, other not; more research is needed on this.

5. Conclusions

The way in which authors collaborate is not well understood. This paper has shown that there are useful insights to be gained from *in vivo*, longitudinal case-studies of distributed collaborative writing practices. Such case-studies can contribute important understanding to the design of systems to support co-authoring over distance.

Our observations have shown some disparity between the creative use of flexible low-tech solutions by the co-authors in our studies, and the (apparent) concerns of many developers of current co-authoring technology to develop technically advanced, but often regulating, features. More case-studies, particularly at the level of detail of group B, should be conducted to further investigate the issues raised.

Implications already apparent, however, include that breaches of agreement may not in themselves be detrimental to the successful working of a group, and may be a natural part of some groups' way of working. For the academic groups we observed, distributed co-authoring was a process characterised by great flexibility in the coordination of individual contributions. Opportunistic use was made of information made available for each other by the co-authors, including information hard to predict the relevance of in advance. This suggests that notions of what is and what is not relevant information; of what is the task being performed, should be critically examined when designing support for people writing together over distance.

Acknowledgments

The greatest thanks are due to the participants in the case-studies for their trust in allowing observation of, and inevitably intrusion into, their work. Thank you to all the friends who at crucial times have provided encouragement and support. A special mention is due to Paul Dourish for his many and varied contributions to this paper. This paper benefited greatly from comments from people at EuroPARC on earlier versions of this paper, and from anonymous reviewers, in particular the suggestion that criticisms of existing approaches be clarified. Financially, the work reported on was supported by a Ph.D. grant from the Norwegian Research Council for Scientific and Industrial Research, and by Rank Xerox Cambridge EuroPARC's Student Internship program.

References

Baecker, R. M., D. Nastos, I. R. Posner, and K. L. Mawby (1993): "The User-Centred Iterative Design of Collaborative Writing Software", in *InterCHI'93. Proceedings of the Conference on Computer Human Interaction. Amsterdam, 21-23 April 1993.*

Beck, E. E. (1993): "A Survey of Experiences of Coauthoring", in M. Sharples (ed.): *Computer-Supported Collaborative Writing*, Springer-Verlag, London 1993, pp. 9-28.

Chandler, D. (1992): *The Experience of Writing. A Media Theory Approach*, Ph.D. Thesis, University of Wales Aberystwyth, Sept. 1992.

Couture, B., and J. Rymer (1991): "Discourse Interaction Between Writer and Supervisor: A Primary Collaboration in Workplace Writing", in M. M. Lay and W. M. Karis (eds.): *Collaborative Writing in Industry: Investigations in Theory and Practice*, Baywood, Amityville 1993, pp. 87-108.

Dourish, P., and V. Bellotti (1992): "Awareness and Coordination in Shared Workspaces", in J. Turner and R. Kraut (eds.): *CSCW'92. Proceedings of the Conference on Computer-Supported Cooperative Work. Toronto, 31 Oct. - 4 Nov. 1992.* ACM 1992, pp. 107-104.

Ellis, C., S. Gibbs, and G. Rein (1990): "Design and Use of a Group Editor", in Cockton (ed.): *Engineering for Human-Computer Interaction*, North-Holland, Amsterdam 1990.

Flower, L. (1989): *Cognition, Context, and Theory Building*, Occasional Paper No. 11, Center for the Study of Writing, University of California, Berkeley, and Carnegie Mellon University, May 1989.

Flower, L. S., and J. R. Hayes (1980): "The Dynamics of Composing: Making Plans and Juggling Constraints", in L.W. Gregg and E. R. Steinberg (eds.): *Cognitive Processes in Writing*, Lawrence Erlbaum Associates, Hillsdale (NJ) 1980.

Forman, J. (1992): "Introduction", in J. Forman (ed.): *New Visions of Collaborative Writing*, Boynton/Cook Heinemann, Portsmouth (NH) 1992, pp. xi-xxii.

Grudin, J. (1991): "CSCW Introduction", *Communications of the ACM*, vol. 34, no. 12, Dec. 1991, pp. 30-34.

Hahn, U., M. Jarke, S. Eherer, and K. Kreplin (1991): "COAUTHOR — A Hypermedia Group Authoring Environment", in J. M. Bowers and S. D. Benford (eds.): *Studies in Computer Supported Cooperative Work. Theory, Practice and Design*, North-Holland, Amsterdam etc., 1991, pp. 79-100.

Kling, R. (1991): "Cooperation, Coordination and Control in Computer-Supported Work", *Communications of the ACM*, vol. 34, no. 12, Dec. 1991, pp. 83-88.

Kraemer, K. L., and A. Pinsonneault (1990): "Technology and Groups: Assessment of the Empirical Research", in J. Galegher, R. E. Kraut, and C. Egido (eds.): *Intellectual Teamwork: Social and Technological Foundations of Cooperative Work*, Lawrence Erlbaum Associates, Hillsdale (NJ) 1990, pp. 375-405.

Law, J., and R. J. Williams (1982): "Putting Facts Together: A Study of Scientific Persuasion", *Social Studies of Science*, vol. 12 (1982), pp. 535-558.

Leland, M. D. P., R. S. Fish, and R. E. Kraut (1988): "Collaborative Document Production Using Quilt", in *CSCW88. Proceedings of the Conference on Computer-Supported Cooperative Work. Portland, Oregon, 26-28 Sept. 1988*. ACM, pp. 206-215.

Lunsford, A., and L. Ede (1990): *Singular Texts/Plural Authors: Perspectives on Collaborative Writing*, Southern Illinois University Press, Carbondale and Edwardsville 1990.

McGuffin, L. J., and G. M. Olson (1992): *ShrEdit: A Shared Electronic Workspace*, CSMIL Technical Report No. 45, Cognitive Science and Machine Intelligence Laboratory, University of Michigan, Aug. 1992.

Mhashi, M., R. Rada, E. Beck, A. Zeb, and A. Michailidis (1992): "Computer-Supported Discussion and Annotation", *Information Processing and Management*, vol. 28, no. 5, pp. 589-607.

Neuwirth, C. M., R. Chandhok, D. S. Kaufer, P. Erion, J. Morris, and D. Miller (1992): "Flexible Diff-ing in a Collaborative Writing System", in J. Turner and R. Kraut (eds.): *CSCW'92. Proceedings of the Conference on Computer-Supported Cooperative Work. Toronto, 31 Oct.-4 Nov. 1992*. pp. 147-154.

Plowman, L. (1992): *Communication, Coordination and Collaboration: The Production of a Co-written Document*, unpublished manuscript, summer 1992.

Posner, I. R. (1991): *A Study of Collaborative Writing*, M.Sc. Thesis, Department of Computer Science, University of Toronto 1991.

Riley, J. (1983): *The Preparation of Teaching in Higher Education*, D.Phil. Thesis, University of Sussex 1983.

Rimmershaw, R. (1992): "Collaborative Writing Practices and Writing Support Technologies", *Instructional Science*, vol. 21, nos. 1/3, pp. 15-28.

Sasse, M. A., S. C. Chuang, and M. J. Handley (1993): "Support for Collaborative Authoring via Electronic Mail: The MESSIE Environment", in: *ECSCW'93. Proceedings of the Third European Conference on Computer-Supported Cooperative Work. Milan, Sept. 1993*. (This volume).

Sharples, M. (1992): "Adding a Little Structure to Collaborative Writing", in D. Diaper and C. Sanger (eds.): *Pauper's CSCW*, Springer-Verlag, London 1992.

Tatar, D. G., G. Foster, and D. G. Bobrow (1991): "Design for Conversation: Lessons from Cognoter", *International Journal of Man-Machine Studies*, vol. 34 (1991), pp. 185-209.

Trimbur, J., and L. A. Braun (1992): "Laboratory Life and the Determination of Authorship", in J. Forman (ed.): *New Visions of Collaborative Writing*, Boynton/Cook Heinemann, Portsmouth (NH) 1992, pp. 19-36.

Proceedings of the Third European Conference on Computer-Supported Cooperative Work
13-17 September, 1993, Milan, Italy
G. De Michelis, C. Simone and K. Schmidt (Editors)

Support for Collaborative Authoring via Email: The MESSIE Environment

Martina Angela Sasse, Mark James Handley
Department of Computer Science, University College London, UK

and

Shaw Cheng Chuang
Computer Laboratory, Cambridge University, UK

Abstact: MESSIE is a collaborative authoring environment to support the production of large-scale documents by teams of geographically distributed groups of authors working with hetereogenous systems. The environment allows authors to submit text at various stages of gestation (e.g. list of topics, first draft) to a shared filestore via email. All authors collaborating on a document can read each others' contributions, and add suggestions, comments and additional material directly to the document. The system integrates automatically answered electronic mail, shared file store administration, and a version control tool in a UNIX environment. The paper describes design and implementation strategy, and reports observations and a number of changes which were made during a 4-month trial period with three collaborative authoring teams.

1 Introduction

Collaboration between geographically dispersed groups is becoming increasingly common. In Europe, there are a number of programmes, such as ESPRIT, RACE and DELTA, to promote research collaboration on an international scale. Most of the projects funded in such programmes require the joint authoring of comprehensive reviews, reports or large-scale technical documentation. Most authoring teams hold regular meetings, and these meetings are a considerable drain on authors' time and travel funds.

Being involved in many such projects, we began to look for collaboration support which could reduce the number of meetings related to joint authoring activities. We conducted a case study to investigate the use of Multimedia Conferencing as a support environment (Baydere et al., 1993). We found that Multimedia Conferencing provided the rich channels of communication which creative groupwork supposedly requires (Chalfonte et al., 1991), and is normally only achieved through face-to-face meetings.

Most teams of authors, however, do not have access to expensive Multimedia Conferencing systems. Even if they did, previous research (Grudin, 1990) has shown that less technology-experienced users than the ones in the case study would be likely to reject such a sophisticated groupware system because of the learning overhead required.

An additional insight gained from the case study was that only the initial phases of document production (generating ideas and determining scope and structure of the document) could be described as *creative*. The other phases did not necessarily require rich channels of communication - authors actually preferred *asynchronous* communication via email, since they felt it was more effective than synchronous sessions. The case study also re-inforced previous observations that considerable time and effort needs to be spent on *managing* a collaboratively authored document. The problems of managing the process of producing large documents between a number of project members in different locations can be summarised as follows:

- Document integrity

  Authors will send copies of their contributions to other authors for information and comment, and amend their contribution as they receive feedback. Since it would require considerable effort to send a new version to all other authors every time a change is made, or only send it to the co-author in response to whose suggestion the change was made, different authors might hold different versions of some parts of the document.

- Duplication of effort

  Several authors might write the same comments or supply the same additions to the document. Authors might repeat explanations or background material which is already covered in other parts of the document.

- Integration of contributions

  Contributions written by different authors are likely to vary in use of terminology and style. Since this does not make for a very readable document, the project member charged with editing the final version has to spend considerable time and effort to (a) integrate the contributions into a coherent and readable document, and (b) provide cross-references between various parts of the document.

- Editing and formatting

  Most authors would prefer to use their favourite word processor or editor and text formatter to produce their contributions. These are likely to be different tools in large authoring teams. If authors do not use the same tool, considerable effort needs to be spent on re-typing and re-formatting parts of the document. Teams in which authors use different tools often supply the person doing the final formatting with an ASCII file and a hardcopy of the formatted version - this approach avoids re-typing text but formatting needs to be done at least twice.

We decided to identify a set of requirements and design objectives for an asynchronous colloboration environment for collaborative authoring to provide support for dealing with these document management problems. The original system requirements and design objectives are elaborated in Section 2, and the implementation is described in Section 3. The user's view of interaction with the environment is described in Section 4, followed by a summary of results from the trial phase in Section 5.

2 Requirements and Design Objectives

The intent was to specify a simple system which could be installed locally and administered independently by each authoring team. We wanted to implement a basic system quickly by using existing tools, and offer it to a number of authoring teams for producing real documents to gain feedback for further development and improvement.

At the outset of the project, we started with two sets of requirements for the environment: requirements of *individual authors* and requirements of the *administrator*, a role assumed by one member in every joint authoring team using the environment.

The *author* requirements we identified we identified for asynchronous collaborative writing support were:

1. Make drafts available as soon as possible

   To ensure misunderstandings are discovered as early as possible, and to ensure that the document grows in a uniform way, it is important that early drafts of sections are made available early in the writing process.

2. Preserve the integrity of the document

In order to preserve the integrity of the document, or its various parts, all authors should have access to the latest version of any file. Authors should have the facility to work on a single master copy of each part of the document. Clearly, authors should not be allowed to edit the master copy of a document section while another author is editing it.

3. Avoid duplication of effort

In order to avoid duplication of effort, all comments and additions to a document should be entered into the document itself, so that authors can identify which comments and additions have been made by other authors.

4. Distribute editing and formatting work

In order to distribute the effort involved in final editing and formatting of document, a prime requirement was to allow authors to exchange *revisable* text as much as possible. Imposing any single document exchange format for authoring teams would preclude this. Whilst it is not possible to support WP and DTP applications which produce non-revisable formats, the environment should support handling of a variety of revisable text formats in addition to ASCII. In order to deal with diagrams, the system should handle PostScript, which, even though it is non-revisable, is so ubiquitous that most authors can view or print such files locally. There is also a requirement for tools which facilitate compilation of reference lists and glossaries.

5. Avoid large learning overhead

The system should be simple and transparent in use, and require users only to learn and remember a small number of commands. Where possible, it should allow users to use familiar tools for familiar activities.

6. Access without direct login

Not all authors have the facility to directly access remote machines today. In addition, it is important to consider that not all sites who might want to install such an environment would want to allow remote logins and give direct access to a shared filestore facility.

7. Deal with heterogeneity

Although there are several synchronous authoring tools available, this system must provide access from a wide range of remote systems. No existing tool would run on all the available remote systems, and the overhead in developing any software to run on all such systems would be too great. Thus the system should only involve one installation - at the site where the authoring team's version of MESSIE and the filestore are kept.

8. Policy-free collaboration

The system should be as policy-free as possible. It should provide the basic collaboration environment, but the users should decide the details of how that environment should be applied to their collaborative task.

The requirements of the authoring team's *administrator* can be summarised as follows:

1. The system should be simple to install, maintain, and port.

2. Storage overhead for the documents should be kept to a minimum.

3. It should be possible to manage documents remotely as well as locally.

We decided that these requirements could be met by integrating and developing the functionality provided by existing tools - shared filestore, electronic mail, and a version control tool - into a support environment which would provide authors with a basic set of facilities to submit, read, edit, delete and list files. The environment allows authors to submit text at various stages of gestation (e.g. list of topics, first draft) to the shared filestore via email. All authors collaborating on a document can request files submitted by the other authors, and add suggestions, comments and additional material directly to the document.

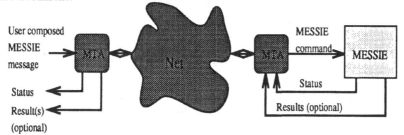

Figure 1: Interacting with MESSIE

3   MESSIE Design and Implementation

All parts of a collaboratively authored document supported by the environment are held in a *shared filestore*, which is administered by one team member. The document can be created and accessed by sending files and requests by *electronic mail* to a MESSIE email account. MESSIE accepts email messages containing MESSIE commands and new text, performs the actions specified by the command (subject to access control), and returns the final status and results. This is shown in Figure 1.

MESSIE places no specific requirements on the end-user environment. An author composes a message using their favourite mail interface program - on a PC, workstation, mini or mainframe, running their respective operating systems. The message is then submitted to MESSIE as a command file. There is no restriction on the type of mail system authors can use, as long as the message can be gatewayed intact to the MESSIE address. When a message addressed to MESSIE arrives in the MESSIE mailbox, MESSIE is activated (using one of the mechanisms described in the following section). A status message will always be returned to the user to provide an overview of the outcome of the command submission. Optionally, if the command generates outputs for the user, these outputs will also be returned to the author in message separate from the status message.

3.1 MESSIE Internal

In this section, we will take a closer look at the MESSIE box as shown in Figure 1. The logical relationship between MESSIE components is illustrated in Figure 2.

MESSIE has been designed to consist of two highly independent parts. The first part is a generic *command interpreter*, which performs validation and execution of commands, user access control, and notifications. The command set and user access and addressing information is stored in separate databases, currently implemented in dbm. This allows MESSIE to be easily expanded to add new functionality.

The *command database* uses the command name as key to locate the actual program which will perform the actions of the command. The access mode of the command can also be indexed. Currently, only *read* and *write* access modes are supported. These access modes are used in conjunction with the user access authorisation. The *user database* uses the mail-id as a key to check the user's access authorisation. For every command to be executed, the user authorisation is checked against the command's access mode. Only users with the correct access authorisation are allowed to execute a particular command. To simplify administration, a wildcard authorisation is also allowed. A wildcard of read-only access would turn MESSIE into an info-server.

The second part of the environment are the MESSIE *command executables*. These could be implemented in any language, independent of the front-end command interpreter. The front-end communicates with the MESSIE commands using shared-file message passing. This avoids using any operating-system dependent IPC mechanisms. Since there are no concurrency activities in MESSIE, very simple message passing mechanisms can be used.

The command executable also writes the status of the command execution to the same status file used by the front-end. Thus, after execution of the commands in a message, a single status message is always returned to the user. The individual commands will also return their own messages where appropriate. By having a separate command status file, the user will always be given feedback on a particular MESSIE job submission. This also enables the command executable to send as many (or as few) messages as are required (e.g. one for each file requested for reading or editing). This helps to avoid the creation of large return messages, which could potentially cause problems with some mail systems.

Since MESSIE's front-end and command set are virtually independent, MESSIE can be used as a generic e-mail based remote command shell (see Section 7).

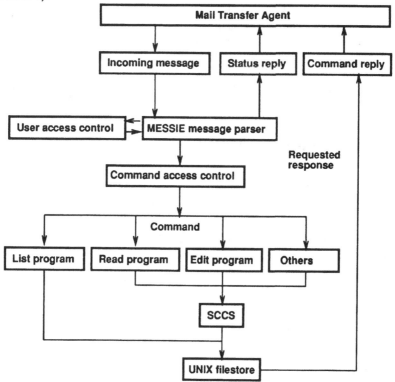

Figure 2: MESSIE Structure

3.2 Implementation Details

Since MESSIE has been implemented using a number of simple C programs (approximately 100 lines of code), and shell/sed/awk/perl scripts, it contains very little system-specific code. It adopts a modular design approach: the components used can be substituted by others. If a team, for instance, wants to use a version control system other than SCCS (e.g. RCS), they can substitute it. The few operating-system dependent details can be easily re-written. The modular design approach also makes it easy to extend existing functionality.

The shell/sed/awk/perl scripts are mainly used for the construction of command executables. We found this approach to be extremely useful for rapid prototyping and experimentation: the current set of commands was coded in less than 40 man-hours. Certain commands were subsequently re-written, either to improve performance or extend functionality, in response to the results of experimentation with the first version. For instance, the *list* command, originally written in *bourne shell*, was re-written in *perl* - this increased the speed with which the command could be executed by a factor of 100.

4 User view of MESSIE

4.1 Email Access

All parts of a collaboratively authored document supported by the environment are held in a shared filestore, which is administered by one of the authors. (During the implementation and evaluation period, all those documents were are held in a filestore at UCL, which was administered by the authors.) The document can be created and accessed by sending files and requests by electronic mail to a MESSIE email account (see Figure 3 for an example message).

```
From: a.sasse@uk.ac.ucl.cs
To: messie@uk.ac.ucl.cs
Subject:
---------------------------------------------------------------
#COMMAND read Race_deliverable/chapter2
```

Figure 3: Example of a email message to MESSIE (for read-only copy of a file)

4.2 MESSIE commands

MESSIE understands a set of commands contained in the body of an email message sent to the email account. All commands have to be placed a the beginning of a line, starting with the instruction #COMMAND, and consisting of a command name and directory/file name (see Figure 3 one for an example of the READ command). The basic command set is fairly small, covering 5 basic activities: *submitting a new file*, *reading an existing file*, *editing an existing file*, *deleting an existing file*, and obtaining a *listing of a directory*.

4.3   Return messages, status reports and notifications

Regardless of the status of the request (i.e. whether it was successful or not), MESSIE will always send a *request status report* back to the sender (see Figure 4 for a successful request, Figure 5 for a failed one).

```
To: a.sasse@uk.ac.ucl.cs
Subject: Request reply read Race_deliverable/chapter2
From: The UCL-CS Messie Service <messie@uk.ac.ucl.cs>
------------------------------------------------------
read Race_deliverable/chapter2: Valid command
Read done
```

Figure 4: Example of request status report (successful)

```
To: a.sasse@uk.ac.ucl.cs
Subject: Request reply read Race_deliverable/chapter2
From: The UCL-CS Messie Service <messie@uk.ac.ucl.cs>
------------------------------------------------------
read Race_deliverable/chapter2: Valid command.
edit error: Race_deliverable/chapter2 does not exist;
    please choose another name
```

Figure 5: Example of request status report (unsuccessful)

For requests that generate a return message (e.g. the *read* command) this return message will always be sent in a separate email message. The message *subject field* in both return messages and status reports will indicate in response to which request the message is sent.

MESSIE can handle multiple commands in one request - it is possible to request more than one file in a single email message. Each file will be returned as separate email message.

In addition to return messages and status reports, MESSIE sends a variety of notifications to authors when requested files are locked, when checkout periods expire, and when changes have been made to a file.

4.4 Shared filestore

The shared filestore is a tree-based structure of directories and files similar to UNIX and MS-DOS filestores (and supports both UNIX and MS-DOS style file naming conventions). To find out what files are available in the directory containing the document, authors can request a listing of the directory contents. MESSIE will return a list of all existing files and their current status along with any embedded meta-data (see 4.8). All files submitted to MESSIE will have one owner - the author who first submitted a particular file become its owner. The owner is notified of any changes made to the file (see 4.5), and only the owner can delete an existing file.

4.5 Version Control

Once a file has been checked out for editing, MESSIE will lock its copy of the file for the specified amount of time - the file cannot be checked out for editing until it is returned, or the timeout period has expired. This locking mechanism is the simplest way to preserve the integrity of the individual files in the document. The tool employed to implement version control in MESSIE is the Source Code Control System (SCCS), though other version control tools can be substituted.

Read-only copies can still be obtained while a file is locked, and are automatically sent when a request for editing a locked file is received. If a file which has been checked out for editing is not returned within 48 hours (or the time specified at check-out), MESSIE will assume that the checked-out copy of the file has been "lost" and unlock the last version. This *timeout* function prevents files from remaining inaccessible if an author requests an edit and then forgets to return the file. When a file is returned, MESSIE registers this as a new version of the file. If an altered version of a file is returned after the timeout has expired, MESSIE will only accept it as a new version if the file has not been checked out by someone else since the lock was removed.

All changes made to a file are registered, and so all versions of a document can be accessed if authors wish to do so, and MESSIE will provide any *diff* file on demand. Furthermore, the owner of a file is notified when changes have been made to a file (through an email message containing the name of the person who has made the changes and a list of the changes). If other authors want to receive these notifications for any file they do not own, they can join a subscription list. This *subscription facility* was added following authors' suggestions.

4.6 Diagrams

Diagrams, figures and drawings are stored as PostScript files. Read-only versions of PostScript files will be sent in response to requests for these files. Authors can print or view copies of these on their home printers. Each new version of a picture will be a new file with its own filename (e.g. pic1, pic2). Each diagram file has an associated text file, into which comments can be entered. The comment filename is naming using the convention of diagram file name suffixed by the word "comment" (e.g. the name of the comment file for diagram pic1 will be pic1.comment). Comments can be appended to this file using the *add_comment* command and read-only copies of the comment file can be requested.

4.7 Glossary and Reference Files

One of the biggest problems associated with collaborative authoring of larger documents tend to be the time and effort involved in compiling a glossary and references as a deadline approaches. The environment provided by MESSIE allows authors to collect such information throughout the project in a joint file for the glossary, and a joint file for references. Authors request a current version of these files, and, if the glossary entry or reference does not exist, send a message which appends the glossary entry or reference to the file.

4.8 Document history

SCCS only provides a mechanism to achieve version control. A set of protocols is still required to ensure effective joint authoring. Typically, sections of a document are held in separate files. The owner of each file is the principal author, who is ultimately responsible for this section of the document. When the first version of a document is submitted to MESSIE, it is automatically put under SCCS control, and then can be commented on by the other authors. A modification history should be kept at the top of each file. An example of such a modification history is shown in Figure 6.

```
#
# MODIFICATION HISTORY
#
#     DATE        YOUR_NAME      MARKER        REMARK
#     14/10/92    MH             W001          2nd draft
#     15/10/92    AS             W002          additions in 3.1
#     26/10/92    TC             W003          Comments
#     28/10/92    MH             W004          3rd draft
```

Figure 6: Example of modification history

This is necessary because although SCCS stores this information, it is not immediately obvious to an author when reading the actual text of the most recent version. [1]The *marker* is used indicate the exact place to in the document text where changes have been, and can be used to locate comments by particular authors. The owner of each file will remove the markers when dealing with the comments. Furthermore, the creator of a file is encouraged (though it is not mandatory) to include at the beginning of the file information about content and status of the document, and actions which should be taken by co-authors. Authors can also issue commands which will prompt Messie to automatically fill in information about dates, confidentiality, and versions of the document.

All information appropriate to these file fields can, if desired, be provided by the document owner using the above commands. The information given in those fields appears in listing of directories requested by authors, thereby making it easier for authors to identify files which they want to request for reading and editing.

4.9   Commenting

It is important that authors can easily recognise which parts of a document have been changed or added, when and by whom. This information can be obtained from *diff* files (Neuwirth et al., 1992). Like Beck & Bellotti (in this volume), however, we found that authors prefer to have this information grounded in the document itself. In order to achieve this, authoring teams need to agree a set of rules - for which we have coined the term *human protocols* - for commenting. A example for human protocols (developed by one of the teams involved in the trials) is:

1. If the change is very small, such as spelling, an omitted word, etc, make the change without marking that you have changed it.

2. Make any additions to the document in such a way that they stand out from the original text. (our convention is [**W003 TC: this is a comment**]). A more complete example looks like this:

```
. . . . . . . . . . . . . .
Synchronous communication occurs when two or more
People interact simultaneously and in real-time,
e.g. in a telephone conversation [**W003 TC do we
need both examples**] or a video conference.
```

---

[1]SCCS does not visibly mark where changes have been made in the file. In order to identify changes, authors would have to view the current version and diff file(s).

The marker (eg. ***W003) should always be at the place of change. It is always useful and convenient to put both the commenter's name and a brief comment next to the marker to give some clue of why changes are made.

3. No text should be deleted by a commenter. Mark the text for deletion or replacement, but let the person responsible for the section include the changes as they see fit:

```
[**W004 Start MH 9/10/91 The above text should be
replaced with: Text should not be deleted...
W004 End **]
```

5 Results of the trial period

In order to evaluate the effectiveness of MESSIE as a support environment for collaborative authoring by email, we released the system to a restricted group of users for a trial period of 4 months. All groups used the system during this period to produce a real, life-size document:

- Group 1: 10 authors at 5 sites in the UK and Germany, producing a 200-page final deliverable for a RACE project over a period of 4 months;

- Group 2: 3 authors at 3 different sites in the UK and Belgium, producing a 40-page intermediate deliverable for a DELTA project over a period of 2 months;

- Group 3: 3 authors at 2 different sites in the UK, producing a 6-page conference paper over a period of 3 weeks.

Altogether, the users issued 856 commands: among them 272 *read* commands, 202 *list commands*, 155 *submit* commands, 96 *edit* commands, 65 *write* commands, 35 *delete* commands, and 10 requests for *help*.

The general response of those users to the system was very positive indeed, the single most important factor being that users could continue to use their own email and text editing facilities, and only had to learn a small number of additional commands in order to use the system effectively - authors felt that the environment provided very useful support for very little investment. Authors were able to produce their contributions, and read others, using the hardware and software that they were familiar with: IBM PCs, Apple Macs, Sun workstations, and IBM and DEC mainframes. All groups started out storing the documents in ASCII format. In Group 1, most authors started to store their files in RTF format, since the final document was to be formatted in MS-Word. The document in Group 2 remained in ASCII format until the very end, and was formatted by one of the authors after the collaborative authoring had finished. Group 3 merged the files halfway through the writing process into a single document, and formatted it using LaTeX. On two occasions, TeX or PostScript files were damaged in transit, a surprisingly low number considering the total number of reads and edits performed on formatted files.

On the basis of the logs of the system use, and authors' comments, we compiled a list of desired changes, which have been incorporated into MESSIE 2.0. These changes fall into two different groups: changes to the commands and messages, and additional functionality. Commands and messages are briefly described here, whereas additional functionality is discussed in section 6.

- *Command recognition*: most frequent cause of failed requests was mistyped command names (e.g. "sumbit" instead of submit or "lsit" instead of list, or lower-case "#command"). Instead of just returning these as errors, the system can be made to recognise typos and execute the "most likely" request, and return it together with the error message.

- *Error recognition*: mis-remembered command names (e.g. "create" instead of "submit", or "write" instead of "submit"). Again, an aliasing mechanism can be set up to recognise the most common confusion, execute the most likely request, and remind the user of the correct command. Obviously this should only happen where no document will be damaged by the assumption.

- *Return files with failed submissions*: There were several cases where "write" commands failed because authors mis-spelt filenames or incorrect directory paths. Even though authors were requested to keep a copy of all submissions until the status request report confirmed successful submission, we found that many did last-minute editing of files in their mail editor, and neglected to save the emailed version. Since MESSIE did not return failed submissions, the last-minute changes were lost to the author (though they could be retrieved from the system backup mailbox). Now, the complete file is returned to an author when submissions fail.

6 Discussion

In developing MESSIE, we have attempted to provide a general-purpose environment to support collaborative authoring with a minimal set of user commands. We decided to start with a simple, basic environment and add functionality as requested by users. We adopted this design strategy in an attempt to dodge the fate of some sophisticated groupware systems, which were rejected by their intended users (Grudin, 1990), and feel that the approach was successful.

Clearly, there is some debate over exactly which commands should be provided for the users. This is largely due to different groups' models for interaction with the system. For instance, if the system is to be strongly locally administered, providing a "delete" command for remote users may be undesirable. However, if the system is to be administered in a more distributed fashion, more powerful (and potentially dangerous) commands (as described by Borenstein, 1992) will need to be provided for remote use. Our current command set lies somewhere between these two extremes, but the advantage of our approach to the overall system design is that the local administrator can decide on the level of support that will be provided, and thus provide the appropriate command set to support this style of management.

Currently, MESSIE does not provide direct support any form of *structured* documents - its model is that a document consists of a set of sections (files), and it is entirely up to the authoring teams to decide whether and how a document should be partitioned into sections. This is in line with our attitude that the system should be as policy-free as possible. However, it may be desirable to also provide some document structuring commands, whereby a user can request, for instance, an entire document. The structuring command would then utilise document meta-data to return the entire document in one piece (rather that as distinct sections). It would also be possible to link such a tool to a text formatter, and return, for instance, a PostScript version of the entire document including diagrams. At the present, we consider such tools outside the scope of what is intended to be a policy-free minimal system, but there is nothing to stop a user group from deciding on a policy, and extending the functionality to by adding such commands.

7 Conclusions and future work

MESSIE has the potential to be used as a general collaboration tool. Although much effort is currently being put into synchronous collaboration tools, many forms of collaboration do not need to be very tightly coupled. It is currently used by the (geographically very much distributed) Executive Committee of the British HCI Group (A Specialist Group of the British Computer Society) as a document store and organizational memory: committee members submit and request PostScript and RTF files for printing letterheaded paper and mailing labels, templates for forms and letters, etc., as well as use it for collaborative production and editing of minutes and policy documents.

It has been suggested that MESSIE be used for collaborative authoring of software. Another project to which we aim to apply it is ESPRIT project MICE (Kirstein, 1992) to handle the booking of resources for full-scale video conferences between a number of European sites. In general, MESSIE may be suitable for many tasks that require loose collaboration, but where the overhead involved in porting synchronous software to all possible remote systems is too great.

Acknowledgements

MESSIE was designed and implemented as part of the RACE CAR project, funded by the Commission of the European Community. The authors would like to thank Jon Crowcroft, of the Department of Computer Science at UCL, for helpful comments and suggestions, and the UK CSCW Special Interest Group and the London Unix User Group for feedback given on earlier presentations on the system. Finally, a tribute to the groups of authors who used MESSIE over the last year - the observations we collected, and the feedback given during the trial period very much shaped the design and implementation.

References

Baydere, S., Casey, T., Chuang, S., Handley, M., Ismail, N. & Sasse, A. (1993): "Multimedia Conferencing for Collaborative Writing: A Case Study." In Sharples, M. [Ed.]: *Computer Supported Collaborative Writing*. Berlin: Springer. pp. 113-135.

Borenstein, N. (1992): Computational Mail as Network Infrastructure for Computer-Supported Collaborative Work. In *CSCW'92: Proceedings of the Conference on Computer-Supported Collaborative Work* (Toronto, Canada, Oct. 31 - Nov. 4, 1992). New York: ACM. pp. 67-74.

Chalfonte, B. L., Fish, R.S. & Kraut, B. (1991): Expressive Richness: A Comparison for Speech and Text as Media for Revision. In *Proceedings of CHI, 1990*, (Seattle, Washington, April 1-5, 1990), New York: ACM. pp. 21-26.

Grudin, J. (1990): Groupware and Collaborative Work: problems and prospects. In Laurel, B. [Ed.]: *The Art of Human-Computer Interface Design*. Reading, MA: Addison-Wesley.

Kirstein, P. T. (1992): Piloting of Multimedia Integrated Communications for European Researchers (MICE). *Proceedings of the Second Packet Video Workshop*, Vol. 2 (Research Triangle Park, NC, Dec. 9-10, 1992). MCNC.

Neuwirth, C. M.; Chandhok, R.; Kaufer, D. S.; Erion, P.; Morris, J. & Miller, D. (1992): "Flexible Diff-ing in a Collaborative Writing System". In *CSCW'92: Proceedings of the Conference on Computer-Supported Collaborative Work* (Toronto, Canada, Oct. 31 - Nov. 4, 1992). New York: ACM. pp. 147-154.

Proceedings of the Third European Conference on Computer-Supported Cooperative Work
13-17 September, 1993, Milan, Italy
G. De Michelis, C. Simone and K. Schmidt (Editors)

Participation Equality and Influence: Cues and Status in Computer-Supported Cooperative Work Groups

Suzanne Weisband, Sherry Schneider and Terry Connolly

University of Arizona, USA

Abstract: We examined status effects in face-to-face and computer-mediated three-person groups. Our expectation that low status members in computer-mediated group discussions would participate more equally, and have more influence over decisions, than their counterparts in face-to-face groups was not confirmed. The results suggest that knowledge of status differences and labels were used to form cognitive impressions of other group members. It seems that when group members are aware of the status characteristics of the group, social cues were magnified rather than reduced. Implications of these findings for mixed status cooperative work groups and for the design of computer communication systems are discussed.

Group members often use physical and social cues such as race, sex, and status to categorize people and organize information about them. These perceptions then shape the members' interactions with one another, the opportunities they give one another to speak, the weight they give each other's opinions, and the influence each has on the decisions the group reaches. A considerable research literature on face-to-face groups (see Hackman, 1976; McGrath, 1984; Stephan, 1985) attests to the power and subtlety of such social cues in shaping the tone and content of a group's communication patterns and social behavior.

Computer-supported communication is of special interest in this context as the social and paralinguistic cues available in face-to-face conversation are greatly attenuated. Several studies have found that when groups use computers to communicate, member status and influence have less impact than they do in face-to-face groups, and there is greater equality of participation (e.g., Rice, 1984; Siegel, Dubrovsky, Kiesler and McGuire, 1986; McGuire, Kiesler and Siegel, 1987; Dubrovsky, Kiesler and Sethna, 1991; Spears and Lea, 1992; Weisband, 1992). In discussions of the equalization phenomenon, it is often assumed that the reduced social cues in computer-mediated group discussions weaken social norms and inhibitions, much like the conditions associated with deindividuation – anonymity, reduced self-regulation and reduced self-awareness (Diener, 1980). Thus, group members communicating electronically are less aware of social distinctions, resulting in increased equality of participation.

In electronic discussions, where social cues and status effects are reduced and participation is more egalitarian, we expect that influence, in turn, will also be more equally distributed. Low status members in computer-mediated groups should have more influence than low status members in face-to-face groups. And they have less reason to defer to the normative influence of powerful, high status individuals. There is, in short, both theoretical argument and empirical evidence to suggest that groups that interact by means of computers are less prone to status effects than are face-to-face groups. As one advocate has written, the medium is "... dizzyingly egalitarian, since the most important thing about oneself isn't age, appearance, career success, health, race, gender, sexual preference, accent, or any of the other categories by which we normally judge each other, but one's mind" (Van Gelder, 1985, p.365).

One goal of this research is to test whether computer mediation raises the influence of a solitary junior member. It is easy to imagine situations in which equalization of the latter sort might be desirable. For example, a lone junior member willing to disagree with the majority in the face of normative pressure may prevent the group from making a disastrous decision (Janis, 1972). Minority opinions have also been shown to contribute to the detection of novel solutions (Nemeth, 1986) and to potentially influence the group outcome when their arguments are presented cogently and consistently over time (e.g., Moscovici, 1985).

But how powerful is this computer effect on participation and influence? In one study that experimentally tested status effects in computer-mediated groups (Dubrovsky et al., 1991), subjects were unaware of the status attributes of their group members (i.e., they were not told that their group was comprised of three freshmen and one graduate student). The considerable literature on category-based impression formation contends that simply knowing the social category of members of our group will strongly affect our perception, memory, and inference of that group or individual member (e.g., Fiske and Neuberg, 1990). That is, once we initially categorize others as members of particular groups – groups about which we have very generalized or stereotypic knowledge – we typically form impressions of them on the basis of the category alone (e.g., Wilder, 1981). We form these initial impressions to simplify our social environment and reduce our cognitive load. Thus, group members who are sufficiently aware of their status differences may behave, and perceive others as behaving, according to their status categories. It is conceivable, then, that providing group members with appropriate status cues could override the computer effect on equal participation.

It is also possible that high status group members differ systematically from low status members on a number of different personal characteristics. They may be smarter, richer, pushier and more talkative than their low status counterparts (e.g., Strodtbeck, James and Hawkins, 1957), and these differences remain unaltered by computer mediation. Using cognitive theories of intergroup relations, we report here an experiment that replicates and extends previous research on mixed status computer groups (Dubrovsky et al., 1991). Our goal is to test whether the equalization phenomenon holds in groups consisting of one low status member, and where members are aware of their group's different status categories. The design compared participation and influence in face-to-face decision making groups (F) with those in three different computer-supported groups: groups in which the participants were identified (C-I), those in which they were anonymous (C-A), and those in which one member was mislabeled (C-M).

Our three-person groups consisted of two MBA students (high status) and one undergraduate (low status). In both the face-to-face (F) and identified (C-I) conditions, we informed each group member of the name and academic level of each of the other members at the outset. The anonymous (C-A) condition provided a low level of anonymity to the participants. We told subjects that their group consisted of two MBA students and one undergraduate, but we did not identify individual members. Subjects only knew the network locations ("Person A", "Person B" etc.) of the other group members. In the mislabeled (C-M) condition, we told subjects that their group consisted of two MBA students and one undergraduate, but the group was actually comprised of three MBA students. We then told two MBA students which one group member (actually an MBA student) was an "undergraduate." This "low status" student was unaware that he or she had been relegated to this position. As in the anonymous condition, we only revealed the network locations ("Person A", "Person B" etc.) of the other group members.

Hypothesized effects of group participation and evaluation

There are several *a priori* comparisons between conditions which allow us to replicate and evaluate status awareness on participation and influence in face-to-face and computer-supported groups. Our first comparison is between correctly-labeled computer-supported and face-to-face groups, i.e., differences between the C-I, C-A, and F conditions. In all three conditions, group members are correctly told that their group consisted of 2 MBAs and 1 undergraduate.

Hypothesis 1: If status awareness overrides other social effects of the medium, then low status members will participate more equally in the anonymous condition (C-A) as compared to the identified (C-I) and face-to-face (F) conditions. This suggests that reduced social awareness in the anonymous condition will protect the low status members from negative evaluations.

Comparisons of the computer-supported groups who are identified by their name and status (C-I) to computer-supported groups who are incorrectly told who the undergraduate is (C-M) are particularly meaningful.

Hypothesis 2: If personal characteristics override other social effects of the medium, then "low status" members will participate equally in the mislabeled condition (C-M) as compared to the identified condition (C-I), and these "low status" members will be evaluated the same as other high status members in both conditions.

Hypothesis 3: If status awareness overrides other social effects of the medium, then "low status" members will participate equally in the mislabeled condition (C-M) as compared to the identified condition (C-I), but "low status" members will be evaluated lower than high status members in both conditions. This suggests the evaluations will be based on stereotypes or negative perceptions of the social category.

Hypothesis 4: If status awareness overrides other social effects of the medium, then "low status" members will participate less than high status members in both conditions, and "low status" members will be evaluated lower than high status members in both conditions. This suggests that "low status" members will infer negative cues from the high status members and be intimidated into not contributing as much to the group outcome.

Method

Subjects

One hundred five business students participated in this experiment: 75 MBA students (53 males and 22 females) and 30 undergraduates (11 males and 19 females) were asked to pick one of four experimental sessions to participate in. Within each experimental session, subjects were randomly assigned to three 3-person groups. Computer malfunctions and other technical difficulties caused the loss of some data, but usable data were obtained from 91 groups. Of those, 27 groups met face-to-face, 24 groups participated in the identified computer condition, 27 groups in the anonymous condition, and 13 groups in the mislabeled condition. Given the proportion of males and females in our subject pool, randomization within experimental session produced representative numbers of mixed-gender groups.

Decision tasks

Three ethical decision tasks were used in this experiment (see Weiss, 1990). Each task required group members to make an ethical evaluation of the conduct of a computer professional in a hypothetical situation. We chose the three scenarios that had the most moderate means and largest standard deviations on pre-test ratings of ethicality. The first task involved a student offering limited access to a pornographic questionnaire ($\overline{x} = 5.8$, $sd = 2.3$), the second involved monitoring others' electronic mail ($\overline{x} = 4.8$, $sd = 2.5$), and the third concerned the development and sale of marketing profiles from public information ($\overline{x} = 5.2$, $sd = 2.4$).

Research design

The design was a 2 x 4 x 3 (status x communication modality x decision task) analysis of variance design in which communication modality and ethical dilemma were repeated. Order of communication condition was counterbalanced within experimental sessions (i.e. during each session, some subjects participated in face-to-face groups first, some participated in anonymous groups first etc.). Order of presentation of decision tasks was also counterbalanced between sessions.

Procedures

Participants in each session were randomly assigned to three 3-person groups prior to their arrival. When subjects arrived for their experimental session, they were handed a uniquely numbered card with instructions on where they were to go for each of the three tasks. For the computer conditions, each participant was assigned to one of 24 terminals in the University of Arizona's Electronic Meeting Room. The terminals were networked into eight groups of three, with group members widely separated from one another, not knowing to which terminals they were connected. Face-to-face groups met in one of three small rooms adjacent to the computer facility.

Electronic groups used a software tool called GroupOutliner. This tool divides the screen into two halves. Messages to be sent are typed and displayed in the bottom half of the screen. Pressing a function key "sends" the message to the top half of the screen, where it is displayed along with messages from other members. Scrolling through the upper screen allows group members to read all previous messages.

On arriving at the experimental session participants in the computer conditions initially took their seats at the first computer terminal number listed on their cards. Those assigned to face-to-face initial conditions were asked to take a seat in the back of the room while general instructions were delivered. All participants were then given paper copies of the experimental tasks and asked to rate privately the ethicality of the actors in the three scenarios. After these initial ratings were collected, the participants were told that the purpose of the experiment was to study how groups communicate and make decisions face-to-face and electronically, and that they would be discussing as a group the same scenarios they had just rated privately. They were told that each 3-person group consisted of two MBAs and one undergraduate.

Further instructions differed by condition. In the face-to-face groups, the sub-jects were asked to introduce themselves by name and educational status, and were prompted to provide both items. Members of computer identified (C-I) groups were asked to sign-on to their group conference by typing in their first and last names and indicating whether they were MBA students or undergraduates. Computer anonymous (C-A) group members were asked to sign in with a non-identifying statement, (e.g., "I am Person A") and were asked not to disclose any personal information. Those in the computer mislabeled (C-M) condition were asked to log on just like anonymous groups. The manipulation was achieved by a note at two of the terminals stating that "Person B" was the undergraduate, while "Person B" (an MBA student) was told that the group was anonymous. In the computer groups, all messages were collected automatically. In the face-to-face groups, all discussions were recorded on audio tape for later transcription.

After the introductions, participants were asked to discuss the problem to con-sensus. When all groups had agreed on a decision a short questionnaire was distributed to evaluate subjects' expertise, comfort and prior experience with com-puter communication systems, perceptions of the task, and perceptions of their own and others' contributions. The face-to-face participants then rejoined the others in the computer facility, and participants moved to the second position on their index card to work on the second task with an entirely new group. Some simply switched terminals, others moved to one of the outside rooms for the face-to-face condition. The procedure was repeated for the third task. At the end of the third task, a longer questionnaire was distributed to evaluate subjects' computer expe-riences, preferences for face-to-face and computer communication technologies, and communication apprehensiveness. Subjects were then debriefed and thanked for their participation.

Dependent measures

Our hypotheses mainly required group-level analyses permitting orthogonal within-group comparisons of high and low status members as a function of the group's communication modality. We predicted that high status members would participate more than low status members. Participation was measured by the number of remarks an individual made during each group discussion as a fraction of the total remarks made in that group. Each separable thought a group member uttered during discussion counted as a "remark" (see Weisband, 1992). Two coders independently divided subjects' statements into remarks and counted them. We also compared the number of remarks made during each "turn" to determine how much participants talked when given the opportunity to do so. As in previous studies, we evaluated differences among groups in choice shift, defined as the absolute difference between the average pregroup preferences of individual members and their group decision (e.g., Myers and Lamm, 1976). We predicted that the final group decision would be closer to the high status members' pregroup opinions than to the low status member's pregroup opinion, especially in the face-to-face group . We also collected questionnaire measures of each participant's rating of his or her own influence on the final outcome relative to that of his or her fellow group members.

We computed Gini coefficients for each group on participation and peer-rated influence. We expected that groups communicating electronically would participate more equally than would face-to-face groups. We predicted that peer-rated influence would reflect this equality. The Gini coefficient sums, over all the group members, the deviations of each from equal participation, normalized by the maximum possible value of this deviation (Alker, 1965). The coefficient thus takes values between 0 and 1, where 0 means perfect equality. For a set of observed participation rates, X_1, X_2, and X_3, the Gini coefficient (G) is calculated as $G = \frac{3}{4} \sum_{i=1}^{N} |X_i - \frac{1}{3}|$.

Results

Preliminary analysis

Not surprisingly, the MBA students were older than the undergraduates ($\bar{x} = 28$ vs 22, $F_{1,193} = 47.6$ $p < .001$), but there were no differences between MBAs and undergraduates in their use of computers and electronic communication.

As a manipulation check, we asked each group member who they thought the undergraduate was. The respondent could either give the name (or letter) of a particular group member or they could reply, "Don't Know." Figure 1 shows the results. Except for some guessing on the part of high status members in the anonymous and mislabeled conditions, on the average a large proportion of group members (80%) responded correctly across all four treatment conditions.

Figure 1. Proportion of group members who correctly answered the question, "Who was the undergraduate?"

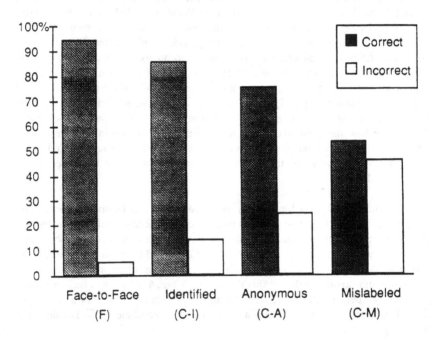

Participation and Influence Effects

Table I reports the results of group participation and influence effects. Looking at participation measures first, we see that face-to-face groups exchanged significantly more total remarks than computer-mediated groups did ($F_{3,73} = 5.9$, $p < .001$), replicating our initial findings. Face-to-face groups also took slightly more "turns" during their discussions than did computer-mediated group discussions ($F_{3,73} = 2.4$, $p < .10$), and they said more during each turn ($\bar{x} = 2.3$) than did members communicating electronically ($\bar{x} = 1.8$), $F_{3,73} = 6.6$, $p < .001$.

Table I. Results of Group Participation and Influence

Group Measures	Mode		Status High	Status Low	Status Diff	Significant F Values Cond.	Status	C x S
Participation Measures								
No. Total Remarks	Identified	(C-I)	28.6	25.0	3.6			
	Anonymous	(C-A)	30.6	25.2	5.4			
	Mislabeled	(C-M)	19.8	23.0	−3.2			
	Face-to-Face	(F)	55.5	44.3	11.2	* * *	*	*
No. Total Turns	Identified		17.0	14.0	3.0			
	Anonymous		16.7	15.1	1.6			
	Mislabeled		13.6	12.9	0.7			
	Face-to-Face		23.8	20.7	3.1	†	*	
No. Remarks/Total	Identified		0.36	0.29	0.07^a			
	Anonymous		0.35	0.28	0.07^a			
	Mislabeled		0.31	0.37	-0.06^b			
	Face-to-Face		0.36	0.28	0.08^a	*	* *	*
No. Remarks/Turn	Identified		1.9	1.8	0.1^a			
	Anonymous		1.9	1.7	0.2^a			
	Mislabeled		1.5	1.8	-0.3^b			
	Face-to-Face		2.4	2.2	0.2^a	* * *	†	
Influence Measures								
Choice Shift	Identified		1.5	2.7	−1.2			
	Anonymous		1.5	2.4	−0.9			
	Mislabeled		1.4	1.7	−0.3			
	Face-to-Face		1.4	2.4	−1.0		* *	
Self-Rated Influence	Identified		0.38	0.36	0.02			
	Anonymous		0.40	0.37	0.03			
	Mislabeled		0.36	0.40	0.04			
	Face-to-Face		0.36	0.34	0.02			
Peer-Rated Influence	Identified		0.33	0.26	0.07			
	Anonymous		0.33	0.27	0.06			
	Mislabeled		0.33	0.28	0.05			
	Face-to-Face		0.34	0.31	0.03	†	* * *	

[a] To test our hypotheses, we conducted planned comparisons using Dunnette's test to compare the identified computer condition (C-I) with the other three modality treatment means. Means not sharing a common subscript differ from each other at the $p < .05$ level. If no subscript is shown, mean comparisons did not differ among modality conditions.

* * * $p < .001$
* * $p < .01$
* $p < .05$
† $p < .10$

Computer-supported interaction can be characterized as relatively large numbers of brief "turns."

But the technology did not change the effect of status. High status members participated more in both face-to-face and electronic groups. Our central measure of group participation is the average proportion of remarks individuals mentioned in their group discussions. High status members talked more ($\bar{x} = .35$) than low status members did ($\bar{x} = .30$), $F_{1,73} = 7.9$, $p < .01$. The significant interaction effect is due to the increased participation in the mislabeled condition. Group members who were labeled as "low status" (but who were unaware of being relegated that status) actually participated more ($\bar{x} = .37$) than the other two members ($\bar{x} = .31$), $F_{3,73} = 3.7$, $p < .05$. This evidence seems to rule out the hypothesis that low status members are intimidated into not participating in the group discussion (Hypothesis 4).

These participation differences are reflected in influence measures. High status members shifted less from their initial pregroup opinions ($\bar{x} = 1.5$) than did low status members ($\bar{x} = 2.4$), $F_{1,77} = 9.0$, $p < .01$, and were perceived by their peers as contributing more to the final group decision ($\bar{x} = .33$) than low status members ($\bar{x} = .28$), $F_{1,81} = 12.2$, $p < .001$. The Gini coefficients of inequality at the group level mimic earlier patterns. Participation was substantially unequal, though not differentially so for electronic ($G = .16$) and for face-to-face ($G = .19$) groups. And computer-supported groups were significantly *less* egalitarian in their evaluation of their peers ($G = .16$) than were face-to-face groups ($G = .10$), $F_{1,45} = 6.4$, $p < .05$.

Results from the two modified electronic conditions are suggestive of possible underlying mechanisms. First, the anonymous (C-A) conditions showed no substantial difference on any measures from the identified (C-I) and face-to-face (F) conditions, leading us to reject Hypothesis 1. Whatever maintains the disproportionate participation and influence of the high status members, it clearly is not the identity of the other members. The finding also appears to weaken any account based on evaluation apprehension on the part of the low status member (e.g., Connolly et al., 1991; Diehl and Stroebe, 1991). It is conceivable that low status members participate less in both face-to-face and identified computer groups because they are dominated by fast talking MBA students (Hypothesis 2), or that the status label confirmed initial expectations of how low status group members should, in fact, behave. We thus have not ruled out support for Hypothesis 4.

The interactions in the mislabeled (C-M) groups proved especially intriguing. The mislabelled individual actually contributed a larger fraction (.37) of the total remarks than did the two (correctly-labelled) high status members (.31). The choice shift measure of influence indicates that this combination of high interaction share and low status label left the mislabeled member as influential as the other group members (see Table I). Peer ratings, however, support Hypothesis 4 and strongly suggest stereotyping: the mislabeled member, though yielding only as much as other MBAs, and contributing proportionately more to the discussion, is rated by the other members as having little influence. He or she is, after all, only an undergraduate!

Discussion

Numerous previous studies examining participation and communication modality effects have found an equalization effect for computer mediation (see Rice, 1984; Culnan and Markus, 1987; Huber, 1990; Sproull and Kiesler, 1991 for reviews). Members have participated in group discussion, and influenced the final result, more equally in computer-based than in face-to-face groups. Our findings are in sharp contrast: High status members dominated the discussions, and exercised disproportionate influence on the final result. These results were replicated for groups whose members knew one another's names as well as for anonymous groups. The progression from face-to-face interaction (presumably rich in social context cues) through identified computer-mediated and finally to anonymous computer-mediated interaction (presumably much less rich in these cues) left untouched the basic inequalities: MBA students participated more than undergraduates, and had greater influence on the group decision.

Consider the notions of undergraduate and MBA "status" we have been using thus far. Compared to undergraduates, MBAs are older, more experienced, quite probably more intelligent, ambitious, self-confident, self-assertive, vocal, affluent – that is, they surely differ from undergraduates on a host of task-relevant dimensions. One account, then, is simply that MBAs are highly verbal, take-charge people. They participate more than, and are at least as persuasive as, undergraduates, and their influence over the group decision reflects this, regardless of communication modality.

An alternative, more cognitive explanation is that participants categorized each other on the basis of their educational status, and subscribed to norms that were consistent with their expectations of how the two groups would differ. Even in anonymous conditions, 12 out of 19 (63%) high status participants were able to make reasonably successful guesses as to which of the others was the undergraduate (see Figure 1). The research in this area indicates that virtually any categorization process can lead to biased evaluations in favor of the in-group (high status majority) and against the out-group (low status minority) (e.g., Billig and Tajfel, 1972; Turner, 1975; Tajfel, 1978). Outgroup members who are relatively deindividuated are also more likely to be targets of negative evaluations than are persons of whom we have greater knowledge.

The computer mediated, mislabeled condition helped to disentangle these accounts. The hint, clearly, is that the mislabeled participant is seen by the others as behaving in a status-inappropriate way and that they react by reducing their participation, unsure how to deal with the deviation. This apparent confusion of status categories in the mislabeled condition is also revealed in Figure 1: even when told who the undergraduate was, 18 out of 39 "high status" members (46%) were unable to figure out who the undergraduate was. Whether or not this conjecture is borne out in subsequent studies, the evidence from the mislabeled condition does suggest that the group interaction is shaped by social impressions beyond simple assertiveness or personality characteristics of MBA students.

Participant ratings of influence are more egalitarian in face-to-face groups, and are clearly stereotyped (to derogate undergraduates) in computer-interactive, mislabeled groups. The evidence suggests that the status cue in computer-mediated discussions was more salient because richer verbal and paralinguistic cues were missing. And with no additional, individuating information available to counter the effects of prior labeling, stereotypical impressions were confirmed on the basis of the social category alone.

The limitations of these studies, based as they are on volunteer student subjects discussing unfamiliar tasks for modest periods of time and for small stakes, are too familiar to need reiteration here. The remedy, too, is familiar: We need to replicate the findings in real-world settings where decisions of consequence are made by experienced, professionally involved participants. A central interest of these extensions, clearly, would be the effect of shared norms for or against equal participation. For example, there will be many decisions in which all participants agree to defer to the superior expertise, knowledge, or judgment of some participants (as perhaps happened here). In other cases, differential influence of, say, hierarchical superiors will be seen as unhelpful to good decision making, in which case the potential of computer mediation for equalizing influence would become more attractive. A full exploration of these issues is, clearly, a substantial undertaking. Perhaps the present demonstration, that a simple status-equalization hypothesis for computer-mediated groups is not tenable, will provide a useful point of departure.

This study has important social implications for the design of computer communication technologies. How communication systems are designed will affect their ability to act as status levelers. Most current electronic mail systems label messages with individuals' personal names, so our results suggest that these technologies will not reduce status inequalities appreciably. Most group decision support systems, however, have the capability for completely anonymous messaging (i.e., without network locations like "Person A," "Person B," and "Person C") which might reduce status inequalities (DeSanctis and Gallupe, 1987, Connolly et al., 1990). As the use of graphic and video technologies becomes more pervasive, and as design features of computer communication systems increase their bandwidth (e.g., by attaching a picture of the sender to each electronic message), group members may find it easier to reveal personal information to each other, making it less likely that people will rely solely on their generalized knowledge of social status categories. Alternatively, it may be easier to transmit status cues in these richer communication environments (e.g., Daft and Lengel, 1986), which could magnify the inequality of participation. Future research will determine whether the availability of such social cues is beneficial to group decision making.

References

Alker, H. R. (1965). *Mathematics and Politics*, Macmillan, New York.

Billig, M. and Tajfel, H. (1973). "Social Categorization and Similarity in Intergroup Behavior", *European Journal of Social Psychology*, vol. 3, pp. 27-52.

Connolly, T., Jessup, L. M., and Valacich, J. S. (1990). "Effects of Anonymity and Evaluative Tone on Idea Generation in Computer-Mediated Groups", *Management Science*, vol. 36, pp. 689-703.

Culnan, M.J. and Markus, L. (1987). "Information Technologies: Electronic Media and Intraorganizational Communication", in F.M. Jablin, L.L. Putnam, K.H. Roberts and L.W. Porter (eds.): *Handbook of Organizational Communication*, Sage, Beverly Hills, pp. 420-444.

Daft, R. L. and Lengel, R. H. (1986). "Information Richness: A New Approach to Managerial Information Processing and Organizational Design", *Management Science*, vol. 32, pp. 554-571.

DeSanctis, G. and Gallupe, R. B. (1987). "A foundation for the Study of Group Decision Support Systems", *Management Science*, vol. 33, pp. 589-609.

Diehl, M. and Stroebe, W. (1991). "Productivity Loss in Idea-Generation Groups: Tracking Down the Blocking Effect", *Journal of Personality and Social Psychology*, vol. 61, pp. 392-403.

Diener, E. (1980). "De-individuation: The Absence of Self-Awareness and Self-Regulation in Group Members," in P. Paulus (ed.): *The Psychology of Group Influence*, Erlbaum, Hillsdale, New Jersey.

Dubrovsky, V. J., Kiesler, S., and Sethna, B. N. (1991). "The Equalization Phenomenon: Status Effects in Computer-Mediated and Face-to-Face Decision Making Groups", *Human-Computer Interaction*, vol. 6, pp. 119-146.

Fiske, S. T. and Neuberg, S. L. (1990). "A Continuum of Impression Formation, from Category-Based to Individuating Processes: Influences of Information and Motivation on Attention and Interpretation", *Advances in Experimental Social Psychology*, vol. 23, pp. 1-74.

Hackman, J. R. (1976). "Group Influences on Individuals", in M. R. Dunnette (ed.): *Handbook of Industrial and Organizational Psychology*, Rand-McNally, Chicago.

Huber, G. P. (1990). "A Theory of the Effects of Advanced Information Technologies on Organizational Design, Intelligence, and Decision Making", *Academy of Management Review*, vol. 15, pp. 47-71.

Janis, I. L. (1972). *Victims of Groupthink*, Houghton-Mifflin, Boston.

McGrath, J.E. (1984). *Groups: Interaction and Performance*, Prentice-Hall, Englewood Cliffs, New Jersey.

McGuire, T. W., Kiesler, S., and Siegel, J. (1987). "Group and Computer-Mediated Discussion Effects in Risk Decision Making", *Journal of Personality and Social Psychology*, vol. 52 pp. 917-930.

Moscovici, S. (1985). "Social influence and conformity", in G. Lindzey and E. Aronson (eds.): *The Handbook of Social Psychology, Vol. 2*, Random House, New York, pp. 347-412.

Myers, D. G. and Lamm, H. (1976). "The Group Polarization Phenomenon", *Psychological Review*, vol. 83, pp. 602-627.

Nemeth, C. J. (1986). "Differential Contributions of Majority and Minority Influence", *American Psychologist*, vol. 93, pp. 23-32.

Rice, R. E. (1984). "Mediated Group Communication", in R. E. Rice (ed.): *The New Media*, Sage, Beverly Hills.

Siegel, J., Dubrovsky. V, Kiesler. S, and McGuire. T. (1986). "Group Processes in Computer-Mediated Communication, *Organizational Behavior and Human Decision Processes*, vol. 37, pp. 157-187.

Spears, R. and Lea, M. (1992). "Social Influence and the Influence of the 'Social' in Computer-Mediated Communication", in M. Lea (ed.): *Contexts of Computer-Mediated Communication*, Harvester Wheatsheaf, Hewel-Hempstead.

Sproull, L. and Kiesler, S. (1991). *Connections*, MIT Press, Cambridge.

Stephan, W. G. (1985). "Intergroup Relations," in G. Lindzey and E. Aronson (eds.): *The Handbook of Social Psychology, Vol. 2*, Random House, New York, pp. 599-658.

Strodtbeck, F. L., James, R., M., and Hawkins, C. (1957). "Social Status in Jury Deliberations", *American Sociological Review*, vol. 22, pp. 713-719.

Tajfel, H. (1978). *Differentiation Between Social Groups: Studies in Social Psychology of Intergroup Relations*, Academic Press, London.

Turner, J. C. (1975). "Social Comparison and Social Identity: Some Prospects for Intergroup Behavior", *European Journal of Social Psychology*, vol. 5, pp. 5-34.

Van Gelder, L. (1991). "The Strange Case of the Electronic Lover," reprinted in C. Dunlap and R. Kling (eds.): *Computerization and Controversy*, Acadmic Press, Boston, pp. 364-375.

Wilder, D. A. (1981). "Perceiving Persons as a Group: Categorization and Intergroup Relations", in D. Hamilton (ed.): *Cognitive Processes in Stereotyping and Intergroup Behavior*, Erlbaum, Hillsdale, New Jersey.

Weisband, S. P. (1992). "Group Discussion and First Advocacy Effects in Computer-Mediated and Face-to-Face Decision Making Groups", *Organizational Behavior and Human Decision Processes*, vol. 53, pp. 352-380.

Weiss, E. A. (1990). "Self-Assessment Procedure XXII", *Communications of the ACM*, vol. 33, pp. 110-132.

Proceedings of the Third European Conference on Computer-Supported Cooperative Work
13-17 September, 1993, Milan, Italy
G. De Michelis, C. Simone and K. Schmidt (Editors)

The Use of Breakdown Analysis in Synchronous CSCW System Design

Silvia Pongutá Urquijo[1], Stephen A.R.Scrivener[2,1], Hilary K. Palmén[3]

[1] LUTCHI Research Centre, University of Loughborough, UK
[2] The Design Research Centre, University of Derby, UK
[3] Institute of Computer Based Learning, Heriot-Watt University, UK

Abstract: CSCW systems are invariably intended to support complex group activities. This complexity is reflected in the richness of the data required to adequately evaluate a system intended to support these activities. Consequently, there is a need for the development of an evaluation technique which can reliably provide diagnostic information quickly from rich data (such as video and audio recordings). In this paper, the development and use of an approach based on 'breakdowns' within the scope of a Model of Interaction is described. Breakdown analysis provides a systematic means of approaching large quantities of communication data, identifying those areas which highlight problems and relieving the evaluator of the task of consulting or becoming an expert in a more complex form of conversational analysis or HCI.

Introduction

The paradigm shift (Hughes *et al.*, 1991) from Human Computer Interaction to that which considers the group work, communication, social, political, and physical aspects within which a CSCW system is used presents numerous design and development problems. The traditional HCI system design approach of an iterative design cycle including both formative and summative evaluation activities is a valuable and potentially productive model. However, the particular methods used within this iterative design cycle to evaluate within a CSCW environment require development to accommodate the paradigm shift. This paper outlines the development of a practical approach to evaluation using the notion of "breakdowns" (Winograd and Flores, 1987). The potential of "breakdowns" in interaction and communication as an evaluation tool has been identified previously (Wright and Monk, 1989). However, the particular relevance of "breakdowns" to the evaluation of real-time CSCW systems is in the way they are produced naturally by users as part of the communication.

In the following section we introduce a set of studies of a prototype CSCW sketching tool for remote co-working (Clark and Scrivener, 1992). The data collection techniques employed in these studies were deliberately wide ranging. The users were video recorded, audio recorded, and detailed logfiles of their drawing activities were created. This approach to data collection produced a wealth of rich data. The problem facing the system developers was how to interpret this data in a meaningful manner that would provide information in a form suitable to direct system development. There are number of popular HCI methods which could provide the diagnostic information required by the system designers. However, given the particular relevance of 'breakdowns' to CSCW systems we developed and applied an analysis approach based on the detection and diagnosis of "breakdowns".

Background

Design at a Distance: The Loughborough-Adelaide Studies

The ROCOCO (RemOte COoperation and COmmunication) project investigated the communicational requirements of remotely sited designers working on a shared problem (Garner *et al.*, 1991; Scrivener *et al.*, 1993a). For the purposes of the project a system, called the ROCOCO STATION, was designed to enable geographically separated designer-pairs to communicate in real-time via an eye-to-eye video-link, a high-quality audio-link, and a shared drawing surface.

A central feature of the ROCOCO STATION is the ROCOCO SKETCHPAD, a computer-based Distributed Shared Drawing Surface (Clark and Scrivener, 1992) which allows persons sitting at different computer workstations to share a drawing surface. The surface takes the form of a large 'shared window' which is displayed on each workstation screen. Users have simultaneous access to the drawing surface (the ROCOCO SKETCHPAD). They are able to draw with a selection of "pen-types" and can point to existing drawings with a "telepointer". The drawing surface can, in principle, be shared by any number of users. The sketchpad is operated via a digitiser and pen. To one side of the workstation screen is a 'Video Tunnel' video-link (incorporating a video camera and monitor). This arrangement, developed by Smith *et al.* (1989), uses half silvered glass and mirrors to allow eye-to-eye contact to be made over the video-link. Users have a high-quality headset audio-link.

In the second phase of the project the communication requirements of group design were investigated in conditions where, typically, communication was impoverished. These experimental conditions were achieved by manipulating the features of the ROCOCO STATION. The four configurations shown in Table I were investigated. Scrivener *et al.* (1993a) found that real-time person-to-person interaction between designers engaged in the initial stages of design could be effectively mediated via a computer-based communications system comprising a shared drawing surface and an audio-link: the Video-off condition.

TABLE I: ROCOCO Workstation Experimental Configurations

Configuration	Sketchpad	Video tunnel	Audio link
1	on	on	on
2	on	on	off
3	on	off	on
4	on	off	off

During February 1992, remote design sessions were conducted between the LUTCHI Research Centre in Loughborough, England, and Flinders University in Adelaide, South Australia (a land distance of over 16 000 km). Using ISDN communications technology and a headset telephone, the Video-off configuration of the ROCOCO STATION was replicated between the two sites. That is, two designers were able to talk to each other via a telephonic link and draw together via the ROCOCO SKETCHPAD. This enabled an assessment of the configuration in a more commercially realistic form (i.e. using standard telecommunications infrastructure).

Four designers took part in this study: two final year BSc in Design and Technology students at Loughborough University of Technology, and two B.A. Industrial Design graduates of the University of South Australia. Each subject was assigned to a test pair. The tasks used in the study were chosen from those used in the ROCOCO project. In the course of the study each subject pair completed the same three design tasks. The six studies were carried out sequentially over a period of three days (i.e. two each day).

At the end of the first and last session each designer was asked to complete a questionnaire that consisted of statements relating to the fitness for the task and the usability of the system. The results obtained from the questionnaire were generally positive in both respects (for a discussion of the results see Scrivener *et al*, 1992 and Scrivener *et.al.*, 1993a, 1993b). However, it was obvious to observers of the studies that communication problems had arisen (for example, coordinating page changes) which were not captured explicitly in either the rated or open question sections of the questionnaire data. It was also obvious that these observed problems were ones that affected usability, and therefore had implications for the re-design of the system. Consequently we investigated methods for evaluating the performance of the system using the audio and video recordings taken during the design sessions.

Issues effecting evaluation approaches

There are numerous techniques that can be used as part of an evaluation approach. Popular research and evaluation methods would include the Interview, Usability Checklist, Focus group, Expert Walkthrough, Incident Diary, and Questionnaire. Each method has strengths and weaknesses which make it either appropriate or inappropriate depending on the resources available to the evaluation activity and the purpose of the system being evaluated. Rather than attempt to comprehensively list and describe the repertoire of techniques available this section intends to introduce some of the practical issues that should be considered when selecting an appropriate technique.

The general aim of an evaluation is to produce recommendations for design improvements. The evaluators have to consider issues such as time, finance, resource availability, the type and quantity of data produced, and the reliability and validity of the methods. These considerations include planning for when recommendations are required, how long, and when resources are available. The resources include users, equipment, money, and effort required (and available) to ensure that the evaluation can be completed. The quantity and type of data required is effected by the extent to which the task and environment are realistic. The evaluator needs to consider questions such as whether the evaluation can take place in the system's intended environment, what data is required, will descriptive information provide a sufficient basis for improvements, and can quantitative information be accurately interpreted?

The selection of evaluation techniques depends on the interaction of all these factors. Using more then one technique can help ensure that the findings are reliable. However, time, money, and resource availability often provide undesirable limitations and the pressure is on evaluators to provide quick, cheap, and effective feedback to the system developers. While an evaluation set in the intended system environment, with the intended user population, may provide the most appropriate data, the intended user population may not be available and the data gathered from a naturalistic study may prove too complex for a reliable interpretation.

CSCW systems are invariably intended to support complex group activities. This complexity is reflected in the richness of the data required to adequately evaluate a system intended to support these activities. Consequently, there is a need for the development of an evaluation technique which can provide reliable diagnostic information quickly from rich data (such as video and audio recordings). An approach based on 'breakdowns' has the potential to provide such a technique.

Breakdowns

Wright and Monk (1989) proposed a design evaluation method founded on two concepts:

1. **Critical incident**: defined as user behaviour which is suboptimal with respect to the functionality provided by the system and the intention of the users. A critical incident occurs in two situations: when the user backs up to some previous state after entering an undesired state, and secondly when the user makes redundant or ineffective actions. Critical incidents can be observed in video records, system logs or even contemporaneous observation.

2. **Breakdown**: defined as the moment when the user becomes conscious of the properties of the system and has to mentally break down or decompose his or her understanding of the system in order to rationalise the problem experienced. Winograd and Flores (1987) described the rationale for breakdowns as follows, " a computer is usable to the extent that it serves to fulfil a task in a 'transparent' fashion. Ideally, the user works without being aware of the system as a separate entity. Only in the case of 'breakdown', and the subsequent need for analytical interpretation of the artifact as possessing properties in its own right, does the system become part of the subjective experience of the interaction".

Wright and Monk (1989) studied a user working with a bibliographic data base for a total of ten hours. They considered four kinds of data: system logs from free use; system logs from the user performing set tasks, retrospective verbal protocol obtained during re-enactment of system logs and concurrent verbal protocol (or co-operative evaluation - i.e. the evaluator co-operates by verbalising during interaction).

Critical incidents were obtained from the first three kinds of data and breakdowns were obtained from the concurrent verbal protocol. They found that critical incidents and breakdowns together provided data that was very effective for system evaluation. They also noted that important problems were uncovered via breakdowns, and that the breakdowns were easier to detect than critical incidents. In conclusion, they advised the use of breakdowns because a critical incident is usually accompanied by a breakdown, but the converse is not necessarily the case.

In collaborative tasks the verbal discourse is unprompted. Participants are not compelled to "think aloud"; and if they do it is in order to cooperate with their partner, not an experimenter. Hence verbal protocols arising during collaboration between two or more people overcome the criticisms usually made of verbal protocols and in general should provide more reliable breakdowns in the sense that these will be reported for the benefit of those involved in the collaboration as a means of bringing the usability problems being experienced by the breakdown reporter into public awareness. It seemed to us, therefore, that Breakdown Analysis could be a useful tool for evaluating the performance of the ROCOCO SKETCHPAD in the Adelaide-Loughborough studies.

Usability Evaluation and CSCW

Evaluating the Usability of CSCW Systems

The importance of achieving usability in human-computer system design is well understood. Shackel (1981, 1991) argues that usability depends upon the design of the tool (i.e. the computer system) in relation to the users, the task, and the environment, and the success of the user support provided (e.g. training, manuals, and other job aids). Each components has its own characteristics which influence the interaction between the user and the computer or, as is becoming increasingly common, between several users and one or more software applications (Benyon *et al.*, 1990). In general, a breakdown in human-computer interaction is an indicator of usability failure. The decomposition of a system in terms of its four principal components (Task, User, Tool and Environment, TUTE) provides a framework for usability evaluation.

A synchronous-remote CSCW system, such as the ROCOCO SKETCHPAD (Clark and Scrivener, 1992), designed to support two or more users working in real-time collaboration can be visualised as a system composed of two (or more) connected human-computer sub-systems. In order to evaluate such a system in terms of TUTE interactions the model must be extended to take these multiple sub-systems into account. In Figure 1 each sub-system is decomposed in terms of it's four principal components, where the boundary separating two components represents a relationship or interface between them, as do the vectors connecting two components. Decomposed in this way, each system can be evaluated independently.

However, when connected for CSCW, as in Figure 1, the evaluation must consider the new relationships in the Model of Interaction between human-computer sub-systems. In Figure 1, which represents two connected sub-systems A and B, the two additional direct relationships are shown that link the sub-systems via connections between User A and User B, and Tool A and Tool B. The Loughborough-Adelaide system fits this model, being composed of different users and instances of the same class of tool replicated in different physical environments.

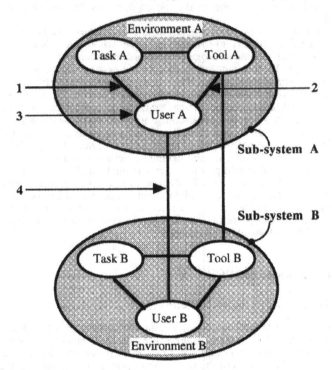

Figure 1   Interaction between Two Human-Computer Sub-Systems

The Role of the Model of Interaction in Breakdown Analysis

In the Breakdown Analysis method described below the Model of Interaction is used as a basis for classifying breakdowns. The aim of the classification is not to put a breakdown event into a neat slot, but to enhance the quality of the information regarding the breakdown such that it is likely to more readily assist the evaluator in identifying its underlying cause (Booth,1990).

Given the definition provided in the previous section, a breakdown occurs between the user and some element of the system with which he or she is interacting. From Figure 1 (see labelled vectors 1,2,3,and 4) it is clear that the user is directly involved in four primary interactions each of which can be subject to breakdown. These interaction are between:

1. **User and task:** where a breakdown can occur when the user has difficulties understanding the task or does not have the necessary knowledge to accomplish the objectives set by the task.

2.	**User and tool**: breakdowns here are related to the two elements that compose a tool: the hardware and software interfaces. Two kinds of problems may occur involving either or both elements. These are tool failure, where a technical problem occurs, and user-tool mismatch, where the user does not understand the tool.

3.	**User and environment**: where a breakdown occurs when the user becomes conscious of some intrusive property of the environment.

4.	**User and user**: here the breakdowns are usually breakdowns in communication. This class of breakdown is elaborated in some detail below.

In the Loughborough-Adelaide studies users communicated via the audio link and the ROCOCO SKETCHPAD. A number of different types of communication breakdown were noted:

4.1	Sufficiency: a sufficiency breakdown occurs when the information provided to a partner is not sufficient for understanding the sender's intention.

4.2	Clarity: a breakdown in clarity occurs when a message is inaudible or illegible, for example poor handwriting.

4.3	Comprehension: a breakdown of this kind occurs when, for example, cultural differences lead to failures of comprehension, such as when one partner refers to religious practices that are alien to the other.

4.4	Attention: a breakdown of attention occurs when the receiver is either absorbed in the task or because some external distraction causes attention loss at a conversationally disruptive moment.

4.5	Coordination: a coordination breakdown occurs when users fail to coordinate their utterances, and consequently interrupt one another.

4.6	Feedback: this class of breakdown occurs when the source does not receive any acknowledgement from the receiver.

Figure 2 shows the full breakdown classification hierarchy together with the corresponding code of each category used during breakdown analysis.

Breakdown Analysis

In this section an evaluation method based on Breakdown Analysis is proposed for use as a part of an iterative system development process.

The method we propose consists of three stages:
Stage 1: Transcription and categorisation of breakdowns.
Stage 2: Causal diagnosis.
Stage 3: Remedy prescription

Using a medical analogy, if we regard a breakdown as the pathology of a system ailment, these stages correspond to the identification of symptoms, diagnosis, and the prescription of a method of treatment. In the following sections we describe and illustrate, using examples from the Loughborough-Adelaide study, each stage of the method.

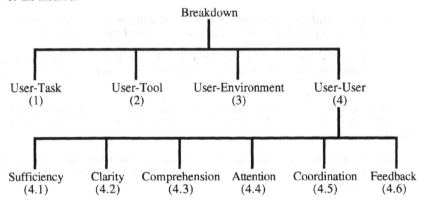

Figure 2. Classification of Breakdowns

Stage 1: Transcription and Categorisation of Breakdowns

The transcription and coding of breakdowns is concerned with the identification of the fact of a breakdown rather than its cause. This stage involves three steps: detection, transcription, and category assignment. Step 1, detection, can be done in two ways: by observation of video-recordings of the user-system interaction, or by direct observation of system use. The rule of thumb in breakdown detection is to record any instance where users' comments indicate self-awareness of user-system interaction, for example:

Subject 1 My pen does not want to work. I can not write anything

In Step 2, the breakdown detected in Step 1 is transcribed. The following data is recorded for each breakdown: time of occurrence, the subject(s) experiencing the breakdown, the sequence of utterances bounding the breakdown, and any comments about the context of the breakdown. The following example illustrates a transcribed breakdown.

Breakdown Analysis				
Experiment: Study 1 Pair 1			Date: July 1992	
Time	Subject	Occurrence	Code	Notes
25:28	OZ UK OZ	What does it say? Good question I've forgotten 'domestic'. It says domestic Oh!! domestic		Pointing at writing

In Step 3 the breakdown definitions associated with the Model of Interaction are used to categorise the transcribed breakdown, which is then assigned a category label. We will illustrate this process using the earlier example. Here subjects are experiencing a breakdown in communication clarity because subject OZ cannot read subject UK's writing, hence the breakdown is assigned the code 4, for communication, and (/)2, for clarity.

Breakdown Analysis				
Experiment: Study 1 Pair 1			Date: July 1992	
Time	Subject	Occurrence	**Code**	Notes
25:28	OZ	What does it say?	**4/2**	Pointing at writing in screen
	UK	Good question I've forgotten 'domestic'. It says domestic		
	OZ	Oh!! domestic		

Stage 2: Causal Diagnosis

So far the fact of a breakdown has been established and coded in terms of the Model of Interaction, however no attempt has yet been made to establish the cause of the breakdown. Hence, the objective of Stage 2 is to establish the underlying causes of the breakdowns documented in Stage 1. Stage 2 takes place once all the breakdowns observed during the analysis have been identified and classified. The crucial question addressed for each breakdown at this stage is "What is causing the breakdowns?"

Consider, for instance, the earlier example of breakdown in communication clarity. A number of plausible explanations can be postulated in this case. First, it may simply be that subject UK's handwriting is illegible. Alternatively, it may be that the UK workstation doesn't adequately support handwriting (for example, the stylus sampling rate might be too slow for effective scribing). Finally, it could be that the interaction between the two sub-systems (i.e. the communication between tools) may be affecting the user-subsystem interactions. Clearly, this example illustrates the point that the cause of a problem may not always be easy to identify, and further studies and tests may be required in order to isolate the specific cause or causes of a given breakdown.

In this case, it turned out that the breakdown in communication clarity could be attributed to the stylus sampling rate which was not fast enough for effective scribing. This conclusion was reached by looking at the set of communication clarity breakdowns as a whole which revealed that the problem was not isolated to one individual or one pair. In fact all subjects produced illegible script, thus suggesting a problem with the tool. This example demonstrates that the grouping of breakdowns in categories is of assistance to the analyst.

Stage 3: Remedy Prescription

In this the final stage, the information obtained from the previous stages, especially information regarding the cause(s) of each breakdown, is used as a basis for remedies to overcome the observed problems associated with the current system.

Distribution of Breakdowns: Session 3 of the Adelaide-Loughborough Study

We have applied the Breakdown Analysis method described above to the data generated in last session of each pairing in the Adelaide-Loughborough study (having evolved the method via analysis of the first and second sessions). Figure 3 represents the number of breakdowns per category experienced by each pair in Session 3.

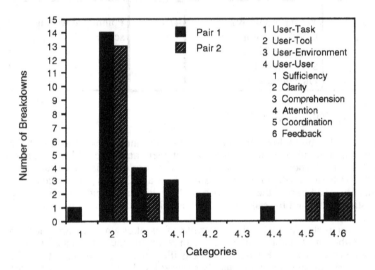

Figure 3   Number of Breakdowns per Category for each Pair

From the graphs it would appear that most of the breakdowns experienced occurred between the user and the tool. On analysis, the breakdowns were found to be caused either because the users had expectations that the tool couldn't support (e.g. freehand writing and sketching) or because of operating performance (eg. inadequate response time).

In the third session the subjects experienced fewer breakdowns in communication than in the previous two studies. One reason for this could be that they developed conventions to avoid certain difficulties. For example, a convention that both pairs adopted was to agree page changes before actually executing them, thus avoiding many of the breakdowns in communication coordination that occured when pages were unilaterally changed.

As users became more familiar with the system their awareness of the environment increased and more breakdowns of this type were reported (as compared to earlier sessions). For example, in the final session subjects discussed matters such as the headset comfort and environmental noises (one subject commented that he could hear a motorcycle going by at his partners end, and in another instance a UK subject commented that he could hear the noise of the marks being made on the board by his partner).

Conclusions

Some of the advantages obtained from analysing breakdowns within the scope of the Model for Interaction are:

1. The Model for Interaction provides the means to focus on the most important aspects of the user-system interaction.
2. Breakdown analysis uncovers problems that users actually register.
3. The focus on users yields insight into how the system is perceived and whether the user finds the system usable or not.
4. Breakdown analysis, by focussing on those parts of the system (i.e user, tool, task, environment) where the user is experiencing breakdowns, isolates areas in need of refinement.
5. By identifying the areas where the user is experiencing difficulties, breakdown analysis can give some indication of how to solve usability problems.

On a more general level breakdown analysis provides a systematic means of approaching large quantities of communication data. The benefits of the approach lie in that each breakdown provides information that indicates a problem with a prototype. Consequently it is not necessary to count each breakdown and use extensive resources analysing vast quantities of data. As it is not necessary to count the occurrences of breakdowns it is also not necessary to pilot the system with a large number of users. While the breakdowns themselves do not necessarily include much interpretive data obtaining this, once a problem has been identified, is a simple matter via querying the original communicants.

The approach provides quick feedback to the system designers - facilitating rapid prototyping. While the lack of interpretative information can be considered a short coming of the approach its important features are that it quickly identifies problem areas, and can handle large quantities of data effectively. Ultimately, it is up to the individual system development team to decide how to use this approach. Breakdowns could be used late in the design cycle, when the prototype has been delivered, to check whether there are still improvements required. Alternatively the approach could be used early in the design cycle for rapid prototyping. We have focussed on the breakdowns in user-system interaction in CSCW systems. However, studies of failures in networking (Rogers, 1992) and the use of shared drawing tutorial system (Sharples, 1992) suggest that the analysis of "breakdowns" may be generally applicable to the socio-technical system as a whole.

It is probable that the type and frequency of breakdowns varies at different areas in the prototype development; this is an area that may benefit from further research. Given the above point, it is highly likely that breakdowns will continue to occur even when the system is delivered and running since breakdowns may not be uncovered because of time and cost limits on the number of design iterations possible. Also differences between the environments and users involved in the evaluation and those of the workplaces into which the system is installed may also be reflected in new breakdowns. However, it is our belief that many on the primary technical, communication, and interaction inadequacies of a system that impact on usability can be uncovered using breakdown analysis. If resources are available the system can be modified to repair for system-in-operation breakdowns.

In the absence of such resources users are obliged to evolve recovery and repair strategies which, whilst not enhancing the systems usability, increase its efficiency and usefulness. It may be that breakdown analysis can be employed in the workplace to aid the development of effective repair and recovery strategies by making explicit to users the nature of the problems encountered; again this is any area worthy of further research.

When planning the evaluation activities for an iterative system development cycle the use of breakdown analysis has the potential to be cost effective because it can:

- handle large amounts of data (eg video recordings)
- provide development feedback with limited user time.
- provide effective feedback using limited evaluator/specialist time (coding activities are quicker than formal methods such as speech act coding).
- be effective when there is limited availability of equipment (minimum of two workstations required).
- provide quick feedback to the developers.

Breakdown analysis provides a means of systematically identifying those areas which highlight problems and relieves the evaluator of the task of consulting or becoming an expert in more complex forms of conversational analysis (eg Heath and Luff, 1991). It does not require an HCI specialist to use this technique, merely familiarisation with the notion of breakdowns.

Acknowledgements

At the time this work was carried out Scrivener was a member of staff at Loughborough University of Technology. The authors would like to thank Sean Clark (LUTCHI Research Centre, Loughborough University, UK) for his advice and assistance during the study, and to the anonymous referees of the paper for their comments.

References

Benyon, D., Rogers, Y.R. and Preece, J. (1990): *A Guide to Usability*, The Open University, Milton Keynes.

Booth, P.A. (1990): "ECM: A Scheme for Analysing User-System Errors", *Human-Computer Interaction-INTERACT'90*, in D. Diaper *et al.* (eds.), Elsevier Science Publishers, North-Holland, 1990, pp 47-54.

Clark, S.M. and Scrivener, S.A.R. (1992) "The ROCOCO Sketchpad Distributed Shared Drawing Surface", LUTCHI Report No. 92/C/LUTCHI/0150, LUTCHI Research Centre, University of Technology, Loughborough, UK.

Garner, S.W., Clarke, A.A., Scrivener, S.A.R., Clark, S., Connolly, J., Palmén, H., Schappo, A., Smyth, M. (1991): "The Use of Design Activity for Research into Computer Supported Co-operative Working", *Proceedings of DATER'91*, Loughborough University, UK.

Heath, C., and Luff, P. (1991): "CSCW: Collaborative activity and Technological design: Task co-ordination in London Underground control rooms", in L. Bannon, M. Robinson & K. Schmidt (eds) *Proceedings of the Second European Conference on Computer-Supported Cooperative Work*, Kluwer Academic Publishers, Dordrecht, The Netherlands, pp 65-80.

Hughes, J., Randall, D. and Shapiro, D. (1991): "CSCW: Discipline or Paradigm? A sociological Perspective", in L. Bannon, M. Robinson & K. Schmidt (eds) *Proceedings of the Second European Conference on Computer-Supported Cooperative Work,* Kluwer Academic Publishers, Dordrecht, The Netherlands, pp 325-336.

Rogers, Y.R. (1992): "Ghosts in the Network: distributed troubleshooting in a shared working environment", in J. Turner & R. Kraut (eds) *Proceedings of CSCW 1992 : Sharing Perspectives,* ACM, New York, USA, pp 346-355.

Scrivener, S.A.R., Harris, D., Clark, S.M., Rockoff,T., and Smyth, M.(1992): "Designing at a Distance: Experiments in Remote-Sychronous Design", *Proceedings of OZCHI'92: CHISIG Annual Conference ,* Gold Coast, Australia, November 1992, pp 44-53.

Scrivener, S.A.R., Clark, S., Clarke, A., Connolly, J., Garner, S., Palmen, H., Smyth, M., Schappo, A. (1993a): "Real-Time Communication between Dispersed Work Groups via Speech and Drawing",*Wirschaftsinformatik,* No 25, Vol. 2, pp 149-156.

Scrivener, S.A.R., Harris, D., Clark, S.M., Rockoff,T., and Smyth, M. (1993b): "Designing at a Distance via Real-Time Designer-to-Designer Interaction", *Design Studies,* (accepted for publication).

Shackel, B.(1981): "The Concept of Usability", in J.L. Bennett, D. Case, J. Sandelin and M. Smith (eds.), *Visual Display Terminals: Usability Issues and Health Concerns,* Englewood Cliffs, NJ Prentice Hall, pp 45-88.

Shackel, B. (1991): "Usability-Context, Framework, Definition, Design and Evaluation", in B.Shackel & S.Richardson (eds.), *Human Factors for Informatics Usability,* Cambridge University Press.

Sharples, M. (1993): "A Study of Breakdowns and Repairs in a Computer Managed Communication System", *Interacting with Computers,* (accepted for publication).

Smith, R.B, O'Shea, T., O'Malley, C., Scanlon, E., Taylor, J. (1989): "Preliminary Experiments with a Distributed Multi-media Problem Solving Environment", *Proceedings of the First European Conference on Computer-Supported Cooperative Work,* September, London,UK, pp. 19-34.

Winograd T. & Flores F. (1987) *Understanding Computers and Cognition: A New Foundation,* Ablex, Norwood, NJ, USA.

Wright P.C. & Monk A.F. (1991): "A Cost-Effective Evaluation Method for Use by Designers", *International Journal of Man-Machine Studies,* 35, pp. 891-912.

Wright, P.C. & Monk, A.F. (1989): "Evaluation for Design", in A. Sutcliffe, & L. Macaulay (eds.) *People and Computers* V, Cambridge University Press, Cambridge, UK, pp 345-358.

Proceedings of the Third European Conference on Computer-Supported Cooperative Work
13-17 September, 1993, Milan, Italy
G. De Michelis, C. Simone and K. Schmidt (Editors)

An Ethnographic Study Of Graphic Designers

Dianne Murray
University Of Surrey, U.K.

Abstract: This paper is about capturing and analysing requirements for Computer Supported Collaborative Work (CSCW) systems, showing that the approach taken differs from that for more traditional IT systems. Social science research paradigms are used to expand the nature of work in constrained environments. Interaction-based studies of office settings and a case study of a set of knowledge workers who manipulate information leads to an investigation of methods for translating their tacit knowledge into more meaningful requirements statements. The work presents views of the organisation through the participants eyes as contrasted with more formal views of the organisation as a business.

Introduction

One of the influences of social science on the field of CSCW is to give a broader understanding of the nature of work. In finding a rationale for how activities are carried out in the office-based societies which form the basis of many studies, it is possible to clarify what it is about working together in groups that make the construction of computer systems to support them so different from that of single-user systems. Such studies document the underlying organisational and social structure of the organisations in which people work and identifies just why they did the work they did in the way that they did. We can use these findings as a basis for design of more effective CSCW systems.

Watching how people act normally as they carry out their job in their usual work situation is not yet a common data gathering technique for collecting user requirements for systems development. The techniques involve non-intrusive observations and some recent researchers have analysed modern office or operations contexts (Anderson and Shorrock, 1992; Bentley et al., 1992; Button, 1992; Dubinskas, 1988; Heath and Luff, 1991; Hughes et al., 1993; Kraut et al,. 1991; Linde, 1988; Nardi and Miller, 1988; Reder and Schwab, 1990; Rogers, 1992).

The technique of ethnography has a number of disadvantages as well as advantages. The large amounts of data it generates are hard to analyse, especially as the techniques for such analysis are not well codified. The observer has no control over what can be observed at any one time so that important but rare events may not be observed at all during the course of the study. There has to be some guidance on what to collect and how to limit fruitless attempts to watch everything that happens in a small project group. This bounding of the field of view seems to be necessary when looking for specific traces of activity and indications of communication episodes.

The advantages are that the observer can obtain a reasonably detailed understanding of the actual social organisation of the work setting and not be reliant upon others interpretation of how things should be. Inside knowledge of the procedures and data that participants really use, not just what they say they use, or what the company guidelines say they should be using, can be derived and experienced at first-hand. An insight into the way things work allows an ethnographer to live inside the organisation rather than apart from it as an external observer. The patterns which individuals make as groups in a particular environmental setting show some of the participation structures which provide accountability of action and the way in which situated learning and the acquisition of competence occurs. The normative rules and actions instantiated in the workplace culture lead to observable rules and interpretation of what these mean in the context of the society being studied. It is critical, however, that the ethnographer remain detached enough to maintain analytical impartiality and scepticism in order to utilise the study for detached analysis and to make connections between the unfolding patterns. In this way, an ethnographic model can be derived (see Figure 1) as a means of representing relevant aspects of social context.

In representing workplace worlds ethnography can illuminate previously hidden and unremarked underlying interaction and shared knowledge. However, that knowledge must also be somehow passed onto systems designers if effective CSCW systems which support work practices as they are constructed by participants and to be built.

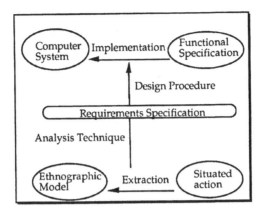

Figure 1. Ethnographically informed requirements specification.

This paper describes a case study, carried out using ethnographic techniques, which tries to bring to light what some of the crucial features of collaborative working might be. The observational studies took place in the offices of two different companies and consisted of watching staff as they went about their day-to-day work, noting activities and environments, conversations and interactions. The people studied are knowledge-workers in that they manipulate information and insubstantial material instead of manufacturing physical products. The distinction is that they handle data, ideas, information and concepts rather than basic material. There will, of course, be a realisation to their work in the real-world in terms of paper-based documents or the artefacts which are the outcome of the processes they engage in.

Case study requirements

Before observational studies can take place, sites must be selected and negotiated and a certain level of site specification has to be gone through. The task specification was based on the premise that small groups producing an artefact, or an identifiable piece of work within reasonably specific short time-scales would be a fruitful starting-point for identifying how knowledge workers operate. It was believed that sufficiently detailed data on a small set of processes in an intensive study, coupled with interviewing and discussion could be collected. The task which the knowledge workers undertook had to be one which was not merely repetitive (as in manufacturing on production-lines) but had to have a number of distinct features which made it individual enough so that, even though a number of the same processes might be carried out for each instance of the operation, it constituted a new information manipulation process each time. One example is that of producing a newsletter to a designated production schedule with each issue being produced by a slightly different set of activities chosen from an overall repertoire. The activity of producing artefacts to a format and, potentially, one mediated by guidelines and quality procedures was a viable source of study. The groups had to be small enough to permit observation of a comprehensive subset of their overall activities; had to demonstrate a certain amount of interpersonal interaction and had to pass material and work-in-progress from one to another.

Some consideration was also given to what features of collaborative work were being sought. Besides identifying typical activities, interaction episodes, procedures and spontaneous events, data was collected on the physical constraints in the work environment, individual workspace organisation and the way in which physical artefacts progressed through the system, focusing on the differing views of such artefacts held by those involved in their production. Visual records, samples of work and photographs helped in analysing data, serving to inform and validate the historical justification of actions. Instances of the following type of activities were used to provide an insight into the work activity:

Traces or a history of passage left behind in the physical world by a document or specific activity, setting up cues that can be read by participants but not readily explained or easily discerned.

Communication codes which demonstrate shared interpretations, not only of language and jargon, but of actions such as the siting of artefacts to indicate their relative importance.

Snapshots of communication episodes which might otherwise be missed because of brevity, location (in passing, outside) or because they are embedded within another activity.

An awareness of the implied procedures that underpin the way in which work is carried out and which allow the use of shared information resources such as filing systems (the knowledge of how it is organised, why an item is placed just there and where to find other items). Such information is usually hard to express but must be learned by novices (and not just be explanation, but by demonstration and observation).

Tacit knowledge which, like expert knowledge, is difficult to quantify, describe and identify objectively but which gives a feel for the work, for anticipating what is to come next, for allocating time and resources and for personal and implicit group organisation

Social organisation observed in situ and which may differ substantially from the official expectations drawn from job descriptions and organisation charts.

Field studies of two work groups within organisations were carried out: the first, a technical writing and authoring group, the second, a graphic design studio. Both adhere to the study requirements identified above. Data from the former, a Technical Publications Unit (TPU) is reported in previous work (Gilbert, Hewitt, Murray and Wilbur, 1991; Murray and Hewitt, 1993) whilst that of the Design Studio is reported on here.

Organisational detail

The Design Studio is part of a medium-sized US-based motivational and rewards company. The design team provide promotional material for the companys clients and the programmes which it sells and organises. The finished material goes out to the sales staff in the client companies in the form of glossy brochures, newsletters, personalised invitation letters, posters and the like. All are highly visual and, like advertising, have a distinct aim: to sell and motivate salespeople to sell more of their companys products; to buy a particular item, or to be persuaded on a course of action. Clients are normally large multi-national companies and are administered by account directors or account managers who tend to have ongoing responsibility for a particular client company. There are five account groups in all. They keep themselves separate because they are dealing with competing clients: like an advertising agency the company's policy is to keep them apart so that one client company does not see what another client company is doing for sales promotion.

The Creative Design Team consists of 7 individual designers, three of whom are Creative Art Directors whilst then others are more junior and are Visualisers/Designers with one being a Senior Visualiser. There is also an Administrator who, additionally, does some basic computer design work; a Print Buyer and two Desktop Publishing (DTP) staff. The Administrator is located in the Design Studio. The others have offices next to that of the Creative Services Manager, a short walk away from the studio itself. The group was observed informally on an initial visit to get a better feel for what the team as a whole did. During the study itself, all members of the Design Studio were observed but attention was focused on two Art Directors following through a number of jobs. Staff were interviewed and material on their general activities and projects collected. Observation, note taking, schematics, audio tape recordings of interactions and photographing of locations and collaborations were followed by structured interviewing of the individuals in the group. Tape transcripts and field notes were made, documents and examples of standard forms used by staff were collected and copies of the designs produced by them at various stages in the different job cycles were collected.

The designers occupy a large room subdivided into small office sections by partitions and with a central space taken up by three Macintosh Quadra computers, light boxes, a colour photocopier, a colour printer and a drawing board. All of these tools of their trade are shared. Each designer has an individual space but not all have an individual machine. Two staff (one an Art Director, one a Visualiser) have their own computer and are more experienced with the drawing and graphic production software they use. The others use the remaining machines, which they call boxes, as need arises. Each person has their own portable hard disk in a distinctive and individually decorated carrying case. Every large project also has its own disk to allow access by everyone and to maintain an up-to-date record of recent work carried out. Each designer has their own drawing board, set of tools and implements, etc. The environment is highly graphic, with visual puns abounding and is decorated with samples of the best of their own and others work. It is extremely colourful and often looks cluttered and rather untidy. Leading off the main workspace is a darkroom and a pasting-up room. There are telephones on some desks but not on all: the main telephone link to the studio has two instruments, one in the central area and one on the Administrators desk. While it rings infrequently, it tends to be ignored by the designers as most of the calls are routine matters which she deals with. If account managers want to discuss work, they visit the designers themselves. Occasionally, a designer will seek out an account manager in another part of the building to show some artwork or to ask a question. The studio has occasional visitors, clients who are being shown around the building, but the designers tend to ignore them completely. Account managers walk in and out frequently, to discuss jobs, to look at slides, or to bring text and supporting material. At least once a day someone from the local DTP company calls to deliver printed output and collect jobs. There are visits from sales representatives, the printer and, occasionally, photographers. This forms part of a normal days work and these people are treated as part of the extended team. There is a lot of banter and noise, with three radios playing music and comments constantly being made. Overall the atmosphere is lively, friendly and outgoing, sometimes quite manic and, when there is little work, subdued and rather bored.

How the work is done: the briefing

The designers have most interaction with the account managers who brief them on the jobs they are to do. The briefing is a central part of a designers work and all the designers interviewed had specific comments and opinions on what an ideal brief might be. To give a procedural account, an account manager has an initial discussion with a client to determine what the focus and needs of a particular campaign will be. Because the underlying administration is handled by clerical staff, what the clients see and what the account managers sell is not the detail (the planning, the handing of mail, the checking of claims, the arranging of travel, the special events which happen) but the way this is portrayed graphically to the eventual users: the salespeople who are to be motivated enough by the thought of rewards for carrying out their work well that they will sell more products. It is the image of exotic locations, luxury goods, special rewards and the way in which these are presented as attractive and desirable that fuels how the company sells its wares. In this way account mangers promote the services of the company but are dependent on the work of the designers to carry the company image to the outside world.

Although the briefing is central to the ensuing design in setting the parameters, in producing initial ideas and suggestions, providing a context in which to generate solutions and is, in some sense, a meeting of minds, it rarely lives up to expectations. Much of a designers work seems to be in amending slight parts of a design to match the clients preconceptions, or the interpretation made by the account managers, or in defending parts of a design and explaining why something works if it looks this way as opposed to that way. A designers account of what briefing should be is:

> The ideal situation should be when one goes to a briefing is the account manager or account director should actually have an idea of a theme, so you can design around it, if there's travel involved, you have locations sorted out, possibly even hotels, normally there's some idea of where theyre going to send stuff to set it up for the clients, so we need to know we can incorporate it into the design. The other things we need to know are corporate colour schemes, logos, some clients are very picky about colours. The other thing we need to know is how much we are going to spend, if there's going to be a limited run of 100, there's no point in doing a 4-colour, glossy 16 page brochure with cut-outs and gold-foil blocking, so we need some idea of budget and run, so we don't do anything daft on it. Basically, once they have given us all this, we should be able to sit down and give them the job an hour, a day or two days later.

In reality, the designer is told something of the form,

> Its for New Campaign *(usually some sort of buzzword with successful connotations)* for Company X and this is something that has been done before, so it wants to be in the same sort of style, its got to have that logo down the bottom. That was one we have done previously for a holiday in Eliat in Israel and the company really liked it so they wanted something similar to that.

The designer and the account manager working together during the briefing will generate ideas, or, more commonly, the designer will generate an idea and the account manager accept or reject them. In the later stages, the designers produce mock-ups, looking for images in image books to generate a design they can draw up very quickly. They develop a layout as an indication of where things should be and this is worked on with the account manager, depending on factors such as how experienced the account manager is, how good a brief has been given, how well the designer knows the client and style preferences, or the time allocated to the work. Given the time pressures they work under (hours and days rather than extended periods) designers tend to talk through with the account manager, before committing to a final design instead of generating design ideas and then asking for feedback. There may be a discussion with the account manager (but not directly with the client) if the designer thinks that criticisms are valid or if it really is a serious criticism such as, You cant have that there because the client say their logo has to go in that bit. The designers explain that things look different on the screen than they do on paper and, since client presentations have to be made with the paper mock-ups, they cannot always tell exactly what the final product is going to look like. Things can change quickly, especially with volatile clients and an account manager could point something out or come up with some new information which means that the design will have to be changed.

Although some account managers seem to have a lot of design knowledge, talk in very technical terms about fonts, colours and sizes and have a level of shared understanding of what the design process involves, they may be intimidated by the Art Directors and so the subsequent briefing will be sketchy and extremely quick. This is accepted as the type of work these individuals produce is known to be good, of high quality and usually successful at selling the concept. It is a factor that has been taken into account when allocating people to the different jobs. Job allocation is an area which they take as read but which shows, like briefings, some of the underlying assumptions they use to construct their work and the taken-for-granted knowledge which they exploit.

How the work is made: job scheduling

The designers do not usually know far in advance what they are going to be working on. A job schedule is prepared and posted either on a Friday afternoon or on a Monday morning. Some jobs from the previous week will run over but others will be new, or be newly approved. There are seasonal fluctuations. Like many commercial businesses, there are time-lags so that they may be working on Christmas promotions during the summer months. However, for the most part the week-to-week part of the job and anticipation of future work depends on the creation of the schedule for each team member. This is actualised in a simple chart on which individuals names have been customised in different typefaces to make it took more designy. The Creative Services Manager is responsible for scheduling and he distributes a copy to each person. An extra copy is stuck on the wall for reference. The charts are subsequently meant to be used for time-coding and costing each job.

The process of job allocation is an interesting one since it appears to be influenced by the personality and manner of the Manager himself in addition to his managerial responsibilities. He is very protective of his designers and will not allow account managers to request work from them directly: others in the company sometimes rail against this but to no avail. They must work through him and he must balance his schedule against a number of constraints. He negotiates his teams time, balancing this against the desires of the account managers. There is a little tension between the two which come out in the briefing process. He says of this activity,

> We try and plan a week in advance to allocate the time and see if we've got any gaps, or whether we've got any problems on timing, but it has to be totally flexible because things get changed and some of the jobs which we've been working on have been in the studio, in and out, over two weeks now because people haven't made up their mind whether they want a visual doing in a particular style or not. I know of two people who aren't in the agency, theyre on holiday, they might well come in on Monday with work to be done.

One reason for tension may be that the work is not long-term: the jobs come, are designed, are printed and sent out. That is the end of the process as far as the designers are concerned and anything which returns is treated as a new piece of work. This attitude is a curious one: the work they produce is essentially disposable, short-life and throwaway. It has to fulfil a purpose for a short period of time, do that job as well as is possible and then be replaced by something else. This attitude seems to permeate much of the working styles they adopt. They concentrate and expend effort on what they do (some are very meticulous and, if time constraints let them, are perfectionist) but in the end that job has to go out and the next one comes in. It was explained that there was no point in keeping archive material because what they design is transitory. They keep original artwork that goes to the printers but not software and computer files. They do not see any value in re-using old designs and claim that it is usually easier to redo a design from scratch, scan in previously worked material, or look in libraries for elements to incorporate into new designs. Some of this may stem from the need to keep the competitive clients of their company apart and to utilise different styles for each client, perhaps it is the result of the way in which training influences designers, or perhaps it is that they treat their computer as tools, as adjuncts and hesitate to explore it too much lest they may become dependent on it. It may be a way of maintaining professional skill and illustrating that design cannot be achieved simply by putting together pre-packaged elements.

The scheduling process is not quite the collaborative process originally expected but it does impact very much on how the design team operates and is based upon a set of assumptions that might not be made clear without an ethnographic focus on collaborative activities. One obvious constraint in most scheduling scenarios is the time and cost of the work to be undertaken whilst another is the availability of each designer. However, the overriding constraint appears to be the desire (or the need) to keep the designers happy by allocating to each the work they like and are best at. Each have different styles and preferences and some may be used to working for a particular account manager on a long-running account. One designer, for instance, produces bi-monthly newsheets for an electrical company and only he works on the account for a particular manufacturing company. Since the image of a campaign is what the company essentially markets, this is heavily instantiated in the designs produced by the design team, which is itself closely tied to the individual graphic style of each designer. The Creative Services Manager discusses how he allocates jobs,

First of all I've got three art directors who are the top Visualisers and I would tend to try and get them booked up first with design and I would discuss with the account director what type of job they saw it being, because Carly can be very illustrative. Jon is very graphic but knows his way round the Apple Mac very well. Tony is middle of the way between them, very illustrative but can do good graphic-type graphic work as well. Kelly is mainly a graphic-type designer, Sam likes to be pretty illustrative, Peter a bit of both. Colin is very good with the Macs and got quite good graphic eye, so really I try and pick the artist who is available that most suits the image that the job might have. Then obviously when it comes to finished art work I would move it ideally away if it was the art directors to one of the others to finish. If it is a job that has already been started by one of the others I would let them see through their own finished artwork. That's the general rule but sometimes through pressure of workload or holidays you have to use someone else to finish the job off. And they don't enjoy doing that particularly.

His reasons can be seen as being:

to give those who are at the top of the design hierarchy the work with the most creative elements and to pass the production of finished art-work (that is, what will be sent off for printing) which is much more tedious and mundane to the more junior people.

to accommodate the different styles of designers.

to maximise the skills each has (for instance, one person is much better on the Macintosh systems than the others who prefer drawing freehand).

to attempt to match the artist to the image the job will have.

The difference between senior and junior is a peculiar one. In this design environment there is not lot of teaching, or apprenticeship, it is more a group of equals and with some being more equal than others, with a strong emphasis on learning-by-doing. Although the boring parts of the work have to be done, all know that the institutionalisation of the graphic design hierarchy means that the Visualisers will themselves be Art Directors at some stage. At times, some of the work will not be divided up in such a simplistic fashion. The Director claims that ...they all prefer to be doing creative work, designing..., but they are flexible enough to cope with seeing through the whole process when the need arises, or when it is actually easier to do so,

> ...if it is designed properly on the Apple Mac by the other artists then they can take it to their own finished art fairly quickly, Carly quite likes doing unfinished art. That's partly because as she designed it how she has constructed it it's easier for her to turn it into finished art than for someone else to get in there and wonder how it has been constructed electronically.

In looking at ways in which computer technology could assist in group processes, one obvious system to investigate is that of an electronic scheduling system. Such a system could easily cope with the mechanical aspects of time logging and costing, perhaps as a spreadsheet. If so, people could just call up the schedule and see what work they had allocated for the day and then log the time spent. However, the Manager claims to prefer a slightly more personal approach with them, acting in a sense as their champion and protector. One reason he gives is that he himself is a designer and takes many of the early briefings. Another is because people who do not know about creative and print using the wrong words in briefings. Again, he says that it is,

> ...also a matter of trying to fit the type of job to the type of artist, the style of the artist, once again its a functional thing, if its just inputting data, then any data entry person can input it, but with this we try and get the jobs where the people will work well with the account people and people have a particular style, if the client wants an illustration we give it to somebody who can illustrate.

Work collaboration

One of the areas investigated was collaboration in working environments. As well as being what is obvious, as in the briefing sessions, when people are actually saying things to each other about what they are doing, there is continual hidden co-operation. When the people observed in this study are at work they are they are not only individual personalities but are also designers, professionals doing a job. But that job takes place in a group situation and, although their part in the group may be as individuals, each designing and creating their own material, they do not operate in isolation. Partly this is because of the actual physical environment, partly because of the way in which they all work, speedily and in sight of the others and, partly through the process of creating an artefact from an idea in a supportive social environment, in which shared perceptions and understandings about the way things work are the norm. They form a distinct entity in the company with a profile known to all account managers, protected from external pressures to a great extent and producing the basic images the company stakes its reputation on.

Since the space they occupy is so open and the machines they use are in the centre of the room, what they do is seen constantly by the others in the team. Briefing sessions take place in the studio in clear sight and sound of everyone. Work in progress is left on drawing boards, discarded sketches, photocopies, printouts and transparencies are left lying around on desks or on the light box. Material is left on the paste-up table and cleared off to one side by the next person who needs to use the table. The transparency books which they have been consulting or the clients design style guidelines are left open at the page they were looking at. The scheduling sheet for the week shows what each individual should be doing and experience of the job gives them an insight into the workload and concerns of each of team that week. They are proud of their work and happy to display it and show it around when satisfied. They know each others style fairly intimately and give credit for good work, displaying it in the open, using as a cover for a disk box, setting it frames for display in the company foyer. Above all, the conversation and constant self-commentary and calling out for assistance on computer problems gives an overall impression that all the group know intimately what the others are doing from hour to hour. Design is not hidden, it is constructed in public so other people can read it and accepting commentary on it from somebody else is part of a tradition they embody. As a consequence, there is a distinct feel of what the team as a whole are doing. People follow through themes, unconsciously picking up on what the other designers are engaged in to make for patterns and correspondences. These may be pertinent to the situation at the time through external events or it may be that what others are doing is fitted in to an individuals own concepts.

They do not often talk to each other directly, asking what is thought of a design. What happens is that people will troubleshoot a problem on the computer. For instance, someone may say, I don't know how to do that...what's happening here? and one of the others will come over to assist or a shouted comment is made by someone who knows what the problem is. They will know if someone is having trouble with a design concept or a layout because his comments and the spread of discarded work will make it obvious: there is a lot of opportunity to know what other people are doing. Information and communication about the overall shared activity they are engaged in filters through an essentially social process demonstrated by the codes of communication they use to inform the group of their activities and which makes external the way in which their own work is undertaken.

Future work

The data from this study are still being analysed and future analysis will concentrate on how workers communicate with each other when they work so closely in a shared environment, doing very similar work. The overall aims of the study itself were: firstly, to give indications of circumstances in which CSCW tools would be effective for a certain type of organisation or business activity and, secondly, to provide commentaries on activities showing the strategies people use in producing artefacts and how being a member of a group process impacts on them. Such features are concerned with aspects of group organisational memory; are examples where individuals co-ordinate actions without explicitly recognised communication; are implied assumptions, behaviours and the societal ethos illuminating hidden organisational and indirect activities; are identifying objects and artefacts that are social products. They may be demonstrated by identifying social roles, relationships and the interplay of the different personalities; in the modes of communication used between group members; in the impact of the shared artefacts (an office design of furniture, trappings and physical layout); in behaviours that demonstrate evidence of the organisation being constructed by participants to their own ends in defiance of the formal organisational model; the idea of inside and outside the group; in satisficing behaviour and in the predominance of the individual over the collective and the personal over the impersonal.

Conclusion

After the experience of observing such a close group of workers and trying to understand how they did their job; what made their work happen; what the limitations of each job were and how those were constructed, it seems that perhaps the group which appears most obviously to work together in teams may not be the most suitable one to consider when introducing new technology. The group studied seem to have little need of shared technology to produce what they produce and have developed a repertoire of sophisticated verbal cues, signals and socially-constructed responses to enable them to work co-operatively in a restricted environment. It would be difficult to transpose such systems of meaning and the whole gamut of both interactions and dependencies to a collaborative environment without resorting to full-scale use of co-location and video-based technologies.

However, it has been demonstrated that such underlying processes do occur and that there are many hidden variables in how groups function which make it essential continue non-intrusive observational studies. Only by having more data will we be able to understand some of the patterns in human communication in working groups and try to derive strategies and assistant systems to support their functioning. It may be that there is a clarification to be made about places that are suited to collaborative working, situations which, on the surface, seem clearly to demonstrate how people work together in groups, but, when investigated, turn out to be individual workers owning their own piece of work and functioning in a group very effectively in a different fashion. If CSCW systems are to be built and used for real applications, we will have to more clearly define those areas of application and the benefits to be gained. The types of workers who might turn out to need CSCW much more than hitherto thought are those such as invoice processors, who have to do the same thing again and again, whose work is essentially disposable (and not creative as in a Design Studio or a Technical Publications Unit) and with no ownership over what they do. Looking at the real world, at ordinary office situations, is not like the studies of process control activities where valid collaborative activity is demonstrably taking place. What workers in what offices actually do from day-to-day may have to reconstructed and reassessed to enable useful and practical collaborative support system to be built.

Acknowledgements

The work reported here has been undertaken as part of the Theories of Multi-Party Interaction (TMPI) project in conjunction with Queen Mary and Westfield College, University of London and sponsored by British Telecom. Thanks are also due staff at the study sites.

References

Anderson, R.J. and Shorrock, W.W. (1992).Can organisations afford knowledge?, *Human Computer Interaction*, in press.

Bentley, R., Rodden, T., Sawyer, P., Somerville, I., Hughes, J.A., Randall, D. and Shapiro, D.Z. (1992).Ethnographically-informed systems design for air traffic control, *Proceedings 4th ACM Conf. on CSCW*, CSCW92, Toronto, Canada, Oct. 31-Nov. 4.

Button, G. (Ed.) (1992) *Technology in Working Order: studies of work, innovation and technology*, Routledge, London.

Dubinskas, F. (Ed.) (1988) *Making time: ethnographies of hi tech organizations,* Temple University Press, Philadelphia.

Gilbert, G.N., Hewitt, B., Murray, D. and Wilbur, S. (1992) TMPI End of Year Report, Chapter 2, University of Surrey, Guildford.

Heath, C. and Luff, P. (1991) Collaborative activity and technological design: task co-ordination in London Underground control rooms, *Proceedings 2nd European Conference on CSCW,* CSCW91, Amsterdam, Sept. 25-27.

Hughes, J.A., Somerville, I., Bentley, R. and Randall, D. (1993) Designing with ethnography: making work visible, *Interacting with Computers,* forthcoming.

Kraut, R.E., Fish, R.S., Root, R.W. and Chalfonte, B.L. (1991) Informal communication in organization: form, function and technology. In: S. Oskamp & S. Spacapan (eds.) *Human Reactions to Technology: Claremont Symposium on Applied Social Psychology,* Sage.

Linde, C. (1988) Who's in charge here? Co-operative work and authority negotiation in police helicopter missions, *Proceedings 2nd ACM Conf. on CSCW,* CSCW88, Portland, Sept. 25-27.

Murray, D. and Hewitt, B. (1993) Capturing interactions: requirements for CSCW. In: D. Rosenberg and C. Hutchison (eds.) *Design Issues in CSCW,* Springer-Verlag, Berlin (forthcoming).

Nardi, B. A. and Miller, J. R. (1988) An Ethnographic Study of Distributed Problem Solving in Spreadsheet Development, *Proceedings 2nd ACM Conf. on CSCW,* CSCW88, Portland, Sept. 25-27.

Reder, S. and Schwab, R.G. (1990) The temporal structure of co-operative activity, *Proceedings 3rd ACM Conf. on CSCW,* CSCW90, Los Angeles, Oct. 10-14. (1990).

Rogers, Y. (1992) Ghosts in the Network: distributed troubleshooting in a shared working environment, *Proceedings 4th ACM Conf. on CSCW,* CSCW92, Toronto, Canada, Oct. 31-Nov. 4. (1992).

Proceedings of the Third European Conference on Computer-Supported Cooperative Work
13-17 September, 1993, Milan, Italy
G. De Michelis, C. Simone and K. Schmidt (Editors)

Building Shared Graphical Editors Using the Abstraction-Link-View Architecture

Tom Brinck and Ralph D. Hill
Bellcore, USA

Abstract: We have written several multi-user graphical editors in the Rendezvous™[1] system. In our approach to building these editors, the applications are first written as single-user editors. When multiple users wish to share a drawing surface, the drawing surfaces of their individual editors are connected using the Abstraction-Link-View (ALV) architecture. "Links" communicate the editing operations among the editors they connect. Links are designed to be invisible to the applications they are attached to, allowing the interface for each user to be highly customized. Links can also attach editors to the interface of a running RENDEZVOUS application, allowing the interface to be edited as the application is being used.

Introduction

We have written several multi-user drawing programs and we describe here an architecture for building such applications. Many multi-user drawing programs have been reported in the literature and several are reviewed by Brinck and Gomez (1992). The design of these drawing programs differ in significant ways, especially with regard to multi-user characteristics. Our goal has been to design an infrastructure which makes it easy for us to build multi-user drawing applications and easily make modifications to explore the implications of various design alternatives.

This paper begins by discussing our architecture as it applies to building single-user drawing programs. Our toolkit provides color palettes, tool palettes, drawing surfaces, and a set of plug-in tools for creating and manipulating object-oriented graphics. These facilities are all provided as part of the

---

1. Rendezvous is a trademark of Bellcore.

RENDEZVOUS system (Hill et al, 1993), a user-interface development system designed at Bellcore. It is important to note that the plug-in tools are supported at the toolkit level and not at the level of drawing programs. This means the plug-in tools are not restricted to being tools for editing drawings.

By viewing a drawing program as a graphical viewer of structured information it becomes possible to use a single-user drawing program written in the RENDEZVOUS system to edit other things, for example, the user interface of any other RENDEZVOUS application. The drawing program is attached to the interface of the other application with "links". Links communicate the results of editing operations between the drawing editor and the application. Toolkit level support for plug-in editing tools makes it possible to build tools for editing user interfaces.

This link-based architecture also allows us to connect a drawing application of one user to the drawing application of another user, resulting in a multi-user drawing application. Because links are separate from the applications, each of the drawing editors can be authored independently, and have different user interfaces. Links can provide various viewing transformations, so the interfaces for each user can be highly customized. This paper discusses our architecture for multi-user applications, explores the impact of multi-user editors on tool design, and discusses other design issues for multi-user graphic editors.

Single-user Graphical Editors

In conventional graphical interfaces, several interaction techniques are common for allowing a user to edit a drawing surface (we'll call it a "canvas"). The most common approach is for the user to select a tool from a tool palette, then click and drag on the canvas to create an object such as a box or line.

Several other interaction techniques are common. The user can push a button or select a menu item to perform a *global canvas operation*, such as clearing the canvas or saving and loading. The user can also *select* an object (possibly using the selection tool) and then operate on the selection by dragging or resizing the selection rectangle or by choosing a menu item that operates on the current selection. The user might also grab an object from a *well*. The user can click on a well to get an object to drag onto the canvas. For instance, an image well provides a stack of images from which you can pull off the top image and add it to the canvas (this could be useful for a deck of cards). A color well allows you to drag a color chip, and by dropping it on an object, the object becomes that color. All of these interaction techniques are available to various degrees in the RENDEZVOUS system.

As an example of a drawing program we've built, the Conversation Board is shown in Figure 1 (Brinck 1992, Brinck and Gomez 1992). The Conversation Board can be used as either a single-user drawing program or a multi-user

Figure 1. The Conversation Board is a multi-user structured graphics editor designed for informal conversational use.

program. It is a structured graphics editor that supports drawing with colored markers, text, and various geometric shapes, such as ovals, lines, and rectangles. It includes telepointers and supports saving and loading drawings, importing images, cut and paste, and undo. At the top-level, a drawing program like the Conversation Board consists of a canvas, a tool palette, a color palette, a line style palette, and various other possible palettes and menu options.

Plug-in Tools

When the user chooses a tool, that tool is used for interpreting what action needs to be taken when the user clicks on the canvas. The canvas acts as a dispatcher for mouse events. When the user clicks on the canvas, the canvas forwards this event to the currently selected tool, informing the tool of where the mouse event occurred and what object was clicked. The tool then performs its appropriate action.

The RENDEZVOUS language is written as an extension to the Common Lisp Object System (CLOS). CLOS provides a flexible object-oriented programming system. To encapsulate the behavior of tools, we define a class called Tool. Any subclass of Tool defines a method for handling mouse events forwarded from the canvas. Whenever a Tool handles a mouse interaction, it registers it's action with the UndoManager (an object associated globally with an application), so that the last action performed can be undone or repeated. A Tool also specifies an icon, a cursor, some explanatory text for providing the user with help information about the tool, and an optional dialog for the user to edit the default parameters of the tool. In order for plug-in tools to be possible, the graphic objects that they manipulate must be in a well-known structure and must have a standard set of properties (such as size and color) that tools can access. The RENDEZVOUS system provides this functionality with a well-specified declarative graphics system.

By incorporating all the functionality of a tool into a single class, it becomes possible to write a new tool without modifying any other part of the application and to simply "plug" the tool into any RENDEZVOUS application that uses tools. Currently we have over 40 standard tools defined, a few of which are in the tool palette of Figure 1. This encapsulation of tools allows us to customize drawing applications quickly. Since graphic objects on the canvas do not have to incorporate any editing behavior, the canvas serves as a generic editor of any graphic elements. As a demonstration of this, the next section describes how a generic editor is used to edit user interfaces.

Graphics Editors as Views

Once a graphical editor is written using the RENDEZVOUS toolkit, it can be linked to another RENDEZVOUS application to edit the interface to that application. For instance, suppose a user is playing a Tic-Tac-Toe game written in the RENDEZVOUS system. A graphical editor can be started and attached with a set of links to the Tic-Tac-Toe game, as shown in Figure 2. In the Abstraction-Link-View (ALV) paradigm described by Hill (1992), the Tic-Tac-Toe game serves as the "abstraction" for which the graphics editor is the "view".

The links between the "abstraction" and view are objects containing constraints that exist outside of both the abstraction and the view. Constraints define relationships between objects (as described, for instance, by Myers et al, 1990), so that when a value of one object gets updated, the constraint will automatically update the value of corresponding objects. The RENDEZVOUS language provides constraints integrated into the base language. Constraints may be specified without making modifications to any of the objects that they specify relations between. Thus, no modifications had to be made to either the Tic-Tac-Toe program or the graphics editor to make this linking possible.

Once linked, any modification made by either application is propagated to the other application, provided that a link has been written for the kind of property that has changed. For instance, if the drawing editor changes the color of a circle to red, the color of the circle in the Tic-Tac-Toe application changes to red. If the Tic-Tac-Toe player places an X into a cell, then an X gets created in the drawing editor. Note that the Tic-Tac-Toe player can continue playing even while the application is being edited!

There are two major types of links involved here. The appendix provides some examples of the code used to implement these links. The most common type of link simply links properties, such as color or position, of an object in the

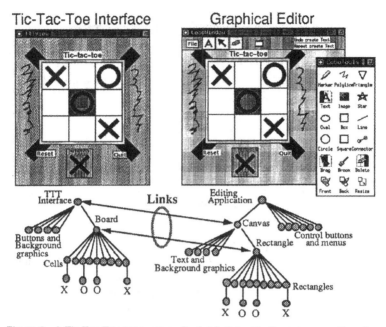

Figure 2. A Tic-Tac-Toe program on the left is linked to the canvas portion of a drawing editor on the right. Using the editor, the user has colored the central cell and added some decoration on the sides and the title text "Tic-tac-toe". The diagram shows the simplified structure of each view, and the top-level objects that get linked.

view with an object in the abstraction. This is implemented with a straightforward equality constraint.

A more sophisticated type of link is the TreeMaintenance link. This maintains the structure of a tree between a view and the abstraction. In the RENDEZVOUS system, all user views are modeled as trees of graphical objects, as in the diagram of Figure 2. The window is the object at the root of the tree. In a drawing program, the canvas is the parent of the objects that are being drawn. In Tic-Tac-Toe, the board is a parent of the cells in which the X and O get drawn. A TreeMaintenance link is attached to a tree node in the view and a tree node in the abstraction. It maintains consistency between the lists of children for the two tree nodes by creating and deleting objects in the lists of children. For the board object in Tic-Tac-Toe, the TreeMaintenance link creates a rectangle object in the graphics editor. It also creates a new link between the board and the rectangle that maintains their position, size, and color. This link must also be a TreeMaintenance link in order to recursively maintain the list of children of the board.

A TreeMaintenance link must work in two directions — when an object gets created or deleted in either the view or abstraction, the corresponding object

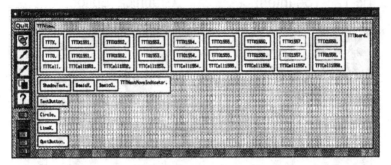

Figure 3. This is a debugger that shows a hierarchical view of the objects of any application it is linked to, using embedded boxes. This one is linked to the Tic-Tac-Toe program.

must be created in the abstraction or view, respectively. A list of maintenance entries indicates what kind of object to create and what kind of link to build. For shared drawing, the standard TreeMaintenance link maps a rectangle to a rectangle, an oval to an oval, and so on, using a standard link for graphics. The Tic-Tac-Toe board (an instance of class TTTBoard) gets mapped to a rectangle because TTTBoard is a subclass of Rectangle.

Other types of TreeMaintenance links are possible. For instance, Figure 3 shows a view used for debugging that maps any abstraction object to a rectangle labeled with the name of the object, and which lays out the children of the object inside of it, resulting in a view of the hierarchical structure of the application. Though this debugger looks nothing like a drawing program, we were able to reuse many of the tools built for manipulating graphics to allow us to query and set properties of the objects viewed in the debugger. This capability of multiple different views onto a single application is similar in spirit to that of Avrahami et al (1989). Their FormsVBT system provides a text and a graphics view of a dialog editor, as well as an operating view of the resulting dialog. The Abstraction-Link-View architecture is not restricted to dialogs, but also allows editors to be attached to highly dynamic and interactive applications.

Multiple Users

To implement two-user drawing, two canvasses are linked with the standard graphical TreeMaintenance link. Links were originally designed for connecting abstraction processes to view processes, but they work equally well for peer-to-peer linking. When two canvasses are linked, any modification one user makes is immediately reflected in the view of the other user.

In order to have more than two users, more graphics editors can be linked to views in the existing session, and the links will maintain consistency among them all. For convenience, we generally designate one of the editors as the central shared abstraction, and link the view of each user directly to the central abstraction.

The ability to connect independently-written applications using links stems from the fact that links are a mechanism built on top of a constraint maintenance system. All the applications that get connected are written in the RENDEZVOUS system, and they therefore run in a common environment in which constraints can be maintained. Similar effects could potentially be achieved in a toolkit without a constraint maintenance system if a standard graphics library is provided and callbacks are attached to all the standard properties of graphic objects. In such a system, "links" would be processes which registered with the callbacks of a view process and an abstraction process and sent updates back and forth between them. A mechanism to prevent cycles would be necessary, either in the links or as part of the callbacks in the standard graphics library. While this approach lacks some of the generality and elegance of a constraint maintenance system, it does allow the interoperability described here, and in a fashion which remains invisible to the application programmer using the standard graphics library.

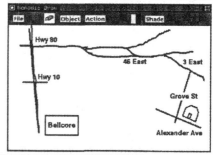

Customized views

Since the drawing application of each user is only linked at the level of the canvas, it is possible to design very different interfaces for each user, while they each edit the same drawing. In Figure 4 we show an example of 3 different editors being used to simultaneously edit the same drawing. Each of these views was developed as an independent

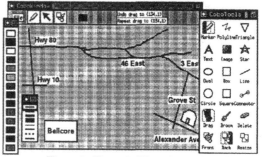

Figure 4. These 3 different graphics editors — SimpleDraw (top), NomadicDraw (middle), and the Conversation Board (bottom) — have their canvasses linked to the same abstraction.

drawing program. The Conversation Board was described earlier. SimpleDraw is an application written to provide minimal drawing functionality so that it would be as simple as possible. NomadicDraw is a drawing program designed to be used on existing portable computers using wireless networks. These editors differ in the set of tools they offer, the interface for accessing tools, and various other drawing options.

Our multi-user architecture has several important advantages over others such as GroupDraw (Greenberg et al, 1992), WScrawl (Wilson, 1992), and Ensemble (Newman-Wolfe et al, 1992). For instance, DistEdit (Knister and Prakash, 1990) is a system for building shared text editors that also allows the editors to be authored independently. However, DistEdit does not allow users to edit the text simultaneously and requires that each editor be modified to make explicit calls to the DistEdit routines. In our approach, customized interfaces which share a drawing surface can easily be authored independently, the users can interact with the application simultaneously and without any sort of locking mechanism, and the programmer can author the editing application independent of the communication, which we embed in the links.

Impact of multiple users on the design of tools

Now that we can build a multi-user graphical editor, it is important to go back and look at what impact this has on the development of our architecture for single-user editing. For almost all the functionality defined, multiple users do not affect the way in which the single-user application is implemented since links act as the sharing mechanism, and the links are not embedded in the applications. However, some of the tools have to be written carefully. For instance, what happens when one user resizes an object while another one drags it or even deletes it? We could easily lock an object so that others can't access it while one person is making modifications. Instead, our default tools simply try to do their own actions, while verifying that those actions are still valid. Thus, a tool for resizing could verify that an object still exists before it tries to change the size of the object. Instead, the resize tool changes the size attribute of an object even after it has been "deleted". Deletion merely removes an object from our graphical tree, but the storage for this object isn't actually reclaimed until all pointers to the object are removed. Therefore, most manipulations remain valid.

Multi-user undo

The implementation of undo is also affected by multiple users. Even in implementing a mechanism for undoing *only* the last action in the view that performed the action, all the problems of multi-user undo appear. For example, suppose user A drags an object across the canvas. To undo this, the application only needs to move the object back to its original position. However, suppose that user B then deletes the object. Now if user A tries to undo the action of dragging, either the object should be undeleted and moved back or the object should just be left deleted. In either case, undo must be able to handle changes that wouldn't have occurred in the single-user case. In fact, since user B can make any number of changes before user A chooses to undo, the implementation of undo must be robust with respect to an arbitrary number of intervening operations. Thus, as each tool implements the method for undoing its actions, it must check carefully that all state that is necessary to undo the action is still valid, and if not, then act appropriately. This may mean that the action cannot be undone. In practice, this isn't a problem for the user since it is rare that an action can no longer be undone, and in the case where an action can't be undone, the user rarely has the impression that the action should still be undoable.

Multi-user undo has also been described by Prakash and Knister (1992) as applied to shared text editors. The issues they discuss are similar to the experiences we've had. Our implementation differs from theirs in where conflicts are detected and resolved. The situation described above, where user B deleted an object that user A dragged, is one example conflict. When user A wants to undo the dragging operation, the deletion operation might also need to be undone.

In their approach, this conflict is detected globally by an algorithm that compares all succeeding operations to determine if they conflict. A conflict between dragging and deleting is potentially resolvable by providing the user the option of first undoing the deletion operation.

In our approach, the conflict is detected locally, by the Tool that originally performed the dragging operation (the DragTool). When the DragTool is told to undo an action, rather than checking the list of operations that have come after it for potential conflicts, it merely checks that the appropriate state is still valid. That is, the DragTool confirms that the object that was dragged still exists before it moves the object back into position. This approach is more efficient than comparing all succeeding operations, since only one property of the current state needs to be tested, whereas an arbitrary number of operations could have followed. Note that both approaches require the programmer to anticipate all potential conflicts between two operations.

Multi-user interface editing of multi-user applications

Since multiple views can be attached to the same abstraction, this paradigm can be extended to allow multiple users to edit a multi-user application. In Figure 5, a two-user Tic-Tac-Toe game consists of a Tic-Tac-Toe abstraction and two views. Each of these views can have multiple drawing editors attached to them, allowing multiple users to be modifying the application simultaneously, even as the two users are playing a game of Tic-Tac-Toe.

While this is a first step in designing a multi-user interface builder, some difficulties remain. Attaching a generic drawing editor to a user interface allows a

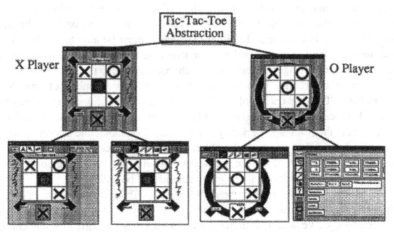

Figure 5. Multi-user editing of a multi-user Tic-Tac-Toe application. The X Player and O Player are the actual players of the game. The bottom row shows a set of editors and a debugger of these running applications.

programmer or designer to manipulate the graphic components of the interface by repositioning or resizing them or to add other graphics which have no behavior, such as static text or freehand sketches. To add components which have *behavior*, the drawing tool needs to be extended to support objects with behavior, such as buttons and menus.

Also, in a multi-user application, it is often not sufficient to be editing only a single view. In the example of Figure 5, modifications to a Tic-Tac-Toe view are not shared with the other Tic-Tac-Toe view unless the appropriate types of objects are linked through the links defined in the Tic-Tac-Toe application. If the developer of the Tic-Tac-Toe application did not anticipate a certain class of objects being created (such as menus), then an appropriate link to create menus in other views is not likely to exist. In addition, the interface developer may want to have an object appear in different ways for different views (a table of numbers in one view might be displayed as a bar chart in another view). This requires that the interface developer of a multi-user application also have a means of editing the links between the views and editing the objects that appear in the abstraction.

Other multi-user policies

SimpleDraw, NomadicDraw, and the Conversation Board all implement a shared canvas where users can all manipulate the objects simultaneously. For example, while one user is resizing an object, another can change its color, or even drag it. We have built a few other drawing editors based on this architecture that implement different multi-user policies.

Floor control

Several types of floor-control policies have been implemented, including token-passing and locks that time out. For example, a token-passing version of SimpleDraw (Figure 6) allows only one user to draw at a time. When a user has the token, drawing is possible. Other users can request the token, and acquire it when the user who possesses it decides to release it.

Figure 6. A token-passing version of SimpleDraw allows only one user to draw at a time. The Lock button is pushed to acquire the token. This user has the token, so the interface indicates that the Lock is Set.

The floor-control mechanism is also built using the Abstraction-Link-View architecture. The view contains buttons which allow a user to request and release a lock. A link sends these requests to the lock-abstraction. The lock-abstraction is shared by all the views, contains information about who holds the lock, and controls transfer of the lock. In the view, the lock determines whether a user's input will be ignored.

The floor-control versions of SimpleDraw cannot be used to edit the interface of any arbitrary RENDEZVOUS application. Since the lock requires a lock-abstraction, any interface being edited must also have a lock-abstraction for the lock to operate.

Other drawing editors, such as the Conversation Board, can be attached to the same abstraction as the floor-control versions of SimpleDraw, but these other editors will not be mediated by the floor-control because their interfaces have no floor-control mechanism. Thus, Conversation Board users will always be able to draw regardless of who has the floor.

CanvasTalk

CanvasTalk (Figure 7) is similar in spirit to the UNIX[2] 'talk' program, except that instead of typing, the users draw. Any number of users can join a session and each user has a personal canvas (in white) to drawn on. Each user sees the canvasses of the other users (in grey), but cannot edit them. A user can drag a copy of a sketch on another user's canvas onto the personal canvas.

CanvasTalk requires every view to be updated when a user enters or leaves a session because there is a canvas for each user in the session. This is done by using a TreeMaintenance link (described earlier) to maintain the number of canvasses between the view and the abstraction. When a new user starts up a

---

2. UNIX is a registered trademark of Unix Systems Laboratories.

Figure 7. CanvasTalk gives each user a personal canvas to edit, and allows the user to view, but not modify, the canvasses of other users.

view, the view creates a local canvas. The TreeMaintenance link then creates a corresponding canvas in the abstraction and across to other views. When a user leaves a session, the view first deletes the local canvas before detaching from the abstraction. The TreeMaintenance link deletes the corresponding canvas from the abstraction and then from other views.

In this case, the view was actually written with explicit knowledge of how the link worked. In previous examples, it was possible to write an editor as if it were a single-user editor and ignoring communication issues. When interfaces provide an explicit representation of other users, it is not entirely possible to ignore how information about those other users is communicated.

Conclusion

We have designed an architecture for building multi-user graphics editors, which serves as the foundation for the applications SimpleDraw, NomadicDraw, the Conversation Board, a simple debugger, several floor-control variations of SimpleDraw, and CanvasTalk. These programs were made possible in the RENDEZVOUS system because of an architecture with the following characteristics:

- A large variety of plug-in tools can be made available to an application, not just to create graphics, but also to modify and manipulate structured graphics. This allows the editing of arbitrary graphic elements in the system, since the graphic elements do not have to handle user input.
- A simple and fast undo mechanism which works equally well for single-user and multi-user applications.
- The links between different views of a shared canvas are invisible to the applications they link, so the editors can be written independently of the communication between them.

- Multi-user editors can easily have a high degree of customization for the individual users.
- Multi-user editing can be done on the interfaces to other applications, allowing those interfaces to be edited even as the applications are running and being used. This is particularly useful in interface design and debugging.

Potentially this approach or a similar one could lead to a standard for interoperability between shared graphics editors that would allow users to purchase different applications, but still be able to draw together.

Acknowledgements

Kimberly Passerella wrote NomadicDraw. John Boyd wrote variations of SimpleDraw with different floor-control policies. John Patterson developed the TreeMaintenance link. Steve Rohall and Anthony Dayao gave helpful comments on this paper.

References

Avrahami, G., Brooks, K.P., and Brown, M.H. (1989): "A two-view approach to constructing user interfaces", *Proceedings of SIGGRAPH '89*, Boston, MA, July 1989. *ACM Computer Graphics*, vol. 23, no. 3, pp. 137-146.

Brinck, T. (1992): "The Conversation Board", *Video Proceedings of CSCW '92*, Toronto, Ontario, Canada, Oct 1992.

Brinck, T. and Gomez, L.M. (1992): "A collaborative medium for the support of conversational props", *Proceedings of CSCW '92*, Toronto, Ontario, Canada, Oct 1992, pp. 171-178.

Greenberg, S., Roseman, M., Webster, D., Bohnet, R. (1992): "Human and technical factors of distributed group drawing tools", *Interacting with Computers*, special edition on CSCW, 1992.

Hill, R.D., Brinck, T., Patterson, J.F., Rohall, S.L., and Wilner, W.T. (1993): "The Rendezvous language and architecture", *Communications of the ACM*, vol. 36, no. 1, Jan. 1993, pp. 62-67.

Hill, R.D. (1992): "The Abstraction-Link-View paradigm: using constraints to connect user interfaces to applications", *Proceedings of CHI '92*, Monterey, CA, May 1992. pp. 335-342.

Knister, M.J. and Prakash, A. (1990): "DistEdit: A distributed toolkit for supporting multiple group editors", *Proceedings of CSCW'90*, Los Angeles, CA, Oct 1990, pp. 343-355.

Myers, B.A. and al. (1990): "Garnet: comprehensive support for graphical, highly-interactive user interfaces", *IEEE Computer*, vol. 23, no. 11, 1990, pp. 71-85.

Newman-Wolfe, R.E., Webb, M.L., and Montes, M. (1992): "Implicit locking in the Ensemble concurrent object-oriented graphics editor", *Proceedings of CSCW'92*, Toronto, Ontario, Canada, Oct 1992, pp. 265-272.

Prakash, A. and Knister, M.J. (1992): "Undoing actions in collaborative work", *Proceedings of CSCW'92*, Toronto, Ontario, Canada, Oct 1992, pp. 273-280.

Wilson, B. (1992): "WSCRAWL 2.0: a shared whiteboard based on X-Windows", *Apple Computer Technical Report*. August, 1992.

Appendix

This appendix provides brief examples of how links are written in the Rendezvous language. Below is the definition of a simple equality link called TypicalGraphicLink which contains constraints to maintain the color, line style, position, and size between an object in the abstraction and an object in the view. When this link is created, the programmer specifies pointers to the abstraction and view objects, and a set of constraints are automatically generated to maintain these equalities.

```
(defClass TypicalGraphicLink (Link)
    (:add-dependencies
            (link= borderColor fillColor
                   lineStyle lineWidth
                   x y deltaX deltaY)))
```

An example definition of a TreeMaintenance link is shown below. This handles creating and deleting rectangles in the view and abstraction. RectangleMaintenanceLink contains a single maintenance entry which states that rectangles map to rectangles, and when rectangles gets created, TypicalGraphicLink should be installed between the corresponding view and abstraction rectangles. Thus, when a user creates a rectangle in a view (for instance, by drawing a rectangle in a graphics editor), another rectangle will be created in the abstraction, and the two rectangles will be linked so that their color and other properties are kept consistent.

```
(defClass RectangleMaintenanceLink (TreeMaintenance Link)
    (:maintenance-list
        (list
            (make-maintenanceEntry
             :abstractionType 'Rectangle
             :viewType 'Rectangle
             :linkType 'TypicalGraphicLink)
        )))
```

Proceedings of the Third European Conference on Computer-Supported Cooperative Work
13-17 September, 1993, Milan, Italy
G. De Michelis, C. Simone and K. Schmidt (Editors)

Beyond Videophones: TeamWorkStation-2 for Narrowband ISDN

Hiroshi Ishii, Kazuho Arita, and Takashi Yagi
NTT Human Interface Laboratories, Japan

Abstract: TeamWorkStation-2 (TWS-2) is introduced to connect two sites with a desktop overlay service using narrowband ISDN (N-ISDN) and the CCITT H.261 standard. Based on the experience gained with TWS-1 use within NTT, we radically simplified the system architecture of TWS-2. Experimental sessions confirmed that TWS-2 is useful for freehand drawing and gesture-intensive design sessions even with the basic rate interface (2B+D). Video delay and jerkiness did not prevent users from concentrating on their task. We are convinced that TWS-2 has a big advantage over ordinary videophones as a narrowband ISDN service.

1 Introduction

In order to provide distributed users with a "seamless shared workspace" that every member can see, point to and draw on simultaneously using various personal tools, we designed the first prototype of **TeamWorkStation-1 (TWS-1)** in 1989 (Ishii, 1990). TWS-1 integrates two existing individual workspaces: computers and desktops. Because each coworker can continue to use his/her favorite application programs or manual tools simultaneously in the virtual shared workspace, the cognitive discontinuity (seam) between the individual and shared workspaces is greatly reduced. We conducted many experiments using the TWS-1 prototype in our laboratories and confirmed the advantage of translucent video overlay approach of TWS over previous computer-oriented approaches (Ishii and Miyake, 1991).

We wanted to conduct further evaluation of TWS in real work environments using the public network. However, the bulky and complicated system architecture of the TWS-1 prototype prevented us from moving the system out of the laboratory.

To overcome this limitation, we started designing a completely new system, **TeamWorkStation-2 (TWS-2).** TWS-2 was designed to use narrowband ISDN (N-ISDN) Basic Rate Interface (2B+D) and the Primary Rate Interface (H1/D). TWS-2 connects two sites via N-ISDN with a *desktop overlay* service and the *ClearFace* interface (translucent, movable, and resizable face windows over the shared workspace) (Ishii and Arita, 1991) using the H.261 standard for moving picture transmission.

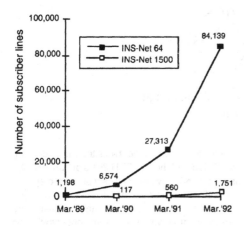

Fig. 1 Growth of Narrowband ISDN Services in Japan

In April 1988, NTT started an ISDN BRI (Basic Rate Interface) service (called INS-Net 64) in Japan using the existing metallic cables[1]. In June 1989, NTT started an ISDN PRI (Primary Rate Interface) service (called INS-Net 1500) using optical fiber cables[2]. Since the introduction of these ISDN services, the number of subscriber lines has grown steadily as shown in Fig. 1.

It is reasonable to target TWS-2 toward these narrowband ISDN services, especially INS-Net 64, because connections are available in most big cities in Japan. However, the question was if TWS-2 would really be usable under the limited 2B+D bandwidth. To find the answer to this question, we started designing TWS-2 in 1990, and completed the first working prototypes in October 1992.

---

1 INS-Net 64 service provides two 64kbps information channels (B channels) and one 16kbps signaling channel (D channel). Using the existing metallic cable, INS-Net 64 service requires only the addition of a compact DSU (Digital Service Unit).

2 INS-Net 1500 service offers digital communications at 64kbps, 384kbps, and 1.536Mbps. This service is accessed by means of optical fiber cable and a DSU (Digital Service Unit).

This paper describes the design evolution from TWS-1 to TWS-2, and discusses the rational of the new design. We also report the initial findings of preliminary experiments of TWS-2 on the basic rate interface (2B+D).

2 TWS-1 Architecture and Problems

TWS-1 was designed in 1989 to provide small work groups (2~4 members) with a seamless shared workspace. The TWS-1 prototype utilized networked Macintosh™ computers. The system architecture of the TWS prototype is illustrated in Fig. 2. In order to connect distributed workstations, a video network (NTSC and RGB) and an input device network were developed, and integrated with an existing data network (LocalTalk™ network) and a voice (telephone) network.

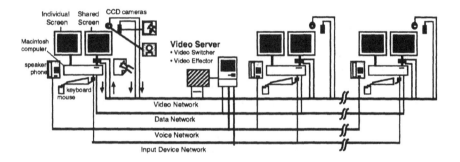

Fig. 2 System Architecture of TWS-1 Prototype (Ishii and Miyake, 1991)

The video network is controlled by a *video server* that is based on a computer-controllable video switcher and video effector. The video server gathers, processes, and distributes the shared computer screen images, desktop images, and face images. Overlay of video images is done by the video server. The results of overlaying are redistributed to the shared screens via the video network.

Each TWS-1 terminal provides a shared screen and an individual screen. The shared screen supports (1) a shared drawing window for concurrent pointing, writing, drawing, and (2) live face windows for face-to-face conversation. Fig. 3 shows the appearance of TWS-1, and Fig. 4 shows an example of the shared screen in a design session.

The individual and shared screens of TWS-1 are contiguous in video memory. Therefore, just by moving the window of any application program from the individual to the shared screen, a user can transmit the application's window to all participants for remote collaboration.

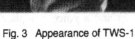

individual screen   shared screen   shared drawing window   face windows

Fig. 3   Appearance of TWS-1   Fig. 4   An Example of Shared Screen of TWS-

Problems of TWS-1 Architecture

TWS-1 was designed to provide a flexible environment for *laboratory experiments* using a variety of video equipment. We made it easy to change the network configuration and to add new video effect functions to the video server.

TWS-1 was originally conceived as a B-ISDN (Broadband ISDN) service so that the video bandwidth was not a problem. We did not pay much attention to the number of cables or the bandwidth. Hubris has its price, and now the system configuration is so complex that only an expert can maintain it.

This complexity of the TWS-1 architecture prevented us from extending its scale and portability and conducting field tests using the public network. The problems are summarized as follows: 1) TWS-1 requires a special video server, and its operation needs special skills and knowledge, 2) The hybrid network (NTSC+RGB analog video network, voice network, input device network, and LAN) is very clumsy and hard to extend over long-distances, and 3) The system is too bulky and expensive. These problems motivated the authors to design the completely new architecture introduced in the following section.

3   Architecture of TWS-2

INS-Net 64 (or 1500)

TWS-2 is designed to run on standard INS-Net 64 and 1500. The main target is INS-Net 64 rather than 1500 because INS-Net 64 is much more widespread in Japan. One advantage of INS-Net 64 is that it uses existing metallic cables, and requires only the addition of a compact DSU (Digital Service Unit) at each site. On the other hand, INS-Net 1500 requires the installation of optical fiber cable in addition to the DSU.

From the HCI (Human-Computer Interaction) research point of view, we are interested in understanding the effect of limited video bandwidth on shared workspace activities. We wanted to know if TWS-2 could be effective or not within the limited 2B+D bandwidth of INS-Net 64.

H.261 Video Compression Standard

TWS-2 uses a video CODEC that supports the video compression standard H.261. H.261 is recommended by CCITT[3] as the compression algorithm for transmitting moving pictures. TWS-2 uses CIF (Common Intermediate Format) whose resolution is 352 pixels/line x 288 lines/picture. Because of the adoption of H.261, TWS-2 can be used with any video CODEC supporting the H.261 standard.

Dyadic Architecture

The centralized video server made TWS-1 network configuration complex, and hard to move out of the laboratory. To make the video server unnecessary, we needed to radically simplify the system architecture and the service functions.

We decided to limit the number of sites (TWS-2 terminals) to be connected at any one time to *two*[4]. This is a critical design decision. We know that there is a need for multi-point connections in video conferencing services. Although the technology of multi-point connection is already available, it definitely increases system complexity and cost.

The main argument for this decision, beyond technical and economic arguments, is our observation that most daily realtime informal communication happen between two persons. The target of *dyadic communication*[5] seems to be most important and appropriate as the first target of TWS-2 usage.

Another reason is that most telephone calls are between *two* people, and most video conferences connect *two* distributed meeting rooms. Although some pre-planned formal meetings are held between more than two points, the main target of TWS-2 use is the informal design sessions established between a small number of users. When the appeal of multi-point connection becomes irresistible, we may extend the TWS-2 architecture.

---

3   CCITT stands for "International Telegraph and Telephone Consultative Committee".

4   Although TWS-2 limits the number of terminals to be connected to two, it is naturally possible that more than two users use each terminal simultaneously. Therefore, multi-user/two location meeting using TWS-2 is possible.

5   Panko and Kenney extensively discussed the importance of dyadic communication in (Panko, 1991). They pointed out that "roughly half of all organizational communication is dyadic."

TWS-2 Architecture

We completed the first working TWS-2 prototype in October 1992. Fig. 5 shows the system architecture which does not use a video server. The two TWS-2 terminals are connected by one ISDN link. Each terminal is composed of three major components: a TWS-2 Box, a PC-9801™ personal computer, and a video CODEC[6]. All video processing functions (e.g. translucent overlay, picture-in-picture) are supported at each terminal. All the hardware for video processing, camera control units, audio amplifiers, and power unit were encapsulated into a single "TWS-2 Box." Therefore the transportability of TWS-2 is much better than that of TWS-1. An MS-DOS™ program running on the PC-9801™ was written to control the TWS-2 Box and the video CODEC.

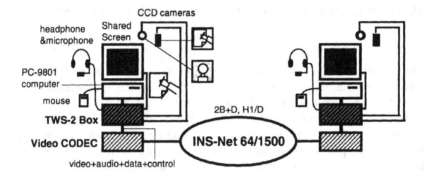

Fig. 5 System Architecture of TWS-2

Fig. 6 shows the appearance of a TWS-2 terminal in use. A headphone with a small microphone is provided for voice communication. Like TWS-1, TWS-2 provides two CCD cameras, one to capture the user's face image and another to capture the desktop image. The TWS-2 Box provides an *external video input port* that can be used to show recorded video clips by connecting a video player. This port is activated by switching the *video source* from the desktop CCD camera to this external video input port.

---

6   As a video CODEC, we are using NTT's product, FaceMate™ FM-C700. FM-C700 provides B, 2B, H0, and H1 channel interfaces and interfaces with INS-Net 64 and 1500.

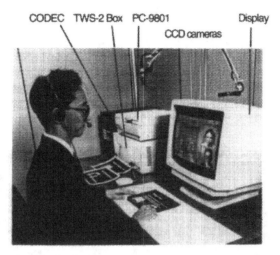

CODEC   TWS-2 Box   PC-9801   Display
                           CCD cameras

Fig. 6   Appearance of TWS-2 Terminal

The most important design requirement of TWS-2 was to implement the desktop overlay service with the ClearFace interface using only *one video channel* and *one video CODEC* for each terminal. It is not realistic to transmit more than one video channel across the 2B+D interface of INS-Net 64 because the speed and quality of each video image would be significantly degraded. The idea of connecting TWS-2 terminals with more than one INS-Net 64 line was turned down because it is not economically reasonable. How to support the full functions of ClearFace with only one video channel and one data channel was a severe design challenge. To solve this problem we devised a new video processing technique.

Face and desktop video processing flows at each terminal are as follows:

(1) Insert own face image into own desktop image using the picture-in-picture function. If desired, the face image can be set to "translucent" mode instead of Picture-in-Picture.

(2) Exchange the resulting video image of step (1) with the remote terminal.

(3) Translucently overlay own image (1) and the image received from remote terminal. In this step, if the face image is set "opaque" mode, mask the face image and translucently overlay to the rest of the image.

If the face images are moved, resized, or their modes are changed between "opaque" and "translucent", the necessary information (e.g. the new coordinates of the moved face image) are exchanged between the control programs via a data channel to keep the display the same at both sites.

4 Multiuser Interface of TWS-2

The multiuser interface of TWS-2 is based on the desktop-overlay function and the ClearFace technique (Ishii and Arita, 1991). Fig. 7 and 8 show typical screen images of TWS-2 in use. In Fig.7, user A and B are discussing the system architecture using hand drawing and gestures. In Fig. 8, user A is teaching calligraphy to user B using red ink to correct B's strokes made in black.

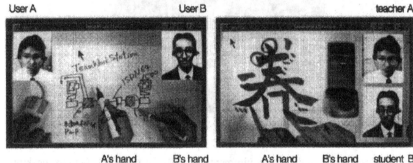

Fig. 7   Design Session via TWS-2   Fig. 8   Calligraphy Lesson via TWS-2

Computer vs. Desktop

The design focus of original TWS-1 was on sharing the information stored in computers. The name "TeamWorkStation" reflects this computer-centered view. The TWS-1 platform is a workstation, and we extended it to incorporate the information on the physical desktop.

Although the principle of "translucent video overlay" is independent of any level of computer architecture (application, window system, operating system, hardware), the TWS-1 prototype depended on the multi-screen architecture of Macintosh to realize the smooth transition of information between individual and shared screens.

The experimental use of TWS-1 for various conceptual discussions and technical design sessions by the subjects led us to observe that computer-screen overlays were seldom used. Most work was done in the desktop-overlay mode. Pointing and marking were usually done by hand (overlaying own desktop) rather than the mouse cursor (overlaying own screen). Even though the documents were stored in Macintosh™ computer files, users preferred to print and share the hard copies (papers) as desktop-overlays rather than using direct computer screen overlays.

This behavior has several explanations. If the collaboration faces tough time constraints, the *speed* of information manipulation is critical. In realtime sessions, even if the users are Macintosh™ experts, computer operations take too long and prevent smooth human-human interaction[7]. Generally speaking, sheets of paper can be manipulated much more quickly than the equivalent computer files. It is also quicker to point to the part of remote documents with own finger than using a mouse pointer. Marking and annotating with a pen is also quicker and easier than using computer programs. Only when data stored in computer memory is extensively manipulated with an application program, does it make sense to share the computer screen directly.

Desktop-Centered Design of TWS-2

Based on these observations of TWS-1 use, we concluded that the support of desktop images is more important than the support of computer screens. We decided to make "desktop overlay" the basic service of TWS-2, and to make "screen overlay" an option. This decision lead to the one screen architecture of TWS-2 instead of the two screen architecture (individual and shared screens) of TWS-1[8].

The desktop-centered design of TWS-2 means that TWS-2 is closer to the service represented by videophones than computers. The PC-9801™ computer of TWS-2 is mainly used to control the video processing in the TWS-2 Box, and the video CODEC. Direct sharing of information stored in the PC-9801™ or any other computer is not supported as the basic TWS-2 service. However, there are two ways of directly sharing data.
(1) Use *screen sharing software* while overlaying desktop video images with the shared computer screen.
(2) Down-convert the computer screen video signal into NTSC, and input the video signal to the *external video input port* of the TWS-2 Box.
Solution (1) requires the existing screen sharing software to be modified so that it simultaneously executes with the TWS-2 control program while sharing the data channel of N-ISDN. Preliminary tests of the two solutions found that solution (1) allows users to share the computer screen at high resolution, while (2) offers only limited quality displays.

ClearFace Interface

Fig. 9 illustrates the mouse operations of TWS-2 that move, change the size, and switch the transparency of the face windows. All the data of these mouse operations are transmitted to the control program running on the other terminal via

---

7   For a similar reason, we implemented simple bitmap paint editor (TeamPaint) instead of object-oriented draw editor as the application for an electronic whiteboard (ClearBoard-2) in realtime meeting environments (Ishii, Kobayashi and Grudin, 1992).

8   Another reason behind this decision is that normal desktops are too limited to support the multi-screen architecture.

the one ISDN data channel to realize the WYSIWIS (What You See Is What I See) principle (Stefik, 86) on both screens.

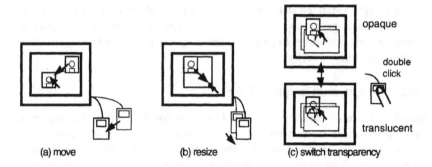

Fig. 9 Operations to Face Images (Move, Resize, and Switch)

Tests of the ClearFace interface confirmed that there is little difficulty in visually separating the translucently overlaid video layers (face and drawing surface). When a subject looked at one layer, he/she found it relatively easy to ignore the other. However, some users said that they preferred to see the partner's face clearly rather than seeing both the face and the desktop image behind it. Therefore, we provided the function that switches the face images between opaque and translucent by double clicking the mouse button (see Fig. 8 (c)).

Who's Face Do You Want To See?

When we demonstrated TWS-1, we were often asked why the user need to see his/her own image on the shared screen. Some of them told us that just the partner's face image is enough, and some other people pointed out that the face images did not add any value to the shared workspace. In order to respond to these various comments, TWS-2 provides users with a menu offering three modes: (a) two face widows, (b) one face widow and (c) no face widow as illustrated in Fig. 10.

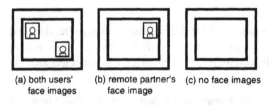

(a) both users'   (b) remote partner's   (c) no face images
    face images   face image

Fig. 10 Selection of Face Images to be Displayed

While mode (a) and (c) provide the WYSIWIS interface, mode (b) does not. In mode (b) each user sees the partner's face image in the face window. We are interested as to which mode will be used most frequently in future tests.

Limitation of Strict WYSIWIS Over Distance

In a geographically distributed environment, it is impossible to keep the WYSIWIS principle in a very strict sense because of the transmission delay caused by the distance. Especially in multimedia groupware such as TWS-2, delayed and jerky video images are inevitable because of the limitations in the communication bandwidth and the current CODEC technology[9]. Resolution of the remote video image is degraded from NTSC (525 lines/picture) to CIF (352 pixels/line x 288 lines/picture). Therefore, the results of overlaying the realtime local video image with the delayed, jerky, and low-resolution remote video image can never be same at the both sites. Thus strict WYSIWIS can never be achieved. One of the TWS-2 field test goals is to understand the effect of this limitation on working efficiency.

Audio is not a major problem because the delay of the remote partner's voice is negligible, and WYHIWIHN (What You Hear Is What I Hear Now) is almost perfect. In the experiments, no subject complained about voice delay. Asynchronism between voice and video can be a problem in videophone-like applications because users notice the motion of lips and the voice are not synchronized. However, in the desktop-centered application of TWS-2, we found asynchronism between hand gestures (video) and voice is not a serious problem in the experiments described in the next section. We discuss the advantages of TWS-2 over videophones in the following section.

5   Initial Findings of TWS-2 Experiments Using INS-Net 64

We implemented the first TWS-2 prototype in October 1992. Two TWS-2 terminals were successfully connected via INS-Net 64 on October 20, and via INS-Net 1500 on November 30. We confirmed that the TWS-2 Boxes functioned properly.

We first tested TWS-2 by connecting our offices in Tokyo and Yokosuka by INS-Net 64 at the end of December. All subjects who joined this experiment were very excited to see that a virtual desktop could be shared over a distance of 60 km. This means that TWS-2 can connect most big cities in Japan via INS-Net 64. This

---

9   When we used INS-Net 64 in our experiments, we assigned 112kbps for the video. In that situation, the frame rate was about 10 frame/sec, and the transmission delay was about 200-300 msec. In the case of H1 (INS-Net 1500), the frame rate became about 30 frame/sec, and the delay was only 10 msec.

excitement could never be gained through small experiments in the same building. Shared drawing activities were much smoother than anticipated by videophone users, most of who had slightly negative impressions of the quality of realtime video communication over INS-Net 64. We believe that TWS-2 can be used for real work over distance. The success of the Tokyo/Yokosuka experiment convinced us of the potential of TWS-2 as a new N-ISDN service.

The main purpose of these experiments was to answer the question: *"Is TWS-2 usable under the bandwidth limitation of 2B+D?"* Before we started the TWS-2 experiments, many people dubious about the ability of INS-Net 64 to support realtime activities because of their previous experience with the jerky displays of videophones. To find out how subjects who were not involved in this project evaluated the usefulness of TWS-2 in a work-like setting, we conducted the following experiments.

Experiment of Remote-Controller Design Using TWS-2

Tasks: Pairs of subjects were asked to design an integrated remote controller for TV and VCR (video cassette recorder), or air conditioner and gas fan heater.

Subjects: Three pairs of subjects (6 people in total) were recruited from other research groups in our laboratories. All had an engineering background. Although none of them had ever used TWS, they knew about TWS through paper reports and video clips.

Conditions: Individual TWS-2 terminals were installed in different rooms on the same floor. They were linked through actual INS-Net 64 connections, and the bandwidth of INS-Net 64 (2B+D) was allocated to each media as follows:
- Video   112 kbps
- Audio   16 kbps
- Data   9.6 kbps

Each pair of subjects spent about 20 minutes doing the design task using TWS-2. Each subject was provided with color markers, an eraser, and a whiteboard placed on the desktop surface. Actual remote controllers for the TV, VCR and air conditioner were also provided. All work activities were videotaped for later detailed analysis. After the design sessions, each subject filled in a questionnaire, and was briefly interviewed about what they liked and disliked about the task environment. A questionnaire was used to obtain a subjective view of TWS-2's usefulness.

Results: In the post-task interview, the subjects generally commented that they were absorbed in the task, and enjoyed interacting with the partner. Although the subjects noticed some delay and jerkiness in the remote desktop video image, these characteristics did not disturb smooth and natural interaction. These comments are consistent with the responses to the questionnaire (Q1, Q2, and Q3) filled in right after the design session by the subjects. Fig. 11 and 12 summarize the results of the questionnaire.

Q1 I could interact with partner smoothly.
Q2 I am satisfied with the design results.
Q3 Video delay did not disturb the work.

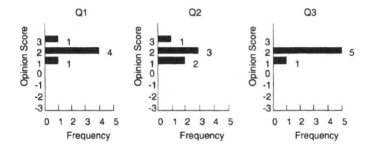

Fig. 11 Responses to Questionnaire (part 1)
(3 = strongly agree, -3 = strongly disagree)

Q4 I could see partner's desktop image clearly.
Q5 I want to have partner's face image on the screen.
Q6 I want to have my own face image on the screen.

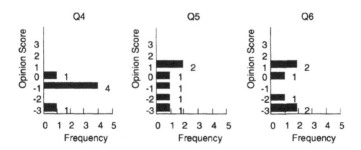

Fig. 12 Responses to Questionnaire (part 2)
(3 = strongly agree, -3 = strongly disagree)

These experiments have convinced us that TWS-2 is effective in drawing and gesture-intensive design sessions even if the basic rate interface (2B+D) is used. We found that delay and jerkiness of the video did not hinder users from concentrating on their work.

However, Q4 of questionnaire confirmed that the CIF (Common Intermediate Format) makes it almost impossible to see the small characters or fine drawings in the remote documents. Since the CIF strongly limits document resolution, we can not resolve this problem by modifying TWS-2. Rather, we think it makes more sense to send documents as facsimile messages if both members need to see fine details. TWS-2 is good at dynamic interaction using hand gestures and hand drawing on paper, while facsimile messages can realize document sharing at fine resolution. We expect facsimile to be the partner that offsets the weakness of TWS-2 in sharing detailed documents.

Regarding the necessity of face images, Q5 and Q6 led to some interesting responses. It turned out that the users do not feel a strong necessity to see the face images. However, we believe face images are useful in preserving the awareness and sense of co-presence between distributed co-workers. Further experiments are needed to understand what kind of roles the face images are playing in TWS-2 design sessions.

An interesting observation is that while explaining a new design, users would often grab the whiteboard eraser as if it were the new device, and gestured by pressing imaginary buttons on the eraser. Although we never expected that the eraser would be used in such a way, we think it indicates one big advantage of video overlay approach over computer-based shared workspace since any solid object can be visually shared as well as papers and hand gestures.

Advantage of TWS-2 over Videophone

Videophone is the most typical application of video communication using N-ISDN, and it represents the traditional concept of "being there" that has long been the goal of telecommunication technologies (Hollan and Stornetta, 1992). VideoWindow (Fish, 1990) pursues "being there" by connecting two distributed rooms with a video wall. Realtime video is used just to see the remote partners' facial expressions, postures and gestures in these applications.

In contrast to these "talking head" applications, TWS-2 demonstrates a new direction for the usage of realtime video; that is the creation of a shared virtual workspace[10]. TWS-2 adds new value for group work through its use of realtime video[11]. The main focus of TWS-2 is not on the face but the desktop.

---

[10] VideoDraw (Tang and Minneman, 1990) pioneered the use of the video to create a shared drawing space.

[11] ClearBoard-1 designed by Ishii and Kobayashi (Ishii and Kobayashi, 1992) is another example of this approach: creation of shared workspace using realtime video. Unlike TWS-2, however, ClearBoard-1 integrates traditional "talking head" service and shared workspace.

The TWS-2 experiments to date confirm that TWS-2 has one large advantage over ordinary videophones as the preeminent narrowband ISDN service. The advantage is due to the bandwidth limitation and human perception. People are especially perceptive to facial expressions. If facial expression is the main means of communication, slight *asynchronism* between the voice and the movement of eye and lips is immediately noticed, and makes smooth conversation difficult. Since the facial expression is always changing and the face and body are always moving, delay in transmitting the partner's image increases the negative impression of users. Since videophones focus on providing the sharing of facial expressions, such devices are inherently unsatisfying.

The main focus of TWS-2, on the other hand, is the sharing of overlaid desktop images, not face images. The main difference of the desktop from faces is that the desktop image is relatively *static*. Image of papers and the marks drawn on the papers do not change quickly. Only the hands move on the desktop when users gesture or draw. Thus the total amount of motion is far less than experienced with videophone displays. This more static nature of the desktop surface increases the *effective video frame rate*. Although quick hand motions suffer from delays and quick drawing looks jerky, TWS-2 users are happier and more productive than their videophone counterparts since they can visually share objects and work on them.

Even using the same N-ISDN interface, the typical image contents of TWS-2 make a big difference to how the user perceives the image. The most important message of this paper is that given existing bandwidth constraints the desktop images of TWS-2 are superior to the face images of traditional videophones for achieving group tasks. We are convinced that TWS-2 is a useful application of INS-Net 64.

6 Conclusion

This paper has described the design evolution from TWS-1 to TWS-2, and the initial findings gained from TWS-2 experiments over INS-Net 64.

To overcome the limitations of the first TWS-1 prototype, we designed TWS-2 to connect two sites with a desktop overlay service using N-ISDN and CCITT H.261 standard. TWS-2 was implemented based on a radically simplified system architecture, and the service functions of TWS-2 are based on the desktop-centered concept.

Through informal observations of the experimental use of TWS-2 over INS-Net 64 (2B+D), we confirmed that TWS-2 is useful in drawing and gesture-intensive design sessions. TWS-2 is a promising application of N-ISDN and is a good example of *"beyond being there"* (Hollan and Stornetta, 1992).

We are going to field test TWS-2 using N-ISDN to clarify the type of collaboration that TWS-2 supports, as well as its limitations.

Acknowledgments

The authors would like to thank to Yasushi Hibino, Takaya Endo, Sadami Kurihara and Gen Suzuki at NTT Human Interface Laboratories for their guidance and discussions on TWS-2 development. Thanks are also due to Minoru Kobayashi, and many other colleagues in NTT who joined the experimental use of TWS-2. We would also like to thank Naomi Miyake at Chukyo University for her insightful comments to the draft of this paper and enjoyable discussions through TWS-2.

References

Fish, R.S., Kraut, R.E., and Chalfonte, B.L. (1990) The VideoWindow System in Informal Communications. *Proceedings of CSCW '90,* ACM, New York, October 1990, pp. 1-11.

Hollan, J. and Stornetta, S. (1992) Beyond Being There. *Proceedings of CHI '92,* ACM SIGCHI, Monterey, May 1992, pp. 119-125.

Ishii, H., (1990) "TeamWorkStation: Towards a Seamless Shared Workspace," *Proceedings of CSCW '90,* ACM SIGCHI and SIGOIS, Los Angeles, 7-10 October 1990, pp. 13-26.

Ishii, H. and Arita, K., (1991) "ClearFace: Translucent Multiuser Interface for TeamWorkStation," *Proceedings of ECSCW '91,* Amsterdam, 25-27 September 1991, pp. 163-174.

Ishii, H. and Miyake, N. (1991) "Toward an Open Shared Workspace: Computer and Video Fusion Approach of TeamWorkStation," *Communications of the ACM,* December 1991, pp. 37-50.

Ishii, H. and Kobayashi, M., (1992) "ClearBoard: A Seamless Media for Shared Drawing and Conversation with Eye-Contact," *Proceedings of CHI '92,* ACM SIGCHI, Monterey, 3-7 May 1992, pp. 525-532.

Ishii, H., Kobayashi, M., and Grudin, J., (1992) "Integration of Inter-Personal Space and Shared Workspace: ClearBoard Design and Experiments," *Proceedings of CSCW '92,* ACM, Toronto, 1-4 November 1992, pp. 33-42.

Panko, R., and Kinney, S., (1991) "Dyadic Organizational Communication: Is the Dyad Different?," *Proceedings of the Twenty-Fifth Annual Hawaii International Conference on System Sciences,* Kauai, Hawaii, January 1991.

Stefik, M., Bobrow, D.G., Lanning, S., Tatar, D., and Foster G., (1986) "WYSIWIS Revised: Early Experiences with Multi-user Interfaces," *Proceedings of CSCW '86,* Austin, 1986, pp.276-290.

Tang, J.C., and Minneman, S.L. (1990) "VideoDraw: A Video Interface for Collaborative Drawing," *Proceedings of CHI '90,* Seattle, 1990.

Proceedings of the Third European Conference on Computer-Supported Cooperative Work
13-17 September, 1993, Milan, Italy
G. De Michelis, C. Simone and K. Schmidt (Editors)

Bringing Media Spaces into the Real World

Daniele S. Pagani
Lucrezio Lab – Formative Networks, Italy
Rank Xerox Cambridge EuroPARC, United Kingdom

Wendy E. Mackay
Rank Xerox Cambridge EuroPARC, United Kingdom

Abstract: This paper describes a field study to evaluate the use of audio and video connections in a "real world" setting, that is a distributed product development organization within a large multinational corporation. We installed two types of media space connections: a focused dial-up video-phone for engineering problem solving between designers in England and the shop floor of a factory in the Netherlands and an unfocused "office share" to support administrative tasks. We observed that users quickly integrated the new video links into their existing media space of telephone, beepers, answering machines, video conference, fax, e-mail, etc. Users easily learnt how to shift from one medium to another. This suggests that "real world" media spaces should be designed to allow a user-driven smooth transition from one medium to another according to the task at hand and the bandwidth available: from live video to stored video, from moving video to still frames, from multimedia spaces to shared computing spaces for synchronous sketching and asynchronous message posting, and from two user conversation to multi-user conference calls.

1 Introduction

A number of research organizations have explored the use of media spaces, which provide distributed users with access to each other via video and audio links (Bulick *et al.*, 1989; Fish *et al.*, 1993; Olson and Bly, 1991; Gale, 1991; Buxton and Moran, 1990; Ishii and Kobayashi, 1992; Mantei *et al.*, 1991). A survey of such research can be found in Bly *et al.* (1993).

The study was conducted in cooperation with British Telecom Laboratories and has been partially supported by the European Community EuroCODE project within ESPRIT III.

The EuroPARC media space is called RAVE and has two main characteristics: first, everyone in the lab, including administrative personnel and researchers on other projects, participate in the media space in their everyday life. Second, RAVE offers the flexibility to shift from peripheral to focused views of the technology (Gaver *et al.*, 1992). The RAVE system offers a range of interaction modes which can be ordered in a scale according to the decreasing level of engagement required: *video-phone*, a two-way connection between two nodes; *office share*, a two-way video connection active for a long time; *glance*, a 3-second one-way connection to one selected office; *sweep*, 1-second connections to various nodes; *background*, one-way view of a public area. These communication modes evolved over time and reflect how individuals in the lab balanced the trade-off between protecting their privacy and increasing their awareness and ability to interact with each other.

We were interested in the next step, which is to bring media space technology to a real user organization. From a technological point of view, the difference between the RAVE system at EuroPARC and the installations described in this paper is that the former is based on traditional analogue video technology (consumer cameras and TV sets, analogue video switch and kilometres of coaxial cable), whereas the latter is based on recent digital technology (ISDN and TCP-IP networks, CCITT H.261 video compression, RISC workstations). The RAVE analogue technology provides PAL quality video but only within the building, whereas the digital technology we used for this field study delivers lower quality video but uses less bandwidth, making it affordable for international links.

This study had three primary goals: i) To discover the thresholds of acceptable video quality for various kinds of media space connections given the bandwidth and cost constraints of long distance links in the "real world". ii) To learn from users and how they reinterpret video technology for their own purposes in the context of their daily work. iii) To develop guidelines for the design of future media spaces.

2 Research Study: Phase 1

This study was conducted in two phases over a period of one year. Researchers from Rank Xerox EuroPARC and British Telecom Laboratories conducted the Phase 1 interviews with members of a design organization and a manufacturing site. Phase 2 involved the installation and evaluation of two video links between these two sites.

2.1 User Organization

The organization is a large multinational manufacturing firm. The European design centre, located in England, has approximately 600 people who are responsible for the design and management of products for sale within the European Community. The organization is structured in a matrix with two dimensions: functions and projects. They work closely with manufacturing centres located throughout Europe, as well as some in Canada and South America. This company is characterized by the typical pressures of high-tech companies in an innovative, competitive and turbulent market: increase customer satisfaction, maintain a technological edge, improve quality while decreasing costs. Product development, in particular, is under great stress: reducing the time-to-market, streamlining processes, concurrent engineering, adapting to fast technical change and efficient use of resources are issues faced at all levels. Process issues are continually readdressed to find new ways to manage the trade-off between accountability and meeting deadlines.

The organization operates as a highly distributed working environment. Some designs originate in Japan or in the U.S. and European versions are created for the European market. A particular product may be designed in England, with components built in France, Canada and the Netherlands, with the final assembly in the Netherlands and a separate conversion process in Mexico. The management control of such a product begins in England during the initial design stages and then transfers to the key manufacturing site. After the product launch, both the designers and manufacturing engineers follow the customer reaction to the product and make changes in the manufacturing process as needed.

The organization uses a fairly sophisticated telecommunications infrastructure: a corporate telephone system based on leased lines (to reach the other site one dials only the extension, no prefix or country code), voice conference calls, answering machines, beepers, fax, electronic mail and video conference facilities for meetings. All engineers and administrative staff have either a workstation or a computer terminal. Even with this infrastructure, engineers spend a great deal of their time travelling to the other site and large percentages of project budgets may be allocated for travel on major projects.

One of the primary motivations for the user organization's participation in the project was to try to reduce travel costs without affecting the quality of the products. A secondary interest was to see if new styles of working could be developed that would improve communication and increase the effectiveness of the development process.

2.2 Interview Procedure

The interviews had two main purposes: to learn about the needs of the people in the user organization and to identify sites for testing the media space hardware and software. Two researchers from EuroPARC and one researcher from British Telecom Labs conducted the interviews. Each interview was audio taped and transcribed for later analysis.

We met extensively with the director of the division, who is a key supporter of the project. He provided an overview of the organization and arranged for us to meet all of his direct reports and many of the second-level managers. He also met with us after each day of interviews.

We began by making a presentation to the managers that described the media space in our lab and the technology available. We then interviewed 22 managers and staff members. We scheduled an hour for each interview and met in the individual's office. The interviews were open-ended, although we asked a set of basic questions of everyone, including their role in the organization, a description of their work, the communication breakdowns they faced and the current strategies for addressing those breakdowns. Finally, we asked each of them to give a recent example of their use of the existing video conference facilities and their general opinions of it. In addition to the interviews, we attended a number of regularly-scheduled meetings, attended by people from each site either live or using video conference.

2.3 Existing Video Conferencing System

Based on the interviews described above, we identified the basic communication patterns within the organization. Here we summarise our findings about the use of the existing video conferencing system. We expected that users would compare the new video links with the existing video conferencing system. As video conferencing is often not very successful for various reasons (Egido, 1988), we were interested in finding out what users thought about it.

The user organization has invested heavily in a corporate television system (CTV) which provides video conferencing facilities at most US and European sites using a mixture of satellite and cable links. Users sit at a long table that can accommodate six people and two video cameras capture each group of three people. In addition, a ceiling-mounted camera provides facilities for transmitting video of a document or object. The users see their remote colleagues on two large video monitors located opposite their table. A third monitor in the middle shows documents from the remote site. (One user said it felt like being on a quiz show on television with the opposing team lined up opposite them.)

The most common use of CTV is a project checkpoint meeting, which has priority. Anyone, however, can schedule a meeting when the room is not already booked. Project meetings are scheduled months in advance and are highly stressful. If successful, the project team receives approval to proceed to the next phase of the project, otherwise the project slips –a highly undesirable outcome. Another common use of CTV is to address critical problems that arise, i.e. those which might make the project slip. These meetings usually involve technical people who know each other. They rarely look at each other, but make use of the ceiling camera to discuss design documents. They cannot discuss the products directly, because there are no facilities for bringing hardware prototypes into the meeting room. There are also no associated computer facilities for sharing electronic documents.

Users expressed mixed reactions to CTV. Some people (usually high-status managers) found it very useful. They tended to be in control of the meetings and found CTV useful for saving travel costs. For example, during the Gulf war, all cross-Atlantic travel was eliminated. One manager said:

CTV really came into its own during the Gulf war; [its] use has really increased since then.

Other managers found it useful as well:

CTV is good for sharing problems and project status; for general information exchange.

CTV is pretty effective... but the 3-4 second delay is off-putting. Also the cross-talk if the time is not sufficient. It's best if it's group to group, rather than just two people talking.

However, most people found CTV to be divisive and felt that it increased the adversarial nature of the relationship among the participants. These users tend to be the individual contributors who must use the system to negotiate issues and solve problems. Several people described their concerns as follows:

CTV is a strange medium – nothing beats face-to-face... For some types of individuals there is lots of friction. If people [already] have positions, being able to see them doesn't help to bridge the gap. You see a panel of people; it's a stand-off situation. It encourages antagonism.

I am anti-CTV. It gets adversarial, like university challenge... It's ok to communicate stuff that's already happened.

One user pointed out the problems when more than one site is connected via video conference:

My group has a regular CTV session with all the regional design centres, but it's not successful really. One control center can view another [but] the other sites can only hear the others on the phone. So they get the lion's share of the activity. We need better multi-site control.

The mechanics of using video conference can also be a problem:

It's a hassle to make bookings and walk to K building [the location of the CTV meeting room].

In summary, most people viewed face-to-face meetings as the optimal form of communication, but were tired of the amount of time they took and the amount of resources spent in travel. CTV was viewed as useful, especially by management, but tended to create antagonism among the participants. We were interested in seeing whether or not a media space could provide better access to each other and reduce the adversarial quality of the interactions found with CTV.

3 Research Study: Phase 2

Phase 2 involved the installation of two different video links and the study of their use. After the analysis conducted in Phase 1, we chose a major product development project in a critical stage within its two-year life cycle. We identified two areas which had the highest coordination and communication needs across the two sites in England and the Netherlands: i) configuration management; ii) cooperation between design engineers and manufacturing engineers on the shop floor, as the first prototypes were produced on the production line.

In both cases, the participants in the link were under tight deadlines and high stress, with extreme communication requirements, which provided a good test of the technology and the concepts underlying it. Furthermore, at the time the field study was conducted, the travel budget was being reduced, so there was great interest in tools for reducing face-to-face meetings.

3.1 Inter-office Link between Planner/Analysts in England and the Netherlands

The first link was designed to support the planner/analysts who are responsible for configuration management. They must maintain an accurate inventory of the thousands of parts which make up a product, which includes keeping track of design changes for each part and evaluating their cost. Although one person is located in England and the other is in the Netherlands, they must keep in constant contact to track changes as the design drawings are received, approved and entered into the database. The planner/analysts at the two sites exchange a lot of information every day and share many online databases. Although planner/analyst is an administrative position with a low hierarchical status, planner/analysts have a key role for all engineers involved in a product development project because they are a bottleneck for handling changes: all change requests must be submitted to them. They register each request, evaluate the cost and submit it to the Change and Control Board (CCB). The CCB meets every Tuesday morning using the video conference facility between England and the Netherlands. At this meeting senior management review all change requests and decide whether to approve them.

The design and manufacturing engineers must be able to work with the most up-to-date drawings possible, yet changes in drawings require a set of approvals that take time. At any point in time, the engineers must decide whether or not a particular drawing change is likely to be approved and take the risk of going ahead with it. If the engineers went strictly by drawings that were officially approved, the project would grind to a halt and large amounts of money would be lost, since incorrect items would be made. The planner/analysts must thus understand what the engineers are "really" doing as well as the "official" state of the drawings. They process thousands of changes in the course of the project and have 30-50 changes under consideration at any point in time. During critical phases of the project, these two are in telephone contact an average of 30 times per day.

3.1.1 Technology

We designed the first video link to provide the two planner/analysts with a constant video connection throughout the working hours of every day. This corresponds to a slow version of an office share in the RAVE media space (Gaver *et al.*, 1992). An office share provides a constant video connection via a small screen or window. The purpose is to provide an unobtrusive way to stay in touch with the remote person without demanding a focussed social engagement. An office share link stays in the periphery of attention and creates a shared awareness among the people connected, who get a feeling of where the other person is and what he/she does without disturbing each other.

Figure 1 shows the first video link between two Sun workstations. In order to provide a constant video connection across countries we could not afford a dial up ISDN link nor a new leased line. The only affordable bandwidth we could find was the corporate TCP-IP network, based on existing leased lines at 128 kbps. To establish the video connection we used two Sun Videopix video digitizing boards running two software packages: Vfctool, which comes with the Videopix board, and IVS, a public domain software developed at INRIA.

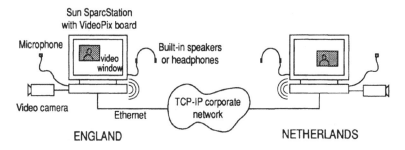

Figure 1. Inter-office Link

Vfctool grabs frames from a video digitising board shared over a local area network. Video frames may be grabbed from one machine and displaying on a remote machine. However, Vfctool does not compress the images, which produces a heavy data stream. Under the average traffic conditions on the TCP/IP network between England and the Netherlands, it took up to 6 minutes to update an image of 320x240 pixels with 8 grey levels, and the software crashed occasionally.

To achieve higher refresh rates we installed IVS, a software package to support video and audio conferences over the Internet (Turletti, 1993). IVS grabs video frames from a Videopix board and compresses them in software on the workstation according to the H.261 standard. IVS transmits the compressed data stream over an IP network using the User Datagram Protocol (UDP) and takes about 20 to 30 kbps of bandwidth. We used QCIF images (176x144 pixels) with 8 grey levels and obtained a refresh rate of one frame every 2-4 seconds. IVS handled packet loss and network overload; the only problem was that sometimes the video window was closed, but the software never crashed and the user could easily restore the link.

3.1.2 User Observations and Results

The inter-office link ran continuously for six days over about one month, during which we installed first Vfctool and then IVS. We spent a few hours observing what users did while the link was up and interviewed the users at various times. We found that the refresh rate of Vfctool was too slow and led to errors. For example, one person thought that the other was at his desk because he could see him on the screen, however when he called him on the phone he found out that he had left a few minutes before. The users enjoyed the link as a new gadget and used it to put up messages in front of the camera such as "Good morning Colin" and "I'll be back at 3 pm", but they did not rely on it as a source of information.

We then switched to IVS, which offered a smaller video window with poorer quality but higher refresh rates. After the initial disappointment about the poorer video quality, the users preferred the new link and kept on using it until the equipment was removed. Even though IVS supports audio communication, the users did not take advantage of this facility but preferred to continue using the telephone on their desk because the audio quality was better.

The users reported that the major use of the IVS link was to see if the other person was busy at his desk before calling him on the phone, which happened several times every day. They could not describe other precise uses, however they said that they liked the office share "because they felt closer". The management evaluation at the end of the project concluded that there were no tangible savings from the specific use of the office share link, and in the final report they wrote: "It's a nice-to-have".

The results of the office share field study are elusive. We need a model of communication to appreciate the meaning and weight of "nice-to-have". An office share can be seen as a medium which specifically supports the *phatic* function of communication (Jakobson, 1960). The phatic function is to keep communication open, to maintain the social relationship between the two partners, to reinforce the physical and psychological connections that must exist to allow cooperation and mutual trust. The phatic function of communication is based on redundancy, which is also the basis of social relations (rituals, conventional behaviour, greetings, tea, beer, etc.); in fact, an office share conveys highly redundant information: the same desk is shown for the whole day.

The best example of how the office share supports the phatic function of communication is the following. The two planner/analysts said they particularly enjoyed the office share on Monday nights, when they have to work late to prepare for the Change and Control Board on Tuesday morning. The configuration managers receive the last data on Monday at 5 pm and work late into the night. When the large open space offices at both sites were deserted and dark after standard working hours, the two planner/analysts appreciated the video link to provide "remote solidarity", to drink coffee together and encourage each other to keep on working until they were done. The video link provided a medium to celebrate the ritual of the long Monday night.

Another way to look at an office share is as a medium to support the communication that takes place by behaving. As the Palo Alto School pointed out, our entire behaviour constitutes a message and since one cannot not behave, "one cannot not communicate" (Watzlawick *et al.*, 1967). An office share delivers behaviour at a distance: not being in the camera view communicates that one is not available, having a lot of paper on the desk communicates that one is very busy, putting the feet on the desk communicates that one is relaxing, etc. All of these messages can be encoded and decoded with no effort or attention by the people sharing the virtual office; in fact, in most cases they are not even aware that communication is taking place, and they cannot stop communicating other than by closing down the link.

It is not surprising that the planner/analysts could not describe precisely how they used the office share link: since they communicated by behaving, it was so natural for them that they were unaware of it. Was communication actually taking place? If we define communication as "anything that changes the probability value of the future behaviour of an organism", then we can find some interesting examples of communication in the behaviour of the planner/analysts. One day during a phone call one planner/analyst mentioned: "Yesterday I saw you were talking with...". The conversation continued without the planner/analysts noticing that the information came from the office share. The link also influenced other people in the open space office; people passing in front of the camera would wave at the other person, and sometimes they asked things like: "Have you seen John around there this afternoon?".

The results of the office share are hard to measure in tangible terms. An office share link creates a virtual office and therefore it produces effects similar to those of building architecture and office layout. It is interesting to observe how easily people adapt to the office share: for a short while users are embarrassed by the camera and "act" in front of it, but after a few hours people forget about it and just behave normally.

3.2 Dialup Video Link between the Engineering Design Centre and the Manufacturing Shop Floor

The second link was designed to support the complex communication and coordination tasks between design engineers in England and manufacturing engineers in the Netherlands. They must transfer and share a large amount of knowledge: the English engineers understand most about product design and the Dutch engineers maintain the relations with the local suppliers. The engineers at the manufacturing site monitor the new prototypes coming off the production line and are the first to see problems. Together with the design engineers, they must decide whether the problem lies in the original design or in the manufacturing process. One of the users' expectations was to use the video link for solving "small" problems arising on the shop floor that require cooperation across the two sites.

3.2.1 Technology

On the English side of the link, we installed one camera clamped on the desktop and one monitor displaying incoming video; for voice we used the speakers built into the monitor and a directional microphone. We also installed a videotape recorder which captured the video coming from the Netherlands and the audio in both directions.

On the Dutch side, the equipment was mounted on a trolley that could be moved around the shop floor to reach various points in the manufacturing line or in the rework area. We installed two monitors (one for incoming and one for outgoing video) and two cameras. One camera was clamped to the trolley and showed a wide angle view of the manufacturing engineers relative to the prototype units on the manufacturing floor. The other was a miniature camera with a flexible cable for showing small details. The people in England could read 2 mm. type sent from this camera. The shop floor had a great deal of background noise, so we used headphones with a built-in microphone.

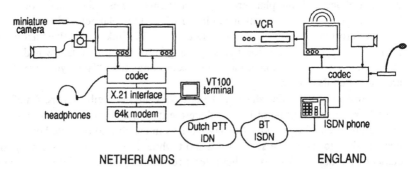

Figure 2. Manufacturing Floor – Design Centre Link

Figure 2 shows the arrangement of the dial-up video and audio link, which was based on two codecs connected by a 64 kbps data line. The codecs implement the H.261 standard and are prototypes of a low end single board model designed for desktop videoconferencing using public ISDN networks. In England the codec was connected to an ISDN telephone via a X.21 interface; the ISDN telephone was used for dialling and for displaying line status messages. In the Netherlands, ISDN was not available in the factory at the time of the field study, so we used a switched 64 kbps IDN line. The lack of a standard ISDN line made the set up on the Dutch side more complicated: a 64 kbps modem was connected to a X.21 controller, which was connected to the codec and to a VT100 terminal. To dial and disconnect the line, users in the Netherlands had to type some commands on the VT100 terminal.

The system had one main problem: it was a research prototype and was not reliable enough for an industrial environment. There were many reasons for the unreliability: we used prototype units of low cost codecs, the codecs were designed for ISDN but in the Netherlands we had to connect it to an analogue 64 kbps line and the system on the Dutch side was constantly moved around the shop floor.

3.2.2   User Observations

The link on the shop floor was available for a total of two weeks. During this period, we spent two days at each site sitting next to the equipment and observing what users did. For the remaining time, we collected videotapes recording the video and audio going through the link and later interviewed the people who used the link. The users tried to use the link eleven times, but could only establish a video connection six times because of the various technical problems described above. The following are examples of tasks carried out using the video link:

- *Packaging problem*. After the design of a part was changed, the packaging for shipping also had to be changed. The change involved making a new cut into the cardboard and assembling the pieces the way that they would fit. Using the video link, a packaging engineer in England was able to show step-by-step how to make the cut and assemble the pieces, with the people in the Netherlands repeating each step at the other site. A problem which would have required a trip was solved in half an hour. When they were interviewed, the users were enthusiastic about the video link and said that it had been particularly useful to do each step of the assembly at both sites, looking at what the other was doing.

- *Software bug*. A manufacturing engineer showed a software programmer in England a software bug by pointing the camera at the display and keyboard of the product so that the programmer could see what was going wrong. Furthermore, the programmer directed the person at the other side to press some key combinations to test some other things, and eventually they found another related bug. The problem could have been described by voice on the telephone, but the manufacturing engineer asked to use the video link because the software programmer was sceptical about the bug: he was confused and thought that the manufacturing engineer was doing something wrong. To actually see the problem and try out some things convinced him of what was happening and allowed him to locate the bug precisely.

- *Paper jam problem*. The paper feed mechanism worked fine on the prototypes, but did not work reliably on some units coming off the manufacturing line. It seemed to be a manufacturing problem, but the manufacturing engineers wanted to have suggestions from the designers. The problem was shown to three designers in England while six people were present on the Dutch side. Many ideas were brainstormed and tested. The main problem in this case was the audio: we had only one set of headphones in the Netherlands, therefore only the person with headphones could communicate with the people in England.

Users complained a lot about the poor audio quality, the poor video resolution, the lack of reliability of the system. However the engineers were really excited when they could solve a problem using the video link without travelling.

3.2.3 Results

What emerges from the field study is that, in spite of the technical flaws, the shop floor video link did support effectively some tasks. The users had to fight with the technical limits of the system, but they suggested a number of ways to improve the system that are described in section 4. The managers rated the potential for such video links very highly and expected that such links would become an essential part of the infrastructure to support product development. They found it most useful for explaining problems on an *ad hoc* basis or when the problem is unique to a particular machine. Most of the complaints were due to specific problems with the particular installation. If fixed, the overall assessment of the video link would be very high. The following kinds of transactions would be well supported by this type of link:

- *Show a problem.* A manufacturing engineer shows something going wrong on the production line and asks the designers for explanations, solutions, changes, etc. (e.g. software bug). For these types of transactions the video is very important not only to improve communication by adding the visual dimension, but also to overcome the initial scepticism and mistrust. Seeing the problem on video supports the typical discussion where the design and manufacturing engineers tend to blame each other for the problem: is it a design problem, which requires a design change, or a manufacturing problem, which requires retooling or a change in the process? In a situation where distance and difference in nationality between manufacturing and design engineers tend to increase the typical tension between design and manufacturing functions, looking at the problem together helps to foster a cooperative attitude towards solving the problem and "getting things done", rather than arguing an abstract problem over the phone to "pass the buck". This is in contrast to the findings from the use of the existing video conference system.

- *Show a solution.* A design engineer shows how to do something on the shop floor (e.g. packaging problem). The video link allows users to go through each step of the process and to perform it simultaneously at both sites, to make sure that both parties have a full understanding of the solution and its consequences. The advantage of the video link is that it is much faster and much more direct; furthermore, it allows users to see the solution working at both sites which increases confidence in the solution and trust between the two sites.

- *Cooperative problem solving.* A problem is shown and engineers at both ends of the link brainstorm solutions, discuss ideas, point at causes, try out experiments on the machine to find out more and test ideas (e.g. paper jam problem). This is not a standard video conference because the video is not used to show the faces of the participants in the discussion, as with a face-to-face meeting, but is used to show the technical problem to be solved and floor passing is done by handing over the portable miniature camera.

4 User Requirements and System Functions

The observation of the problems engineers and planner/analysts encountered when they used the media space connections suggests a number of user requirements to be addressed. The following list identifies the most important user requirements and related system features to be implemented:

- *Audio quality and voice conference calls.* Users discussed and argued a lot during the connections on the shop floor. They therefore expected at least what they already get from their telephone system: reasonable audio quality and conference calls. Audio quality is a critical factor: if audio quality was too poor, the users interrupted the video/audio link. Future systems have to deliver good audio quality (at least telephone standard) and have to support multi-user conference calls.

- *Smooth transition between low resolution moving video and high resolution still pictures.* People could cope with the low resolution of moving video at 64 kbps and appreciated the interactivity of the live connection ("show me this, try that..."). However they sometimes needed more resolution to see fine details. In such cases, they were definitely ready to trade off moving images for resolution (assuming the bandwidth remained constant). The system could therefore be improved by providing a tool to pause the video and send a frame at a higher resolution. Furthermore, it would be useful to save the captured frame and sketch over it.

- *Smooth transition between stored and live video.* In some circumstances live video in not convenient. For example, sometimes it was difficult to recreate the conditions of a problem or to shoot the video and discuss with people at the other end at the same time. In these cases users prefer to be able to shoot a video first, save it and edit it off-line, then play the stored video during a live connection and discuss it, with the possibility of going back and sketching over it. From a technical point of view, this approach offers the opportunity to perform asymmetric compression of the stored video and therefore increase the resolution of the video transferred. One interesting application of this feature can be exploited if live video connections are recorded. The participants in the discussion can go back to the recorded session and watch or hear again something that happened before.

- *Sketching and annotation tool.* The packaging engineer, after using the link as described above, suggested that it would have been very useful to have "a light-pen to sketch over the video as they do in football matches on TV". As the user suggested, it is important to integrate media spaces and computing spaces. It would be useful to have a synchronous shared sketching tool to draw over video and still images, such as the TeamWorkStation system (Ishii,

1990). Furthermore, the system should be improved with an asynchronous multimedia annotation tool for editing stored video.

- *Shared virtual pin-board*. The users of the office share link often put up notices or pictures in front of the camera. However they did so only when they were not there because the message had to take over the whole video window to be readable. This desire to exchange written notes can be addressed with a computer tool that allows the two people sharing a virtual office to share a computer window where they can put up short messages and sketches, or even icons of documents that can be double-clicked. The difference between this and e-mail is that the content of the shared area is always visible on the screen, but it is not permanently stored and lives until you write something else on top of it or close the window. This would be like sharing a virtual pin-board with the colleague.

5 Summary and Conclusions

The main purpose of the study was to test the media space concepts outside of a research lab. We chose an engineering organization within a large multinational firm characterised by having product development and manufacturing distributed across many countries. We focused on a major product development project in a critical stage within its two-year life cycle. Members of the project were divided between two sites: a design centre in England and a factory in the Netherlands. After analyzing the distributed organization and work patterns, we installed two media space connections: an office share between the desktops of two people sharing administrative tasks across the two sites and a dial up video-phone between the desktop of an engineer in England and the shop floor of the factory in the Netherlands.

The office share improved the cooperation between the two planner/analysts by opening up new levels of communication at a distance: phatic communication and communication by behaviour (see section 3.1.2). The office share supported various levels of communication whose effects could be detected in the behaviour of planner/analysts and other people in the office. It created a shared awareness allowing to feel the "presence" of the remote person without demanding a focused social engagement, it maintained social relationships by reinforcing the physical and psychological contact and it delivered the information produced by people's behaviour.

The video-phone link was used to solve problems arising on the shop floor (see section 3.2.2). It was never used for face-to-face communications: people did not stay in front of the camera but always used the video to show technical problems. The visual dimension not only speeds up and eases communication, but also increases cooperative attitudes, confidence in the solution and mutual trust. This is in contrast to what users said about the existing video conference system, i.e. that it creates an adversarial relationship among the participants. We think that the attitude towards the two systems was different because the video-phone and office-share links are more integrated into the workplace, readily available and more flexible for solving specific problems and supporting informal communication. CTV is perceived as a tool used by upper management to control the status of the project minimizing travel, whereas the media space links are viewed as tools to improve the quality of work.

Users complained about the low video and audio quality available because it was below their expected standards, respectively television and telephone. Users however could cope with the low quality video when it became clear that the media space connections allowed them to acquire new degrees of freedom, to do new things that before were impossible. On the other hand, sometimes users gave up when the audio quality was too bad or when it took too long to set up a connection.

Users were very quick to adapt to the technology and its limitations. Users understood very easily that bandwidth was the bottleneck, and they were extremely good at shifting from one communication medium to another for solving the various problems they encountered: they used telephones, beepers, fax and e-mail together with the video links, using a lot of creativity and *bricolage*. However the system we provided was not flexible enough; for example, it was not possible to print a frame from the video and send it by fax, or store video on tape and transmit it later to the other site, or sketch over the video.

For media spaces to be effective in the "real world" we have to design systems that allow people to shift smoothly from one medium to another according to the problem at hand, the current situation, the various technological constraints and the resources available (e.g. bandwidth, resolution, background noise, etc.). Furthermore, the media space should be integrated with the existing communication infrastructure, which is usually very rich but very fragmented: telephones, beepers, answering machines, faxes, e-mail, etc. The user requirements that emerged are: smooth transition between live video and stored video; smooth transition between moving video and high resolution still pictures; smooth transition between multimedia links and shared computing spaces of two kinds: synchronous shared sketching over video or still images, and asynchronous message posting on a shared pin board area; smooth transition between voice two-users conversation and multi-user conference call. These requirements add new dimensions of flexibility besides the transition between focused and peripheral use of the technology originally conceived at the beginning of the project.

Acknowledgements

Special thanks to Bob Anderson, Graham Button, Ian Daniel, Richard Harper, Michel Hessoir, Ian Mair, Mike Molloy and Alistair Rogers for their contributions to the field study. We also thank all the users who cooperated with us in spite of their other commitments.

References

Bly, S.A., Harrison, S.R. and Irwin S. (1993): "Media Spaces: Bringing People Together in a Video, Audio and Computing Environment", *Communications of the ACM*, Vol. 36, No. 1, January 1993, pp. 28-47.

Bulick, S., Abel, M., Corey, D., Schmidt, J. and Coffin, S. (1989): "The US West Advanced Technologies Prototype Multi-media Communications System", *GLOBECOM '89: Proceedings of the IEEE Global Telecommunications Conference*, Dallas, Texas, 1989.

Buxton, W. and Moran, T. P. (1990): "EuroPARC's Integrated Interactive Intermedia Facility (iiif): Early Experiences", *Proceedings of the IFIP WG8.4 Conference on Multi-User Interfaces and Applications*, Herakleion, Crete, September 1990.

Fish R.S., Kraut R.E., Root R.W. and Rice R.E. (1993): "Video as a Technology for Informal Communication", *Communications of the ACM*, Vol. 36, No. 1, January 1993, pp. 48-61.

Egido, C. (1988): "Videoconferencing as a Technology to Support Group Work: A Review of its Failure", *Proceedings of the Conference on Computer Supported Cooperative Work*, September 26-28, 1988, Portland, Oregon. ACM, New York, 1988, pp. 13-24.

Gale S. (1991): "Adding Audio and Video to an Office Environment", in Bowers and Benford (eds.): *Studies in Computer Supported Cooperative Work*, Elsevier Science Publishers, 1991.

Gaver, W. W., Moran T. P., MacLean A., Lovstrand L., Dourish P., Carter K. and Buxton W. (1992): "Realizing a Video Environment: EuroPARC's RAVE System", *Proceedings of CHI '92*, Monteray, California, 3-7 May, 1992. ACM, New York, 1992.

Ishii, H. (1990): "TeamWorkStation: Towards a Seamless Shared Workspace", *Proceedings of the Conference on Computer Supported Cooperative Work*, October 7-10, 1990, Los Angeles, CA. ACM, New York, 1990, pp. 13-26.

Ishii, H. and Kobayashi, M. (1992): "Integration of Inter-personal Space and Shared Workspace: ClearBoard Design and Experiments", *Proceedings of the Conference on Computer Supported Cooperative Work*, October 31-November 4, 1992, Toronto, Canada.

Jakobson, R. (1960): "Closing Statement: Linguistics and Poetics", in Sebeok, T. (ed.): *Style and Language*, MIT Press, Cambridge, Mass., 1960.

Mantei, M., Baecker, R.M., Sellen, A., Buxton, W., Milligan, T. and Wellman, B. (1991): "Experiences in the Use of a Media Space", *Proceedings of the CHI '91*, New Orleans, Lousiana, April 28-May 2 1991, pp. 203-208.

Olson, M.H. and Bly, S.A. (1991): "The Portland Experience: a Report on a Distributed Research Group", *Int. J. Man-Machine Studies*, 34.

Turletti T. (1993): *H.261 Software Codec for Videoconferencing Over the Internet*. INRIA Technical Report N° 1834, Sophia Antipolis, France, 1993.

Watzlawick P., Bravin J. H. and Jackson D. D. (1967): *Pragmatics of Human Communication*. Norton Publishing, New York, 1967.

ECSCW '93 Directory:
Authors and Committee Members

Martin Ader
BULL S.A
7, Rue Ampere
91343 Massy Cedex
France
phone: +33 1 6993 8359
email: M.Ader@frmy.bull.fr

Robert J. Anderson
Rank Xerox Cambridge EuroPARC
61 Regent Street
Cambridge, CB2 1AB
UK
phone: +44 223 341500
fax: +44 223 341510
email: anderson@europarc.xerox.com

Kazuho Arita
NTT Human Interface Laboratories
1-2356 Take, Yokosuka-Shi,
Kanagawa, 238-03
Japan
phone: +81 468 59 4266
fax: +81 468 59 2332
email: arita@aether.ntt.jp

Liam Bannon
Dept. of Computer Science & Information
    Systems
University of Limerick
Limerick
Ireland
phone: +353-61-333644
fax: +353-61-330876
email: bannon@ul.ie

Eevi E. Beck
School of Cognitive and Computing
    Sciences
University of Sussex
Brighton BN1 9QH
UK
phone: +44 273 678524/699255
fax: +44 273 671320
email: eevib@cogs.sussex.ac.uk

Victoria Bellotti
Rank Xerox EuroPARC
61 Regent Street
Cambridge CB2 1AB
UK
phone: +44 223 341 516
fax: +44 223 341 510
email: bellotti@europarc.xerox.com

Steve Benford
Communications Research Group,
    Department of Computer Science
The University of Nottingham
University Park
Notthingham NG7 2RD
UK
phone: +44 602 514203
fax: +44 602 514254
email: sdb@cs.nott.ac.uk

Gordon Blair
Computing Department
Lancaster University
Lancaster LA1 4YR
UK
phone: +44 524 65201
fax: +44 524 381707
email: gordon@comp.lancs.ac.uk

Tom Brinck
Human-Computer Systems Research
Bellcore
445 South Street, MRE 2A 219
Morristown, NJ 07962
USA
phone: +1-201-829-5238
fax: +1-201-829-5963
email: hammer@bellcore.com

Graham Button
Rank Xerox Cambridge EuroPARC
61 Regent Street
Cambridge, CB2 1AB
UK
phone: +44 223 341500
fax: +44 223 341510
email: button@europarc.xerox.com

Shaw Cheng Chuang
Computer Laboratory
Cambridge University
Pembroke Street
Cambridge CB2 3QG
UK
phone: +44-223-33-4645
email: shaw.chuang@uk.ac.cam.cl

Claudio Ciborra
Università degli Studi di Bologna
Dipartimento di Organizzazione del Sistema
   Politico
Strada Maggiore 45
40125 Bologna
Italy
phone: +39 51 6402727
fax: +39 51 234036

Terry Connolly
Department of Management and Policy
College of Business and Public
   Administration
University of Arizona
Tucson, Arizona 85721
USA
phone: (602) 621-5937
fax: (602) 621-4171
email: connolly@ccit.arizona.edu

Giorgio De Michelis
Dipartimento di Scienze dell'Informazione
Università degli Studi di Milano
Via Comelico 39
20135 Milano
Italy
phone: +39 2 55006 311
fax: +39 2 55006 276
email: gdemich@hermes.mc.dsi.unimi.it

Peter Docherty
Institute of Management and Innovation
   Technology
Stockholm School of Economics
PO BOX 6501 Saltmåtargatan 13-17
S-11383 Stockholm
Sweden
phone: +46 8 736 9445
fax: +46 8 326 524
email: pmopd@hhssun.sunet.se

Paul Dourish
Rank Xerox EuroPARC
61 Regent Street
Cambridge CB2 1AB
UK
phone: +44 223 341512
fax: +44 223 341510
email: dourish@europarc.xerox.com

Pelle Ehn
Department of Information and Computer
   Science
Lund University
Sölvetagan 14 A
S-221 00 Lund
Sweden
phone: +46 46 108029
email: Pelle.Ehn@ibadb.lu.se

Clarence Skip Ellis
Department of Computer Science
University of Colorado
Campus Box 430,
Boulder Colorado 80309 - 0430
USA
email: skip@cs.colorado.edu

Lennart Fahlen
Distributed Systems Laboratory
The Swedish Institute of Computer Science
   (SICS)
Kista, Stockholm
Sweden
email: lef@sics.se

Geneviève Filippi
Unité de Recherche CNRS,
"Langages, Cognitions, Pratiques et
   Ergonomie",
Laboratoire d'Ergonomie Physiologique et
   Cognitive,
Ecole Pratique des Hautes Etudes
41 rue Gay Lussac
75005 Paris
France
phone: +33 1 46 33 63 23
fax: +33 1 43 26 88 16

Mark James Handley
Department of Computer Science
University College London
Gower Street
London WC1E 6BT
UK
phone: +44-71-387 7050 ext 3666
fax: +44-71-387 1397
email: m.handley@uk.ac.ucl.cs

Christian Heath
Rank Xerox Cambridge EuroPARC
61 Regent Street
Cambridge CB2 1AB
UK
phone: +44 223 341500
fax:
email: Heath.EuroPARC@rx.xerox.com

and also

Department of Sociology
University of Surrey
Guilford GU2 5XH
UK
phone: +44 483 300800
fax: +44 483 306290
email: Christian.Heath@soc.surrey.ac.uk

Ralph Hill
Human-Computer Systems Research
Bellcore
445 South Street, MRE 2D295
Morristown, NJ 07962
USA
phone: +1-201- 829-4581
fax: +1-201-829-5963
email: rdh@bellcore.com

Jon Hindmarsh
Centre for Requirements and Foundations
 Programming Research Group
University of Oxford
Oxford OX1 3QD
UK
phone: +44 865 272 578
fax: +44 865 273 839
email: Jon.Hindmarsh@prg.oxford.ac.uk

Elke Hinrichs
Institute for Applied Information
 Technology
GMD - German National Research Center
 for Computer Science
Postfach 1316
D-53731 Sankt Augustin
Germany
phone: +49 2241 14 2442
fax: +49 2241 14 2084
email: hinrichs@gmd.de

Anatol Holt
Dipartimento di Scienze dell'Informazione
Università degli Studi di Milano
Via Comelico 39
20135 Milano
Italy
phone: +39 2 55006 333
fax: +39 2 55006 334
email: holt@hermes.mc.dsi.unimi.it

Hiroshi Ishii
NTT Human Interface Laboratories
1-2356 Take, Yokosuka-Shi,
Kanagawa, 238-03
Japan
phone +81 468 59 3522
fax: +81 468 59 2332
email: ishii.chi@xerox.com or
 ishii@aether.ntt.jp

Marina Jirotka
Centre for Requirements and Foundations -
 Programming Res. Group
University of Oxford
11 Keble Road
Oxford OX1 3QD
UK
phone: +44 865 272578
fax: +44 483 273839
email: Marina.Jirotka@prg.oxford.ac.uk

Philip Johnson
Department of Information and Computer
 Sciences
University of Hawaii
2565 The Mall
Honolulu, HI 96822
USA
phone: (808) 956-3489
fax: (808) 956-3548
email: johnson@hawaii.edu

Scott D. Kalter
Twin Sun Inc.
360 N. Sepulveda Blvd., Suite 2055
El Segundo, CA 90245-4462
USA
phone: +1 310 524 1800
fax: +1 310 640 2180
email: sdk@twinsun.com

Simon M. Kaplan
Human-Computer Interaction Laboratory
Department of Computer Science
University of Illinois
1304 W. Springfield Avenue
Urbana, IL 61801
USA
phone: +1 217 244 0392
fax: +1 333 3501
email: kaplan@cs.uiuc.edu

Robert E. Kraut
Bellcore
445 South St.
Morristown, NJ 07962
USA
phone:
fax:
email: kraut@bellcore.com

Thomas Kreifelts
Institute for Applied Information
Technology
GMD - German National Research Center
for Computer Science
Postfach 1316
D-53731 Sankt Augustin
Germany
phone: +49 2241 14 2643
fax: +49 2241 14 2084
email: kreifelts@gmd.de

Paul Luff
Rank Xerox Cambridge EuroPARC
61 Regent Street
Cambridge, CB2 1AB
UK
phone: +44 223 341 528
fax: +44 223 341 510
email: luff.europarc@rx.xerox.com

Wendy E. Mackay
Rank Xerox Cambridge EuroPARC
61 Regent Street
Cambridge, CB2 1AB
UK
phone: +44 223 341 500
fax: +44 223 341 510
email: mackay@europarc.xerox.com

Boris Magnusson
Department of Computer Science
Lund University
P.O. Box 118
S-221 00 Lund
Sweden
phone: +46 46 10 80 44
fax: +46 46 13 10 21
email: Boris.Magnusson@dna.lth.se

Sten Minör
Department of Computer Science
Lund University
P.O. Box 118
S-221 00 Lund
Sweden
phone: +46 46 10 96 41
fax: +46 46 13 10 21
email: Sten.Minor@dna.lth.se

Dianne Murray
Social and Computer Sciences Research
Group
Department of Sociology
University of Surrey
Guildford GU2 5XH
UK
phone: +44 483 509292
fax: +44 483 509356
email: dianne@soc.surrey.ac.uk

Daniele S. Pagani
Lucrezio Lab - Formative Networks
Via Stampa, 4
20123 Milano
Italy
phone: +39-2-8901.0667
fax: +39-2-8901.0646
email: pagani@sophia.inria.fr

Hilary K. Palmén
Institute of Computer Based Learning
Heriot-Watt University
Riccarton
Edinburgh, EH 14 4 AS
UK
phone: + 44 31 449 5111 ext 4187
phone: + 44 31 449 5111 ext 3282
fax: + 44 31 451 3283
email: hilary@icbl.hw.ac.uk

Dorab Patel
Twin Sun, Inc.
360 N. Sepulveda Blvd, Suite 2055
El Segundo, CA 90245-4462
USA
phone: +1 310 524 1800
fax: +1 310 640 2180
email: dorab@twinsun.com

Wolfgang Prinz
Institute for Applied Information
Technology
GMD - German National Research Center
for Computer Science
Postfach 1316
53731 Sankt Augustin
Germany
phone: +49 2241 142730
fax: +49 2241 142084
email: prinz@gmd.de

Mike Robinson
Computer Science Department
University of Aarhus
Ny Munkegade, Bygning 540
Aarhus C. DK-8000
Denmark
phone: +45 8612 7188 (reception) +45
8620 2711 X 5105 (direct)
fax: +45 8613 5725
email: mike@daimi.aau.dk

Tom Rodden
Computing Department
Lancaster University
Lancaster LA1 4YR
UK
phone: +44 524 65201
fax: +44 524 381707
email: tom@comp.lancs.ac.uk

Martina Angela Sasse
Department of Computer Science
University College London
Gower Street
London WC1E 6BT
UK
phone: +44-71-380 7212
fax: +44-71-387 1397
email: a.sasse@uk.ac.ucl.cs

Thomas Schäl
HDZ/KDI der RWTH Aachen
Rolandstraße 7-9
D-5100 Aachen
Germany
phone: +49-241-918290
fax: +49-241-9182922
email: schael@cs.vu.nl

and also
Istituto RSO
Via Leopardi 1
20123 Milano
Italy
phone: +39-2-72000583 (x39-2-984-
937109)
fax: +39-2-86450720
email: schael@crai.crai.it

Kjeld Schmidt
Cognitive Systems Group (KOG)
Risø National Laboratory
P.O. Box 49
DK-4000 Roskilde
Denmark
phone: +45 4237 1212
fax: +45 4675 5170
email: kschmidt@risoe.dk

Sherry Schneider
Department of Management and Policy
College of Business and Public
Administration
University of Arizona
Tucson, Arizona 85721
USA
phone: (602) 621-9324
fax: (602) 621-4171
email: sherry@ccit.arizona.edu

Stephen A.R. Scrivener
The Design Research Centre
University of Derby
Kedleston Road
Derby, DE22 1GB
UK
phone: +44 332 47181 ext 1517
fax: +44 332 294861
email: S.A.Scrivener@lut.ac.uk

Abigail Sellen
Rank Xerox EuroPARC
61 Regent Street
Cambridge CB2 1AB
UK
email: sellen@europarc.xerox.com

Wes Sharrock
Department of Sociology
University of Manchester
Manchester, M13 9PL
UK
phone: +44 61 2752510
fax: +44 61 2752514

Carla Simone
Dipartimento di Scienze dell'Informazione
Università degli Studi di Milano
Via Comelico 39
20135 Milano
Italy
phone: +39 2 55006 289
fax: +39 2 55006 276
email: simone@hermes.mc.dsi.unimi.it

Ian Sommerville
Computing Department
Lancaster University
Lancaster LA1 4YR
UK
phone: +44 524 65201
fax: +44 524 381707
email: is@comp.lancs.ac.uk

Lucy Suchman
Work Practice and Technology Area
Xerox Palo Alto Research Center
3333 Coyote Hill Road
Palo Alto, CA 94304
USA
phone: +1 415 812-4340
fax: +1 415 812-4380
email: suchman@parc.xerox.com

Jacques Theureau
Unité de Recherche CNRS, "Langages,
    Cognitions, Pratiques et Ergonomie",
Laboratoire d'Ergonomie Physiologique et
    Cognitive,
Ecole Pratique des Hautes Etudes
41 rue Gay Lussac
75005 Paris
France
phone: +33 1 46 33 63 23
fax: +33 1 43 26 88 16

Danu Tjahjono
Department of Information and Computer
    Sciences
University of Hawaii
2565 The Mall
Honolulu, HI 96822
Hawaii
phone: (808) 956-3489
fax: (808) 956-3548
email: dat@uhunix.uhcc.hawaii.edu

Jonathan Trevor
Computing Department
Lancaster University
Lancaster LA1 4YR
UK
phone: +44 524 65201
fax: +44 524 381707
email: jonathan@comp.lancs.ac.uk

Michael Twidale
Computing Department
Lancaster University
Lancaster LA1 4YR
UK
phone: +44 524 65201
fax: +44 524 381707
email: mbt@comp.lancs.ac.uk

Silvia Pongutá Urquijo
Department of Human Sciences
University of Technology
Loughborough
Loughborough LE11 3TU
UK
email: husep@lut.ac.uk

Gerrit van der Veer
Department of Cognitive Psychology
Free University of Amsterdam
de Boelelaan 1111
1080 HV Amsterdam
The Netherlands
phone: +31 20 548 4405
fax: +31 20 548 4443 / 542 6275
email: gerrit@psy.vu.nl

Suzanne P. Weisband
Department of Management Information
Systems
College of Business and Public
Administration
University of Arizona
Tucson, Arizona 85721
USA
phone: (602) 621-8303
fax: (602) 621-2433
email: sweisband@bpa.arizona.edu

Gerd Woetzel
Institute for Applied Information
Technology
GMD - German National Research Center
for Computer Science
Postfach 1316
D-53731 Sankt Augustin
Germany
phone: +49 2241 142 648
fax: +49 2241 142 084
email: woetzel@gmd.de

Takashi Yagi
NTT Human Interface Laboratories
1-2356 Take, Yokosuka-Shi,
Kanagawa, 238-03
Japan
phone: +81 468 59 3750
fax: +81 468 59 2332
email: yagi@aether.ntt.jp